THE ITALIAN LEGAL SYSTEM

The Italian Legal System

An Introduction, Second Edition

MICHAEL A. LIVINGSTON, PIER GIUSEPPE
MONATERI, AND FRANCESCO PARISI

Based on the First Edition by

MAURO CAPPELLETTI, JOHN HENRY
MERRYMAN, AND JOSEPH M. PERILLO

STANFORD LAW BOOKS

An Imprint of Stanford University Press

Stanford, California

Stanford University Press
Stanford, California

The first edition of this book by Mauro Cappelletti, John Henry Merryman, and
Joseph M. Perillo was published in 1965; the second edition contains revisions by
Michael A. Livingston, Pier Giuseppe Monateri, and Francesco Parisi in 2015.

Printed on acid-free, archival-quality paper

Printed and bound in Great Britain by
Marston Book Services Ltd, Oxfordshire

Library of Congress Cataloging-in-Publication Data

Livingston, Michael A., author.
    The Italian legal system : an introduction / Michael A. Livingston, Pier
Giuseppe Monateri, and Francesco Parisi.—Second edition.
        pages cm
    "Based on the First Edition by Mauro Cappelletti, John Henry Merryman, and
Joseph M. Perillo."
    Includes bibliographical references and index.
    ISBN 978-0-8047-7495-6 (cloth : alk. paper)
    1. Law—Italy.   I. Monateri, P. G., author.   II. Parisi, Francesco, 1962–
author.   III. Cappelletti, Mauro. Italian legal system. Revision of: IV. Title.
    KKH68.C367 2015
    349.45—dc23

                                                                2015021623

    ISBN 978-0-8047-9655-2 (electronic)

Typeset by Newgen in 10/14.5 Minion

Contents

Preface to the Second Edition

When I first became interested in Italian Law more than a decade ago, I naturally asked if there was an English-language treatise that summarized the topic for a curious but otherwise novice reader. It didn't take long until I learned that there was only one truly serious contender for the title. "The Cappelletti," as people called it, is not only the single best book on the Italian legal system in a foreign (and perhaps in any) language but a classic work in the field of comparative law as a whole. With its identification and description of a peculiarly "Italian style" of law and legal thinking—a background music, as it were, that makes even the same words and concepts take on a different meaning—it captures the tension between sameness and difference that defines the comparative field. The question implicit in the book, whether the special Italian style can survive in a world of shrinking distances and converging norms, remains as relevant today as it was when the book was first published. While questions remain the same, answers change with time.

When the First Edition was published in 1967, the Italian Republic was barely two decades old; the European Union (EEC) was a purely economic arrangement; and *globalization* was a term used only by a few futuristic thinkers. Few Italian lawyers or law professors spoke English, even as a second language; it is safe to say that none used a computer or knew anyone who did. The Constitutional Court was in its infancy, and the idea that democratic or constitutional values should inform legal interpretation, at both the judicial and scholarly levels, remained a novelty. Changes of this magnitude affect not only the substance of legal rules but the way of thinking about them: the music of the law, to follow the previous analogy, as well as the lyrics. Yet, through all of this, something of the original Italian style remains in force, buffeted by global phenomena but stubbornly refusing to give way altogether.

Out of respect for the original work—and a justified modesty regarding our own ability to improve it—we have taken as light an editing approach as possible, making only those changes that are necessary to keep the book factually accurate and useful for contemporary readers. Thus, while certain materials regarding Italian law and institutions have been updated, the essential core of the book remains largely as it was in the previous edition. At times the combination may prove jarring: discussions of globalization or the EU are followed by citations from the 1950s or observations about the passage from fascism to the democratic era. It is hoped that these superficial incongruities will be compensated by the overall flow and cadence of the book and the recognition that its principal themes remain as relevant today as they were forty years ago.

Although this book remains a vital source on Italian law, it is also a case study in the persistence of national styles and ways of thinking about law in an increasingly interconnected world. Indeed, it is not an exaggeration to say that the question of "convergence" and "divergence" of national legal systems—which aspects of national legal systems become more similar and which remain or even become more different with the passage of time—has become the predominant theme of modern comparative law. While continuing to be a vital source for understanding Italian law, it is hoped that this work may prove part of this broader, continuing conversation.

I wish to thank my coauthors, whose knowledge of Italian law essentially contains my own, for their patience and perseverance in bringing this project to fruition. Special thanks are due to the original authors, Professors Merryman and Perillo, for their assistance, advice, and encouragement. Professor Merryman's death, as this book was headed to publication, was an incalculable loss to the comparative law and the broader academic community. Extra special thanks to Professor Cristina Costantini for help with Chapters 2, 3, and 4, and to Mauro Balestrieri and Davide Gianti for reading the manuscript and preparing the index: without them, it would have been quite impossible to finish the book on schedule. Thanks also to Rebecca Mamone and Sara Gattazzo for outstanding research assistance, and to Diego Corapi, Vincenzo Varano, and the participants at a symposium at the Roma Tre Law Faculty for insightful and helpful comments. Finally, I wish to thank my wife, Anne F. Weiss, without whose support and encouragement I would remain quite lost (*perduto*) in this and other endeavors.

Michael Livingston

Preface to the First Edition

The purpose of this book is to open the way to the study of Italian law and, through it, the civil law system. Italian law has its own characteristics, just as French and German law, for example, have theirs. Indeed, the differences between legal systems commonly classified as belonging to the civil law family often seem of a higher order than the differences between those, say of California and England. But Western European jurisdictions also share a common legal culture that gives meaning to their law and tends to limit the importance of formal differences in norms, institutions, and processes. This common culture, much of which is Italic in origin, is readily accessible through the study of Italian law.

Although there is a good deal of writing in English about other continental legal systems, little exists that would be helpful to one seeking an introduction to Italian law. The decision taken in 1961 to focus on the Italian legal system in the basic foreign and comparative law courses at Stanford consequently created the need that this book attempts to fill.

The collaborative effort that produced this book grew out of a chance meeting of the authors in Florence in 1962. From that beginning we have all participated in planning and preparing its contents. Professor Cappelletti took initial responsibility for Chapters 1 and 4; Professor Merryman for Chapters 5, 6, and 7; and Professor Perillo for Chapters 2 and 3; and Professors Cappelletti and Merryman for the Appendixes. Professor Perillo translated Professor Cappelletti's work into English, and Professor Merryman coordinated production of the book and saw it through the press. Each of us read, criticized, and supplemented the work of the others, and it is accurate to say that this volume is the product of our joint, as well as our several, endeavors.

There is much in this volume that departs from the traditions of scholarship in foreign and comparative law. We have decided to let the reader discover these departures for himself, with only one exception. We cannot resist calling attention to Appendix B, which represents the complete history of a civil action from trial through appeal, cassation, and decision on remand. Anyone who would like to get the feel of Italian law in action should find this account fascinating. [Note: This Appendix is not included in the Second Edition.]

We thank the many colleagues in Italy and the United States who have generously given us their ideas and criticism. Professor Cappelletti wishes to acknowledge the assistance of Dr. Lamberto Pansolli in the preparation of Chapter 1, and Professor Merryman that of Drs. Paolo Scaparone, Giorgio Schiavoni, and Vincenzo Varano in the preparation of Chapters 5, 6 and 7. All of us express our gratitude to Mrs. Evelyn Roodhouse for her assistance in the preparation of the manuscript and for her expert management of the complicated logistics involved in producing a book by three widely scattered authors. Finally, we thank the Ford Foundation for financial support in connection with the research for this volume.

M.C.

J.H.M.

J.M.P.

THE ITALIAN LEGAL SYSTEM

CHAPTER ONE

History of Italian Law

1.01 *Introduction.* Even a summary exposition of the history of Italian law must begin with its matrix: Roman law.[1] Roman law had a thousand-year history, from the primitive XII Tables in the fifth century B.C. to the Codification of Justinian in the sixth century A.D. In the course of this millennium, radical changes occurred in legal institutions.[2]

Justinian's Codification, as it was interpreted and developed by Italian jurists from the twelfth century onward, is the direct source of the Italian legal system.

---

1. A history of Italian law in English is Calisse, *A History of Italian Law* Vols. I and II (2001). See also the *Continental Legal History Series: A General Survey of Events, Sources, Persons and Movements in Continental Legal History* (1912), by various European authors, available at http://archive.org/details/ageneralsurveyeo1wigmgoog; part 2, pp. 85–199, dedicated to Italy. For the main features of the Italian legal system, see Lena and Mattei, *Introduction to Italian Law* Vol. 9 (2002) and Watkin, *The Italian Legal Tradition* (1997). Also important, although limited to procedure and evidence, is Engelmann et al., *A History of Continental Civil Procedure* (1927). For a general history in English, see Salvatorelli, *A Concise History of Italy: From Prehistoric Times to Our Own Day* (1940).

2. On Roman private law, see Kaser, *Roman Private Law* (Dannenbring trans., 1980); Buckland, *A Text-book of Roman Law from Augustus to Justinian* (3d ed. 1963); Arangio-Ruiz, *Istituzioni di diritto romano* (14th ed. 1960); Schulz, *Classical Roman Law* (1951, reprinted 1992). On the history of Roman law, see De Francisci, *Storia del diritto romano* (1943–44); Kunkel, *An Introduction to Roman Legal and Constitutional History* (Kelly trans., 1973); Siber, *Römisches Recht in Grundzügen für die Vorlesungen, I: Römische Rechtsgeschichte* (1925–28). For a comparative study, see Buckland and McNair, *Roman Law and Common Law: A Comparison in Outline* (2008).

However, it is necessary to turn to the law of the late Roman Empire in order to understand the materials with which the juridical schools of the twelfth and succeeding centuries began the remarkable process of developing a legal system that marked the renaissance of juridical civilization in continental Europe.

1.02 *The Principal Periods of Italian History.* The history of Italian law can best be understood in relation to the cultural, political, social, and economic histories of Italy. This is, of course, a very large subject which can only be touched upon here. The interested reader will find it valuable to supplement this chapter with other readings[3] on Italian history.

Italy's period of greatness began early in the eleventh century, rising on foundations created by the blending of two cultures: Roman and Germanic. This period was marked by the birth of Italian law and the Italian language[4] and the rebirth (Renaissance) of the arts, commerce, and the liberties of the townspeople. For four centuries, Italy was the principal center of European civilization. In a great burst of creativity, Italians of genius transformed the worlds of art, thought, and action.[5]

The creative ferment in Italy in the eleventh through the sixteenth centuries had been preceded by centuries of barbarian invasions and was followed by centuries of economic, political, and moral decadence. The liberties enjoyed by the Italian cities degenerated into the pomp, plots, and despotism of the new nobility. New invasions by the French, Spanish (the most devastating, both materially and morally), and Austrians began at the end of the fifteenth century; foreign domination lasted until liberation and unification in the nineteenth. The scars of this period

---

3. Hughes, *The United States and Italy* (2d ed. 1965) is a good place to begin. See also generally Duggan, *A Concise History of Italy* (1994).

4. See ch. 6 of Haskins, *The Renaissance of the Twelfth Century* (1957). See also note 41 and accompanying text.

5. Leonardo (1452–1519) perhaps best personifies the qualities of the Renaissance man. The catalog of other notable men from this period is far too long to set out here. A highly selective list would include among the painters, sculptors, and architects, Cimabue, Giotto, Brunelleschi, Ghiberti, Donatello, Beato Angelico, Paolo Uccello, Masaccio, Piero della Francesca, Mantegna, Bramante, Botticelli, Ghirlandaio, Michelangelo, Giorgione, Raphael, Titian, Cellini, Tintoretto, and Palladio; among the writers, philosophers, and divines, St. Francis of Assisi, St. Thomas Aquinas, Dante, Petrarch, Boccaccio, Lorenzo the Magnificent, Savonarola, Machiavelli, Ariosto, Tasso, and Giordano Bruno; and among the explorers and adventurers, Marco Polo, Columbus, and Amerigo Vespucci.

remain, especially in the South, where the wounds inflicted by foreign rule were deeper. Indeed, the fascist dictatorship, with its nationalistic rhetoric, its resentment of the outside world, and its isolationism, may have been a kind of ultimate consequence of this period.

Despite the relative decline in creativity, "none of the successive epochs of Italian history has failed to leave its mark. . . . As opposed to a country like Greece, which lived for centuries in the backwaters of history, in Italy the record is continuous, the stream of civilized activity has never been interrupted."[6] Even in the darkest centuries, creative figures appeared. The sixteenth and seventeenth centuries produced the painter Caravaggio and the sculptor Bernini, whose baroque architecture changed the face of Rome. Galileo (1564–1642) "built the foundations of modern science and led the struggle against the Aristotelians and their narrow-mindedness."[7] The eighteenth century had its geniuses: the historian-philosopher Giambattista Vico and the legal scholars Beccaria and Filangieri.[8] The eighteenth century also had the art of Tiepolo, the comedy of characters and costumes of Goldoni, and above all the sublime music of Antonio Vivaldi, the "red priest" who inspired Johann Sebastian Bach.[9] In the following centuries came the poetic grandeur of Leopardi, Foscolo, Manzoni, and Carducci; the strong realistic novels of Verga; the *ante litteram* "existential" works of Pirandello; and the operas of Bellini, Donizetti, Rossini, Verdi, and Puccini.

---

6. Hughes, *op. cit.* n. 3, at 42.

7. *Italian Literature*, in 12 *Encyclopaedia Britannica* available at http://www.britannica.com/ EBchecked/topic/297281/Italian-literature.

8. See *Filangieri Gaetano*, in 7 *Novissimo digesto italiano* 296–97 (1961); and *Beccaria Cesare*, in 2 *ibid.*, at 290 (1958); see also Cotta, *Gaetano Filangieri e il problema della legge* (1954); and Calamandrei's *Introduction* to Beccaria, *Dei delitti e delle pene* (2d ed. 1965). Beccaria's book, *Of Crimes and Punishment*, "was the most influential volume on the reform of criminal justice ever produced." 3 *Encyclopaedia Britannica* 285 (1961). Filangieri's *The Science of Legislation* "showed him to be an ardent reformer and vehement in denouncing the abuses of his time. [Its] success was great and immediate not only in Italy but throughout Europe at large." 9 *Encyclopaedia Britannica* 237 (1961).

9. The roll of notable Italian composers who preceded and followed Vivaldi includes the Gabrielis, Palestrina, Monteverdi, Frescobaldi, Lulli, Corelli, the Scarlattis, Albinoni, Tartini, Pergolesi, Boccherini, Cimarosa, Clementi, Cherubini, Paganini, and many others. It almost seemed, particularly in the seventeenth and eighteenth centuries, as if the artist, unable to express himself with words (foreign rulers spoke foreign languages, and Italians were denied freedom of expression), turned instead to music.

The history of Italian law during these great periods is intricately involved with, and consequently tends to reflect, the cultural, social, political, and economic histories of Italy. It begins with the great creative achievement of the Glossators and the University of Bologna in the twelfth century, dominates the legal life of Europe for several hundred years, and then subsides in the sixteenth century. In the years that follow there are substantial, sometimes brilliant, legal achievements, but they stand out as unusual. In the early 1500s, the center of legal creativity shifted, first to France and Holland and then to Germany, and Italy received the ideology of the French Revolution and the French codes, and later in the nineteenth century German legal scholarship.

With the fall of fascism and the end of World War II, Italy entered a new period. The new Constitution of 1948 came into force, and Italy experienced an economic miracle of industrial and commercial development, as well as drastic changes in the patterns of rural and urban life throughout the peninsula. Many aspects of Italian law were successfully reformed, and the project of European integration brought further changes to the Italian legal system.

1.03 *The Pre-Justinian Compilations and Justinian's Corpus Juris.*   The sources of the Roman law at the end of the third century A.D. may be divided into two categories: *leges* and *iura*. In the late Empire, the term *leges*[10] included all general enactments of the emperors, particularly in public law. The entire complex of opinions of those juris-consults endowed with *ius respondendi ex auctoritate principis*[11] was known as *iura*, and may be crudely analogized to case law in the common law systems. By the middle of the third century A.D., this kind of authoritative source lost the creativity it had enjoyed in the preceding centuries, and the decay of juridical culture

---

10. In the first three centuries of the Empire, a distinction was made between *leges generales* and *leges speciales*. The latter, encompassing *decreta*, *mandata*, *rescripta*, and *adnotationes*, were rules formulated to resolve individual cases or orders directed to officials. The fourth century A.D. saw the progressive abandonment of these various acts. For a bibliographic orientation, see Berger, *Encyclopedic Dictionary of Roman Law* (1953).

11. The *ius respondendi* is an institution of the principate of Augustus. The power could be conferred only by the emperor (*ex auctoritate principis*). It was conferred upon jurists who were consulted by judges about the proper resolution of a legal question. With the passage of time, it seems that the opinion given was binding upon the judge. Although never explicitly abolished, *ius respondendi* seems to have fallen into disuse in the period between Diocletian and Constantine (the end of the third century). See Schulz, *History of Roman Legal Science* (1946); Kunkel, *Herkunft und soziale Stellung der römischen Juristen* (1952).

had become, in the West, an irreversible phenomenon. During this same period, it became apparent that the bulk of imperial legislation, which was both massive and disorganized, needed systematic reorganization. This necessity gave birth to two private collections: the *Codex Gregorianus*,[12] compiled about 292 A.D.; and the *Codex Hermogenianus*,[13] the continuation of its predecessor, of which we possess but a small part of the text. As private collections, they had no official authority.

Of much greater importance was the *Codex Theodosianus*,[14] compiled, like the others, in the East. This was the product of a commission of jurists named by the Emperor Theodosius II. The Code was divided into sixteen books and contained only the enactments (*constitutiones*) dating from Constantine's reign, with certain nonradical modifications made by the compilers. It was extended to the West on January 1, 439, by solemn vote of the Roman Senate. During the early Middle Ages, it was widely known and used in the West, especially in the transalpine regions, which, unlike Italy, did not receive the compilation of Justinian.

In 527, Justinian took the throne of the Eastern Empire. His first work as legislator was the drafting of a new *Codex*, the *Novus Justinianus Codex*.[15] This work,

12. No one definitive reconstruction of either the *Codex Gregorianus* or the *Codex Hermogenianus* exists. See Corcoran, *The Empire of the Tetrarchs: Imperial Pronouncements and Government*, A.D. *284–324*, 25–35 (1996). The original edition of this book cited the version published in 3 Krüger, *Collectio librorum iuris anteiustiniani* 221 (1890), available at http://books.google.com/books?id=PSwGAAAAQAAJ, which was prepared from the Visigothic abridgment. Another reconstruction, which does not include material not explicitly attributed to the *Codex Gregorianus*, is found in Haenel, *Codicis Gregoriani et codicis Hermogeniani fragmenta* 1 (1837), available at http://books.google.com/books?id=015EAAAAcAAJ. For a discussion, see Schulz, *op. cit.* n. 11, at 287–309, Scherillo, *Teodosiano, Gregoriano, Ermogeniano*, in *Studi in memoria di Umberto Ratti* 249–323 (1934), and Sperandio, *Codex Gregorianus: origini e vicende* 389–95 (2005).

13. The original edition of this book cited to the version published in 3 Krüger, *op. cit.* n. 12, at 249. Another version is available in Haenel, *op. cit.* n. 12, at 57. A more recent edition is Cenderelli, *Ricerche sul "Codex Hermogenianus"* (1965). A chronological arrangement of rescripts from the period of the *Codex Gregorianus* and *Codex Hermogenianus* is provided in Honoré, *Emperors and Lawyers, Second Edition, Completely Revised, with a Palingenesia of Third-Century Imperial Rescripts 193–305* A.D. (1994). For a discussion, see Scherillo, *op. cit.* n. 12.

14. Published in *Theodosiani Libri XVI cum constitutionibus sirmondinis . . . ediderunt Mommsen et Meyer* (1904), available at http://books.google.com/books?id=eWkNAAAAI AAJ. There is a translation into English, edited by Pharr, *The Theodosian Code and Novels and the Sirmondian Constitutions* (1952).

15. The text has been lost. A fragment of its index has been found on a papyrus.

which was based on three preceding compilations, was published in 529. The following year, Justinian began the compilation of the *iura*, entrusting this labor to a commission presided over by the jurist Tribonian. After ransacking 1,625 works by 39 ancient jurisconsults, almost all of whom had been endowed with *ius respondendi*, the commission produced fifty books of widely differing sizes. This work, known as the *Digesta* or *Pandectae*,[16] became effective on December 30, 533. In the same year, the *Institutiones*, an elementary manual of four books modeled on the *Institutiones* of Gaius,[17] was promulgated.

The publication of the Digest made necessary a second edition of the Code in order to unify and harmonize the parts of the legislative system and to add the enactments of Justinian made after 529. The result was a revised edition, the *Codex repetitae praelectionis*, in twelve books. The revised edition, effective from December 29, 534, replaced its predecessor.[18] All of Justinian's legislation, including the *Novellae Constitutiones*,[19] his enactments from 535 to 565, was extended to

16. The critical edition of the Digest is by Mommsen, *Digesta Iustiniani Augusti . . . adsumpto in operis societatem Krüger* (1868–70), available at http://books.google.com/books?id=Vi8GAAAAQAAJ. An English translation that contains the text of Mommesen's Latin edition is Watson, *The Digest of Justinian* (1985). For a discussion, see the works cited above and Collinet, *Le genèse du Digeste, du Code et des Institutes de Justinien* (1952).

17. The *Institutiones* of Gaius, an elegant profile of Roman law in the classical era, was written about 161 A.D. It is our most important source of classical Roman law, and its discovery was as fortunate as it was fortuitous. It was found in 1816 on a palimpsest in the Capitolare library of Verona by Niebuhr. There is so much literature surrounding the work that no bibliography is necessary here. The original edition of this book recommends the English translation, together with a commentary, of De Zulueta, *The Institutes of Gaius* (2 vols., 1946 and 1953). Another translation, Poste, *Institutes of Roman Law by Gaius* (4th ed. 1904), is available at http://oll.libertyfund.org/title/1154, and a more recent translation is Robinson and Gordon, *The Institutes of Gaius: With the Latin Text of Seckel and Kuebler* (1988). A biography of Gaius is Honoré, *Gaius: A Biography* (1962). The critical edition of the *Institutiones* of Justinian is by Krüger. Published in 1867, it was included in the Berlin edition of the *Corpus Juris Civilis*, edited by Mommsen, Krüger Schöll, and Kroll, available at http://archive.org/details/corpus-juriscivilookrueuoft. An English translation of Krüger's text is Birks and McLeod, *Justinian's Institutes* (1987). On the materials utilized by the compilers of the *Institutiones* of Justinian, see Ferrini, *Sulle fonti delle Istituzioni di Giustiniano*, in 2 Ferrini, *Opere* 307 *et seq.* (1929).

18. The critical edition by Krüger (1877) has been reprinted several times. An English translation is Blume and Kearley, *Annotated Justinian Code* (2d ed. 2010), available at http://uwacadweb.uwyo.edu/blume&justinian/.

19. The critical edition by Schöll and Kroll (1894) has been reprinted several times. An English translation is Blume and Kearley, *op. cit.* n. 18.

Italy after he reconquered the peninsula from the Ostrogoths, who had ruled there since the end of the fifth century.

Justinian's goal was to compose a body of practical law that would meet the needs of the times. By innovating and reforming in accordance with new exigencies, he hoped to eliminate antiquated institutions, academic controversies, and scholarly differences. In addition, however, he wanted to salvage the treasures of ancient learning and to restore the level of legal culture. Thus, Justinian pursued two mutually contradictory goals; while he attempted to restore faithfully the Roman legal tradition by reorganizing an enormous body of materials that already had normative force (the compilation), he also enacted new legislation, repealing all acts not contained in the compilation and forbidding any manner of interpretation.[20] His efforts and those of his staff of jurists reached the limits of the possible in reconciling these opposing goals.

1.04 *The Langobard Period.*   Justinian's war to reconquer Italy had barely ended when, in 568, the Langobards, a Germanic people of the Saxon group, invaded. Their conquest, which took place slowly and in a disorganized manner, eventually extended to a great part of the peninsula. Byzantium continued to dominate the Venetian lagoons; Ravenna and the Exarchate;[21] the Pentapolis;[22] Latium (the area around Rome) and a series of fortified Umbrian castles connecting Latium with the Pentapolis; the cities of Gaeta, Naples, and Amalfi; the areas of Puglia and Calabria; and the islands of Sicily and Sardinia.[23]

The Italian territories remaining under the Eastern Empire were the only ones in Italy in which the Roman legal tradition continued in relatively genuine form. Roman law continued to be the territorial law binding everyone living on imperial soil. The Byzantine areas continued to receive the legislation emanating from the

20. The prohibition is contained in Constitutio Tanta § 21.

21. The Exarchate, the territory around Ravenna, was so designated because its ruler, appointed by the Byzantine emperors, was called the exarch. On Byzantine administration of this territory, see Diehl, *Etudes sur l'administration byzantine dans l'exarchat de Ravenne (568–751)* (1888).

22. The Pentapolis consisted of the five cities of Rimini, Ancona, Pesaro, Fano, and Senigallia.

23. A number of useful maps illustrating the extent of this conquest may be found in Hallenbeck, *Pavia and Rome: The Lombard Monarchy and the Papacy in the Eighth Century* (1982), published in the *Transactions of the American Philosophical Society.*

imperial court, and the study of Roman sources survived, bridging the ancient imperial schools of law and the Italian schools which, beginning in the twelfth century, diffused Roman law throughout Europe.

The Langobards introduced into Italy the principle of the personality of law, the norm among the Germanic peoples. In accordance with this principle, subjects of the same legal system were governed in their private relationships by the law of their tribe (*natio*).[24] This was in contrast to the principle of the territoriality of law in Byzantine Italy. In Langobard Italy, therefore, a large part of the subject population, and the Church, continued to live under Roman law. However, in the absence of any authority capable of applying it correctly, what passed for Roman law often involved customary practices of diverse origins and structures.

The Langobards, like the rest of their Germanic kin, had no written law. It was not until 643, seventy-five years after their invasion of Italy, that the Langobard king Rothari gave his people a complex of laws. Written in incredibly coarse Latin, this work, known as the *Edictum*, was divided into 388 chapters. It is considered to be the most complete statement of the customary law of any of the Germanic tribes. The legislative efforts of Rothari were pursued by his successors. The body of Langobard legislation, consisting of the *Edict* of Rothari and the additions made by his successors, goes under the name *Edictum regum Langobardorum*.[25]

1.05 *The Frankish Capitularies and the Legislation of the Holy Roman Empire.*   Even after the Frankish Conquest of Langobard Italy in 774, Langobard private law, with its basic principle of the personality of law, continued to be applied. This principle remained in effect even after the coronation of Charlemagne as Holy Roman Emperor on Christmas Day, 800, and the establishment of Frankish public law.[26] Indeed, it was fundamental to the new political structure. Hence, the old and relatively simple dichotomy of Roman law and Langobard law was superseded by

24. A series of rules existed to determine the applicable law when the parties to a relationship belonged to different systems of personal law.

25. Many manuscripts have survived. The best critical edition is Bluhme, *Monumenta Germaniae Historica, IV Leges* 1–225 (1868), available at http://books.google.com/books?id=DGL29SuQymcC. An English translation and commentary is Drew, *The Lombard Laws* (1973).

26. On public law in the Carolingian period, see Kleinclausz, *L'Empire Carolingien: ses origines et ses transformations* (1902); Fichtenau, *The Carolingian Empire* (Munz trans., 1957).

numerous systems of personal law. Coexisting in the peninsula with Roman and Langobard law were the national laws of other Germanic nations—the Salic and Ripuarian Franks, the Alemans, the Bavarians, the Burgundians, and the Visigoths. The Gallo-Romans, who had emigrated to Italy before Charlemagne, were governed by the Theodosian law of the *Lex Romana Wisigothorum*. The Italian territories continued to constitute a distinct kingdom. The Regnum Italicum, as it was called, was ruled at first by Charlemagne's son Pippin and later by his grandson Bernard. It enjoyed a certain autonomy, with a court and administrative offices located at its capital, Pavia, and it had its own popular assembly.[27]

To minimize the inevitable inconveniences of diverse legal systems, there was an abundant production of legislation called *capitula* or *capitularia* promulgated by the sovereign, both in his capacity as national king and as emperor. The Carolingian capitularies applicable in Italy were compiled under private auspices in a collection known as the *Capitulare Italicum*. The *Capitulare Italicum* was permanently joined to the Langobard *Edict* at the beginning of the eleventh century. There were two reasons for this consolidation: the scriveners customarily transcribed the *Capitulare* immediately after the *Edict*, and the legislation of the Frankish sovereigns was considered to be a continuation of that of the Langobards. This corpus of Langobard-Frankish law, entitled in the manuscripts the *Liber Legis Langobardorum*, is commonly known today as the *Liber Papiensis*.[28] The greater part of the *Liber Papiensis* is accompanied by detailed glosses written by generations of Langobard jurists; it was definitively completed by an anonymous jurist, perhaps in Pavia in the second half of the eleventh century.

1.06 *The Sources of Canon Law before Gratian.*   In studying the sources of Italian law, it is necessary to consider, along with the statutory and customary law, the canon law of the Roman Catholic Church. The history of canon law, the law of a universal organization, naturally exceeds the boundaries of Italian law. However, the two are inextricably woven together because of the Church's great influence on Italian history and because of the particular relationship between Italy and the Church resulting from the fact that Rome, almost from the beginning, was the center of Christendom.

---

27. On the legal system of this kingdom, see Leicht, *Dal "regnum Longobardorum" al "regnum Italiae,"* in 3 Rivista di storia del diritto italiano 5 (1930); see also Solmi, *L'amministrazione finanziaria del regno Italico nell'alto medioevo* (1932).

28. See the edition of Boretius in Bluhme, *op. cit.* n. 25, at 595 *et seq.*

The Church distinguishes two fundamental categories of law: divine and human. The former is said to have its origin in the divine will and is further divided into divine positive law (as revealed in the Bible and in tradition) and natural law (rules taught by nature, discovered by human reason, and applicable equally to all men). Human law is divided into canon law, consisting of the canons and decretals,[29] and civil law.

The most ancient Western canonical collections, witnesses to the consolidation of the constitution and hierarchical structure of the Church, appear in the fifth century. Of these, the most important is the *Collectio Dionysiana*,[30] edited in Rome by the monk Dionysius about 500. This text, which was brought up to date from time to time, was sent by Pope Hadrian I to Charlemagne in 774, and at the Diet of Aachen of 802, it was solemnly adopted as the general code of the Frankish Church. This modernized compilation, called *Dionysio-Hadriana*, thus became an official text and was diffused throughout the West.

A new period in the history of the Western canonical compilations began in the middle of the ninth century with a series of collections blending genuine and forged sources (the well-known Frankish forgeries, so called because they were written to defend the rights and interests of the Gallic Church against the interference of public officials). From the same era came the famous "Donation of Constantine," a document which purported to be a cession of temporal power over the City of Rome and other central Italian territories by the Emperor Constantine to the Papacy. The donation, which was thought to be genuine until the humanist Lorenzo Valla showed it to be a forgery in the fifteenth century, was prepared to strengthen the claim of the Papacy to temporal power.

The most important phenomenon of this period was the progressive increase in the use of Roman legal materials from Justinian's era in compilations of canon law. One of these compilations, made at the beginning of the ninth century and known

29. In general, the canons are enactments of councils, while decretals are normative provisions issued by the popes.

30. See Strewe, *Die Canonessammlung des Dionysius Exiguus in der ersten Redaktion* (1931). Transcriptions of material from *Collectio Dionysiana* and *Dionysio-Hadriana* are available from the Carolingian Canon Law Project, at http://ccl.rch.uky.edu/dionysiana-article. For a guide to critical editions of canon law texts, see Lotte, *Canonical Collections of the Early Middle Ages (ca. 400–1140): A Bibliographical Guide to the Manuscripts and Literature* (1999).

as the *Lex romana canonice compta*,[31] contains the *capitula romanae legis ad canones pertinentia*, the Roman law applicable and adapted to the ecclesiastical legal system. The materials were selected from the *Institutes*, the *Code*, and to a greater extent from the *Novels* of Justinian. Probably at the end of the ninth century from Northern Italy came the *Collectio Anselmo dedicata*,[32] the first collection to contain the canonical and Roman texts of Justinian's era arranged in systematic form. These works were important manifestations of the progressive penetration of Roman into canon law, and vice versa. This interrelationship may be characterized as a true reception, through which Roman norms formally came to be part of the legal system of the Church.

1.07 *Knowledge of Roman Sources and Legal Literature in the Early Middle Ages.*   We now turn to a brief consideration of the legal culture of the times. Knowledge of the *Digest* had disappeared; other Roman sources had become corrupted. Part of Justinian's corpus of law was known in Italy from the seventh to the eleventh centuries, but the part that was known often contained errors and omissions. Still, Italy was the only country in the West where Justinian's work was known before the eleventh century.[33]

Naturally, because of its bulk and its complexity, the *Digest* was the first to disappear. The last certain citation to it is found in a letter by Saint Gregory the Great in 603, and no citation is again found until 1076 in a judgment rendered by Nordilo, the delegate of the Marchesa Beatrice of Tuscany, at Marturi, near Poggibonsi.[34] In the interim, however, there is no citation to the *Digest* by writers,

---

31. See the edition of Mor, *Lex romana canonice compta. Testo di leggi romano-canoniche del secolo IX pubblicato sul ms. parigino Biblioteca Nazionale* 12448 (1927).

32. See the edition (although incomplete) of Thaner, *Anselmi episcopi Lucensis Collectio canonum etc.* (1906–15), reprinted as Thaner, *Collectio canonum, una cum collectione minore* (1965). Another edition, which contains the Roman law texts as found in one particular manuscript, is Russo, *Tradizione manoscritta di leges romanæ nei codici dei secoli IX e X della Biblioteca capitolare di Modena* (1980). See Fournier and Le Bras, *Histoire des collections canoniques en Occident depuis les fausses décrétales jusqu'au Décret de Gratien* 25 et seq. (1931–32).

33. On the knowledge of Roman sources before Irnerius, see Conrat, *Geschichte der Quellen und Literatur des römischen Rechts im frühen Mittelalter* (1889–91, reprinted 1963); Flach, *Etudes critiques sur l'histoire du droit romain au moyen âge* (1890).

34. Published in 4 Ficker, *Forschungen zur Reichs- und Rechtsgeschichte Italiens*, no. 73, p. 99 *et seq.* (1874), available at http://books.google.com/books?id=EEM0AAAAIAAJ.

grammarians, or historians. No knowledge of it is shown in court or private records or in any compilation that can be attributed with certainty to this period.[35]

The *Code* was known, but in reduced form. At the end of the seventh or at the beginning of the eighth century, it was edited into a compendium from which the last three books were excised and which contained only about one-quarter of the first nine books. The reason for the disappearance of the last three books is simple; they were concerned with the public offices of the Empire—administrative, fiscal, and military matters of little relevance to the Italy of the Middle Ages. These three books, called the *Tres Libri*, were not rediscovered until the middle of the twelfth century, at the height of the Bolognese renaissance.

The *Novels*, too, were known during the early Middle Ages in compendium form: the *Epitome Juliani*, a private condensation written about 555 by one Julian, perhaps a professor at the school of Constantinople. This compendium was used until the twelfth century, at which time it was replaced by a larger collection called the *Authenticum*.

Only the *Institutes* of Justinian was known in its entirety, as numerous manuscripts from the era attest. Like the other manuscripts of Justinian's corpus, these were frequently, if crudely, supplied with glosses. Most of them are chiefly remarkable for the legal ignorance of their authors. They serve to illustrate the cultural decadence of the era and suggest the difficulty of the effort of reconstruction and research that was necessary before the rebirth of legal culture of which we speak below.

1.08 *Legal Science and Law Schools before Irnerius.*   It is clear that a school of law existed in Rome at the time of Justinian, but it certainly disappeared in the following century. The letters and sermons of Saint Gregory the Great testify to the shocking barbarization of customs and the decadence of all aspects of civilization.[36] A tradition that goes back to Odofredus (d. 1265) tells us of the existence of a school at Ravenna that could have been the bridge between the ancient Roman

---

35. See Mor, *Il Digesto nell'età preirneriana e la formazione della Vulgata*, in *Per il XIV centenario della codificazione giustinianea. Studi di diritto pubblicati dalla Facoltà di Giurisprudenza della Università di Pavia* 557–679 (1934) (a work now substantially outdated).

36. Justinian's conquest of Italy and the ensuing Langobard invasion, with their sequels of famine and epidemic, had practically depopulated Rome. See the vivid description in Gibbon, *The Decline and Fall of the Roman Empire*, ch. 45. At the time of Gregory the Great (590–604), there was only one banker in Rome, and even he was beset with the general financial troubles of the times. Of the ancient aqueducts only one functioned. It was not

school and that of Bologna. Since the fifth century, Ravenna had been a center of the arts, especially architecture and mosaics, and since the ninth century, the city had frequently been an imperial residence. Though it is clear that there were judges, lawyers, notaries, and public officials stationed there from the Byzantine era until the tenth century, there is no contemporary source attesting to a school of law, nor is there any written work attributable with certainty to such a school.[37]

A different conclusion must be reached with regard to the Langobard school at Pavia, where the study and interpretation of legal sources was conducted in a less barbarous manner. Studies were not based solely on empirical interests but were carried out according to the processes of formal logic just beginning to be developed by the first scholastics.[38]

As the capital of the Italian kingdom and the seat of a supreme court with a corps of judges and notaries, Pavia was the site of vigorous activity in interpreting and applying the law to cases. Although this growth was born of purely practical needs, it encouraged legal studies and improved standards of legal culture. The fruit of several generations of study was the *Expositio ad Librum papiensem*,[39] an enormous collection of glosses that was consolidated in a definitive edition around the second half of the eleventh century. Its author distinguishes the various interpreters into *antiquissimi*, *antiqui*, and *moderni*. The principal difference between the last two groups was the use of Roman law in the exegesis of the Langobard sources. For the *antiqui* such use was rare, but the *moderni*, who consciously strove to find the spirit of the law, tended to turn to Roman law, especially in cases of gaps in the Langobard-Frankish law.

---

until the fifteenth century that Rome became once again an important center of learning, art, and wealth.

37. On the school of Ravenna, see the classic works of Fitting, *Zur Geschichte der Rechtswissenschaft am Anfange des Mittelalters* (1875); Conrat, *op. cit.* n. 33, at 601; Patetta, *Per la storia del diritto romano nel medio evo*, in 12 Rivista italiana per le scienze giuridiche 307 (1891). For a balanced appraisal, see Astuti, *Lezioni di storia del diritto italiano: Lefonti, età romano-barbarica* 339 et seq. (1953); Calasso, *Medio evo del diritto* 279 et seq. (1954). See generally Mor, *Scritti di storia giuridica altomedievale* (1977).

38. On the school at Pavia, see 3 Ficker, *op. cit.* n. 34, at 44 et seq.; Mengozzi, *Ricerche sull'attività della scuola di Pavia nell'alto medio evo* (1924) (a work which, however, suffers from an excessively narrow local outlook); Solmi, *La persistenza della scuola di Pavia nel medio evo fino alla fondazione dello studio generale*, in *Contributi alla storia del diritto comune* 285 (1937).

39. Published in Bluhme, *op. cit.* n. 25.

The early Middle Ages, although rich in legal history, did not enjoy a high level of legal culture. With a few exceptions, legal scholarship, and schools devoted to other than practical ends, did not exist. The surviving literature demonstrates the poor state of knowledge of the Roman sources and of legal culture as a whole.

1.09 *Birth of the Universities.* We have sketched the legal history of the centuries preceding the legal renaissance at Bologna in order to put that great age into perspective. The period to which we now turn marks the genesis of Italian civil law, and the civil law of half the world. From the Italian civil law came the *jus commune*—the European common law—which spread from Europe to Latin America (and much of the rest of the world) and became the basis of the "civil law system," which is so often contrasted with the Anglo-American "common law."[40]

The school of Glossators, which developed in Bologna, was an integral part of the tremendous revival of intellectual life that began around the end of the eleventh century and characterized the entire late Middle Ages. This cultural revival—marked by the rediscovery of Aristotle and the development of scholastic philosophy—was favored by a rise in population and economic activity. The rustic feudal economy was destroyed; new lands were put to the plow; commerce flourished; the great markets, fairs, and banks were born; the cities once again became economic centers; the ships of the Italian maritime republics (Venice, Genoa, Pisa, Amalfi) took to the sea to find new markets. During the same period the Italian language was shaped from crude transformations of spoken Latin.[41]

40. There is a large body of literature on the origins of the *jus commune*. We will limit our citation to Koschaker, *Europa und das römische Recht* 79 and *passim* (1953).

"They [the Glossators] laid the foundations of the system of modern Roman law, the system which is at the base of most of the legal systems of modern Europe." 4 Holdsworth, *A History of English Law* 221 (1924); see also Haskins, *op. cit.* n. 4, at 193–94; Coing, *Zur Geschichte des Privatrechtssystems* 14–15 and *passim* (1962).

41. The three great "creators" of the Italian language, Dante, Petrarch, and Boccaccio, lived in the years 1265–1321, 1304–74, and 1313–75, respectively. These three men spent most of their lives in Florence. Tuscany, whose capital is Florence, is still the area in which purest Italian is spoken.

Before Dante, the most important center of literary art in the vernacular was the Sicilian school of poetry, which flourished at the court of Frederick II (1194–1250), and the school of the "*dolce stil nuovo*" (sweet new style), which flourished mostly in Tuscany during the second half of the thirteenth century.

The same era marked the beginning of the great age of figurative art. Giotto, a Florentine, was a contemporary of Dante; Simone Martini (who was highly influential in France

In this cultural awakening the study of law was separated from the study of rhetoric, with which it had been integrated during the early Middle Ages.[42] The intellectual activity of the Glossators was not spent on Langobardic-Frankish law, which was too crude and too firmly tied to primitive conditions. The Glossators turned instead to a law that was more fully developed, the law of Justinian's day, adapting it to the newly developing civilization. Their first need was to reconstruct accurate texts of Justinian's law, in particular the fundamental text that the early Middle Ages had ignored: the *Digest*.

The beginnings of the school of Bologna were modest.[43] Of its founder, Irnerius, we know very little.[44] He appears in thirteen documents as attorney or judge during the years 1112–25. Modern critical historians have disproved his authorship of all the works attributed to him by the Glossators who followed him. Nevertheless, what little we do know about him as a scholar and teacher is enough to confirm that his teaching gave rise to the school of Bologna and that after his death his spiritual legacy was preserved by numerous disciples, among them the famous "four doctors," Bulgarus, Martinus, Ugo, and Jacobus.

Within a few decades Bologna became the center of legal studies, and to it came students from all Italy and, later, from all Europe.[45] Around the middle of the

---

as well, having worked for many years at the Papal court at Avignon) and Ambrogio and Pietro Lorenzetti, three of the foremost masters of the Sienese school, were more or less contemporaries of Petrarch and Boccaccio.

42. See Calasso, *op. cit.* n. 37, at 276.

43. On the history of the medieval universities, see Denifle, *Die Entstehung der Universitäten des Mittelalters bis 1400* (1885). For Bologna, see 1 Rashdall, *The Universities of Europe* 87–268 (2d ed. in 3 vols. 1936); see also *Storia dell'università di Bologna* by Sorbelli (Middle Ages) and Simeoni (modern age) (1940); Calcaterra, *Alma mater studiorum (L'università di Bologna nella storia della cultura e della civiltà)* (1948). A more recent work is Passeri, *Piccola storia dell'universita' di Bologna* (1986). See generally Janin, *The University in Medieval Life* 1179–1499 (2008).

44. On Irnerius, see Besta, *L'opera d'Irnerio* (1896). See also Genzmer, *Die justinianische Kodifikation und die Glossatoren*, in 1 *Atti del Congresso Internazionale di diritto romano—Bologna e Roma*, 1933, 345–430 (1934), and Winroth, *The Making of Gratian's Decretum* 162–68 (2000).

45. The original edition of this book cites to an unpublished version of Coing, *Die europäische Privatrechtsgeschichte der neueren Zeit als einheitliches Forschungsgebiet*, ultimately published in 1 Jus Commune 1–33 (1967), available at http://data.rg.mpg.de/iuscommune/ic01_coing.pdf. The original edition describes and quotes from this unpublished version thus:

In this study the author demonstrates the probability, indeed the necessity, of a Unitarian history of European law. The school of Bologna stands at the beginning of this

twelfth century there were about ten thousand law students there, an enormous figure for that day.[46] The students chose their own teachers and contracted with them concerning the place and manner of instruction and the amount of tuition. The relationship between teacher and student was juridically characterized as a *societas*, that is, a partnership. The ever-growing body of students organized itself for purposes of internal discipline, mutual assistance, and defense. The various *societates* formed a larger organization called *universitas scholarium* (university of students) within which the students were grouped by nations. Within the university the students elected their chiefs from among fellow students. These at first were called *consules*, and later *rectores*.

The university was a product of communal liberty. It was formed at the time of the birth of the free city-state as a private association. However, after the second half of the thirteenth century it was considered necessary to obtain an imperial or papal decree to give official status to a university. The only state university was at Naples; it was founded in 1224 by Frederick II of Swabia, emperor of the Holy Roman Empire and king of Sicily, to compete with the school of Bologna.

1.10 *The Work of the Universities in the Formation of the Jus Commune.*   The age of formational development of the universities (Bologna c. 1100, Padua 1222, Perugia 1308, Pisa 1343) coincided with the birth of Italian law and the *jus commune*. The two essential elements of the *jus commune*,[47] fused into a single normative system,

---

unity. Its curriculum, organization, and examinations were the model for later schools in Italy (Padua, 1222; Perugia, 1308; Pisa, 1343, etc.) and abroad (Salamanca and Orléans, around 1230; Prague, 1348; Vienna, 1365; Cracow, 1367; Heidelberg, 1388, etc.). In this manner there came to be "a unity of legal culture and education" among all educated European jurists. At the base of this education was Roman law, as glossed and commented upon. "Throughout the late Middle Ages," he writes, "even during the sixteenth century, the Italian universities, especially Bologna, Padua, Perugia, and Pavia, were the meeting place of the international student body; not even the English were absent." Coing, ch. 3, p. 2.

And when universities were founded outside of Italy, "at first many of the law professors were Italians." Vinogradoff, *Roman Law in Medieval Europe* 127 (3d ed. 1961).

46. The population of the city itself was about thirty or forty thousand.

47. A bibliography of works on the concept of the *jus commune* would be vast. Only major contributions to the literature are cited here. Besta, *Introduzione al diritto comune* (1938); Calisse, *Il diritto comune con riguardo speciale agli Stati della Chiesa*, in 2 *Studi di storia e diritto in onore di E. Besta* 415 (1939); Calisse, *Intorno alle relazioni fra statuti e diritto*

were: (a) the Roman law of Justinian's time as rediscovered and developed by the Glossators and Commentators, and then received by a great part of continental Europe as the civil law of the Holy Roman Empire (the so-called Roman common law); and (b) canon law, the law of the universal Church. The *jus commune* was considered to be the law of Christendom, the *societas christiana*, which was ruled by two supreme authorities: the emperor, its temporal head, and the pope, its spiritual head.[48] Each system of law retained its distinct area of application, its individual character and content. It was the work of the scholars to define the respective fields of application of the two systems. Intrinsic to both systems was a potential universality, a factor that helps to explain their reception in a great part of the world.

In juxtaposition to the law of the universal organisms—the law of the Holy Roman Empire and of Christendom—was the *jus proprium*, or local law of particular organisms.[49] The local and universal laws were not antithetical; they were complementary, and each influenced the other. Many statutes born out of the need to regulate situations not provided for by the *jus commune* were formulated and interpreted according to concepts forged by the scholars for the *jus commune*. The scholars, in turn, with their concern for the concrete problems of the day and their need to deal with the law as it actually existed, took the local law into account, thus enriching their work.

---

comune, in 1 *Studi di storia e diritto in memoria di Guido Bonolis* 154 (1942); Engelmann, *Die Wiedergeburt der Rechtskultur in Italien durch die Wissenschaftliche Lehre* (1938); 1 Ermini, *Corso di diritto comune* (3d ed. 1952); and last, three works by Calasso (who made the major contribution to the clarification of the subject matter of the *jus commune*): *Introduzione al diritto comune* (2d ed. 1970); *I glossatori e la teoria della sovranità* (1951), and *Medioevo del diritto* (1954).

48. Starting in the twelfth century, the Empire based its claim to universality on Roman law as interpreted in the glosses. It is significant that the Glossators added new imperial *constitutiones* and the text of the Treaty of Constance (1183) to the *Corpus Juris*, indicating that they considered the emperors of the Holy Roman Empire to be legitimate successors to the Roman emperors.

49. Particular, or local, law was enacted in the form of statutes (see 1.14) and, especially at the beginning, grew out of custom. It was primarily applicable to new matters not provided for in Roman law, such as certain aspects of commercial and maritime law. Through the centuries, statutory law increased in volume at the expense of Roman law. Nonetheless, the *jus commune* continued for centuries to be the living law in Europe and elsewhere. In Germany, for example, only with the Zivilprozessordnung of 1877 (effective 1879) and the bürgerliches Gesetzbuch of 1896 (effective 1900) was the *jus commune* entirely abrogated.

There was a progressive growth in the various European countries of a class of jurists with a common background of study of Roman law at Bologna or at another school modeled on Bologna. In their roles as judges, lawyers, and administrators, these jurists frequently treated the local law as an exception to the *jus commune*, and therefore as something requiring restrictive interpretation. In addition, they tended to interpret the local law with the concepts and terminology of the Roman law, thereby adapting it to and harmonizing it with the *jus commune*.

Thus, the *jus commune* became the law of a great part of Europe; it continued as such until the modern era of national codification. Even these codifications of civil and commercial law and procedure did not involve a total rupture with the past; what they did represent was a rejection of the idea of the universality of law contained in the concept of the *jus commune*. If today we may speak of the law of Italy, France, Germany, Holland, Spain, Latin America, prerevolutionary Russia, and much of Eastern Europe as "civil law," it is because the national codifications retained as their basis the conceptual framework and the principal institutions of the *jus commune*.

1.11 *The Glossators.*   In no era has the activity of interpreters been so important in building a legal system as it was in the age of the Glossators (the first teachers and scholars at the University of Bologna).[50] The legal scholars who developed the case law of the classical Roman era operated within a system containing other sophisticated and important sources of law, such as the *senatus consulta* and imperial *constitutiones*. The Glossators, working with the inadequate legislation of the medieval empire, had to face the enormous task of forging juridical tools suitable to a new age. Their achievement is even more impressive when one considers the low cultural level of the time.

The first important problem the Glossators faced and resolved was that of restoring the text of the *Corpus Juris* by eliminating the various compendia, summaries, and extracts that had been used in the earlier Middle Ages. The Glossators are also responsible for the rediscovery of the *Digest*. According to tradition, this occurred in three stages: first, the initial twenty-four books, the *Digestum Vetus*; second, the last twelve books from XXXIX to L, the *Digestum Novum*; and third,

---

50. From the vast body of literature on the Glossators, we cite Kantorowicz, *Studies in the Glossators of the Roman Law* (1938, reprinted in 1969); Calasso, *op. cit.* n. 37, at 521 *et seq.*; Paradisi, *Storia del diritto italiano. Le fonti del diritto nell'epoca bolognese*, parte I (1962).

the central books called by the strange name *Digestum Infortiatum*, the meaning of which philologists still dispute. These three parts of the *Digest* were contained in three volumes. A fourth consisted of the first nine books of the *Codex*, and a fifth volume held the *Institutiones*, the last three books of the *Codex*—the so-called *Tres Libri*—and the *Novellae* as found in the *Authenticum*. The fifth volume also contained several medieval texts, the *Libri Feudorum*,[51] certain *constitutiones* of the emperors of the Holy Roman Empire, and the peace treaty of Constance (1183). These five volumes were called by the Glossators the *Corpus Juris Civilis*, the name by which we now call Justinian's compilation.

The Glossators considered the compilation to be a truly organic corpus, containing no contradictions or interpolations. Even if they had known of any, they could not have removed them because the work of Justinian was considered living law, incapable of being corrected. This made more difficult their task of harmonizing obscure and contradictory points, filling gaps, and understanding oversights. They were compelled to create new concepts in order to satisfy their great need for systematizing. The Glossators were in no sense historians or scholars of ancient law; they were interpreters and adapters of an ancient text considered to be living law.

Their typical literary form was the gloss,[52] explanations written between the lines and in the margins of the text.[53] The gloss evolved from concise and purely literal, explanatory interpretations to more elaborate interpretations systematically

---

51. The nucleus of the *Libri Feudorum* was two letters outlining the fundamental institutions of feudal law; the letters were written between 1137 and 1156 by Oberto dell'Orto, an imperial judge of the tribunal of Milan, to his son Anselmo, a student at Bologna. The text was rearranged and added to by the Bolognese jurist Jacopo di Ardizzone. After undergoing further additions, it was divided into two books and placed by Accursius in his *magna glossa* edition of the *Corpus Juris*. Ugolino de' Presbiteri was responsible for inserting the *Libri Feudorum* into the collection of legislative texts, where it came to be studied along with Roman law. In this way Germanic institutions of the feudal law entered into the *jus commune*. A facsimile edition of *Libri Feudorum*, taken from a 1573 printing, is available as part of Montorzi, *Diritto feudale nel Basso Medioevo: materiali di lavoro e strumenti critici per l'esegesi della glossa ordinaria ai Libri feudorum: con la ristampa anastatica dei Libri feudorum e della loro glossa ordinaria* (1991).

52. On the various literary forms employed by the Glossators, see Kantorowicz, *op. cit.* n. 50, at 229 *et seq.*

53. Of course, the texts were hand written on parchment. As these passed from scholar to scholar, the apparatus of glosses grew. Usually new glosses were marked with a personal seal. Still, it is difficult and sometimes impossible to determine the authorship of a gloss.

connected, known as an apparatus of glosses. Other literary forms employed by the Glossators included (1) the *dissentiones*, the opposing and irreconcilable opinions that had been expressed by various Glossators; (2) the *quaestiones*, or disputes concerning controversial situation-types about which the arguments on all sides of the questions were expounded and resolved pursuant to the author's *solutio*; (3) the *casus*, glosses on hypothetical and, later, actual cases to which a rule of law was applied (a form used only infrequently); (4) the *brocarda* or *aphorismata*, maxims or definitions of general applicability, expressed succinctly for easy memorization; (5) the *summae*, which were treatises (like the *summae* of the theologians) on particular areas or institutions of the law.

No purpose would be served here by listing the principal Glossators. We have already mentioned Irnerius and the "four doctors," and mention should be made of Azo, whose work was used in Italy by Accursius and in England by Bracton.[54] There were many others, and they left an enormous body of written scholarship.

By the beginning of the thirteenth century, the method of the Glossators, as Azo had previously seen, had exhausted its purpose. The accumulation of glosses had suffocated the text, which was no longer studied directly but only through its glosses. This state of affairs was ended by one of the great scholars, the Florentine Accursius (d. about 1260), who undertook to select the best of the glosses that his predecessors had produced. The task was enormous; the final selection amounted to about 96,000 glosses. Accursius's work had great success. It was called the *Glossa Ordinaria* or *Magna Glossa* and was regularly published with editions of the *Corpus Juris* so that they were received together throughout the continent. Accursius's work was the final great product of generations of Bolognese scholars.

Accursius has been criticized for partiality, for a lack of originality, and for historical and philological ignorance (the last criticism has been directed at all of the Glossators). Although there is an element of truth in such criticisms, one must give Accursius some credit for originality in the task he selected. A more serious criticism has been directed at all of the Glossators: that they neglected the evolving canon law and the statute law enacted by local political organs, especially the city-states. It is true that the school of Bologna was interested in neither of these phenomena. The study of Roman law was more than enough to occupy the Glos-

---

54. On the influence of Azo on Bracton, see *Select Passages from the Works of Bracton and Azo* (1895).

sators, for here was a system of legislation more fully developed than either the current statute law or the nascent canon law.

For the Glossators, Roman law was the law of a universal empire. They studied it and taught it as such to students who came from all of Europe to Bologna to study according to what would later be called the *mos italicus*. In this way, their methods of studying and teaching Roman law quickly spread throughout Europe. The Glossators also traveled: Piacentino founded a school for the study of Roman law at Montpellier; Azo probably taught in Provence; and Vacarius founded the law school at Oxford. In this way the legal culture of the great school of Bologna permeated European civilization.

1.12 *The Commentators.*   It is usually asserted that the work of Accursius marks the end of the era of glosses. That assertion is inexact: the method of the Glossators was not completely abandoned with the appearance of the *Magna Glossa*. However, beginning with the second half of the thirteenth century, examination of the letter of the *Corpus Juris* was almost entirely abandoned in favor of new methods.

The cultural climate during the latter part of the thirteenth century was different from the one in which the work of the Glossators had begun. Scholastic philosophy reached its apogee with the work of St. Thomas Aquinas (d. 1274), and the new dialectic that this philosophy had forged was not limited to metaphysical-theological speculations but permeated studies in both private and public law. The study of public law was given new impetus by a changed political system in which the traditional dualism of a universal Empire and a universal Church was slowly but inexorably emptied of content by the crises affecting both institutions,[55] by

---

55. The last emperor of this period who retained a unitary view of the Empire and actively participated in the life of the Italian peninsula was the king of Sicily, Frederick II of Swabia. After his death in 1250 there was a long interregnum until 1273. Frederick's successors preferred to consolidate the fortunes of their dynasties in Germany rather than to deal with the Empire as a universal organism.

The Church entered the fourteenth century in a state of crisis. Evidence of this was the transfer of the Holy See to Avignon, where the pope remained subject to the control of the kings of France for some seventy years. This "Babylonian Captivity" was followed by the great schism, which terminated only with the election of Pope Martin V in 1417. These difficulties permitted "lesser" organs, such as the nascent European states and the Italian city-states, to develop their political structures with little interference from the higher universal organisms.

the rise of new nation-states in Europe, and by the growing strength of the communes[56] in Italy and some other areas of Europe.

The new method, called the "comment," was born and developed in complete harmony with the contemporary dialectical methods of inquiry of scholastic philosophy. Legal study no longer rested on a literal reading and exegesis, as it had during the time of the Glossators. It was now based upon a search, through a process of synthesis and abstraction, for the principles running through the law and the rationale of legal rules. Thus, there was a change from the literal interpretation of law to the building of an analytic structure (or, as it is still called in Italy, a "dogmatic construction") of the law within the legal system. With this method, the Commentators created a good part of the dogmatic or analytic structure that still differentiates the style of modern continental legal systems from their Roman antecedent.[57] In addition, the Commentators addressed themselves, in their roles as judicial consultants, to the development of case law, which also resulted in a progressive refinement of their concepts and their logical tools. Many of their theories and dogmatic constructions were born out of the pressures of actual cases.[58]

The application of scholastic methods to the law began in France with the work of Jacques de Révigny and Pierre de Belleperche, respectively professors at Toulouse and at Orléans in the second half of the thirteenth century. Cino of Pistoia (1270–1336) studied under both. On his return to Italy, Cino revolutionized legal scholarship. His method consisted, first of all, of a *lectio literae*, a literal rendition of a legislative text. This was followed by a *divisio legis*, a subdivision of the text into its component provisions. The *divisio* was followed by the *expositio*,

---

56. The centuries which followed the year 1000 saw the rise of the communes, the free city-states. Although this phenomenon also occurred elsewhere (for example, Flanders and parts of Germany), it was more widespread and accentuated in Italy.

57. To quote the words of the German jurist Paul Koschaker, "They drew from the treasures of Roman wisdom and legal technique which could be used at the time and made of it a basic part of the law of their time, thus preparing the unification of Italy in the field of private law; they in addition made of Roman law the substratum of a legal science, which was later to become European legal science." *Op. cit.* n. 40, at 93. "All the peoples of Europe contributed to it, but its creation will always remain an Italian glory. And history has recognized it, giving it the name *mos italicus*." *Ibid.*, at 91.

58. The Commentators, especially Bartolus and Baldo, wrote the first analyses of commercial law, which grew primarily from the customs of the merchants and became law by virtue of their corporate autonomy. Beginning in the eleventh century, these customs were reduced to writing. The Commentators were the first exegesists of these customs.

which summarized the content of the text, and by the *positio casuum*, which gave examples of practical cases in which the text was relevant. Next came the *collectio notabilium*, a collection of the more important observations suggested by the law; the *collectio* was followed by the *oppositiones*—that is, possible counterarguments. The commentary on the text closed with the *quaestiones*, problems that might arise. The method involved subjecting a legislative provision to a dialectical process and a systematic analysis that permitted a thorough exegesis, with the rationale of the law as the goal of the process. For centuries this was to be the typical method of Italian legal scholarship, the *mos italicus*.

With Cino, the school of Commentators begins. His pupil was Bartolus of Saxoferrato (1314–57), one of the great jurists of all time. In addition to teaching law at Pisa and Perugia and performing judicial services, Bartolus commented upon every part of the *Corpus Juris Civilis*, dictated legal opinions, and wrote some forty monographic treatises on the most diverse subjects. The complete edition of his works runs to ten folio volumes.

His premature death did not interrupt the new scholarly movement. It was said then, and it was repeated for centuries, *nemo est bonus iurista nisi est bartolista*, "no one is a good jurist who is not a Bartolist." His principal follower was Baldo degli Ubaldi (c. 1327–1400), a man of philosophical temperament, with uncommon powers of abstraction. Sometimes these gifts brought him to constructions so original that they forced the legislative text beyond recognition. Unlike Bartolus, Baldo was a canonist and a feudalist as well as a civil lawyer: he commented upon the Decretals of Gregory IX and the *Libri Feudorum*. With Baldo, the distinction between civil lawyer and canon lawyer ends. From this point on, jurists studied both systems (many law schools in Europe still award the degree of J.U.D., "Doctor of Both Laws"). However, they continued to be called either civil or canon lawyers, depending on their field of concentration.

1.13 *The Codification of Canon Law.*   At the time when the Glossators were "rediscovering" genuine Roman law, the canonists were reorganizing the vast body of canonical sources.[59] The compilations of the early Middle Ages had consisted

---

59. On the history of the sources of canon law, a fundamental work is von Schulte, *Die Geschichte der Quellen und Literatur des canonischen Rechts von Gratian bis auf die Gegenwart* (4 vols., 1875, 1880). See also Ferme, *Introduction to the History of the Sources of Canon Law* (2007); Van De Wiel, *History of Canon Law* (1992).

of the most varied materials: conciliar canons, both ecumenical and local, both Eastern and Western; pontifical letters and writings of the early Church Fathers and a variety of other ecclesiastical writers; lay sources such as fragments of the Theodosian Code and the Justinian compilation; Carolingian enactments; and other materials.

Gratian of Chiusi, a monk at the monastery of Santi Felice e Naborre in Bologna, set about in the years 1139–42 to put this unorganized mass of materials into some kind of order. His product was the *Concordia discordantium canonum.*[60] Its title indicates the author's purpose; Gratian wished to make a single systematic collection of all of canon law, eliminating theological matters and eliminating or harmonizing contradictions inevitably arising in such heterogeneous sources. The work, which appeared a few years after the death of Irnerius, is divided into three parts: these, in turn, are subdivided into *distinctiones* or *causae*, with the latter again divided into *canones*. Gratian added his own comments and illustrations, so the work had the characteristics of both a compilation and a treatise. Although it never acquired official standing, it was of extraordinary importance in the doctrinal development of canon law. In testimony to the importance of his labors, his contemporaries changed the title to the *Decretum Gratiani*, and they and their successors added an apparatus of glosses, synthesized in the *glossa perpetua* of the canonists Giovanni Teutonico and Bartolomeo da Brescia.[61]

In the course of the twelfth and the first quarter of the thirteenth centuries, the *Quinque compilationes antiquae,*[62] five collections of papal decrees and conciliar canons, followed the *Decretum Gratiani.* The third of these, sanctioned by Innocent III, and the fifth, sanctioned by Honorius III, had official character.

---

60. Edited under the title of *Decretum Magistri Gratiani*, by Friedberg (1879), available at http://web.colby.edu/canonlaw/category/canon-law/. (It forms the first part of the *Corpus juris canonici*.) An English translation of the first part of Gratian's work is Thompson and Gordley, *The Treatise on Laws (Decretum DD. 1–20)* (1993). On Gratian, see Sohm, *Das Altkatholische Kirchenrecht und das Dekret Gratians*, in *Festschrift der Leipziger Juristenfakultät für Dr. Adolf Wach zum 16. November 1915*, 3–674 (1918). See also *Studia Gratiana post octava Decreti saecularia* (8 vols., 1953–62) (studies by various authors edited by Forchielli and Stickler).

61. The *glossa perpetua*, together with the other ordinary glosses mentioned in the text, can be read in all editions of the glossed *Corpus iuris canonici*.

62. Also edited by Friedberg, *Quinque compilationes antiquae, nec non collectio canonum Lipsiensis* (1882), available at http://works.bepress.com/david_freidenreich/21.

Pope Gregory IX (1227–41) was responsible for a definitive official collection in five books of the *constitutiones* and *decretales* of his predecessors. Repetitions and contradictions were eliminated and interpolations made where deemed necessary. A Spanish Dominican, Raymond of Peñafort, was the compiler; the model was Justinian's compilation. The collection was promulgated by the papal bull *Rex pacificus* on September 5, 1234, and was sent to the Universities of Paris and Bologna to be studied and to be used in the courts. Its official title, *Decretales Gregorii IX*,[63] was infrequently used. It was commonly called the *Liber Extravagantium* or *Liber Extra* (i.e., outside the *Decretum*). The compilation was repeatedly glossed until 1256, when Bernardo da Parma composed the standard gloss.

The appearance of the *Liber Extra* did not end the normative enactments of popes and councils. Within a short time, there was confusion and uncertainty. To correct this situation, Boniface VIII promulgated a systematic collection of five books, which was entitled *Liber Sextus Decretalium*,[64] to indicate that it was a supplement to the five books of Gregory IX. The *Liber Sextus* was promulgated by the bull *Sacrosanctae Romanae Ecclesiae*, March 3, 1298.

By order of Pope Clement V in 1313, the *Liber Sextus* was supplemented by the *Constitutiones Clementinae*,[65] completed by Pope John XXII in 1317 and published by the bull *Quoniam Nulla*. The compilation completed the official codification of Church law.[66] The compilation is of course important in ascertaining the law of the Church; it is also essential in understanding the effect of canon law upon the *jus*

63. Edited by Friedberg in the second volume of the *Corpus juris canonici* at 1–928, available at http://www.columbia.edu/cu/lweb/digital/collections/cul/texts/ldpd_6029936 _002/index.html. See note 60.

64. *Id.*, at 934–1124.

65. *Id.*, at 1130–1200.

66. Other unofficial compilations were made after the *Clementinae*, such as the *Extravagantes Johannis XXII* (twenty decretals later than 1317) and the so-called *Extravagantes communes*, which collected decretals promulgated by various popes from Boniface VIII, 1294–1303, to Sextus IV, 1471–84. The French jurist Jean Chappuis added these private compilations to the Paris edition (1500) of all the canonical compilations from the *Decretum* of Gratian onward. He gave it the name *Corpus juris canonici* in imitation of the *Corpus juris civilis*. Finally, the increasing number of printed editions, often filled with errors, induced Pius V to create a commission of thirty-five revisors (the *Correctores romani*) to determine a definitive text. This commission, granted the usual powers to correct and supplement the text, completed its work in 1580. Their product was approved by the bull *Cum pro munere* on July 1 of that year and was given its now traditional title of *Corpus juris canonici*.

commune. From the time of the Commentators, the *jus commune* was understood to consist of a coordination of two distinct normative systems: the *jus civile* and the *jus canonicum*. Canon law, unlike civil law, was purely a medieval creation and developed directly out of the forces operating during this era.

1.14 *Statutory Law.*   Alongside Roman and canon law there was the local law of political bodies and the particular law of the mercantile corporations or guilds.[67] In addition there was law growing out of the need to regulate certain activities, such as maritime trade. This kind of law is customarily spoken of as statutory law or *jus proprium* in contrast with the *jus commune* of which it was a necessary supplement.

There was almost always a prior history of customary law behind the statutory law. Customary law exerted its greatest influence in the eleventh, twelfth, and thirteenth centuries. The first written drafts of city customary law appeared at the end of the twelfth century (Venice, 1195; Bari, between 1180 and 1200). As a rule, these collections of customs were succeeded by what strictly speaking may be called statutes. By definition, a *statutum* was legislation enacted by an inferior legislative body. An enactment of theoretically universal application, a *lex*, could be promulgated only by the Emperor. The *statutum* was subordinate and could supplement but not modify or derogate from the *lex*. Nevertheless, the statutes often were irreconcilable with the *lex*, and despite this fact they prevailed in the practice of the legal system in which they had been enacted.[68]

67. A bibliography of statutory sources, still of value, is the *Bibliografia degli statuti dei comuni dell' Italia superiore* compiled by Leone Fontana (3 vols. 1907). Still more definitive is Biblioteca del Senato della Repubblica, *Catalogo della raccolta di statuti, consuetudini, leggi, decreti, ordini, e privilegi dei comuni, delle associazioni e degli enti locali italiani dal medioevo alla fine del secolo XVIII.* The catalogue, along with updates to previously published volumes, is available at the website of the Biblioteca del Senato della Repubblica at http://notes9.senato.it/w3/Biblioteca/catalogoDegliStatutiMedievali.nsf/.

For a critical evaluation of the statutory law and a classification by regions and families, see 2 Besta, *Fonti: legislazione e scienza giuridica dalla caduta dello impero romano al secolo decimosesto* (volume 1 of *Storia del diritto italiano pubblicata sotto la direzione di Pasquale Del Giudice*) 455–770 (1925).

68. There is an extraordinary similarity here with the development of English law. The *jus commune* of Europe claimed to be superior to, and not derogable by, statutory law. This view, firmly held in theory, failed in practice. In England, before the "glorious revolution" of 1688, it was commonly held that statutes "contrary to the laws and customs of the realm" should not be applied. See Corwin, *The "Higher Law" Background of American Constitutional Law*, 27, 49 n. 27 (1955). At the time of Coke, the tradition that the common law was fundamental law and prevailed over statutory law was at least four centuries old.

Monarchies also enacted legislation. In the flourishing Kingdom of Sicily, the Norman laws, of which the most important was the *Assise di Ariano Irpino*[69] (1140), were replaced during the time of Frederick II of Swabia by the *Liber Constitutionum Regni Siciliae* (1231). This legislation (usually called the *Liber Augustalis*),[70] was the work of Pier delle Vigne and Jacopo, archbishop of Capua. For centuries the *Liber Augustalis* was the principal body of law in the Southern Kingdom; it was kept in effect by the Angevin kings, who succeeded the Swabians in 1268, and by their various successors until the eighteenth century.

In the domains of the Church the most important legislation was the *Constitutiones Sanctae Matris Ecclesiae*[71] promulgated at Fano in 1357 by Cardinal Gil of Albornoz, the legate to the papal state during the period of pontifical residence at Avignon. Other monarchical legislation was enacted in the County (later Duchy) of Savoy, the provinces (*giudicati*) of Sardinia, the patriarchate of Aquileia (now Friuli), and many other areas.

1.15 *The Birth of Commercial Law.*   Italian cities developed the first great system of commercial law.[72] The burghers, beginning in the second half of the twelfth century, organized themselves into autonomous corporations known as guilds. These organizations consisted of the "masters" of the crafts, their coworkers, and

---

See additional references in Cappelletti, *Alcuni precedenti storici del controllo giudiziario di costituzionalità delle leggi*, 21 Rivista di diritto processuale 52, 62 *et seq.* (1966).

69. The law is also known as *The Assizes of King Roger*. The Latin text, edited by Brandileone, appears as an appendix to his book, *Il diritto romano nelle leggi normanne e sveve del Regno di Sicilia* 94 *et seq.* (1884), available at http://books.google.com/books?id= bGUMGABk5WoC. An English translation is available at http://www.medievalsicily.com/ Docs/04_Kingdom_of_Sicily/Roger%20II%20Assizes.pdf.

70. The legislation is also known as *The Constitutions of Melfi*. In addition to the numerous medieval editions generally accompanied by the standard gloss of the great southern jurist, Marino da Caramanico, a modern edition is Huillard-Bréholles, *Historia diplomatica Friderici Secundi* (tome 4, pt. 1) 1–177 (1854), available at http://books.google.com/ books?id=VFYBAAAAYAAJ. An English translation is Powell, *The Liber Augustalis* (1971).

For a historical evaluation of Frederick II as a legislator, see Calasso, *Rileggendo il "Liber Augustalis,"* in *Atti del Convegno Internazionale di studi federiciani* (December 1950) 461 *et seq.* (1952).

71. A critical edition is Sella, *Le costituzioni egidiane dell'anno MCCCLVII* (1912). (Vol. 1 of the *Corpus statutorum italicorum*.)

72. For an overall view of the history of commercial law and its institutions, see L. Goldschmidt, *Universalgeschichte des Handelsrechts* (1891). See also the fascinating pages in Ascarelli, *Corso di diritto commerciale* 1– 43 (3d ed. 1962).

their apprentices. The guild had a dual historical role. First, it was an economic entity with monopolistic powers over the practice of a particular craft; only those enrolled could legally practice the trade. Indeed, its power grew so that it alone had the power to adjudicate commercial disputes among its members. Second, the guilds became, in many cities, the fundamental units of the communal government; enrollment in a guild was often a prerequisite to participation in public life.

The commercial law created in the medieval Italian cities took on an international character. Although it was born as "particular" law, it became a common commercial law. It succeeded in penetrating areas where even the Roman law met with resistance. Thus, in England, where the Roman law was unable to displace the common law, the merchant law, containing rules that had their origins first in the customs and statutes of the Italian cities, became the law of the land because it was better suited to the needs of domestic and international trade.[73] Since this was the era of commercial dominance by such Italian cities as Venice, Florence, and Genoa,[74] it was natural that commercial institutions, if they did not originate in Italy (a search for origins would take one back to the dawn of civilization), had their modern development there.

73. "At the same time as the revival of Roman law and the development of Canon law were proceeding . . . in the great centers of trade and commerce such as Venice, the Italian merchants were laying the basis of the body of mercantile and maritime custom which was to form another vital strand in the law of Western Europe, not excluding, in this case, the law of England." Millner, *Note on Italian Law*, 14 Int'l & Comp. L.Q. 1028, 1031 (1965). Similarly, see Coing, *op. cit.* n. 45, at IV, 6 c: "In the seventeenth century the bases for the reception in England of the Italian-Continental commercial and maritime law were laid, a reception which was completed by Lord Mansfield in the eighteenth century." See also, in greater detail, 5 Holdsworth, *op. cit.* n. 40, at 65 *et seq.*, 129 *et seq.* (1924).

74. The earliest records of commercial insurance are found in the fourteenth-century Italian cities, and the earliest insurance policies found in English court records (1545 and 1547) are written in Italian. See Vance, *The Early History of Insurance Law*, 8 Colum. L. Rev. 1 (1907).

The most important book on maritime law, the *Libro del consolato del mare*, is principally based on statutes of Italian cities, even though it was published in Barcelona in 1494. On the problems relating to the history of this text, see Besta, *op. cit.* n. 67, at 673 *et seq.*; Zeno, *Storia del diritto marittimo italiano nel Mediterraneo* 195 *et seq.* (1946). On maritime law, see Bonolis, *Il diritto marittimo medievale dell' Adriatico* (1921); Zeno, *op. cit.*

On the origins of the law of bankruptcy, see Santarelli, *Per la storia del fallimento nelle legislazioni italiane dell' età intermedia* 21 *et seq.* (1964).

1.16 *The "Reception" of the Jus Commune in Europe and Elsewhere.*   We now come to the central part of this historical study: the spread and "reception" of the *jus commune* in Europe and in the continents conquered and colonized by Europeans.[75] The reception did not involve the entire body of the *jus commune*, since the canon law had previously been received and accepted by all Catholic peoples by virtue of their allegiance to the Church. The Roman part of the *jus commune*, however, was received in a variety of historical situations and often met with opposition. The basis for its acceptance varied: in some areas (Castile, León, and Germany) it was received by will of the monarch; in other areas it was received because of its value as customary law or because of its appeal as a rational system (*ratio scripta*).

A preliminary distinction should be made between those nations that had been constituent parts of the ancient Roman Empire, those that had never been subjected to Rome, and those, like England and Hungary, in which Roman civilization had once held sway and had been obliterated. In areas where the Romans had ruled for a long time, the Roman legal tradition continued and was favored by the principle that law was personal. Where the Roman tradition was weak or nonexistent, the reception occurred upon substrata of institutions and cultures of the most varied kinds. The acceptance of Roman law (whether official or not) was always a fact of more than legal significance. It was the acceptance of a system deemed superior and more civilized—the acceptance of an ideal of a universal order that was later shattered by the rise of the nation-state.

The Roman legal tradition survived in those sections of France that had been constituent parts of the Empire. At the beginning of the twelfth century, the country was divided into central-southern regions inhabited by Gallo-Romans and a northern region inhabited mostly by Franks, a Germanic people. This geographical division, whose boundaries are still a matter of historical controversy, was reflected in the law.[76] The central-southern regions were areas of written law (*pays de droit écrit*), adhering to the Roman law of the Theodosian era. This law was compiled

75. On the penetration of the *Corpus juris* and Italian legal science into European countries, see generally Calasso (*Introduzione*), *op. cit.* n. 47, esp. *Saggio VIII: In orbem terrarum* 305–40; *op. cit.* n. 37, at 607–29; Vinogradoff, *op. cit.* n. 45; Kurtscheid, *De utriusque iuris studio saec. XIII*, in 2 Acta congressus iuridici internationalis 309–42 (1934); Koschaker, *op. cit.* n. 40.

76. For France, as for the other countries discussed, we cite only some of the principal works: Glasson, *Histoire du droit et des institutions de la France* (8 vols. 1887–1903); Viollet, *Histoire du droit civil français* (3d ed. 1905); Chénon, *Le droit romain à la "Curia Regis" de Philippe-Auguste à Philippe-le-Bel*, in 1 *Mélanges Fitting* 197–212 (1907); Declareuil, *Histoire*

(perhaps in the first decade of the fifth century) in the *Lex Romana Burgundionum* for the Romans living in the Kingdom of Burgundy, and in the more important *Lex Romana Wisigothorum* (also called the *Breviarium Alaricianum*) compiled by order of King Alaric II in 506 for the Romans of the Kingdom of the Visigoths. The northern regions were lands of Germanic customary law (*pays de droit coutumier*) where only a few Roman institutions, such as certain kinds of contracts and the will, had penetrated.

At the beginning of the twelfth century, the regions of written law accepted Justinian's texts, which had been revived by the school of Bologna. Together with the texts, these areas received the results of the Glossators' interpretative efforts. In France, and in every other country that received the *jus commune*, the glosses were considered to be an integral part of the legislative texts.

The acceptance of Roman law did not stop at the borders between central and northern France. French students came to Bologna, Padua, and other Italian centers of legal learning. Teachers from Bologna came to France to teach Roman law (for example, the Glossator Piacentino abandoned Bologna for political reasons and founded the law school at Montpellier in the second half of the twelfth century). Nevertheless, the monarchy tried to keep Roman law out of the north. To accept it would have been tacit admission of the sovereignty of the Holy Roman Empire, from which France proclaimed itself completely independent. The written (Roman) law was said to be effective only *ex permissione regis,* only by the consent of the king and by strength of custom. Despite the opposition of the monarchy, Roman law succeeded in permeating the various *coutumes*, especially during the period in which they were being written down in accordance with the *ordonnance* issued by Charles VII in 1453. Moreover, both in scholarship and in practice, Roman law was an accepted source even in northern France, to be used as a residual common law when neither local custom, the custom of neighboring communities, nor the custom of Paris provided a solution.[77] Here Roman law was accepted not because of imperial command

---

générale du droit français des origines à 1789 (1925); Chénon, *Histoire générale du droit français public et privé des origines à 1875* (2 vols., 1925–29).

77. The custom of Paris, although not formally valid elsewhere in France, was often looked upon as the common law of France. On the custom of Paris, see Martin, *La coutume de Paris trait d'union entre le droit romain et les législations modernes* (1925).

but because of *imperio rationis*, its appeal to reason and equity. The movement toward the unification of French law that lasted for centuries and terminated in the Napoleonic codes proceeded on a normative system substantially permeated by Roman law and conceptually unified by Roman categories that were adopted because of their superiority.

Spain, too, had a substratum of Roman law.[78] For a time, Roman personal law, expressed in the *Lex Romana Wisigothorum*, coexisted with the laws of the Visigoths. With the fusion of the two peoples, a territorial law, permeated in form and substance by Roman law, was promulgated by King Recceswinth (perhaps in 654). This *Liber iudiciorum*, commonly called the *Lex Wisigothorum*, was the fundamental basis of Spanish law until the fifteenth century. At about the same time, local customary laws with a primarily Germanic content, called *usus terrae* or *fueros*, began to appear. In later centuries these *fueros* became obstacles to national legal unification.

In the twelfth, thirteenth, and fourteenth centuries, Spanish legal culture underwent a more thorough process of Romanization. Students from Spain were so numerous at Bologna that in 1364 the Spanish Cardinal Gil of Albornoz founded a boarding institution there for them. (The Collegio di Spagna is still in existence.) Spanish universities sprang up: Palencia (1208–9), Salamanca (c. 1227–28), Seville (1254–60), and Lérida (1300). These institutions were to spread the knowledge of Roman and canon law, and the methods of the Glossators and the Commentators, throughout the Iberian peninsula.

The major product of this vigorous growth of the study of Roman law was the principal legislative monument of medieval Spain: the *Libro* (or *Fuero*) *de las leyes*, commonly called the *Ley de las Siete Partidas*, compiled in 1265 by order of Alphonso the Wise, the king of Castille and León. This work, divided into seven books, was intended to unify law throughout his realm. The text, drafted largely by doctors of the University of Salamanca, brought together various parts of the compilation of Justinian, the *Decretum* of Gratian, and the *Decretales* of Gregory IX,

---

78. For a history of Spanish law, see Mayer, *Historia de las instituciones sociales y políticas de España y Portugal durante los siglos V a XIV* (2 vols., 1925–26); Merêa, *Estudios de direito hispanico medieval* (2 vols., 1952–53); Sánchez and Rubio, *Curso de historia del derecho* (10th ed. 1972); Garcia-Gallo, *Manual de historia del derecho español* (1959); Merino-Blanco, *Spanish Law and Legal System* (2006).

as well as the textual interpretations made by the most famous of the Glossators, especially Azo and Accursius on civil law and Goffredo of Trani and Raymond of Peñafort on canon law. With this text, Roman and canon law would have become, by will of the king, the common law of Spain. However, Spanish traditionalists, loyal to their local customs, were so strongly opposed to the *Siete Partidas* that it was not promulgated until 1348 and then only as an appendix to the *Ordenamiento de Alcalá*. It was relegated to the role of a subsidiary statute, effective only where the *Ordenamiento* and the local customs were silent. Despite the lack of its promulgation as the common law of the realm, the fate of Roman law in Spain was decided: the *Siete Partidas* was recognized and applied as the official law of Spain. The accompanying reception of Italian legal doctrine was so massive that the monarchs decreed that the courts, in case of gaps or doubts in the law, should rely on the authority of the major Glossators and Commentators, and should not follow the opinions of jurists later than Bartolus on the civil law and Giovanni d'Andrea on canon law.[79]

Thus, Roman law, although opposed by some kings and local interests and objected to because of the pretensions of the Empire, became the nucleus of Spanish legal life and the basis for the scientific study of law in the universities. Indeed, until the eighteenth century the only subject studied in the universities was Roman and canon law.

In nearby Portugal the legislation at first was the same as in Visigothic Spain: the *Liber iudiciorum*, with additions in 1054 by Alphonso V of León, as well as the various local customary laws. Portugal, too, received the *jus commune* with the foundation of legal studies at its universities (Coimbra and Lisbon). The consequences are clear in Portuguese legislation. The first systematic collection, the *Ordenações Alfonsinas*, promulgated by Alphonse V in 1446, in large part consisted of Roman and canon law. This collection was followed by the *Ordenações Manuelinas* of King Manuel in 1521, and finally in 1603, after Philip II became king of Portugal, by the *Ordenações Filipinas*, which remained in effect until modern times not only in Portugal, but also in its colonies, including Brazil. These enactments embody the principle that Roman law, the glosses, and the comments are the common law of the kingdom and applicable whenever the local legislation or customs are silent or ambiguous.

---

79. Edict of John II of Castille and León of 1417. Later, by a law of 1499, Baldo was included.

In England,[80] throughout the early Middle Ages, traces of ancient Roman law remained, and it is not unlikely that Lanfranc, a teacher of law at Pavia and subsequently Archbishop of Canterbury, used his knowledge of Roman law to assist William the Conqueror in his legislative and administrative reorganization of the kingdom. In the middle of the twelfth century, the Italian Glossator Vacarius arrived in England to found the law school at Oxford.[81] The success of the school raised the fear that Roman law would be received as the law of the land and provoked a quick reaction from the monarch, who did not appreciate the implication in Roman law of imperial sovereignty. The barons, too, reacted against the threat of a reception because Roman law provided a foundation for royal absolutism. Thus, King Stephen forbade Vacarius to teach at Oxford,[82] and in 1234, Henry III prohibited the teaching of Roman law in London.[83] Two years later, the barons, gathered at Merton, replied to those who proposed to accept the Roman law on illegitimacy: *Nolumus leges Angliae mutare*.[84]

This firm legislative policy corresponded to the practice of the courts and permitted the autonomous and original development of English law. Nonetheless, Roman concepts were not without influence on English doctrine. This is evident from the two most influential legal treatises of the era. Glanvill's *Tractatus de legibus et consuetudinibus regni Angliae*, of 1187, and Bracton's treatise of the same title, written about seventy years later, show a good knowledge of Roman law, and Bracton made intelligent use of the glosses, especially the *Summa Codicis* of Azo.[85]

Though Roman law was known in England as a sort of general jurisprudence, English lawyers resisted a legal system that would have impeded the spontaneous development of the common law. While Roman and canon law continued to be studied for centuries in the university, the common law was learned in the Inns of Court from practitioners. Hence, in England, the lawyers were not trained in the study of Roman texts, and an essential prerequisite for the reception of Roman law

---

80. See generally Rashdall, *op. cit.* n. 43; 5 Holdsworth, *op. cit.* n. 40; Vinogradoff, *op. cit.* n. 45, ch. 4; and *Romanistische Einflüsse in angelsachsischen Recht*, in 2 *Mélanges Fitting* 499 (1907); Sarfatti, *Influenza reciproca del diritto romano e del diritto anglosassone*, in 3 *Studi in memoria di Aldo Albertoni* 563–75 (1938).

81. See 2 Holdsworth, *op. cit.* n. 40, at 147 *et seq.*

82. *Id.*, at 148.

83. See Koschaker, *op. cit.* n. 40, at 213; Vinogradoff, *op. cit.* n. 45, at 98.

84. 2 Holdsworth, *op. cit.* n. 40, at 218.

85. See *Select Passages from the Works of Bracton and Azo*, cited in full in note 54.

did not exist. The *jus commune* penetrated only into limited areas, for example, into certain aspects of equity. The later attempts of the monarchs (especially Henry VIII) to introduce Roman law as a foundation for their absolutist pretensions[86] were unsuccessful.[87]

The fate of the *jus commune* in Germany was quite different.[88] It was brought to Germany by the great many German students who received their doctorates in Italy and returned to their homes to introduce it into the practice of the tribunals and in the drafting of legal instruments. The rise of the German universities gave further impetus to the trend. The methods of study and the texts used were substantially the same as in Italy. In addition there was a common political structure. The emperor of the Holy Roman Empire was at the same time the king of Italy and of Germany. On this cultural and political base, Emperor Maximilian I in 1495 created the Reichskammergericht, the central court of the Empire, which heard appeals from regional and local German courts. The judges were required to adjudicate *nach des Reichs und gemeinen Rechten*—that is, in accordance with the common (Roman and canonical) law as well as the local laws of the Empire. With this act of sovereign will, Roman law was officially received. German doctrine speaks of "*Rezeption in complexu*"—that is, "full reception" of the Roman law. Moreover, as elsewhere in Europe, the gloss was accepted with the *Corpus Juris Civilis*.

---

86. See Holdsworth, *The Reception of Roman Law in the Sixteenth Century*, 27 L.Q. Rev. 387 (1911), 28 L.Q. Rev. 39, 131, 236 (1912). It is noteworthy that the *regu professores* created by Henry VIII for Oxford and Cambridge were required to teach Roman law at the same time that the study of canon law was forbidden. See Koschaker, *op. cit.* n. 40, at 124 n. 2; Plucknett, *A Concise History of the Common Law* 299 (5th ed. 1956).

87. Nonetheless, it is certain that the teaching of Roman law in the universities exercised a certain influence even in England. According to a noted historian, this influence is present in the *Commentaries* of Blackstone, especially "in the framework and structure of the work itself, which presented a complete picture of English institutions, public and private, digging out the secret of their historical genesis and showing their evolutionary process, on the guidelines of the Roman legal system, which offered surprising similarities, even if Blackstone has been accused of often misunderstanding the meaning of the technical terms of this law." Calasso (*Introduzione*), *op. cit.* n. 47, at 318.

88. A rich body of literature exists on the reception in Germany. Citations here will be limited to Stintzing and Landsberg, *Geschichte der deutschen Rechtswissenschaft* (3 vols., 1880–1910); von Below, *Die Ursachen der Rezeption des römischen Rechts in Deutschland* (1905); Wieacker, *A history of private law in Europe with particular reference to Germany* (Weir trans., 1995).

Within a few years Germany was rocked by the Protestant reformation. Anything emanating from Rome was suspect, but the intrinsic worth of Roman law, coupled with the favor shown it by educated German jurists, overcame popular fears. It was considered the law of imperial unity or, at least, capable of becoming the common law of an area that, although politically fractured into countless subdivisions, was unified in theory. Despite the reception of Roman law by educated German jurists, local law never disappeared. Rather, local law complemented the *jus commune*.

Elsewhere in Europe the foundation of universities, whether at Prague or Dublin, further spread Roman law and the methods of the Italian school. A true *koiné*, a union of legal thought and practice, existed throughout Europe in the late Middle Ages. Naturally the penetration of Roman law often caused reactions, opposition, and confusion, especially in areas without a substratum of Latin culture and institutions.

Even where Roman law was not received in a normative sense, there was nonetheless a doctrinal reception. Roman rules might be rejected, but the conceptual structure created by the Italian scholars gave a Roman form to indigenous rules. For example, in Norway and Hungary, although there was no adoption of the *jus commune*, local legislation was marked by a certain Romanist influence. The Code of 1274 of King Magnus VI of Norway, the *Lagaböter* (law-giver), while intended to be a written draft of ancient Viking custom, shows the influence of Roman and canon law in its organization and in many of its institutions.[89] In areas as far off as Byelorussia and the Ukraine, where there was no reception but where Roman law from Byzantium was applied, for example, to matrimonial matters, Roman law was looked to as a remote paradigm to be used as a guide.[90] Aside from the "re-

---

89. See Rindal and Berg, *King Magnus Håkonsson's Laws of Norway and Other Legal Texts* (1983). On the influence of Roman law in Hungary, see Zajtay, *Sur le rôle du droit romain dans l'évolution du droit hongrois*, 2 *L'Europa e il diritto romano. Studi in memoria di Paolo Koschaker* 183 *et seq.* (1954). He writes that despite the absence of a normative reception in Hungary, "*elements* of Roman law nevertheless penetrated into Hungarian law from the beginning of its history," and that "because of its great perfection Roman law was given, in a certain measure, the role of subsidiary law." He concludes by stating that the concepts, classifications, principles, and structure of Hungarian law are a legacy of the Roman spirit, which exercised "a decisive influence on the formation and the methods of work of the jurists and, therefore, on the development of the science of law" (pp. 209, 210, 211).

90. See Koschaker, *op. cit.* n. 40, at 133.

ception," Roman law impregnated all of the indigenous systems of law in Europe, accomplishing a civilizing mission.

1.17 *Legal Humanism.*   By the end of the fifteenth century, Italian legal science showed signs of excessive rigidity and pedantry. Nevertheless, during the sixteenth and seventeenth centuries, students from all over Europe continued to enroll in the Italian universities, and the style of the Commentators—the Bartolistic method—was widely used in many European universities.

The movement known as legal humanism[91] arose in the fifteenth and sixteenth centuries in reaction to the Bartolistic method. Liberty of interpretation was its slogan. It rejected doctrinal precedent and the supine acquiescence of many scholars to the *communis opinio doctorum.*[92] It had its genesis in the world of letters, where jurists were criticized for their wretched Latin, their lack of sensitivity in facing the problems of a critical reconstruction of the Roman texts, their neglect of literary style, and, indeed, their lack of intelligence. The more able jurists accepted much of this criticism and acknowledged the need to deepen their knowledge of philology and history. From this era came the first critical editions of Justinian's texts and of works of postclassical Roman law. The first proposal to put together a critical edition of the *Digest* was made in the fifteenth century by Politian, a master of erudition as well as a great poet.

During this period Italian legal science lost its preeminence. The humanist school centered elsewhere in Europe, for the most part in the French universities. There came to be a clear contrast between the *mos italicus jura docendi*, the Italian manner of legal teaching, and the *mos docendi gallicus*, the French manner.[93]

91. For an original critical analysis of legal humanism in Italy, see Garin, *Umanesimo e rinascimento*, in *Questioni e correnti di storia letteraria* 349 *et seq.* (1949); and *La cultura filosofica del rinascimento italiano. Ricerche e documenti* (2d ed. 1979). On legal humanism, see Calasso (*Introduzione*), *op. cit.* n. 47; Koschaker, *op. cit.* n. 40, at 185–213; Brugi, *Per la storia della giurisprudenza e delle università italiane* (2 vols. 1915 and 1921); Piano Mortari, *Considerazioni sugli scritti programmatici dei giuristi del secolo XVI*, in 21 Studia et documenta historiae et iuris 276–302 (1955); Maffei, *Gli inizi dello umanesimo giuridico* (1956).

92. Both among the scholars and the courts there was an increasing tendency to cite the opinions of the principal jurists, especially Bartolus and Baldo. Reliance on such authority was frequently required by legislation. As a result the work of the legal scholars and the courts was rigidly bound by the authoritarian pronouncements of their predecessors.

93. On the contrast between *mos italicus* and *mos gallicus*, see Riccobono, *Mos italicus e mos gallicus nella interpretazione del Corpus iuris civilis*, in 2 *Acta congressus iuridici interna-*

The former, in the tradition of the Glossators and Commentators, looked to Roman law for practical ends. The latter sought to obtain an historical, scientific knowledge of Roman law without practical preoccupations. The French school was interested in Roman law as an historical phenomenon rather than as an existing body of law. They sought to reconstruct the original texts, freeing them from interpolations made by Justinian's codifiers and from the Glossators.

The leader of the French school, Andrea Alciato (1492–1550), was an Italian.[94] He was both an expert philologist and a master jurist. Born in Lombardy, he taught in Italy and in France (Bourges). To comprehend his importance it is enough to know that he founded the so-called "School of the Cultured Men" or "Cultured Jurisprudence" (*Scuola dei Culti*), which reached its apex with Jacques Cujas (Cujacius). In Germany the principal exponent of the French approach was Ulrich Zasius. It is commonly stated that the teaching of Alciato, followed to such a great extent in France, had extremely limited influence in Italy. This statement is essentially true, although there were a number of scholars who continued his work in Italy.

Implicit in the formation of the "*Scuola dei Culti*" was the birth of legal nationalism.[95] When, in France and Germany, scholars claimed to study the *Corpus Juris Civilis* as if it were just another ancient text, they obscured its status as living law. In this era of refined classicism it was natural that scholars would search for the original textual formulation and meaning of the components of the *Corpus Juris*. The difficulty was that for centuries the practice and doctrine had been based on the interpolated text and the glosses. The contradiction could be resolved by a new codification designed to govern organically and completely given subject matters, such as civil, criminal, or procedural law. This idea appears, for example, in the *Antitribonien* (1567), the celebrated work of the Frenchman Francis Hotman.[96] The

---

tionalis 377–98 (1934); Astuti, *Mos italicus e mos gallicus nei dialoghi "De iuris interpretibus" di Alberico Gentili* (1937). Astuti also edited the critical edition of *De iuris interpretibus* of Alberico Gentili (1937) (preface by Riccobono), the fundamental work for an understanding of the dichotomy and for full examination of the various opinions.

94. On Andrea Alciato, see Viard, *André Alciat 1492–1550* (1926) and the studies by Abbondanza published in the first several volumes of *Annali di storia del diritto*. See also Phillipson, *Andrea Alciati and His Predecessors*, in *Great Jurists of the World*, 58–82 (1914).

95. Concerning this aspect of legal humanism, see Piano Mortari, *Diritto romano e diritto nazionale in Francia nel secolo XVI* esp. 79–170 (1962).

96. An English translation is found in Franklin, *Constitutionalism and Resistance in the Sixteenth Century: Three Treatises* (1969).

Antitribonien is an indictment of Justinian and his chief scholar, Tribonian, and a plea for the codification of French law. The idea triumphed two centuries later.

1.18 *The Universities and the Teaching of Law in Italy in the Sixteenth through the Eighteenth Centuries.*   In the sixteenth through the eighteenth centuries the Italian universities continued for the most part to be governed by regulations developed in the preceding centuries. Teaching continued, with few exceptions, along Bartolistic lines. The Bartolistic method, however, had lost much of its scientific rigor; its ambitions were reduced to the training of practitioners. The period was characterized by a growing interference of the individual Italian states in the life of the universities and a suffocating surveillance exercised by the Church. This was the period of the counterreformation. The fate of Galileo symbolized the era.

This period saw the birth of learned historiography, which concentrated upon researching and evaluating Roman and medieval documents. The very term *Middle Ages* was coined by these historiographers. Old documents, especially the legislation of the early Middle Ages, began to be published. It was during this baroque era—generally, but not entirely accurately, considered an era of decadence in Italy—that the historiography of law originated. The leading Italian historiographer of the period was Ludovico Antonio Muratori (1672–1750) of Modena, the author of two monumental collections, the most important yet made, of sources from the medieval period: *Rerum italicarum scriptores* (24 volumes in folio containing narrative and documentary sources from the years 500 to 1500 with an introduction and notes); and *Antiquitates italicae medii aevi* (six volumes containing seventy-five well-documented dissertations in Latin, discussing political, legal, economic, religious, and social problems of the Middle Ages).

According to a noted legal historian, the school of natural law[97] was the third of the three great common bases of European legal history.[98] While the first two

---

97.   There is a vast body of literature on natural law doctrine. See Stahl, *The Philosophy of Law* (Alvarado trans., 2007); von Gierke, *Iohannes Althusius und die Entwicklung der naturrechtlichen Staatstheorien* (1880); Solari, *La formazione storica e filosofica dello stato moderno* (4th ed. 2000); Thieme, *Das Naturrecht und die europäische Privatrechtsgeschichte* (2d ed., 1954).

98.   Thieme, *Einheit und Vielfalt in der europäischen Rechtsgeschichte*, in 10 Juristenzeitung 65, 67 (1955); Thieme, *op. cit.* n. 97, at 10–11. Coing, *op. cit.* n. 45, sub VI–VII, adds a fourth common factor, the common economic and social transformations and ideological movements of the nineteenth and twentieth centuries.

of these—Roman and canon law—had their principal development in Italy, the natural law school of the sixteenth through the eighteenth centuries had its major development elsewhere. Unlike the Thomistic ideas of natural law, the natural law of this era was rigidly secular. This accounts for its weaker development in Italy, where, especially in the seventeenth century, the cultural climate of the counter-reformation suffocated new ideas.[99]

A more fruitful current of thought was the movement toward consolidation of law (it is still too early to speak of codification), a movement that was in harmony with the rationalistic and antihistorical temper of the eighteenth-century enlightenment. The problem is examined by Muratori[100] in a spirited polemic entitled *Dei difetti della giurisprudenza*, published in Venice in 1742.[101] According to Muratori, the legal system had two kinds of defects: internal and external. Internal defects are the lack of clarity of legislation, the inability of laws to foresee every case, the fact that laws express the intentions and purposes of men but must be interpreted by other men, and, lastly, the fact that justice depends on "the minds, the comprehension of judges." These defects are incurable, since they flow from the limitations of human nature.

The external defects consist of "the flood of law books," especially those by practicing lawyers, which serve only "to make the law more difficult, entangled, and thorny, and the judgments of those who must administer justice more uncertain and doubtful." Muratori proposes that the princes decide "with the mature counsel of the most gifted and wise the questions disputed by the legists," authoritatively determining the solutions that the judges must adopt. In fact the time was ripe, if not for a codification, at least for a major step in that direction—the "consolidation" of existing law.

99. Nonetheless, an Italian, Alberico Gentili (1552–1611), was a famous and influential "father" of the European natural-law school. Because of his ideas he was suspected of heresy and had to seek refuge in England. While a professor of law at Oxford he wrote the celebrated classic on the law of war, *De jure belli* (1588). For a discussion of the man and his work, see Del Vecchio, *Ricordando Alberico Gentili. Con un saggio di bibliografia gentiliana* (1936). In addition, a collection of essays on Gentili appears in Kingsbury and Straumann, *The Roman Foundations of the Law of Nations: Alberico Gentili and the Justice of Empire* (2010).

100. On this phase of Muratori's activities, see Donati, *Lodovico Antonio Muratori e la giurisprudenza del suo tempo* (1935).

101. Available at http://books.google.com/books?id=MA9NAAAAcAAJ.

1.19 *Development of Legislation and Legislative Policy in Italy before the French Revolution.*   On the Continent the period from the sixteenth to the latter part of the eighteenth century was one of increasing princely absolutism and a corresponding decline in the autonomy enjoyed by the communes. In contrast with France, where the *ordonnances* of the kings were enacted as instruments in the unification of the kingdom, there was little in the way of important legislative compilation in Italy. The medieval legal system remained the basis of law in Italy. Numerous laws were promulgated to supplement or modify the inherited mass of legislation, but these changes tended to be fragmentary, unsystematic, and designed to meet the contingencies of the moment. In the seventeenth century, to facilitate research in the mass of legislative, judicial, and doctrinal material of diverse origin and authority, there was an outpouring of private compilations of law organized in chronological or systematic order.

A discussion of the enlightenment in Italy would involve too great a digression. It is important to mention, however, that Italy was influenced by various contemporary European cultural movements. As a result, Italian culture became considerably less provincial and pedantic. The effects on legislation were considerable. Ancient feudal privileges, guild-controlled economic structures, and rules and customs that hindered the free circulation of goods and persons were in part removed. Punishment became more humane. Torture was abolished in Tuscany[102] and in other Italian states. The abolition was in large part due to the enormous impact of Beccaria's book *Of Crimes and Punishments* (1764), an acute and lucid indictment of torture, the death penalty, and other evils of criminal law.

This climate of renewal was evident in much of the legislation that preceded the Napoleonic codes, but an overview of the legislative work of the eighteenth century demonstrates that, important as it was in the simplification and development of the law, it was at best a prelude to codification. It did not completely abrogate the ancient Roman common law and substitute new, complete, coher-

---

102. Peter Leopold, Grand Duke of Tuscany in enacting (in 1786) an organic reform of all criminal law also abolished "forever" the death sentence. Even though it was reinstituted on August 30, 1795, this would seem to be the first time the penalty was abolished in Europe. It should also be noted that the system of "legal proof," binding on the judge (see 4.15), was first abolished in penal proceedings in Tuscany in 1786. Cf. Fiorelli, *La tortura giudiziaria nel diritto comune* (2 vols., 1953–54); Gilissen, *La prevue en Europe du XVIᵉ au début du XIXᵉ siècle*, in 2 *La preuve*, XVII *Recueils de la Société Jean Bodin* 755, 830–31 (1965). For an English translation of the Edict of 1786 of the Grand Duke of Tuscany, see 3.04, n. 41.

ent laws to govern matters heretofore regulated by Roman law. Nevertheless, the codifications of the nineteenth century owe much to the legislative compilations of the eighteenth.

1.20 *Revolutionary and Napoleonic Legislation in Italy.*[103]   With the arrival of the French revolutionary armies in Italy in 1796, and the foundation of several Italian republics and, later, vassal kingdoms,[104] came the new revolutionary legislation. This legislation was generally well received in Italy, both because it satisfied social and economic needs and because France and Italy shared a common legal tradition based on the Roman law and the standard glosses and comments. This tradition, in great part, was absorbed into the Napoleonic codes.

The republics that were formed on the French model usually copied the legislation of revolutionary France; they abolished feudal rights, the procedural privileges of the clergy and nobility,[105] and most future interests in property; they confiscated a part of the ecclesiastical mortmain, introduced civil marriage, and lowered the age limits of majority. Even what was probably the most organic of the legislative enactments of the Cisalpine Republic, the *Corpo di leggi organiche giudiziarie* of 1797, which set up the new court system headed in imitation of the French system by a Corte di cassazione,[106] was but a revision of the corresponding French law.

103. On the legislation enacted in Italy during the revolutionary and Napoleonic periods, see Del Giudice, *Storia del diritto italiano*, vol. 2: *Le fonti* 143–83 (1923); Ghisalberti, *Le costituzioni "Giacobine"* (1796–99) (1957).

104. The political geography of Italy in those years underwent radical changes. The Cisalpine Republic (Lombardy and Emilia) was formed in 1797 and transformed in 1802 into the Italian Republic under Napoleon's presidency. In 1797, a Ligurian Republic (centering in Genoa) was instituted; in 1798, a Roman Republic was formed; in 1799 a Parthenopean (Neapolitan) Republic was formed. With the proclamation of the French Empire in 1804, the Italian Republic, plus Venice, became the Kingdom of Italy, and Napoleon was crowned as king. A Kingdom of Naples was also created, with Joseph Bonaparte as king.

105. Among the more important reforms of the revolution was the unification of the courts previously divided into royal, feudal, and ecclesiastical jurisdictions. Unification involved abolition of the privilege of the nobility and clergy to be judged in special courts. Judicial office was radically transformed. Previously, such an office was frequently a property right. "Feudal judgeships were hereditary; royal judgeships, formerly sold to the highest bidder, had also become hereditary. Judges were among the more rabid opponents of the French Revolution, and many paid for their opposition at the guillotine." Cappelletti and Perillo, *Civil Procedure in Italy* 38 (1965).

106. On the Corte di cassazione, see 2.06, 4.16.

The French Civil Code of 1804[107] was made effective in the Kingdom of Italy in 1806. The Civil Code was followed by the Code of Civil Procedure, the Commercial Code, and the Penal Code, all mere translations of the corresponding French codes. The same process occurred in the Kingdom of Naples.[108] An exception in the Kingdom of Italy was the Code of Criminal Procedure, in effect on September 8, 1807; although inspired by the principles of the French code, it varied from the model in several notable respects—for example, elimination of the jury.

The new codes were an expression of the power of the middle class at the expense of the aristocracy. In addition, they represented both a substantive and a formal departure from the preceding consolidations. Prior organic collections of law were normally compilations of preexisting legislation; the codes born from the revolution were new law that would entirely replace the old. Even the many rules and institutions with ancient roots incorporated into the codes were effective (in theory) only because of their reenactment as part of the new, complete legislative system. There was a formal rupture with the *jus commune*; no longer was it to be considered as a kind of general residual law. Despite the formal rupture with the past, however, the codes were, of necessity, built up of culturally familiar concepts, institutions, and ways of thinking about law derived from the preceding system.[109]

107. Space does not permit a discussion of the history of the enactment of the French Civil Code. See Portalis, *Discours, rapports et travaux inédits sur le code civil* (1844). On the influence of the French Civil Code in Italy, see Chironi, *Le code civil et son influence en Italie,* in *Le code civil 1804–1904. Livre du centenaire* (tome II) 761–77 (1904).

108. The French codes were also adopted in other Italian states, such as the Kingdom of Etruria and the Principate of Lucca, which were formed in this period.

109. See the concise discussion of the codes in Ryan, *An Introduction to the Civil Law* 15–19, 26–29 (1962). The legal geography of France had contained two principal zones: the *pays de droit coutumier* and the *pays de droit écrit* (cf. 1.16). In the zone of "written law," the reception of Roman law and the glosses was nearly complete, while in the zone of "customary law," the *jus commune* permeated important areas of the law and as *ratio scripta* had a general supplementary function. The main task of the four principal draftsmen of the Civil Code—two of whom, including the great Portalis, were from the zone of "written law"— was to unify French private law. A great many Roman elements converged in the final draft. The true novelty of the code, other than its bourgeois liberal ideology, was the formal rupture with the *jus commune*. Substantively, however, much of the legal tradition, with a new ideological base, was carried over into the code. Cf. David and DeVries, *The French Legal System* 12 (1958): "the Napoleonic codification in France . . . did not represent a violent departure from tradition." Even more linked with the past was the Code of Civil Procedure of

Among the elements that spurred the rising Italian ruling class to seek political unity in the era of the Risorgimento was the realization that unitary legislation, such as the Napoleonic codes, was a necessary condition for the material and moral development of the country. Its fractioned legal systems, the direct consequence of political disunity, constituted a serious impediment to the improvement of its standard of living.

1.21 *The Legislation of the Restoration.*[110]   After the restoration of the old regime in 1815, most Italian princes ordered the immediate reenactment of the prerevolutionary legislation. Soon thereafter, they authorized the drafting of new codes, almost always turning to the French codes as models. The Napoleonic codification contained too many legal and technical virtues to be ignored in the changed ideological and political context of the time.[111]

1806, defined by David and DeVries as "a barely revised edition of the *Ordonnance* of 1667" (at 13). See also, generally, West et al., *The French Legal System* (1998).

110. Although there are numerous studies of individual codes, there is no unified study of the legislation of this period. See 2 Del Giudice, *op. cit.* n. 103, at 184–267.

111. The first Italian state to enact a code after the restoration was the Kingdom of Naples, where, in 1819, the Code of the Kingdom of the Two Sicilies, in five parts (civil, penal, civil procedure, criminal procedure, and commercial law), took effect. The Neapolitan codification was followed by that of the Duchy of Parma, ruled by Maria Luisa, former wife of Napoleon and empress of France. The French Civil Code was here revised and adopted in 1820. In the same year, codes of civil procedure, military crimes, common crimes, and criminal procedure were promulgated. In the Duchy of Modena, Duke Francesco IV at first reenacted the Code of 1771. In 1835 he promulgated a markedly reactionary Penal Code. Not until October 1851 was a new Civil Code enacted; it was followed by a Code of Civil Procedure (1852) and a new Code of Criminal Law and Procedure (promulgated 1855, effective 1856).

In the Kingdom of Lombardy–Venetia, ruled by a king who was also the emperor of Austria, the Austrian Civil Code promulgated in 1811 by Francis I was adopted in 1816, and remained in effect in the now-Italian provinces of Trent and Trieste until after World War I. The Austrian Criminal Code of 1804 was introduced in 1815 and remained in effect until 1852. In the Papal States an initial violent reaction against the French codes was followed by partial codification. A characteristic of the codes of the Papal States was that the *jus commune* continued to be applicable to matters not covered by the codes. In the Grand Duchy of Tuscany the French Code of Commerce was retained as well as the French laws concerning mortgages and rules concerning testimonial evidence. For other matters, the old system was reinstituted with the promise of the enactment of new codes. But the only new code

In Piedmont the restored King Victor Emmanuel I of Savoy reenacted pre-Napoleonic compilations. His successor, Charles Albert, was responsible for the drafting of a constitution that later became the constitution of a united Italy,[112] and an almost complete codification, including a Civil Code, Penal Code, Military Penal Code, Commercial Code, and Code of Criminal Procedure. The work was completed by his successor, Victor Emmanuel II, the last king of Piedmont (officially known as King of Sardinia) and the first king of Italy, with the promulgation in 1854 of the Code of Civil Procedure, and in 1859 of a new Penal Code that was later extended throughout Italy (with the exception of Tuscany) and remained in effect until 1890.

Despite the conservative, if not reactionary, intentions of almost all of the restored monarchs, the Napoleonic experience left its mark on the Italian law of the restoration. It was not possible to reestablish the ancient feudal jurisdictions, municipal and noble privileges, and restrictions on the alienability of property. Indeed, the restored princes found many of the Napoleonic reforms congenial to their aims because they involved the suppression of privileges of the aristocracy, who, in the ancient régime, had set boundaries upon the central power of the monarch. Despite the repeal of some reform legislation, Italy's legal condition did not regress to its pre-Napoleonic state.

1.22 *Legislative Unification.*[113]   The proclamation of the new Kingdom of Italy in 1861[114] brought about a rapid and sometimes artificial process of unification of law and centralization of administration. At first the process involved the simple

---

was a Penal Code, enacted in 1853, considered the masterpiece of the "classical school" of criminal law.

112. The Statuto, as this constitution was called, was "flexible"; it could be overridden by simple legislation. Although much modified and of little effect in limiting the activities of the fascist regime, it was entirely abrogated only on January 1, 1948, by the present "rigid" constitution, which may be amended only by special procedures. The Statuto was a typical example of constitutions granted by previously absolute sovereigns, especially after the European revolution. The sovereigns sought to placate popular aspirations while divesting themselves of as little power as possible. The text of the Statuto is available at http://it.wikisource.org/wiki/Statuto_albertino.

113. See the well-documented book, Aquarone, *L'unificazione legislativa e i codici del 1865* (1960).

114. The House of Savoy, in alliance with France, conquered Lombardy in 1859. Savoy then annexed, on the basis of plebiscites, Emilia, Tuscany, Umbria, the Marches, Naples,

introduction of the codes and principal public laws of Piedmont (the Kingdom of Sardinia headed by the House of Savoy) into the annexed territories.[115] In some cases the introduction of these codes involved a regression to local laws. The second stage was the promulgation, in 1865 and following years, of new codes for the Kingdom of Italy: the Civil Code, Code of Commerce, Code of Civil Procedure, Navigation Code, and Code of Criminal Procedure.

The most complex and most important of these codes was the Civil Code. It consisted of three books, dealing respectively with persons (arts. 1–405); goods, property interests, and their modification (arts. 406–709); and the manner of acquiring and transmitting property interests (arts. 710–2147). Its general structure was modeled on the Napoleonic Code, although it varied from its model by adhering to Italian legal traditions in some places and by innovating in others.[116] Italian doctrine in the decades following the enactment of the code, especially in the years after the German Pandectist school had become influential, criticized it for its poor analytic structure. The compilers had been moved more by practical motivations than by scientific spirit.[117] The lack, for example, of legislative treatment of the "legal transaction" (*negozio giuridico*), a key concept in Italian legal analysis, led the courts and scholars to extract principles and rules from the most diverse sources to formulate a general theory of the concept.[118]

A more serious gap was the lack of regulation of labor relations. But the government, with its conservative middle-class orientation, was primarily concerned about the protection of property rights. As under the French Civil Code, the stress on individualism gave the employer more power than the employee. And as the industrial revolution swept down into Italy, the code, which was postulated on an

---

and Sicily. The Kingdom of the Two Sicilies (Naples and Sicily) had been conquered by Giuseppe Garibaldi. The conquest was ratified by plebiscite.

115. Tuscany retained its own laws for a number of years. At first, in the former Kingdom of the Two Sicilies, only the Penal Code and the Code of Criminal Procedure were introduced. These were amended in many respects to take into account southern customs and certain aspects of Neapolitan legal scholarship.

116. For example, legal persons were permitted to enjoy the same private rights as individuals (art. 2). Without conditions of reciprocity, aliens were granted the same private rights as citizens (art. 3). Dowry property was made alienable (art. 1404).

117. This kind of criticism was directed at all civil codes based on the French model. For a more general discussion of Italian legal science, see Chapter 5.

118. For a description of the *negozio giuridico* and other concepts employed by Italian (and other civil law) scholars, see 5.05.

underdeveloped state, soon showed itself inadequate to meet the needs of a radically changing society.

There were two exceptions to legislative unification. In Tuscany the Penal Code of 1853, notably superior to the Piedmont Code of 1859, which applied in the rest of Italy, remained in effect. And in Venetia, which was annexed in 1866 as a result of a war with Austria, the excellent Austrian mercantile legislation remained in effect.

Partial unification ended with the promulgation of the new Commercial Code in 1882, which was followed, after lengthy preparation and many drafts,[119] by the Penal Code of 1889. The Commercial Code, although following the structure of the French Code de commerce of 1807, was a marked improvement over its model. It took into account the evolution that had occurred in commercial law, especially in Germany, as well as the great transformations in the nineteenth-century economy: the introduction of railroads, electricity, the telegraph, new kinds of industrial organizations, and the widespread circulation of wealth in the form of bearer paper. It was particularly influential in the legislation of Latin America and Eastern Europe. In 1886, Rumania adopted it nearly in its entirety.[120] The Penal Code, in formulation and content, was markedly superior to preceding legislation. It was characterized by the abolition of the death penalty, milder punishments, and a liberal spirit throughout.

The last codification prior to the enactment of the current codes of 1930 and 1940–42 was the revision in 1913 of the Code of Criminal Procedure of 1865. This code produced a workable system of procedure, but because it was motivated by liberal, antiauthoritarian ideals, it was quickly repealed and replaced by the Rocco Code of 1931.[121] The Code of 1913 marked the end of the first period of codification in unified Italy. Although not marked by great originality, these codes contributed much to the consolidation of the youthful Italian state.[122]

---

119. The drafts of 1868 and 1870 were taken into account in the formulation of the German Penal Code of 1871 and the Penal Code of the Canton of Ticino of 1873. See Vassalli, *Codice penale*, in 7 *Enciclopedia del diritto* 261, 266 (1960).

120. See Asquini, *Codice di commercio*, in 7 *Enciclopedia del diritto* 250, 251 (1960).

121. See Delitala, *Codice di procedura penale*, in 7 *Enciclopedia del diritto* 284 (1960).

122. Another important effort at legislative unification was made in the field of administrative law by the Law of March 20, 1865, no. 2248, entitled law "on the administrative unification of the Kingdom." It was subdivided into six important laws called "allegati," parts of which are still in effect. On *allegato* E and administrative jurisdiction in Italy, see 2.07 and 4.04.

1.23 *Italian Legal Science in the Era between Codifications.* The local codifications in the restoration period were enacted at a time when Italian legal scholarship had neither the vigor nor the originality to come to grips with the codes. The natural consequence was a general reliance upon French legal science. There were few legal scholars of particular note in the early decades of the nineteenth century. Legal writing consisted largely of paraphrases and comments on the codes (themselves French in origin) along the lines of the corresponding French commentaries. Doctrinal creativity was also inhibited by the reactionary policies of state and church in the restoration period.

The level of legal culture slowly began to change toward the middle of the century, in conjunction with the political awakening of the country. After 1848, exiles from all over Italy sought refuge in the small but free Kingdom of Sardinia; in this liberal atmosphere, they exchanged ideas and problems. Exiled legal scholars participated in the political and legislative unification of Italy and opened a new period in the history of Italian doctrine.

The renewal of Italian doctrine at first followed the French influence, but it soon took a more productive direction under the influence of Roman law scholars educated in the German Pandectist school.[123] They put the study of Roman

123. It is possible here only to summarize the German "historical school" and the "Pandectist school" which followed it. The historical school was founded by F. C. von Savigny (1779–1861). Its fundamental premise was that the systematic analysis of law must be based upon the knowledge of Roman law and its development in the Middle Ages. Significantly, Savigny's best-known work is *Geschichte des römischen Rechts im Mittelalter* (*The History of Roman Law in the Middle Ages*). Its approach was antithetical to natural-law conceptions. The school gave birth to modern methods of studying legal history and also to a dogmatic construction of law on the basis of legal history.

Germany was divided into about thirty states until 1866–70. In these years the Prussian House of Hohenzollern, guided by Otto von Bismarck, succeeded in unifying the Reich. There was no civil code until 1896–1900. The *jus commune* was existing law and was considered to be the law of the German nation. As stated by Bernard Windscheid, "the law of the Pandects" was "German private law of Roman origin." In nineteenth-century Germany, the Pandectists produced the most refined and organic systemization of Roman law and theory. The successors of Savigny tended to accentuate the importance of dogmatics to the detriment of legal history. Impatience with this approach is evident in the work of the great Jhering, who, starting from a framework that was clearly dogmatic and systematic, moved on to new approaches that were to become the basis of the "jurisprudence of interests," a movement in many respects similar to American legal realism.

Despite the criticisms which may today be made of the Pandectists, it is incontrovertible that all continental Europe (and certain English and American scholars led by Austin) used

law on a new basis, showing the need to approach it not as a mere study of the past but as a necessary basis for the comprehension of the existing Civil Code.[124] This new approach to Roman law studies consequently had its effect on the study of contemporary civil law. Thus began the modern flowering of the Italian *scienza civilistica*: the "science" of civil law. Its beginning was strongly characterized by a historical approach, nourished by a tradition stretching back two millennia, in which the Napoleonic and post-Napoleonic codification was only the latest phase. Together with this historical approach there was an analytical and dogmatic emphasis on the search for precise definitions of the concepts—the general principles and dogmas upon which positive law is based and upon which scholars could build their systematic analyses. This analytic emphasis was characteristic of the German Pandectist school. Unfortunately, in Italy, as in Germany, it soon prevailed, often becoming excessively abstract and losing contact with the historical roots of existing law. By and large, the excesses of the analytic or dogmatic school prevailed.[125]

This school of civil lawyers led the movement for reform of the Civil Code of 1865[126] that resulted in the adoption of the present Civil Code, in effect since

the powerful doctrinal constructions of the Pandectists as a tool for refining national doctrinal constructions. It is not surprising that Italy, at a time when its own juridical production was in crisis, turned to contemporary German legal science. Some of the consequences are discussed in Chapter 5.

124. Prior to this important movement initiated by Serafini, "Roman law, having lost [in Italy, in contrast with Germany] the validity of a common law, was neglected in the schools, and civil law was explained on the basis of French doctrine." Del Giudice, *op. cit.* n. 103, at 317–18; see also Pacchioni and Grassetti, *Diritto civile*, in 5 *Novissimo digesto italiano* 800, 804–5 (1960).

125. See Chapter 5; Nicolò, *Diritto civile*, in 12 *Enciclopedia del diritto* 904 (1964), at 919 states: "In the period between the two world wars, the principal task undertaken, more or less consciously, by Italian civil law science was to delineate a geometric system of concepts." This was partly a consequence of the "propensity to overevaluate the requirement of legal formalism," but also partly a more or less knowing defense against the seductions and risks of fascism. On this latter point, see Cappelletti, *Il processo civile italiano nel quadro della contrapposizione "civil law–common law,"* 9 Rivista di diritto civile (pt. 1) 31, 59 (1963); 5.09.

However, especially among the younger civil law scholars emerging in this postwar period, there is a strong tendency toward consideration of the sociological and ideological basis of law, accompanied by a greater interest in comparative law. The teacher of all in this respect was Tullio Ascarelli (1903–59). See 5.10 and 7.12.

126. For a discussion of the defects of the Civil Code of 1865, see 6.07.

1942.[127] The movement toward the new code, for propaganda purposes, was presented by the regime as an expression of fascist ideology. In fact, however, the new code had relatively little to do with fascism and much to do with the economic, social, and cultural climate of this century.[128]

Doctrine in the field of civil procedure developed along similar lines. The starting point was, of course, the Code of Civil Procedure of 1865, which, although in the Italian procedural tradition, had its immediate source in the French Code de procédure civile of 1806. It was therefore markedly inspired by principles of individualism and nineteenth-century liberalism. The physiocratic doctrine of laissez-faire had, however, lost its impetus in Europe by the mid-nineteenth century. In 1877–79 the German Zivilprozessordnung, rich in new procedural techniques, came upon the scene; it was followed by the much more modern Austrian Zivilprozessordnung of 1895–98, with its "social conception" of procedural law. These modern codes employed institutions and concepts of Roman and Italian origin in order to change radically the formalistic procedure inherited from the canon law and the *jus commune*.[129] The examples given by these codes, together with a general rise in the level of legal studies, stimulated Italian procedural scholars toward a search for the historical origins of procedural institutions and rediscovery of the Roman, Italian, and Germanic traditions behind existing rules. The leader of the new school was Giuseppe Chiovenda, whose disciples included Piero Calamandrei, Enrico Redenti, and Antonio Segni.[130] Their

127. There is a detailed discussion of the Civil Code of 1942 in 6.09–6.15.

128. The ideology of the 1942 Civil Code is discussed in 6.08.

129. For the characteristics and the defects of the Romano-canonical and *jus commune* procedures, see Cappelletti and Perillo, *op. cit.* n. 105, at 1.33. On the contrast between them and classical Roman procedure, see *ibid.*, at 1.31; see also 4.15.

130. On Italian procedural doctrine in the era between the two codes (1865–1942), see, in greater detail, Cappelletti and Perillo, *op. cit.* n. 105, at 1.38–1.39. On the codes of civil procedure in France, Germany, and Austria, see *ibid.*, at 1.35–1.36.

Among scholars in the field of civil procedure, as with the civil law doctrine, utilization of a dogmatic-systematic approach tended to prevail in later decades and to lose itself in high-level abstraction, out of touch with reality (which is not geometry but history and, therefore, change). The greatest system-builder of Italian procedural doctrine was Francesco Carnelutti (1879–1965) who, however, especially in his later years, felt the inadequacy of the purely systematic approach and the need of the jurist to turn to the human problems at the basis of legal phenomena. Strongly open to the consideration of these problems and their social roots was Piero Calamandrei (1889–1956), who, although like Chiovenda openly

work achieved partial expression in the Code of Civil Procedure of 1940, in force since 1942.[131]

There is a debate in Italian circles regarding the impact of fascism on the legal system. The Code of Civil Procedure and the Civil Code were both presented as the product of the fascist regime, but the original edition of this work argued that in reality these Codes were "the combined result of a renaissance of legal scholarship and practical and doctrinal pressure for reform antedating the regime." The authoritarian ideology of fascism was felt to a greater extent in the Penal Code,[132] and, to an even greater extent, in the Code of Criminal Procedure, both made effective on July 1, 1931, through the efforts of Fascist Minister of Justice Alfredo Rocco.

The Penal Code has since been extensively amended in the postwar period, and the Code of Criminal Procedure was replaced in 1989,[133] but the lingering influence of fascism on Italy's criminal law continues to be debated.[134] Substantive provisions of the Penal Code have even been challenged before the European Court of Human Rights, in part based upon their fascist origins.[135] Beyond this, commentators have argued that the language and structure of the Penal Code continue to bear stylistic marks indicative of their fascist origins.[136] The original edition of this work argued that the Code required "fundamental reform."[137]

---

anti-fascist, was, together with Carnelutti and Redenti, the principal author of the Code of Civil Procedure of 1942 and later one of the "fathers" of the republican Constitution of 1948.

131. For a discussion of the enactment of the code and the historical and ideological reasons for the failure to realize needed reforms, see Cappelletti and Perillo, *op. cit.* n. 105, at 1.38–1.39; 4.15. On the amendments to the Code in 1950, see *id.*, at 1.40.

132. For concrete examples of the manifestation of fascist ideology in the Penal Code, see Vassalli, *The Reform of the Italian Penal Code*, 20 Wayne L. Rev. 1031 (1974). These included more severe punishments, as well as efforts to "rationalize" and integrate the administration of the penal system.

133. But see Grande, *Criminal Justice: The Resistance of a Mentality*, in Lena and Mattei, *op. cit.* n. 1, for a critical assessment of the replacement of the Code of Criminal Procedure.

134. Skinner, *Tainted Law? The Italian Penal Code, Fascism and Democracy*, 7(4) International Journal of Law in Context 423 (2011) provides an overview of the Italian literature on the subject.

135. *Giuliani and Gaggio v. Italy* [2011] ECHR 513, para. 202–4 (24 March 2011).

136. See Skinner, *op. cit.* n. 134, at 436–42.

137. See also Delitala, *op. cit.* n. 121, at 286–87.

Fascism, in power in 1922 with dictatorial power after 1925, caused paralyzed doctrinal development in the field of constitutional and public law. A vigorous recovery, however, occurred in the postwar period. Like scholarship in private law, that in public law was first

1.24 *Conclusion.* The period since 1945 has been a time of change but also continuity in Italian law. The postwar period has seen the birth of the Italian Republic, which marked the rise of a new, at least formally, democratic political system and its accompanying institutions, most notably the constitutional court. It has also seen the accession of Italy to the European Union, whose laws and institutions have complemented or supplanted those of the country in several areas. There have also been numerous changes to substantive law, including amendments to the civil and criminal codes and a new Code of Criminal Procedure; extensive institutional changes; and an increasing Anglo-American influence which—especially in criminal law—have led some to wonder whether Italy remains a purely civil law country or has achieved a sort of mixed, hybrid status.[138]

Notwithstanding these changes the country's fundamental patterns of legal thought and behavior—what later chapters refer to as the "Italian style"—have remained remarkably consistent over time and, to a large extent, distinct from those in other countries. Italian law remains the product of over twenty-four centuries of more or less continuous legal development. The Italian legal system was older at the time of Justinian's compilation than the Anglo-American common law is today. This long history includes important events, movements, institutions, and persons generally thought to be extraneous to the common law: the XII Tables; the jurisconsults and the *ius respondendi*; Gaius; Justinian, Tribonian, and the *Corpus Juris Civilis*; the canon law of the Church of Rome; the Holy Roman Empire; the University of Bologna, and the revival of Roman legal studies; the *mos italicus*; the revival of commerce and the development of commercial law; humanism and the Enlightenment; nationalism, the Risorgimento, and legislative unification and codification; Italian fascism and its overthrow; and the new codes and the Constitution of 1948.

In terms of legal geography, Italy was the source of the *jus commune* of Europe, as it was earlier been the source of the Roman law. By the time the *mos italicus* went into decline the legal tradition of Europe and of Europe's colonial empires had been formed out of the revived Roman law, the canon law, and the commercial

---

influenced by French thinking, then by the more scientific method of the German scholars, who built on concepts taken from civil and procedural legal theory. See Giannini, *Diritto amministrativo*, in 12 *Enciclopedia del diritto* 855, 868–69 (1964).

138. On the influence of the common law upon postwar Italy, see Alpa, *The Age of Rebuilding: Sketches of the New Italian Private Law* 392–400 (2007).

law as studied, taught, and practiced in Italy. The demise of the Holy Roman Empire, the rise of the nation-state, and the ideology that received partial expression in the movement toward codification have not destroyed this common legal base. Although these codes took different forms from nation to nation they were built up of concepts and institutions from the same legal tradition, a tradition that still lives in Italy.

The French and German codifications, in particular, reflect contrasting attitudes toward the nature and functions of codification, and are cast in quite different forms. In a sense they constitute the polar extremes of the European codification movement. Each has strongly influenced the legal development of unified Italy. The first Italian codes were French in form, and Franco-Belgian exegetic scholarship for a time dominated the Italian doctrine. Later the rise of the Pandectist school in Germany and the enactment of the German codes profoundly affected the style of Italian legal thought and, through it, of the new Italian codifications of the 1930s and 1940s. More recently, reforms in criminal procedure have brought Anglo-American influences to Italy, and accession to the European Union has given pan-European laws a place in Italy's legal order

The result of these forces is a legal order that combines (1) the legal tradition and many of the historically derived concepts and institutions of the *jus commune*, (2) the quite different French and German contributions of the nineteenth century, and (3) reforms and innovations brought about by the current era of globalization. When the original edition of this work was published in 1967, its authors characterized the Italian legal system as, more than any other legal system, "a kind of paradigm of the civil law system" because of the way it had integrated the first two of these influences.[139] Readers of the ensuing chapters may judge whether this evaluation remains accurate or whether Italy's legal order has morphed into something new and different.

---

139. See also Millner, *Note on Italian Law*, 14 Int'l & Comp. L.Q. 1028, 1035 (1965): "Similarly, in other parts of the Code, departures were made from the 1865 Code in order to make good inadequacies, weaknesses and hiatuses, which time had brought to light. In so doing, the Italian compilers had the advantage of the post-Napoleonic codifications, more particularly the German Civil Code and the Swiss Code. The new Code has not stuck rigidly to the Napoleonic formulations, so that it represents, in some degree, a blend between the French and German families of Civil law codes, interlaced with certain native Italian trends."

CHAPTER TWO

Italian Government

2.01 *Introduction.* Italy as a State is a creature of the nineteenth century.[1] Before 1861, Italy was a conglomeration of petty states, dismissed by the European powers as nothing more than a geographical expression.[2] Since the downfall of Rome—with a few parentheses—Italian territory had been fragmented into numerous

---

1. A concise and readable history of modern Italy is Albrecht-Carrié, *Italy from Napoleon to Mussolini* (1950), which also contains a short but useful bibliography. Smith, *Italy: A Modern History* (2d ed. 1969) and Smith, *Modern Italy: A Political History* (1997) are also comprehensive in nature and contain a helpful list of suggested readings. For other insightful arguments, see Riall, *Risorgimento. The History of Italy from Napoleon to Nation State* (2008) and Patriarca and Riall, *The Risorgimento Revisited: Nationalism and Culture in Nineteenth-Century Italy* (2012). The historical perspective and the construction of a national tradition are analyzed and discussed in several volumes, among them Ginsborg, *A History of Contemporary Italy: Society and Politics 1943–1988* (2003); Ginsborg, *Italy and Its Discontents: Family, Civil Society, State 1980–2001* (2006); Kirk, *The Architecture of Modern Italy: 1. The Challenge of Tradition, 1750–1900* (2005); and Gilmour, *The Pursuit of Italy: A History of Land, Its Regions and Their Peoples* (2011). An economic, political, and social history, with emphasis on labor relations, is Neufeld, *Italy: School for Awakening Countries* (1961). An economic history is Clough, *The Economic History of Modern Italy* (1964). A gender-based approach is developed in Marotti and Brooke, *Gendering Italian Fiction: A Feminist Revision of Italian History* (1999).

2. The statement that Italy is nothing more than a geographical expression has been attributed to Metternich. Adams and Barile, *The Government of Republican Italy* 6 (2d ed. 1972). Politically, the statement was correct. However, educated Italians have been conscious of their common nationality since at least Dante's day.

states, often existing in some form of dependence on non-Italian rulers. When, during the Renaissance, Italians controlled their own destiny, constant warfare between cities and constant uprisings in cities were the rule.

Unlike many other new nations, Italy was not organized as a political entity by her German, French, Spanish, or Austrian overlords. Territorial fragmentation combined with ideological disunity to delay and hamper a national effort for independence. On the eve of the formation of the Italian state, Italians were divided into monarchists, papists, and republicans, and further split into federalists, regionalists, and nationalists. Within each of these factions, liberals, radicals, and conservatives vied for primacy. Others preferred to collaborate with the dominant foreign power of the day. Millions were apathetic.

The formation of the Italian State in 1861 (with Venice, Rome, Trent, and Trieste not yet included) did not unify Italian society. Disunity continued in a different framework. Elections were sometimes rigged, and violent demonstrations, although always kept in hand, showed a deep social malaise.[3] World War I exhausted Italy economically, killed 600,000 of her men,[4] and brought little reward at the peace table. The postwar struggles between Marxist, reform, clerical, liberal (conservative), and nationalist groups disrupted state action and provided the opportunity for a fascist coup.

The downfall of fascism, brought about by the Allied armies in conjunction with widespread popular uprisings in northern and central Italy, was the occasion for a coalition of parties, dominated by the Church-inspired Christian Democrats, ranging from the Communists to the conservative Liberals. Fascists and the previous royal family were excluded. In retrospect, the degree of sound compromise that went into the 1948 Constitution, adopted by a national convention representing such a spectrum of parties, is striking. It can only be explained by one of the central facts of Italian history: the resistance. Over 100,000 Italians died in the fight

---

3. See Kogan, *The Government of Italy* 6–9 (1962); Neufeld, *op. cit.* n. 1, at 18–19, 100–102, 105, 166–74, 211, 213–16, 219–22, 231; Germino and Passigli, *The Government and Politics of Contemporary Italy* (1968); Putnam, Leonardi, and Nanetti, *Making Democracy Work: Civic Traditions in Modern Italy* (1993); Newell, *The Politics of Italy: Governance in a Normal Country* (2d ed. 2010).

4. Albrecht-Carrié, *op. cit.* n. 1, at 109. For greater statistical detail, see Morgan, *The Fall of Mussolini. Italy, the Italians and the Second World War* (2007); Riemer and Simon, *The New World of Politics: An Introduction to Political Science* (4th ed. 1997), at 338.

against fascism, more persons than the allies lost in the long Italian campaign.[5] The ideal of anti-fascism and the memories of a common struggle against the fascist regime temporarily overcame ideological difficulties, but the lack of a national consensus on fundamental political principles prevented more systematic progress. However, despite the lack of a national consensus, constitutional if highly imperfect government survived for about 45 years, implementing many reforms and other important legislation and transforming an almost wholly agricultural State into a fully developed industrial country.[6]

After the collapse of the Berlin Wall in 1989, Italian democracy entered an era of deep structural change, and with the election of 1994, it is a commonplace that a Second Republic was inaugurated, including a large-scale reversal of values and constitutional practices.[7] The First Republic was dominated by a proportional system and two main coalitions, one centered on the Christian Democrats and the other on the strongest Communist Party of the West.[8] Because of this situation the Christian Democrats remained effectively in office for almost 50 years, and the changes of cabinets were not provoked by general elections but by internal agreements between the members of this party and their allies.[9]

After 1994 the Christian Democrats collapsed and the Communist Party changed its name and substance.[10] The Left gave rise to newer forms of coalition,

5. Adams and Barile, *op. cit.* n. 2, at 13.

6. In-depth political studies of Italy include Adams and Barile, *op. cit.* n. 2; Hughes, *The United States and Italy* (rev. ed. 1965); Kogan, *op. cit.* n. 3.

7. On the Italian transition to the Second Republic, see Gundle and Parker, *The New Italian Republic: From the Fall of the Berlin Wall to Berlusconi* (1996); Koff, *Italy from the First to the Second Republic* (2000); Furlong, *Modern Italy. Representation and Reform* (1994); Janni, *Italy in Transition: The Long Road from the First to the Second Republic* (1998); Mershon and Pasquino, *Italian Politics: Ending the First Republic* (1995).

8. Giammanco, *The Catholic-Communist Dialogue in Italy: 1944 to the Present* (1989). On Italian political parties in the First Republic, see Virga, *Il partito nell'ordinamento giuridico* (1948); Predieri, *I partiti politici*, in 1 Calamandrei and Levi, *Commentario sistematico alla costituzione italiana* 171 (1950); Mortati, *Note introduttive ad uno studio sui partiti politici nell'ordinamento italiano*, in 2 *Scritti giuridici in memoria di V. E. Orlando* 111 (1957).

9. Leonardi and Wertman, *Italian Christian Democracy: The Politics of Dominance* (1989); Webster, *Christian Democracy in Italy 1860–1960* (1960); Deutsch, *The Political Ideology of Italian Christian Democracy: Case Studies of the Genesis, Structure and Goal of an Ideology* (1978).

10. White, *Political Parties and the Collapse of the Old Order* (1998); Weinberg, *The Transformation of Italian Communism* (1995) at 64; Busky, *Communism in History and*

whereas the Right reorganized itself mainly under the leadership of Silvio Berlusconi.[11] The electoral system shifted toward a more majoritarian voting paradigm.[12] In this way the life span of Italian cabinets became longer, and the Left and the Right began an uneasy alternation in power.

In terms of political theory, the shift from the First to the Second Republic can be captured by the concept of a change in the "Material Constitution" of Italy, meaning that the text of the Constitution remained the same but the spirit of the Constitution and the conventions under which a Constitution is implemented in practice were reversed.

2.02 *Fundamental Provisions of the Constitution.*   The Constitution of January 1, 1948, adopted certain fundamental principles that have traditionally been recognized by liberal states. Separation of powers,[13] checks and balances,[14] procedural due process,[15] equal protection of the laws,[16] universal suffrage,[17] freedom of expression,[18] association,[19] and assembly,[20] freedom from unreasonable search

---

Theory: The European Experience (2002) at 57; Drake, *Apostles and Agitators: Italy's Marxist Revolutionary Tradition* (2003) at 230.

11. Shin and Agnew, *Berlusconi's Italy: Mapping Contemporary Italian Politics* (2008); Ginsborg, *Berlusconi: Television, Power and Patrimony* (2004).

12. Renwick, *The Politics of Electoral Reform: Changing the Rules of Democracy* (2010); Ruzza and Fella, *Re-inventing the Italian Right* (2005).

13. See Balladore Pallieri, *Appunti sulla divisione dei poteri nella vigente Costituzione italiana*, 2 Rivista trimestrale di diritto pubblico 811 (1952). On the Italian Constitution in general, see Mortati, *Istituzioni di diritto pubblico* (6th ed. 1962); Barile, *Corso di diritto costituzionale* (2d ed. 1964); Balladore Pallieri, *Diritto costituzionale* (8th ed. 1966); Crosa, *Diritto costituzionale* (4th ed. 1955); Virga, *Diritto costituzionale* (5th ed. 1961). See also Calamandrei and Levi, *op. cit.* n. 8.

14. E.g., Constitution arts. 89, 94, 134.

15. Constitution arts. 24, 25, 27.

16. Constitution art. 3.

17. Constitution arts. 48, 56, 58. But see Constitution, Transitory and Final Provisions art. XII, para. 2; art. XIII, para. 1.

18. Constitution art. 21.

19. Constitution arts. 18, 49. But see Constitution, Transitory and Final Provisions art. XII.

20. Constitution art. 17.

and seizure,[21] freedom to travel,[22] and other fundamental liberties[23] find expression in the Constitution. Judicial review of legislation, not traditionally recognized as a fundamental principle of government outside the Western Hemisphere, was also adopted, and with the passage of time has become a factor of striking importance.[24]

Social goals were also incorporated into the Italian Constitution. Paragraph 2 of article 3 states, "It shall be the task of the Republic to remove obstacles of an economic or social nature that, by restricting in practice the freedom and equality of citizens, impede the full development of the human personality and the effective participation of all workers in the political, economic, and social organization of the country." The right to employment,[25] free medical aid to the indigent,[26] eight years of compulsory free education,[27] paid vacations for all workers,[28] the right to strike and to form trade unions,[29] and other social goals were proclaimed.

Some of the provisions of the Italian Constitution were said to be enforceable (*precettive*) and others to be programmatic (*programmatiche*),[30] but this theory was essentially superseded during the 1970s, as the Constitutional Court began to play a very active role in promoting a liberal and progressive reading of the text.[31]

A significant part of this progress was induced by social and economic change. Socially, it was, for the first time in Italian history, deemed proper for women of all classes to seek employment. Economically, industry made rapid progress, especially in the 1960s and the 1980s, distributing benefits more broadly throughout

21. Constitution arts. 13, 14, 21.

22. Constitution art. 16.

23. E.g., Constitution arts. 15, 22, 26, 27.

24. Constitution art. 134. See Cappelletti and Adams, *Judicial Review of Legislation: European Antecedents and Adaptations*, 79 Harv. L. Rev. 1207 (1966).

25. Constitution art. 4, para. 1.

26. Constitution art. 32, para. 1.

27. Constitution art. 34, para. 2.

28. Constitution art. 36, para. 3.

29. Constitution arts. 39, 40.

30. The former theory was discussed in various publications, among which we could mention Azzariti, *La nuova Costituzione e le leggi anteriori*, in *Problemi attuali di diritto costituzionale* (1951); Crisafulli, *La Costituzione e le sue disposizioni di principio* (1952); Calamandrei, *La Costituzione e le leggi per attuarla* (1955).

31. Paladin, *Le fonti del diritto italiano* (1996) at 134 ss.; Occhiocupo, *Costituzione e Corte costituzionale: percorsi di un rapporto genetico dinamico e indissolubile* (2010).

Italian society. The times, in this case, caught up to the Constitution. A "Constitutional reading" was likewise extended to the Civil Code, shaping a new way of interpreting its norms so as to promote the values and rights of the a democratic society.[32]

Provisions granting equal protection of the laws and procedural due process received especially progressive interpretation. It was held, for example, that the imposition of security for costs in civil proceedings was unconstitutional— despite the fact that poor litigants were exempted from this requirement— because it placed an unfair burden on those plaintiffs who have limited economic resources.[33] Since court costs include the successful party's attorney's fees, the posting of security for costs was a significant factor in causing persons with limited cash resources to abandon prosecution of meritorious claims. In a more significant decision, based on similar reasoning, the Court abrogated a provision of law requiring prepayment of a tax assessment as a condition precedent to judicial review of the assessment.[34] The Court held that the requirement constituted a de facto limitation on equal protection of the laws by placing a serious burden on taxpayers of limited means: since it placed a burden on the constitutional right to obtain judicial redress of a wrong, it also unconstitutionally limited due process. The Court also abrogated some of the more obnoxious provisions of the fascist police laws,[35] but some arguably unconstitutional provisions of these laws remained in effect since procedural access to the Court was limited.[36]

---

32. The recurrent expression used at this regard is "constitutionalisation of private law." See Rodotà, *Il diritto privato nella società moderna* (1971); Salvi (ed.), *Diritto civile e principi costituzionali europei e italiani* (2012).

33. Corte costituzionale, Nov. 29, 1960, no. 67, 5 Giurisprudenza costituzionale 1195 (1960) (note by Satta); 16 Rivista di diritto processuale 283 (1961) (note by Denti); 10 Giustizia civile (pt. 3) 209 (1960) (note by Bianchi d'Espinosa); 113 Giurisprudenza italiana (pt. 1, § 1) 273 (1961) (note by Pizzorusso). See also Gualandi, *Cauzione per le spese e costituzione*, 15 Rivista trimestrale di diritto e procedura civile 283 (1961).

34. See *Stroppa v. Intendenza di finanza di Pavia*, Corte costituzionale, March 31, 1961, no. 21, 6 Giurisprudenza costituzionale 138 (1961) (notes by Treves, Esposito).

35. In its first six years of existence (1956–1961), the Constitutional Court declared approximately 150 provisions of national and regional laws to be unconstitutional. A complete listing of such laws is published annually as a preface to the publication Giurisprudenza costituzionale.

36. This issue is discussed further in subsequent chapters.

The matter of church–state relations has been and still is crucial in the Italian Constitution, which incorporates by reference the Lateran agreements entered into by Italy and the Vatican in 1929. The latter place the Roman Catholic Church in a privileged position[37] and recognize Vatican City as an independent state, an arrangement which gives church–state relations not only an internal but also an international status.

The Lateran agreements were comprehensively reviewed and reframed by the Socialist government led by Bettino Craxi in 1984.[38] The revised agreements grant Catholic priests the power to perform marriage ceremonies that have civil validity if the civil norms governing the family are read and explained during the ceremony. However, the ecclesiastical courts have jurisdiction only over the "canonical" aspects of marriages, and their decisions must receive an *exequatur* by Italian courts in order to have legal effect.

Salaries of priests are subsidized by a taxpayer election (known as 8/1000)[39] agreeing to devote a small amount of taxes to this or other approved charitable purposes, but the state has renounced any residual control over the appointments of bishops.

Although the Constitution provides that private schools may be established "without burden to the state," such schools may receive state grants.[40] The proponents of these grants argue that parochial and other private schools ease governmental burdens by relieving the state of part of the cost of education, while opponents of the grants point out that the constitutional provision was drafted by the agnostic philosopher Benedetto Croce for the purpose of prohibiting grants to parochial schools. Religious instruction continues to be provided in public

37. Constitution art. 7. The Lateran agreements were signed on Feb. 11, 1929, and made effective by the Law of May 27, 1929, no. 810. On the legal relationship between church and state in Italy, see Jemolo, *Lezioni di diritto ecclesiastico* (1962); Jemolo, *Chiesa e Stato in Italia: dalla unificazione ai giorni nostri* (1977); Acerbi (ed.), *La Chiesa e l'Italia: per una storia dei loro rapporti negli ultimi due secoli* (2003); Pertici, *Chiesa e Stato in Italia: dalla Grande Guerra al Nuovo Concordato* (2009). The Jemolo treatise is available in English as *Church and State in Italy: 1850–1950* (1961).

38. The agreement between the Italian government and the Holy See was ratified with the Act of March 25, 1985, no. 121.

39. As it has been established according to the provisions of the Act of May 20, 1985, no. 222 (art. 47).

40. Constitution art. 33, para. 3. The great majority of private schools are Roman Catholic.

schools but is no longer compulsory in nature, and students (or their parents) decide whether they wish to receive it.[41]

Acquisition of real property by, and donations and testamentary gifts to, churches and religious organizations are contingent upon state approval.[42] The amount of real property taxes to be paid by the church for its religious buildings remains a significant issue, given the fact that these buildings, and the enormous collections of art and historical objects that they contain, constitute a substantial portion of the Italian cultural heritage.

Freedom is guaranteed to all religions, and organized non-Catholic faiths do find toleration. Article 8 of the Constitution provides that relations between the state and non-Catholic religions are to be regulated by laws based on agreements entered into by the state and representative of those religions. Evangelical preachers who are not ministers of religions that have reached agreements with the state have sometimes been hampered in the performance of missionary work.

Article 11 of the Constitution consents to the limitations of sovereignty necessary to achieve peace and justice among nations. Postwar Italian governments have implemented this provision by membership in the United Nations, the European Economic Community (later European Union), EURATOM, and NATO. Perhaps no other Western State has as firmly and as persistently favored the expansion of the roles of these international organizations.

Article 11 has also become the legal cornerstone for the implementation of European legislation, providing a constitutional platform for all European Union (EU) sources of law.[43] The Constitutional Court has further held that European law may expand itself at the expense of pure Italian law, as a form of its general

41. According to Act of March 25, 1985, n. 12.

42. Codice civile art. 17. Although this requirement applies to all legal persons, its purpose, when imposed in 1850, was to discourage church and charitable ownership of real property, which had previously resulted in the withdrawal of immense areas of land from the market. See Ferrara, *Le persone giuridiche*, in 2 *Trattato di diritto civile italiano* (tome 2) 242–53 (1938). For other rules of Italian law designed to encourage free marketability of land, see Merryman, *Policy, Autonomy, and the Numerus Clausus in Italian and American Property Law*, 12 Am. J. Comp. L. 224 (1963).

43. For a general overview, see Adam-Tizzano, *Lineamenti di Diritto dell'Unione Europea* (2010) at 245; Tesauro, *Diritto dell'Unione Europea* (2010) at 194 ss.; Villani, *Istituzioni di Diritto dell'Unione europea* (2011) at 272 ss. The EU's role as a source of Italian law is discussed further in 6.02 *infra*.

acceptance by the country.[44] The Supreme Court of Cassation has adopted an additional doctrine under which a judge may give Italian norms an interpretation in conformity with European law including the decisions of the European Court of Justice and the European Court of Human Rights.[45] In this way not only has European legislation entered directly into Italian law, but the preexisting legal system is constantly adapting to European developments. However, European legislation cannot violate the principles of the Italian Constitution and the rights accorded by it to Italian citizens.[46]

2.03 *Local Government.*   Government in Italy was traditionally based on the centralized system instituted in France by Napoleon.[47] Centralized government was favored and implemented by the leaders of Italian unification, who feared divisive regionalism, and was further extended by fascist leaders who feared any opposition to dictatorial control. In recent decades this system has begun to change as the regions, provinces, and communes of Italy have become increasingly autonomous.[48]

The Constitution granted a significant degree of autonomy to the twenty regional governments of Italy.[49] Five regions—Sicily, Sardinia, Valle d'Aosta, Trentino–Alto Adige, and Friuli–Venezia Giulia—were, for historical reasons, granted greater autonomy than the other fifteen.[50]

44. Corte costituzionale, December 27, 1973, no. 183; Corte costituzionale, October 30, 1975, no. 232.

45. Corte di cassazione SS.UU., Jan. 26, 2004, nn. 1338–1341; Corte di cassazione, Dec. 23, 2005, no. 26507; Corte di cassazione, Sept. 22, 2005, n. 35616.

46. Corte costituzionale, June 8, 1984, no. 170; Corte costituzionale, July 11, 1989, no. 389.

47. See Adams and Barile, *op. cit.* n. 2, at 118, 120, 122, 130.

48. This goal has been achieved by means of complex regulations adopted during the 1990s. The principal statements were the Act of June 8, 1990, no. 142, and the so-called "Legge Bassanini" (Act of March 15, 1997, n. 59; Act of May 15, 1989, no. 127). A Consolidation Act on the regulation of local authorities was adopted in 2000 (D. Lgs. of August 18, 2000, n. 267). On the reform of local government, see Piterà, Vigotti, and Barberis, *La riforma degli Enti locali: Commentario al D. Lg. 18 agosto 2000*, n. 267 (2002).

49. Constitution arts. 114–33 originally foresaw the institution of nineteen regions. The Constitutional Law of Dec. 27, 1963, no. 3, raised this number to twenty.

50. Royal Legislative Decree of May 15, 1946, no. 455 (Sicily); Constitutional Laws of Feb. 26, 1948, nos. 3, 4, 5 (Sardinia, Valle d'Aosta, and Trentino–Alto Adige); Constitutional Law of Jan. 31, 1963, no. 1 (Friuli–Venezia Giulia).

The Constitution, as it was implemented in the first few decades, authorized the state to delegate to the regions administrative competence in matters of regional and local concern.[51] It also invested the regions with legislative competence as long as their legislation did not conflict with the national interest or the interests of another region in such matters as urban planning and the promotion and regulation of tourism and the hotel industry. In addition, local public works, hunting and fishing, artisans, and local police were to be placed under regional control.[52]

These powers of the regions were further expanded by the Constitutional Law of October 18, 2001, which redrafted Chapter V of the Constitution and was adopted under political pressure from the "Lega Nord," a semi-independentist movement based in the Northern regions (especially Veneto and Lombardy), although it rejected demands for a kind of "federal" system displacing the power of the central State.

Regional government is vested in a single-chamber legislative council, which elects an executive committee. Since 1994, the President of the Region has been directly elected by the people, and his or her coalition receives a bonus prize in legislative seats to assure firm government while in office.[53] Because of this popular legitimation, the figure of the regional president has become so important that the American term "governor" is normally used to designate her in informal speeches.

The acts of the region are laws to all effects within their proper sphere of jurisdiction. Like other laws, they are subject to the judicial review of the Constitutional Court, which also has the power to decide any issue over competence and jurisdiction between the regions and the central state.

The basic working units of local government today are the approximately 8,000 communes.[54] Some communes consist of a large city, such as Rome, whereas others may be a collection of rural hamlets and their countrysides, but all have

---

51. Constitution art. 118.
52. Constitution art. 117.
53. Constitution art. 122, para. 5, as modified by the Constitutional Law 1/1999.
54. On the communes and on other local authorities, see the works cited at note 48; see also Roversi, Monaco, and Vandelli, *Codice di diritto amministrativo* (10th ed. 2010); Pinto, *Diritto degli Enti Locali* (2012); Caretti, Tarli, and Barbieri, *Diritto regionale* (3d ed. 2012); Caringella, Giuncato, and Roano, *Ordinamento degli Enti Locali* (2d ed. 2007); Mastragostino and Vandelli, *I comuni e le province* (1998); 3 Zanobini, *Corso di diritto amministrativo* (6th ed. 1958); Sandulli, *Manuale di diritto amministrativo* (7th ed. 1962); Colzi, *La provincia ed il commune nell'ordinamento costituzionale*, in 2 Calamandrei and Levi, *op. cit.* n. 8, at 381.

the same governmental structure. A communal council is chosen by popular election, but the mayor is elected independently, receiving, as in the regions, a bonus prize for his coalition and thus a form of independent political legitimation.[55] The mayor is a state as well as a local official and serves as registrar of the office of vital statistics, supervising the local health office as well as the issuance of building permits.

Most of the functions of communes are delineated by state and regional laws. Communes are entrusted with zoning power, police powers in matters of food marketing, and traffic control. Some communes have assumed ownership of utilities. The communes have power to levy taxes within limits set by the state but are still heavily dependent on state grants-in-aid.

The provinces are geographical units that are larger than the communes but have narrower functions. Local elections provide a provincial council, which in turn selects a provincial executive committee, and a president who is directly elected by the people. The provinces maintain roads, undertake certain public works, and engage in some welfare functions. The prefect, a provincial officer appointed by the Minister of the Interior, remains in existence but now has limited power, primarily the coordination and control of police forces and the maintenance of public order.

Although the provinces no longer have a great practical role, stretched as they are between the communes and the regions, they remain important for historical reasons. A province may be thought as the territorial extension of old Italian city-states. Everyone in Italy feels himself strongly attached to his or her province (to be a "florentinian"—not precisely from the city center of Florence, but from its outskirts—produces a sense of pride even stronger than being a tuscan, and especially important against the other tuscans, the pisans, the livornese, and so forth). Provinces are frequently under attack because of budgetary and other concerns, but none of these has been able to defeat these strong elements of heritage and identity.

2.04 *The Constitutional Court.* Before 1948, the Constitution of Italy was the so-called Statuto, granted in 1848 by Carlo Alberto, king of Sardinia and Piedmont. Because it could be overridden by simple act of Parliament or by Royal Decree, the Statuto was the type of constitution that was historically called "flexible." No

---

55. Caciagli and Di Virgilio, *Eleggere il Sindaco: la nuova democrazia locale in Italia e in Europa* (2005).

court could refuse to enforce, or strike down, a law as "unconstitutional."[56] Such an attempt would have been regarded as a violation of the principle of separation of powers. This was the traditional Italian view until fascism showed the dangers of legislative power unchecked by some form of binding legal control.

The present Constitution, which is stronger in nature and can be overridden only by a special amending procedure, is said to be "rigid." The constituent assembly that approved the Constitution considered and rejected the American system under which an ordinary court can, under the rule of *Marbury v. Madison*, refuse to apply a law that it deems unconstitutional.[57] Since in Italy *stare decisis* is not a recognized principle,[58] there was a concern that the highest ordinary court (Corte di cassazione) might find a law to be unconstitutional, and lower courts might refuse to follow the decision. Instead, a Constitutional Court with power to abrogate a law *erga omnes* was felt to be necessary. It was also considered desirable to concentrate in one court all constitutional matters, including the power to adjudicate controversies on the division of powers among the supreme organs of the state as well as among the regions, and between the state and the regions, to decide the admissibility of referenda, to try the President of the Republic for high treason or an attempt to overthrow the Constitution, and to try a minister for crimes committed within the scope of his functions.

In creating a separate Constitutional Court, the framers of the Constitution also took into account that the ordinary judiciary had neither the prestige nor the importance of the American judiciary and moreover that the incumbent Italian judges had been selected, trained, and promoted under the fascist system and could not be relied upon to interpret the Constitution in the progressive spirit intended by the framers. Traditional notions of separation of powers also may have played a role. There was some feeling that the Constitutional Court was to be

56. However, if a law lacked the formal requisites for validity—for example, if the law lacked the requisite signature—any court could refuse to enforce it. See Esposito, *La validità' delle leggi* (reprint 1964).

57. For an analysis of the reasons for instituting a separate constitutional court, see Cappelletti and Adams, *Judicial Review of Legislation: European Antecedents and Adaptations*, 79 Harv. L. Rev. 1207 (1966); Pierandrei, *Corte costituzionale*, in 10 *Enciclopedia del diritto* 874–87 (1962).

58. On the role of precedent in Italy, see Chapter 7.

not a judicial but a legislative control body;[59] however, this theory has lost general acceptance.[60]

The Constitutional Court consists of fifteen judges who serve for nine-year terms.[61] Five are chosen by the President of the Republic, five by Parliament in joint session, and five by the judges of the highest ordinary and administrative courts. Judges of these high courts, law professors, and lawyers who have practiced for twenty years are eligible.[62] Largely because of the difficulty of selecting judges in a turbulent political climate, the Court was not instituted until 1956. From the promulgation of the Constitution until 1956, the ordinary courts could rule on the constitutionality of laws, refusing to apply those they deemed unconstitutional.[63]

The Constitutional Court may not rule on the constitutionality of a law except in a concrete case. In any civil, criminal, or administrative proceeding, a party or the court in which the case is pending has the right to refer a constitutional issue to the Constitutional Court if the court in which the proceeding unfolds finds the issue relevant and not patently groundless.[64] This preliminary finding is designed to avoid the raising of constitutional issues for merely dilatory reasons.

Actions also may be initiated in the Constitutional Court by the state against a region, or by a region against the state or against another region, on the charge of invasion of the plaintiff's competence.[65] The Court may adjudicate conflicts of competence between the fundamental organs of the state, such as the President of the Republic, Parliament, the Council of Ministers, the Corte di cassazione, and

---

59. See Calamandrei, *Corte costituzionale e autorità giudiziaria*, in 6 Calamandrei, *Studio sul processo civile* 210, 215 (1957). For more recent scholarship on the Constitutional Court, see Zagrebelsky, *Principi e voti: la Corte costituzionale e la politica* (2005); Celotto, *La corte costituzionale* (2004).

60. See, e.g., Cappelletti, *Il controllo di costituzionalità delle leggi nel quadro delle funzioni dello Stato*, 15 Rivista di diritto processuale 376 (1960).

61. According to art. 135 Cost., as it has been modified by constitutional law no. 2/1967.

62. Constitution art. 135.

63. Constitution, Transitory and Final Provisions, art. VII, para. 2.

64. Procedural access to the Court is governed by Constitutional Law of March 11, 1953, no. 1; Law of March 11, 1953, no. 87. See Cappelletti, *La pregiudizialità costituzionale nel processo civile* (1957); Adams and Bartle, *The Italian Constitutional Court in Its First Two Years of Activity*, 7 Buff. L. Rev. 250 (1958); Treves, *Judicial Review of Legislation in Italy*, 7 J. Pub. L. 345 (1958).

65. Constitution art. 134, para. 2.

the Constitutional Court itself.[66] Parliament is charged with the duty of creating a list of persons, sixteen of whom are to be selected by lot, to serve as additional judges on the Court in a prosecution against the President of the Republic or a minister.[67]

When compared to the activities of Parliament and the Council of Ministers, the Constitutional Court, although having principally the negative function of abrogating laws, seems to be the body that has done the most to make the 1948 Constitution a living document. The Court early on decided that it has power to abrogate laws enacted prior to the promulgation of the 1948 Constitution. Since political inertia prevented Parliament from repealing and replacing much of the legislation of the fascist era, it was the Court's function to declare many of these laws unconstitutional. Although the Constitution cannot be implemented merely by abrogating legislation, the decisions of the Court have served to remind Italians of the existence of the Constitution and of the large chasm that inevitably separates political reality from constitutional mandates.

2.05 *The Civil and Criminal Courts.*   Italy has a unified national court system. No regional, provincial, or municipal courts exist. The ordinary courts, which exercise civil and criminal jurisdiction, are the justices of the peace, tribunals, courts of appeal, and Corte di cassazione.[68]

At the bottom of the pyramidal organization of the ordinary courts are the justices of the peace, established by Act 468/1999 and replacing the office of Conciliation Judge, who have first instance jurisdiction both in criminal and in civil cases.

The criminal jurisdiction of the justices of the peace is limited to small claims and minor criminal matters. Their civil jurisdiction includes actions relating to movables with a value not in excess of €5,000, actions for damages caused by road accidents with a value not in excess of €20,000, actions concerning specific matters related to real immovable property (e.g., disputes on land boundaries, on the use of common parts of shared apartments, and on neighborhood relationships),

---

66. Constitution art. 134, para. a. See Calamandrei, *op. cit.* n. 59, at 249–50.

67. Constitution art. 135, para. 6; art. 134, para. 3.

68. On the organization and competence of the courts, see Cappelletti and Perillo, *Civil Procedure in Italy*, chs. 3–4 (1965). For a schematic representation of the Italian judicial system, see http://www.csm.it/documenti%20pdf/sistema%20giudiziario%20italiano/inglese.pdf.

and actions concerning failure to provide certain welfare services, regardless of their value.

Tribunals have first instance jurisdiction over all cases which are not expressly allocated to other courts. They also have exclusive jurisdiction in matters relating to capacity of individuals, honorific rights, some forms of taxation, forgery complaints, enforcement, and over any claims having an undetermined value.

Tribunals have second instance jurisdiction over decisions and judgments pronounced by justices of the peace. They can be composed of only one judge ("composizione monocratica") or of three judges ("composizione collegiale"), according to the type of case they are dealing with.

Although in theory unitary, tribunals are often divided into sections that are in practice specialized in particular subject matter. In addition, the law provides for specialized sections for cases dealing with minors, such as adoptions or emancipation (Family Proceeding Court); certain agrarian problems (Land Estate Court); and suits between employers and employees (Labor Tribunal). Laymen serve on these cases, not as jurymen but as "popular" or "expert" judges, deciding along with ordinary judges issues of law and fact.

Criminal cases that are not within the competence of the justices of the peace are allocated to the tribunals and the courts of assizes. The courts of assizes are now organized as specialized sections of the tribunals; nevertheless, there is a division of competence between the tribunals as tribunals and the courts of assizes. Many of the most serious criminal cases are heard by the courts of assizes.[69] Here, two ordinary judges and six laymen, acting as "popular" judges, sit on the bench for a case. All eight vote on the facts and the law. A majority vote convicts; a tie vote acquits. Specialized units settled in the courts of appeal, and named assize courts of appeal are in charge of appeals on decisions by the courts of assize.

The courts of appeal, sitting in panels of three, hear appeals on questions of fact and law from the tribunals. They have limited competence as courts of first instance: they alone may give a foreign judgment domestic effect or approve a consensual adoption. Courts of appeal of assizes, in panels of two ordinary judges and six "popular" judges, hear appeals on questions of law and fact from the courts of assizes and are organized as special sections of the courts of appeal. The court

69. In particular, the courts of assizes have jurisdiction over all cases where people are charged with crimes, with a maximum penalty of at least 24 years.

of appeal is normally located in the regional capital and has territorial jurisdiction within its geographic proper district.

Criminal cases involving defendants under eighteen years of age are decided by the tribunals for minors that are attached to each court of appeal. Each case is adjudicated by a panel consisting of two ordinary judges and two social workers—one male, one female. Appeals are taken to the courts of appeal. A section consisting of three judges and two lay experts—one male, one female—adjudicates the appeal.

Cases involving water rights in public streams, springs, and lakes are heard by regional tribunals of public waters attached to some of the courts of appeal. Cases are adjudicated by panels consisting of two judges and one technician. Appeals are taken to the superior tribunal of public waters, which consists of five ordinary judges, four councilors of state, and three experts, sitting in panels of five or seven, depending on the subject matter.

The highest of the ordinary courts is the Corte di cassazione, often called the Supreme Court, which may either uphold or quash decisions of the lower courts. Its review is limited to questions of law. The Corte di cassazione also has the power to decide conflicts of jurisdiction and competence among the various lower courts at lower levels.

Since there is a constitutional right to obtain the review of all provisional orders relating to personal liberties and of all judgments of the ordinary courts,[70] the Corte di cassazione has a heavy workload. It is divided into several criminal and civil sections. A panel of seven judges sits on each case. In an attempt to maintain uniformity of interpretation of the laws, united civil and criminal sections, composed of judges of each of the regular sections, hear and determine cases that involve particularly controversial issues.

2.06 *Administrative Courts.*   Judicial review of administrative acts in Italy has a fundamentally different basis than in the United States.[71] Special courts have been

---

70. Constitution art. 111, para. 2.

71. On Italian administrative law, see Galeotti, *The Judicial Control of Public Authorities in England and Italy* (1954); Miele, Coki, and Falconi, *Italian Administrative Law*, 3 Int'l & Comp. L.Q. 421 (1954); Treves, *Judicial Review in Italian Administrative Law*, 26 U. Chi. L. Rev. 419 (1958–59). A classic work in Italian is Zanobini, *Corso di diritto amministrativo* (6 vols., 1958–59). For a contemporary source, see Cerulli Irelli, *Lineamenti del diritto amministrativo* (2012).

instituted to review administrative acts, and the ordinary courts may also entertain certain actions against the state or a public body.

The jurisdictions of the administrative courts and the ordinary courts are related to the dichotomy between the Italian concepts of "rights" and "legitimate interests." A "right" is defined as an interest directly guaranteed by law to an individual, whereas a "legitimate interest" is defined as "an individual interest closely connected with a public interest and protected by law only through the legal protection of the latter."[72] For example, if an individual enters into a contract with a public body, the contract gives him contractual *rights*. Redress for breach of the contract may be obtained in the ordinary courts since they are vested with jurisdiction when an individual's rights are violated. If, however, the state requests competitive bids from the public for the formation of a contract, an individual who is unlawfully excluded from competing for the contract cannot show that a right has been violated. Italian law deems that the public competition was opened in the public interest and not for the benefit of individual bidders. A qualified individual, however, has a legitimate *interest* in competing and can seek relief in the administrative courts.

In an action against the state in the ordinary courts, only declaratory judgments and judgments for a sum of money may be obtained. The administrative court may vacate the administrative act attacked and sometimes may substitute its own. It may not, however, render money judgments, except for costs.[73] Ordinarily, a complainant must exhaust administrative remedies before seeking relief in an administrative court.

In determining whether a legitimate interest has been violated, the administrative courts determine whether the administrative organ issuing the act (1) was

---

Although Italian *diritto amministrativo* and French *droit administratif* may seem on first impression to be cut from the same cloth, there are fundamental differences. On the French system, see Hamson, *Executive Discretion and Judicial Control* (1954); Schwartz, *French Administrative Law and the Common Law World* (1954); Uhler, *Review of Administrative Acts* (1942).

72. 1 Zanobini, *op. cit.* n. 71, at 185, 187.

73. There is doctrine to the effect that damages should be awardable for interference with a legitimate interest. See Miele, *Risarcibilità dei danni derivanti da ingiusta lesione di interessi legittimi ad opera della pubblica amministrazione*, 86 Foro Italiano (part 4) 23 (1963); Micheli, *Sentenza di annullamento dil un atto giuridico e risarcimento del danno partimoniale derivante da lesione di interessi legittimi*, Rivista di diritto processuale 396 (1964).

incompetent, (2) exceeded its powers, or (3) violated the law. In some cases the courts may determine whether or not the administrative act involved a wise exercise of discretion.

Any dichotomy of court systems (law-equity; federal-state) creates a certain amount of uncertainty in borderline situations about the proper choice of court. In order to reduce uncertainty, a large number of the cases that involve mixed questions of rights and legitimate interests have been invested exclusively in the administrative courts. The Corte di cassazione determines, in the last resort, issues of jurisdiction.

The Council of State (Consiglio di stato) is, by far, the most important of the administrative courts. Councilors of State are appointed by the President of the Republic upon the recommendation of the Council of Ministers, but they enjoy considerable independence. The Consiglio has seven sections, three of which carry out a jurisdictional function, and four a consultative function.[74] Each section requires a quorum of seven members.

The Council of State has appellate jurisdiction over decisions delivered by the Regional Administrative Tribunals, instituted by Constitutional Law no. 1034/1971. These in turn have jurisdiction over claims between citizens and the public administration relating to the protection of claimant's legitimate interests. Moreover, in special cases dictated by the law, the Council of State has original jurisdiction over compliance proceedings. Cases against local organs are heard by judicial sections of the provincial executive committees. Their decisions may be appealed to the Council of State.

A provincial executive committee, when sitting as a judicial section, consists of the provincial prefect, two prefectural officers, and two members chosen by the elected provincial council. Since the prefect is the chief administrative officer of the province, the executive committees are not completely independent. In areas such as Sicily and Valle d'Aosta, where regional governments have been instituted, other bodies have replaced the executive committees.

74. The Consiglio di Stato may also meet as a court in plenary session, which usually consists of the Consiglio's president and twelve councilors, four being chosen from each section. In addition to the three permanent sections, special minor judicial sections were set up after World War II to deal with specific problems emerging from that conflict. The Consiglio di Stato also has three advisory sections that advise the ministries and other administrative bodies on matters such as the legality and merits of proposed contracts, property condemnations, and grants of citizenship.

An aggrieved party may instead follow another procedure which, although attacked as anachronistic, is nevertheless remarkably simple and inexpensive. Within eighty days, instead of the sixty days to which an applicant to the Council of State is limited, she may make an "extraordinary application to the Chief of State." The responsible minister, acting for the Chief of State, seeks an advisory opinion from the Council of State. If he does not choose to follow the advisory opinion, he must present his decision to the Council of Ministers for approval.

Independent of the Council of State is the Court of Accounts (Corte dei conti), which is primarily concerned with the handling of public money. It hears cases against public officials involving their management of public funds. Six of its eight judicial sections in Rome are concerned with pension claims. Another judicial section functions in Palermo. A quorum of five judges is required to hear a case. Appeals may be taken to the joint section of the same Court, which consists of eleven judges selected from the regular sections. The Court also hears appeals from lower special courts concerned with financial matters. Issues of jurisdiction may be taken to the Corte di cassazione.[75]

There are many other special courts which, except for the courts-martial, are largely administrative in competence. Many of these courts are invested with tax questions. Often a question that has been adjudicated by one of these courts and appealed through the appropriate appellate levels may then be brought to the ordinary tribunals and relitigated through to the Corte di cassazione.

The Constitution imposes the duty upon the legislature to "review" all the special courts, except the Council of State, the Court of Accounts, and the courts-martial, and prohibits the institution of additional special courts.[76] This duty, which seems to indicate that the special courts are eventually to be abolished or else reconstituted as specialized sections of the ordinary courts, strengthened by the granting of independence to the special court judges, has not been fulfilled.

---

75. Constitution, art. 111, para. 3.
76. Constitution, art. 102, para. 2, and Transitory and Final Provisions art. VI.

CHAPTER THREE

The Law Professionals

3.01 *Introduction.* Italy has many legal professions.[1] Although attorneys, notaries, state's attorneys, and judges share a common legal education and are all known as jurists, they are members of distinct professions, among which only minimal interchanges of personnel occur. Since the content of law school instruction significantly affects the manner in which all jurists approach law, discussion of these professions requires an understanding of Italian legal education.

3.02 *Legal Education* Forty-five of the forty-seven schools of law[2] (*facoltà di giurisprudenza*) are units of the state university system, and two are sponsored by private agencies.[3]

The Ministry of Education assigns a minimum number of credits in certain broad areas of law (e.g., twenty-five credits for private law, nine credits in legal

1. The Italian bench and bar are the subject of chapters 2 and 3 of Cappelletti and Perillo, *Civil Procedure in Italy* (1965). Foreign nationals may practice as lawyers (*avvocati*) if their professional qualifications from their country of origin are recognized in accordance with European Directives 89/48/EEC and 98/5/EC. These Directives were transposed by Legislative Decrees Nos. 115/92 and 96/2001.

2. A good discussion of Italian legal education is contained in Lena and Mattei, *Introduction to Italian Law* (2002). See also Certoma, *The Italian Legal System* (1985).

3. See Attanasio and Capursi (eds.), *Statistical Methods for the Evaluation of University Systems (Contributions to Statistics)* (2011).

history, and so on) that a student must take to reach the final stage of graduation.[4] Within these limits schools are permitted to arrange the credits as they see fit, requiring, for example, more for international law, constitutional law, or other subjects, and to shape the courses within these areas.

Considerable autonomy is conferred upon the universities in other academic matters, and they have some degree of financial independence, although they are subsidized by the State. However, the Ministry retains the power to intervene and reframe the structure and the governance of these units, since they remain subject to State bylaws.

As a result of recent reforms, schools are organized in departments, and the old faculties have officially disappeared, but the departmental directors are elected by academic colleagues. The president of the university and the the board of directors are similarly elected, although seats on the board are reserved for public or private representatives who do not belong to the university community.

The quality of an Italian law school is generally gauged by the caliber of its faculty. Of all the careers in law, the academic is the most sought after and the most difficult to attain. The title "professor" is a coveted and prestigious one. Among the most famous and successful practicing lawyers, professors have historically predominated.

A law graduate who aspires to an academic career begins as an assistant to a sponsoring professor. (Officially the term *assistant* does not exist any longer, but it is still used in informal speech.) The academic career is structured as a doctorate program, which includes three years of study and a final dissertation; a degree of research-fellow (ricercatore), which may be for a term of years or tenured; a degree of associate professor, which is tenured; and finally the position of full professor (*professore ordinario*), from which one may not be removed (except for cause) until a mandatory retirement age. It is also possible to receive teaching contracts for specified times and periods.

A young faculty member does the research and, sometimes, performs the teaching duties assigned to her by her department. Her progress depends on how well she does in a series of national competitions (concorsi), in which the quality and quantity of publications is the primary measure. In recent years legislation has repeatedly shuffled and reshuffled the details of these competitions. At the moment, in order to become a professor, one must receive an *Abilitazione nazionale*, which

4. See Rossi, *Legislazione universitaria* (2011).

is conferred by a panel drawn from professors in the same subject matter. (An Italian law professor is not appointed merely as a professor of law but as professor of criminal law, administrative law, civil procedure, or some other specialty.) Once this Abilitazione is obtained, the scholar may participate in local competions in the various universities to be appointed at the appropriate level and receive tenure. The period required to obtain a professorship is frequently dependent on timing and other fortuitous circumstances.

To enter law school, an applicant must have completed thirteen years of primary and secondary education.[5] The last five of these years must have been in a liceo or equivalent institution. No preliminary university studies are required for admission to law school. However, the intensive liceo course is considered to be about equivalent to an American junior college education.[6]

Primary and secondary education in Italy is in many respects similar to that in the United States: attendance is recorded, homework is assigned, Socratic methods of discussion are employed, and promotion is dependent on successful results in periodic examinations. Law school education was historically radically different. Instruction was by lecture, and attendance by a small fraction of the class was the rule. Now the Socratic Method has become more widespread, and attendance has often become compulsory.

Examinations are normally based on assigned textbooks (*manuali*). Often, printed or photocopied lecture notes are published by the professors. The texts and lectures are concerned largely with the explanation and classification of definitions and concepts, although the case method has become more widespread in recent years.[7] As a general rule, legal education is concerned not with the techniques of problem solving but with the inculcation of fundamental concepts and

5. Article 34, para. 2 of the Constitution provides that eight years of tuition-free education are compulsory. This article was implemented by the Law of December 31, 1962, no. 1859, which also provided penalties for nonattendance.

6. Because the curriculum of Italian secondary schools differs considerably from that of American schools, and because the caliber of different licei and high schools varies within the two countries, it is difficult to evaluate the relative weights of liceo and high school diplomas. Italian universities have historically required two years of American college work as a prerequisite to admission.

7. The fallacy of confusing a system of case law with the case method of instruction is still very well exposed in Eisenmann, *The University Teaching of Social Science: Law* 116 (1954).

principles. The analysis of factual situations is not as important as the analysis of the components of the law. This is consistent with an underlying philosophy where law school is not considered merely a professional training ground but a cultural institution where law is taught as a science.

Some of the flavor of an Italian law textbook may be observed by comparing a typical *manuale* with a casebook in a comparable American course. For example, a leading tax manual begins with a chapter on the so-called institutes or principles of tax law (the idea of a tax, differences between taxes and fees, and so forth); proceeds to the sources, interpretation, and constitutional principles underlying the field; and continues with a total of twenty-five units on theoretical subjects (taxpaying units, administrative procedures, etc.), all essentially textual in nature, with few if any references to cases or other decisions. Only in chapters 17 through 25 are practical issues like income, deductions, and so on addressed, and even then primarily with references to idealized fact patterns (*fattispecie*) rather than real-world cases.[8] A manual of civil (private) law is similarly organized around broad categories like sources of law, legal actors, and concepts such as *atti giuridici* (legal acts) and *negozio giuridico* (legal transaction), with little if any reference to real-world problems.[9] These materials tend to proceed from general to specific themes and to emphasize abstract legal principles over the resolution of actual cases: more or less the opposite of the approach in a similar American course. (One of the most popular American tax casebooks begins with a case about a man who received free meals and lodging at a hotel in Hawaii, while a classic contracts book begins with a man whose hand became hairy after a flawed skin transplant.) While many of these features are common to all civil law systems, some of them are especially true in an Italian context: together they have profound implications for Italian education and for the "mental machinery" that Italian lawyers bring to their studies and their work.

Examinations also differ from the American model, usually oral in nature and frequently conducted in the classroom in the presence of other students. The lack of interest in problem solving as a pedagogical tool is carried over into the examinations. In a criminal law examination, for example, a student may be asked to discuss the concept of causation. As he proceeds with the discussion, he will be

---

8. See Tesauro, *Compendio di diritto tributario* (4th ed. 2010).

9. See Edizioni Giuridiche Simone, *Istituzioni di diritto privato* (Diritto civile) (16th ed. 2010).

asked more specific questions such as "Which authors espouse the sine qua non theory of causation, and what theory does the penal code adopt?" The examination consists of a discussion of perhaps three such topics. The student is not expected to know detailed rules of law: these may be looked up in the codes or learned in a law office.

Although legal education is designed to be completed in five years, the student is not required to take examinations at the end of any school year. In fact, she does not have to take any examination until she considers herself prepared. Failed examinations may be retaken. No student is dismissed for failure. The student may remain enrolled for up to ten years without taking exams as long as the required tuition is paid.

The final hurdle to the law degree (*laurea*) is the thesis examination. The candidate must write a thesis under the close supervision of a professor or professorial assistant. Upon successful completion of an oral examination, which is conducted by a panel of professors, on his thesis, the student is awarded the degree of *Dottore in giurisprudenza*. Italian universities also grant master's degrees and the equivalent of a Ph.D. degree, that of *dottore di ricerca*.

Many of the merits and demerits of the Italian system of legal education are readily apparent. On the positive side, the student must exercise considerable self-reliance since there is little student-teacher contact. From oral examinations he or she acquires considerable verbal fluency in discussing difficult concepts and principles. On the negative side, the learning process is passive, with much memorization and with little room for individual thinking. With the exception of the thesis requirement, there is normally no significant training given in legal research. Certainly, the student is not specially trained to handle a concrete case. Above all (and whether this be positive or negative is debatable), legal education gives the student a strong orientation toward doctrine as opposed to precedent and toward the orthodox dogmatic approach of the academic establishment.

3.03 *The Law Graduate.*   More than half of the graduates end their legal careers upon graduation. They have acquired the title of *dottore* and will be addressed by that title in social intercourse, much as American M.D.'s are addressed as "Doctor." The degree grants access to jobs that are steppingstones to executive positions in industry and to the higher reaches of the civil service. In short, it serves much the same purpose as the bachelor of arts degree in the United States.

The minority of graduates who do intend to pursue careers as jurists usually make a choice soon after graduation whether to set out for the bar, the notariat, the bench, or a position as state's attorney. A number of obstacles inhibit a subsequent change from one to another of these careers. Most of these graduates decide to seek entrance to the practicing bar.

3.04 *The Bar.*   Attorneys who represent clients in the courts are called *avvocati.*[10] The *avvocato* is considered the modern successor to the Roman *jurisconsultus*, the legal artist-scientist who prepares and prosecutes the party's substantive claims and defenses.

After an apprenticeship of eighteen months in a law office (usually without pay), a law school graduate is qualified to take a state examination for admission to practice as an *avvocato*. As such, he or she may practice, except in the highest courts, anywhere in the country. Eight years of practice as an *avvocato* is the sole prerequisite for admission to practice before the highest courts.

Membership of *avvocati* in the Attorneys' Guild (*ordine forense*) is compulsory. The guild is a semiautonomous quasi-governmental agency that is responsible for maintaining the rolls of attorneys and for disciplining violators of professional ethics. Its local and national officers are elected by its members.

The legal status of attorneys is similar in many respects to that in the United States, with several important differences. Attorneys may not accept full- or part-time employment, either in a professional or nonprofessional capacity, and may not engage in business. Violation of these rules results in removal from the rolls.

Some of the rules regarding legal practice have begun to change under the pressures engendered by the growth of modern industrial and commercial enterprises. For example, partnerships between *avvocati*, which were previously forbidden, are now permitted. Although a corporation may not *employ* house counsel, it may *retain* attorneys for a yearly retainer fee and provide space in the corporation's offices.

Notwithstanding numerous changes, the Italian economy is still dominated in many areas by owner-managed small enterprises. In these areas, attorneys do conform to the legislative ideal of individual practice. The independent practitioner is idealized because attorneys are deemed to be independent participants in the administration of law. "The lawyer is the lord, not the serf. Professional freedom

---

10. The legal profession is now governed by the Law of December 31, 2012, n. 247, published in *Gazzetta ufficiale* on Jan. 18, 2013, n. 15.

of the lawyer in relation to his client means this: that he is free to accept or refuse, in accordance with the dictates of his conscience, the clients who solicit his services and the cases offered him; and that when he has accepted a case, he is the only one who determines how it is to be conducted."[11] In the light of this thinking, it is apparent that the attorney's status is designed to prevent his subordination to clients, partners, or employers.

The attorney-client relationship is governed, along with similar relationships in such professions as journalism, medicine, and engineering, by articles 2229–38 of the Civil Code, which are entitled "The Intellectual Professions." The attorney is given broad discretion in carrying out his client's mandate. Imposed upon him is the concomitant duty to safeguard and to attend, with a minimum of delegation, to his client's interests. The client may discharge his attorney without cause, paying for services rendered on a *quantum meruit* basis. The attorney, however, may withdraw only for good cause and on the condition that his client's interests are not prejudiced by his withdrawal; he retains his right to payment for services rendered. The lawyer is enjoined from divulging any information that came to him by virtue of his professional activity—a rule of professional secrecy that goes far beyond its American counterpart.[12]

In theory the attorney incurs no liability to a client by mere negligence. Liability attaches only to the immediate and demonstrable consequences of professional errors caused by gross negligence or gross ignorance. In practice courts interpret certain errors on a *res ipsa loquitur* basis so that the error is in itself evidence of a fault, such as allowing the time to appeal a decision to lapse.[13]

Contingent fee agreements are forbidden, but legal fees are now free to be contracted under European Competition Law. The current system deviates from a long tradition of State-fixed minimum fees when it was deemed a violation of professional ethics to charge less.

11. *Gli avvocati dello Stato e l'inamovibilità*, in 5 Calamandrei, *Studi sul processo civile* 277, 280 (1947), republished in 2 Calamandrei, *Opere giuridiche* 412, 415 (1966). This volume contains the writings of Calamandrei on law professionals and legal education.

12. Violation may result in a disciplinary proceeding as well as up to one year of imprisonment. Codice penale art. 622. Secrecy is further protected by a privilege not to give evidence upon the matters protected. Codice di procedura penale art. 351; Codice di procedura civile arts. 118, 249.

13. See Favale, *La responsabilità civile del professionista forense* (2011) and ref.

Upon decision of a case, the judgment must order that the unsuccessful litigant reimburse the victor for his counsel fees. By American standards, legal fees are quite high for extrajudicial matters but quite low for litigation. This seeming paradox is perhaps explained by two factors. First, Italian courtroom procedure does not suffer from rigidity of form, and except to a limited extent in criminal cases, the expertise required of an American trial specialist has no counterpart in Italy. Second, the drafting of typical contracts and other legal instruments does not ordinarily require the services of an attorney. These are prepared by notaries. Consequently, only complex legal instruments involving affluent clients are ordinarily prepared with the aid of attorneys.

The system of legal aid—although criticized as less than adequate by many Italians—is in many respects superior to that in the United States. As early as 1786, the Criminal Laws of Tuscany provided, "In all criminal trials, in places where there is no lawyer appointed as the defender of accused persons who are poor, an advocate shall be named ex officio for the poor and unfortunate who are accused, and who have no advocate of their own."[14] This in essence continues to be the law. In all except specified minor cases, a party to a civil case, or a defendant in a criminal case, must be represented by an attorney.[15] The Constitution guarantees free legal aid to indigent parties in civil, criminal, and special courts.[16] No public defender system is in effect. Rather, the burden of defending the poor is placed, at least theoretically, upon the whole profession. An applicant for legal aid petitions a committee of judges and lawyers attached to each court. The committee then assigns an attorney to serve the applicant. Unfortunately, in practice, the whole profession does not share the burden. The volunteers assigned are usually the more inexperienced and unsuccessful practitioners in the profession, although this is one way young attorneys can display their abilities and gain important experience.

---

14. See article 50 of the *Edict of the Grand Duke of Tuscany for the Reform of Criminal Law in His Dominions: Translated from the Italian: Together with the Original* (Warrington, Byrnes 1789). The Edict was issued under the influence of Cesare Beccaria's famous book *Of Crimes and Punishments* (available in various English translations), the impact of which revolutionized European criminal law, especially in the abolition of legalized torture and capital punishment.

15. Codice di procedura civile art. 82; Codice di procedura penale art. 97.

16. Constitution art. 24, para. 3. The basic law governing legal aid is Testo unico in materia di spese di giustizia D.P.R., testo coordinato 30.05.2002 n° 115. See AA.VV., L'avvocatura dello stato, Istituto Poligrafico dello Stato, Roma, 1999.

Sometimes a case so outrages public opinion that attorneys, fearing financial repercussions or social ostracism, are reluctant to accept it. When substantial numbers of attorneys refuse to involve themselves with unpopular causes, the rule of law is vitiated. In Italy such occurrences are rare. If such a situation arises, however, the tradition is that the president of the local council of the Attorneys' Guild gratuitously undertakes to represent the unpopular cause.

The modus operandi of attorneys in the administration of law is best examined in connection with a discussion of Italian procedure. It suffices to say here that the lawyers who stand out are the lawyers who have the best grasp of legal dogmatics and the greatest facility in writing briefs in the doctrinal style. This in part explains the historic preeminence of law professors among the practicing bar.

As a rule, people have always had ambivalent feelings about lawyers. The Italians are no exception. On the one hand, lawyers are regarded as pillars of society and are generally elected to public office in preference to others. On the other hand, they are seen as hair-splitting quibblers and suspected of practicing brinkmanship on the edge of law and ethics. This ambivalent reputation seems universally to have afflicted the profession from ancient Greece to the modern world.

3.05 *State's Attorneys.*   One agency (Avvocatura dello Stato) represents and provides legal advice to the state and most state organs.[17] It has no role in criminal prosecutions, and it does not intervene to represent the public interest in proceedings to which neither the state nor a state agency is a party. The centralization of government lawyers into one organ is the product of a long historical process during which various specialized bureaus, such as the attorneys' office of the state railways, were consolidated into a semiautonomous agency, responsible only to the prime minister. Agency personnel act as attorneys only; they have no power to compromise claims or otherwise dispose of the substantive rights in issue. This power belongs to the governmental organ that holds the substantive rights.

A district office of the agency is established in each of the twenty-three court of appeals districts. The office in Rome is headed by the Avvocato Generale dello Stato, who also exercises supervisory functions over the entire agency and determines its overall policy. The staff of the Avvocatura dello Stato is selected by competitive civil service examinations, which are partly oral and partly written.

---

17. The basic laws governing the agency are the Royal Decree (testo unico) of Oct. 30, 1933, no. 1611, as modified by the Law of April 3, 1979, n. 103.

The examinations are open to apprentice judges (*uditori giudiziari*) and law school graduates who are eligible for examination for admission as *procuratori*. Upon successful completion of the examination, the applicant is appointed *procuratore dello Stato*, a position in the lower echelon of professional service in a state's attorney's office. Three years of service as *procuratore dello Stato* is the usual prerequisite to examination for the position of *avvocato dello Stato*. Ordinary judges and military judges who have three years of service are also eligible for the examination. Promotions within the Avvocatura dello Stato to the position of office chief and other responsible posts are made, upon the recommendation of a committee consisting of high officers within the agency, by the prime minister.

A career in the Avvocatura dello Stato carries tenurial rights. These are not as firm, however, as those held by judges. The agency's top officials, if they have been found failing in diligence or lacking in ability, may be retired by the Cabinet. Personnel on the next lower level, if passed over for an increase in salary three consecutive times, are dismissed.

The agency has developed a considerable amount of autonomy. Although the prime minister and the Cabinet have the authority to control its functioning through their powers to dismiss and appoint key personnel, these powers are not generally exercised for this purpose, and it is common to find statements that state's attorneys are accorded independence similar to that granted judges. In general, agency personnel are not affected by changes in political fortunes. These career civil servants, insulated from the spoils system, help preserve the principle that governments should be founded in law and not in men. The agency has somewhat divergent goals: at the same time, it must represent the interests of the state and protect the rights of individuals against arbitrary state action. That the system effectively achieves both goals seems borne out by the respect with which practicing lawyers regard it.

3.06 *Notaries.*　　The functions of the American notary public are little more than vestiges of those of his Italian counterpart. The Italian *notaio* drafts and authenticates important legal instruments, including wills, corporate charters, conveyances, and contracts.[18] Any instrument that on its face purports to have been drafted by and executed under the supervision of a notary is known as a "public

---

18. See generally Casu and Laurini, *Codice del notaio* (2006); Gibboni and Russo, *Codice del notariato* (2012).

act" and is conclusive evidence that it was in fact so drafted and executed; that the recitals and agreements expressed in the instrument are accurate reports of the parties' statements and agreements; and that any fact that the instrument recites to have occurred in the presence of the notary did occur and any act the instrument recites to have been performed by the notary was in fact performed.[19] The conclusive nature of a public act can be upset only in a *querela di falso*, a special proceeding with criminal overtones.[20] The faith and credit granted a notarial instrument has been termed a potent force for civilization and order.[21] Although it is only rarely that an instrument has to be prepared by a notary,[22] notarial services are obtained in many transactions because of the evidentiary value of a notarial instrument and because notaries are trained and experienced draftsmen.[23]

The notary profession is constantly under scrutiny because of aggressive interpretations of European Antitrust Law which have attempted to open up the market for these services but also threaten to reduce the profession's status, rendering the *notaio* a simple private counsellor of the parties. So far, only minor reforms have been introduced, such as the ability to register transfer of vehicles without the assistance of a *notaio*, thereby lowering the fees required for such transactions. A more significant proposed reform would permit the management of the office of a *notaio* incorporate or company form: in this way real estate developers, for instance, could invest in such small "firms," making the *notaio* a kind of employee and undermining his professional independence. Up to now the Consiglio Nazionale del Notariato has been successful in repelling this kind of reform.

Notaries are also authorized to draft and present in court certain petitions in noncontentious matters. Frequently they are appointed by court order to take inventories, draw up partition plans, take custody of sequestrated property, and perform other duties in connection with litigation.

19. Codice civile art. 2700.

20. Codice di procedura civile arts. 221–27.

21. See Bartolini, *Manuale del notaio* (6th ed. 1957), n. 57, at 5.

22. See Codice civile art. 782 (donations); arts. 14, 2328, 2464, 2475 (corporate and partnership charters); arts. 162–63 (marital agreements); arts. 2504 (corporate mergers), 2538 (corporate meetings); and Codice della navigazione art. 328 (contract of enlistment in the maritime service).

23. In addition, a public act calling for the payment of a sum certainly may be brought directly to a marshal (*ufficiale giudiziario*) for execution, without the necessity of a court action on the merits. See Cappelletti and Perillo, *op. cit.* n. 1, at 12.02 b.

Successful completion of a difficult national examination is a requirement for admission to the notariat. Before taking the examination, the candidate must have completed law school and have served a two-year apprenticeship in the office of a notary. When a vacancy occurs in one of the approximately 4,700 notarial positions, preference is given to notaries already in service. In the ensuing national competition for the position, such factors as seniority, publications, and public service are evaluated. Vacancies that are not applied for by any incumbent notary are filled by the successful examination candidates.

Before assuming her position, the notary must post security. This fund guarantees redress to the public in the event of malpractice and also serves to ensure payment of certain taxes and fees owed to public bodies. Soon after appointment, the notary is obliged to open an office in the district to which she is appointed and to be present during office hours fixed by the president of the court of appeal. Unlike a lawyer, she must serve any person who requests her services; the notary also may not advertise services or compete for clients. To prevent competition, she is forbidden to perform any official function outside the district to which she is appointed.

The keeping, filing, and indexing of notarial records are minutely governed by law. Ordinarily, a notary must retain the original of any instrument he prepares or that is filed with him. Upon demand he is required to prepare and deliver a copy of any instrument—except a will—that is in his official custody. A notarial copy usually has the same evidentiary value as an original.[24]

Although a notary is a public official, he receives no salary but is remunerated by his clients. The fees charged are rigidly fixed by law and fixed high. The transfer of a parcel of land for $25,000 involves a notarial fee of about $300. In nonstandardized transactions, parties frequently retain lawyers as well as a notary, thereby increasing the financial burden of legal services.

Notaries elect, from among their number, a national council of fifteen members whose principal function is to study and recommend proposals for the improvement of laws that affect the notariat and notarial duties. The council also exercises limited disciplinary powers. It may warn privately or censure publicly any notary whose professional or private conduct adversely affects the dignity or prestige of the profession. Charging fees less than what the law requires is also grounds for censure. More serious penalties are within the competence of the civil tribunals, which, in a proceeding instituted by the National Council of the Notariat or the

24. Codice civile art. 2714; Codice di procedura civile art. 212.

public prosecutor, may impose a fine on or suspend or remove an offender from office. The notariat is subject to the national supervision of the Ministry of Justice and to the local supervision of the public prosecutor. Supervision is exercised by periodic and special inspections of the records of each notary.

The profession offers its members generous financial rewards and performs a highly useful function. The implicit trust that is granted notaries is rarely abused. Lawyers consider the profession a dull, plodding one, but many envy it for its secure earning power and the universal respect it is accorded.

3.07 *Judges and Prosecutors.*   The Italian judiciary (*magistratura*) is organized along lines radically dissimilar to those followed in common law systems. The principle of separation of powers is pushed toward its logical conclusion: the judiciary is not only a separate but also an autonomous branch of government. Judges are appointed, promoted, and supervised by judges. Moreover, the judicial function is deemed to be fundamentally distinct from advocacy; consequently, a judgeship is not the culmination of an advocate's career but a post to be earned by apprenticeship within the judiciary. And in Italy it is the impartial judge, not the fiery advocate, who is chosen to carry out the prosecutorial function.[25]

The governing body of the judiciary is the Superior Council of Magistrature (Consiglio Superiore della Magistratura), which bears this name because a judge (*giudice*) and a public prosecutor (*pubblico ministero*) are both considered magistrates.[26] Fourteen of the twenty-four members of the Council are elected by

25. In addition to his function in criminal proceedings, the public prosecutor (pubblico ministero) may or must initiate or appear in many civil cases deemed by law to affect public interest. These include such proceedings as declarations of mental infirmity, annulment of marriages, and recognition of foreign judgments. He may intervene in any case affecting the public interest. He is empowered to introduce evidence, make motions, and file briefs. In a limited class of cases, he may appeal, irrespective of the wishes of the other parties to the litigation. He is a necessary party to all proceedings before the Corte di cassazione, where his function is to advise the Court of what he deems to be the correct decision. He participates in the Court's deliberations in chambers but has no vote in the decision.

26. Before 1958, a council with this name existed, but its functions were primarily consultative. The fundamental powers of the Council derive from articles 104–10 of the Constitution. The basic law governing the Council is the Law of March 24, 1958, no. 195. The matter is now covered by Law 44, 2002. See Bartole, *Il potere giudiziario* (2012); Di Federico (ed.), *Ordinamento giudiziario: uffici giudiziari, CSM e governo della magistratura* (2012); Pomodoro, *Manuale di ordinamento giudiziario* (2012).

magistrates from their own ranks. The electoral provisions assure that six will be magistrates of the Corte di cassazione, four of the courts of appeal, and four of the tribunals. Weighting of the Council in favor of higher-court judges has been attacked—especially by lower-court judges—as a violation of the spirit and perhaps the letter of the Constitution, which provides that "judges are to be distinguished among themselves only by reason of diversity of function."[27] The intent of this provision, it is argued, is to prevent any hierarchical control of lower-court judges and to ensure the judiciary self-government along democratic (one man, one vote) lines. However, the Constitutional Court has upheld the validity of the electoral provisions of the law instituting the Council.[28]

The Constitution also assigns membership on the Council to the President of the Republic,[29] who acts as its chairman, and to two magistrates from the Corte di cassazione—the first president and the public prosecutor.[30] By convention, the actual chairmanship for "business as usual" is assumed by the Vice-President of the Council, who is elected by the members. In addition, Parliament appoints seven members to the Council. Eligible for appointment are *avvocati* who have practiced for fifteen years and law professors.[31] The Council is empowered to admit applicants to the judiciary and to promote and discipline those who are already members.

Candidates for the judiciary must be law school graduates, Italian citizens between the ages of 21 and 30 years, and persons of unquestionable moral reputation.[32] As with civil service posts, entrance is attained by competitive examinations. Since 1963, women as well as men have been eligible. Qualified applicants are examined by a commission consisting of judges and law professors appointed by the Superior Council of Magistrature. The examinations, usually held yearly, are difficult.

27. Constitution art. 107, para. 3.

28. Corte costituzionale, Dec. 23, 1963, no. 168, 89 Foro italiano (part 1) 3 (1964).

29. Constitution art. 104, para. 2. The chairmanship of the President of the Republic is a check on the autonomy of the judiciary.

30. Constitution art. 104, para. 3.

31. Constitution art. 104, para. 4.

32. The basic law, known as the Ordinamento giudiziario, governing the appointment and apprenticeship of judges and the organization of courts is the Royal Decree of Jan. 30, 1941, no. 12, as amended. The matter is now covered by the Law of July 25, 2005, n. 150, published in the *Gazzetta ufficiale* on July 29, 2005.

A successful applicant is appointed to the post of "magistrato ordinario in tiro-cinio" (MOT) and is assigned to a court of first instance or to a prosecutor's office to begin an apprenticeship that theoretically lasts at least two years. Vacancies in the courts are not, however, filled swiftly, and a shortage of judges is the result. To fill this shortage, auditors are usually assigned to sit on the bench as judges after one year of apprenticeship, even though they have not attained judicial status.

Eighteen months after his appointment as judicial auditor, the candidate may apply for the examination for the status of judicial adjunct. The examination takes a fairly practical form. The candidate must write three judicial opinions on problems presented and answer orally questions on the practical application of rules of law. Successful completion of the examination entitles him to be appointed to perform the functions of tribunal magistrate. (In fact, however, he may have been performing these functions prior to the examination.) After three years of service in this position, the District Council of Judges determines whether he has demonstrated the necessary aptitude to acquire the title of tribunal magistrate. If the judgment is adverse, the candidate is removed from service. If the title of tribunal magistrate is conferred, the candidate acquires tenurial rights and cannot be transferred without his consent or removed from office except for legal cause duly proved. The title of tribunal magistrate is somewhat misleading. A person bearing that title may be appointed to serve as a judge or as a public prosecutor attached to a tribunal.

Wages and promotion—for many years a hotly contested issue—are controlled by the Law of April 30, 2007, n. 111. Wages are calculated on the basis of seniority, but promotion to the higher courts also takes into account the aspirant's ability. In this way the Judge of a Tribunal may earn as much as a Justice of the Cassazione without being actually a member of it.[33]

There are three roads to promotion from court of appeal to Corte di cassazione. The first of these—based almost entirely on a competitive examination—provides an avenue to promotion for the brightest and most ambitious judges. Only 10 percent of vacancies in the higher courts may be filled in this manner.

---

33. According to article 106 of the Constitution, professors of law and outstanding avvocati who have practiced for fifteen years may be appointed to the Corte di cassazione. In recent years law professors have started applying and being appointed to such positions, an additional fact demonstrating the shift of power from universities toward courts in managing the development of law.

The other two avenues of promotion are based on a complex evaluation of ability and seniority: they diverge only in the degree of emphasis placed on seniority or ability, and they will not be distinguished here. In both cases the candidate's ability is calculated by complex formulas and then assayed by a commission of judges appointed by the Superior Council of Magistrature. The local judicial council, on the basis of a report made by the chief judge of the candidate's court, reports to the commission on his "culture, diligence, and reputation." The candidate submits a specified number of his written judicial decisions. In the early years of the Republic, the candidate was permitted wide latitude in selecting these decisions, with the result that she often selected decisions that were not necessarily representative of her day-to-day work but were written with an eye toward the promotion competition. Starting in 1963, a candidate is required to submit decisions that she has written during specific trimesters arbitrarily selected by the Superior Council. A candidate may also submit publications or any other relevant material. All of the material submitted is considered in relation to her years in service.[34]

As of this writing there are 8,369 judges in office, 4,461 men and 3,908 women, of whom 360 are Justices of the Corte di cassazione. As has been indicated, the titles of these positions tend to be misleading. For example, the position of president of a tribunal section is occupied by a court of appeal magistrate. Prosecutors are also included in these categories, and a number of magistrates are assigned to administrative posts in various ministries but nevertheless bear the titles of magistrates of specified courts.

The excessive caseload led to the introduction in Italy of the "Giudice di pace" (Justice of the Peace) position by the Law of November 21, 1991, n. 374, and there are now 2,206 such officials. These judges are honorary judges selected among *avvocati*, not younger than thirty years and not older than seventy, by the president of the Court of Appeal, with the advice of the Consiglio Superiore della Magistratura, and are appointed by the Minister of Justice. According to article 7 of the Code of Civil Procedure, they have jurisdiction over petty offenses and minor cases, including nuisance cases, car accidents with less than €20,000 in damages, and controversies over the possession of goods less than €5,000 in value. Under articles 113 and 114, they are permitted to award up to the sum of €1,200 as an "equitable" judgment, not based on the "strict" law, and they may likewise

---

34. The competitions described in the text apply only to judges. Magistrates who have been assigned to prosecutorial or other nonjudicial duties are evaluated by other standards.

award larger sums on an "equitable basis" if so requested by both parties to the proceeding.

Not only is the judiciary largely independent of the other branches of government, but the magistrates themselves possess a large measure of independence. The Constitution provides that "judges are subject only to the law." This is an elliptical way of stating that judges need not heed unlawful orders from judicial superiors or other governmental authorities. Magistrates may not be removed from office—until the mandatory retirement age of seventy—except for causes established in a proceeding conducted by the Superior Council of Magistrature. A judge against whom charges are brought must be apprised of the charges made, given an opportunity to be heard, and permitted to read the transcript of the evidence against him.

Disciplinary sanctions include warnings, censure, loss of seniority, removal from office without loss of pension rights, and dismissal from office with loss of pension rights. These measures may be applied on grounds as varied as physical incapacity to perform judicial duties and conviction of a crime. Indeed, any magistrate whose public or private conduct reflects adversely on the judiciary may be penalized. Disciplinary proceedings are infrequent, and corruption is believed to be almost nonexistent.[35] Judges are subject not only to criminal prosecution and disciplinary sanctions for unjudicial behavior but also to civil liability for willful acts of fraud or corruption.[36]

Judicial independence is further protected by the rule that no magistrate may be transferred without his consent. The rule is intended to prevent the influencing of judicial conduct by threats of exile to a desolate community. This rule is, however, subject to some interesting exceptions. A magistrate of a court other than the Corte di cassazione must be transferred if a relative or a relative of his or her spouse (the degree of consanguinity is specified) practices law in the same community. Moreover, if two magistrates of the same court are related, one may be transferred.

The status of public prosecutors as members of the judiciary is the result of a long historical development. Previously they had been a *sui generis* category of civil

35. An application may be made to revoke a civil judgment tainted with judicial fraud. Codice di procedura civile art. 395 (6); see 4.16. It is indicative that applications of this kind have been extremely rare.

36. Law 177, 1988. Judges are held liable only for gross negligence, as the application of an unexisting law, and no action can be brought against them without the prior authorization of the Consiglio Superiore della Magistratura.

servants, loosely dependent on the Ministry of Justice. Since the enactment of the 1948 Constitution and implementing legislation, the position of public prosecutors in the judiciary has been more firmly established. The rationale behind the granting of judicial status to prosecutors is that they, like judges, must be impartial and free from political and governmental pressures. Judges and prosecutors may exchange roles, but this occurs infrequently. A judicial candidate serves his apprenticeship in either a prosecutor's or a judge's office and generally continues in the role in which he or she began.

Italian courts, especially the criminal courts, suffer from congestion. The pressure to create new judgeships is constant, but many judges oppose this increase on the grounds that a rapid influx of many new judges would dilute the quality and reputation of the judiciary. They argue that the courts need more clerical help, not more judges. For lack of such help, many, if not most, judges, even on the appellate level, must perform their own clerical tasks. Judicial law clerks are essentially nonexistent.

The number of judges assigned to particular courts is determined by Presidential Decree based upon proposals made by the Minister of Justice after consultation with the Superior Council of Magistrature. This power has not been used with great flexibility. Statistics of the number, kind, and disposition of proceedings are meticulously kept and published but are not used to develop flexible responses to problems identified in the published data. Delays in civil matters tend to be quite long. More than two years are typically needed for a decision of first instance and two more years for an appellate decision. One may expect to receive a final decision by the Court of Cassazione in approximately six or seven years from the start of the original proceeding.

Delays in civil cases are not, for the most part, attributable to calendar congestion but to the opportunities presented to litigants by the Code of Civil Procedure to stall and hamper the rapid disposition of cases. Civil cases are deemed to be a private matter of the parties, and judges have very limited power to speed up the matter. In contrast with American practices, one must also remember than in Italy the phase of pretrial discovery is considered an integral part of the trial. Since this phase normally takes a year or more in the United States, in order to make the comparison meaningful, one should arguably subtract this figure. One must further consider that routine business matters are ruled by special provisions of the Code of Civil Procedure, so one may receive an injunction for payment on a business account or bill in as little as two weeks. (Italian civil procedure and evidence are discussed further in Chapter 4.)

Although Italian judges are respected, they, unlike their common law counterparts, are not regarded as occupying the pinnacle of the legal profession. Rather, they are considered important bureaucrats. And in parts of northern Italy where the standard of living is high, their earnings are good but not exceptional. A tribunal judge earns about €3,500 per month after taxes, an appellate judge about €4,500, and a justice of the Court of Cassazione about €6,000 — respectable but not extraordinary amounts.

In comparison with the past, the current perception of the Italian judicial system is quite poor. It is regarded as accurate but habitually slow and inefficient in nature. The increasing involvement of criminal prosecutors, especially, in the political arena, contributes further to this negative perception.

3.08 *Conclusion.*   A major characteristic of the legal professions in Italy is the almost complete lack of lateral movement among personnel. Career decisions must be made early; for example, applicants for the judiciary must be no more than thirty years of age. Promotion of judges, prosecutors, and state's attorneys is largely dependent on seniority, which tends to discourage most individuals from leaving one legal career to start another at the bottom of the ladder. Similarly, a notarial or academic position must be preceded by an apprenticeship. Some movement from these public and quasi-public offices to the private practice of law occurs; movement in the opposite direction is highly unusual.

Lack of lateral mobility creates a degree of insularity. Almost invariably, an Italian judge will attribute any malfunctioning of the courts to the dilatory tactics of lawyers. Lawyers tend to resent "bureaucratic" interference by judges in the conduct of their cases. Lawyers and judges fail to think of themselves as members of a common profession, and except for occasional conferences, they do not join together in professional associations to discuss and solve mutual problems of judicial administration.

Emphasis on seniority tends to discourage the more able law school graduates from entering the judiciary and the state's attorneys' offices. These careers, it is frequently said, offer a life without fear and without hope: from the acquisition of tenure until retirement, the career follows a predetermined course. This is not entirely true; ability is recognized in the award of promotions. However, the difficulty of measuring ability and the fear of political interference mean that there is continuing pressure to make seniority the dominant, if not exclusive, criterion.

Compartmentalization of the legal professions has its drawbacks, but it also has numerous and important advantages. Specialization and emphasis on apprenticeship and seniority usually result in depth of experience and competence, even if in a limited area. The continuing insulation of judges, prosecutors, and state's attorneys from politics inhibits some of the more unsavory aspects of judicial administration that can result from the spoils system. The elevation of notaries to impartial, almost judicial, draftsmen of legal instruments results in community reliance on a great number of legal instruments and certainty in legal relations, and it inhibits overreaching in many transactions.

Although the Italian bench and bar are organized pursuant to conceptions that are sometimes foreign to those developed in common law systems, both systems have similar goals. The objective of an independent bench and an independent bar in both systems is an outstanding example. The desire to make legal services available to all on a nondiscriminatory basis is another. However, the methods used to achieve these and other goals tend to diverge and to produce characteristics unique to their legal orders. The Italian system of legal education, the tradition of Italian legal scholarship, and the nature and organization of the various Italian legal professions all contribute to the "style" of Italian law. This style, which is different in many ways from the one familiar to common law lawyers, is discussed in Chapters 5 through 7.

Civil Procedure and Evidence

4.01 *Introduction.* This chapter describes the basic characteristics of Italian adjective law, with emphasis on those aspects that are most interesting to a common lawyer.[1] Prevalent conceptions and misconceptions concerning European procedure in general, and Italian procedure in particular, are stressed, and a comparative viewpoint is employed.[2]

4.02 *Relationship between Procedure and Evidence.* Usually, European doctrine considers evidence to be a branch of procedure. Textbooks on procedure typically devote only one chapter—albeit an important chapter—to evidence. In Italy some of the greatest Italian legal scholars are known for their works on procedure.

---

1. For a more detailed discussion of the principal topics in this chapter and their historical development, see Cappelletti and Perillo, *Civil Procedure in Italy* (1965). A more recent discussion is Varano, *Civil Procedure Reform in Italy*, 4 Am. J. Comp. L. 657 (1997).

2. On the distinction between foreign and comparative law, see, e.g., Hall, *Comparative Law and Social Theory* 1–21 (1963). On the diverse approaches to comparative law, see Monateri, *Methods of Comparative Law* (2012); Hoecke (ed.), *Epistemology and Methodology of Comparative Law* (2004); Mattei, Ruskola, and Gidi, *Schlesinger's Comparative Law: Cases, Texts, Materials* (7th ed. 2009). For further discussion of the principal issues raised by comparative law as an autonomous discipline, see Smits (ed.), *Elgar Encyclopedia of Comparative Law* (2012); Clark, *Comparative Law and Society* (2012); Engelbrekt and Nergelius, *New Directions in Comparative Law* (2009); Örücü and Nelken, *Comparative Law: A Handbook* (2007); Tay, Doeker-Mach, and Ziegert, *Law and Legal Culture in Comparative Perspective* (2004).

Some of these have also done important work in evidence, without departing, however, from a procedural framework, being aware that the basic characteristics of a procedural system are strictly connected with the characteristics of the law of evidence adopted.

Rules of evidence in civil cases are in the Code of Civil Procedure[3] and the Civil Code,[4] and rules of evidence in criminal cases are mostly in the Code of Criminal Procedure.[5] Italian law books do not deal with a "law of evidence" but with a "law of civil evidence"[6] and a "law of criminal evidence."[7] In this chapter, only the rules of evidence in civil cases are considered.

4.03 *Relationship between Civil and Criminal Procedure.* There are radical differences between Italian civil procedure and Italian criminal procedure. Civil procedure is largely governed by the Code of Civil Procedure, enacted in 1940, effective since 1942, and modified many times from 1950 to Law 134 of 2012. Criminal procedure is governed primarily by the Code of Criminal Procedure, which was essentially redrafted in 1988 and has been further modified up to Law 172 of 2012. Despite the distinct procedures employed, the courts that have civil competence are also competent in criminal cases. Within these courts, however, there are sections that hear only civil or criminal cases. The differing functions of civil and criminal law are thus to some extent reflected in the structure of the court system.

---

3. Mostly in articles 115–16; 191–266.

4. Mostly in articles 2697–2739. In Italy, as well as in France, legal scholars have criticized the inclusion of rules of evidence in the Civil Code, maintaining that a more logical placement would be in the Code of Civil Procedure. See Liebman, *Norme processuali nel codice civile*, in *Problemi del processo civile* 155 (1962); Morel, *Traité élémentaire de procedure civile* 376 (2d ed. 1949); Cuche and Vincent, *Précis de procedure civile* 575 (13th ed. 1963).

5. Mainly in Book III (arts. 187–271.

6. The best-known monograph on evidence in civil cases is Carnelutti, *La prova civile* (2d ed. 1947). See also Denti, *Le prove nel processo civile* (1973); Grasselli, *L'istruzione probatoria nel processo civile* (2d ed. 2000); Taruffo (ed.), *La prova nel processo civile* (2012).

7. On evidence in criminal cases, see Florian, *Delle prove penali* (1924); Cordero, *Tre studi sulle prove penali* (1963); Taormina, *Il regime della prova nel processo penale* (2007); Furgiuele, *La prova per il giudizio nel processo penale* (2007); Fiorio, *La prova nuova nel processo penale* (2008); Gaito, *La prova penale* (2008); Ferrua et al., *La prova nel dibattimento penale* (4th ed. 2010); Conte et al., *Le prove penali* (2011); Tonini and Conti, *Il diritto delle prove penali* (2012). On evidence in administrative proceedings, see Tentolini, *La prova amministrativa* (1950); Gallo, *La prova nel processo amministrativo* (1994).

Not infrequently a judge will spend his whole career engaged almost exclusively in either civil or criminal cases, thereby developing expert knowledge and an outlook different from colleagues on the other side of the court.

Article 185 of the Penal Code requires a criminal, or a person civilly responsible for a criminal's conduct, to make restitution or to pay damages to her victim. Traditionally the civil action was thought of as dependent on the facts established in the criminal trial. This doctrine was revised by the reform of 1988 (d.p.r. N. 447), which added new articles 75, 651, and 652 of the Code of Criminal Procedure. The new principle is laid down in article 75, and it is that of *independence* of the two actions: civil and criminal.[8] In this way the victim may enforce liability in an ordinary civil action, but he may also join as a party plaintiff in the criminal proceeding brought by the *pubblico ministero*.

As a consequence of the above, the judgment of the civil law about the existence of a fault, or intention, may differ from that of the criminal court. The criminal decision is to be followed by the civil judge only when the criminal case has been settled before the civil judgment and only with respect to factual matters. A further consequence is that there may be two different decisions regarding a crime and a tort arising from the same facts. While the civil judge cannot establish the facts differently from the criminal court if this process ended before the civil process, she has the discretion to adopt a paradigm different from the criminal process and to assume the existence of a "civil" fault on the part of the defendant with a resulting duty to pay damages (arts. 651–52 c.p.p.).

The joinder of criminal and civil proceedings becomes more comprehensible when the substantive rule of the Penal Code is considered. It lays down the startling—to Americans—rule that the negligent infliction of personal injuries always constitutes a crime. This rule is enforced (usually by suspended sentences), and as a result, a great number of personal injury claims are adjudicated in nominally criminal proceedings. No real analogue to the joinder of criminal and civil proceedings exists in the United States.[9] Italians have not found the varying stan-

---

8. Maniscalco, *L'azione civile nel processo penale* (2008); Lavarini, *Azione civile nel processo penale e principi costituzionali* (2009).

9. It is well known, however, that prosecutors frequently decline to prosecute and that judges frequently impose more lenient sentences if the criminal makes restitution or pays damages. Practicing lawyers are well aware of the effect of potential penal sanctions in collecting civil claims.

dards of proof in the two kinds of proceedings to be an insuperable obstacle to the achievement of this economy of effort.[10]

4.04 *Relationship between Civil and Administrative Procedure.* Before 1865, in obeisance to a rigid concept of separation of powers, judicial review of administrative acts was forbidden.[11] If an individual was aggrieved by an administrative act (for example, a breach of contract), his only recourse was to certain organs within the executive branch called *tribunali del contenzioso amministrativo*. These organs were not true tribunals but administrative boards of review subject to the executive power.[12]

Radical changes were made by the Law of March 20, 1865, no. 2248, *allegato E*, which is still in effect, although it has been modified by the New Code of Administrative Process (*Nuovo codice del processo amministrativo*; D.Lgs. July 2, 2010, n. 104; and D.L. 160/2012).

The law of 1865 reflected the era in which it was enacted—an era when traditional liberal principles were at their height. The law vested the ordinary civil courts with the power to adjudicate claims against the state by individuals whose political or private rights had been violated. In compliance with then-current ideas of separation of powers, the courts were not permitted to revoke or amend any administrative determination. They were permitted merely to award damages to individuals whose rights had been violated.

The reform of 1865 left a serious gap in administrative law. If an unlawful administrative act did not violate an individual's rights but only his inchoate "legitimate interests" (*interessi legittimi*), judicial redress was unavailable. The only remedy was to petition the administrative body to which the wrongdoing admin-

---

10. For example, civil liability may be presumed in certain circumstances. Criminal liability must be proved. Cf. *Helvering v. Mitchell*, 303 U.S. 391 (1938) (acquittal in criminal prosecution for tax evasion does not bar a civil action on the same facts for a civil penalty); *United States v. National Association of Real Estate Boards*, 339 U.S. 485 (1950) (acquittal in criminal prosecution for antitrust law violations does not bar civil action to enjoin the same violations).

11. Leading works on administrative law are cited at 2.06. In addition, see Sandulli, *Il giudizio davanti al Consiglio di Stato e ai giudici sottordinati* (1963); Giannini, *Discorso generale sulla giustizia amministrativa*, 18 Rivista di diritto processuale 522 (1963).

12. See, e.g., 1 Calamandrei, *Istituzioni di diritto processuale civile* § 42 c (2d ed. 1943); 2 *id.*, at § § 76 c, 86, 87 (1944).

istrators were subordinate. Consequently, a great many administrative acts were subject to no check outside the executive branch of government.

The need for greater checks on administrative power soon became obvious, and the movement for reform was led by Silvio Spaventa, who campaigned with the slogan "Justice in the administration."[13] A proposal was advanced to permit any citizen to bring an action (*azione popolare*) in the courts to contest the validity of any administrative act. After long debate, around the turn of the century, an ingenious but less radical solution was found. The 1865 reform, permitting individuals whose rights had been violated to sue in the ordinary courts, was left intact. New organs, known as administrative courts, were created as sections of administrative bodies known as the Consiglio di Stato and the Giunte Provinciali Amministrative.

The system above has shaped the "classical model" of Italian administrative jurisdiction. Under this model only citizens who have a legitimate interest in an administrative act are permitted to contest the act. They must be personally aggrieved; for example, they must have been excluded from public bidding or from a civil service competition, or had their property affected by an invalid zoning regulation. They may complain of the violation of laws which do not vest individuals with rights but which protect the public interest by governing the competence of administrative bodies, the forms and procedures they are to follow, and the purposes they are to serve. The administrative courts are given the power to enforce this kind of law by revoking improper administrative acts, and in some cases by modifying them.[14]

Nowadays administrative jurisdiction is exercised by Regional Administrative Tribunals (TAR) with the Consiglio di Stato working as an appellate court, and the matter of "damages" provoked by illegitimate acts of the Public Administration is covered by article 30 of the Code of Administrative Process. An action for damages for the infringement of a "right" (such as property) is exercised with a five-year

---

13. See 1 Calamandrei, *op. cit.* n. 12, at § 42 c.

14. The most important enactments governing the powers of administrative courts are the Royal Decree of June 26, 1924, no. 1054 (*Testo unico delle leggi sul Consiglio di Stato*); Royal Decree of June 26, 1924, no. 1058 (*Testo unico sulle attribuzioni delle giunte provinciali amministrative in seds giurisdizionale*); Royal Decrees of Aug. 17, 1907, nos. 642, 643 (*Regolamenti* of procedures before the Consiglio di Stato and the Giunte Provinciali Amministrative, respectively, when sitting as courts); Royal Decree of July 12, 1934, no. 1214 (*Testo unico delle leggi sulla Corte dei conti*); Royal Decree of Aug. 13, 1933, no. 1038 (*Regolamento* of procedures before the Corte dei conti).

statute of limitations in the Administrative Tribunals but following the rules of the Civil Code on torts (arts. 2043 ss.). In these cases the plaintiff may also bring a claim for specific performance against the Public Administration. In case of the infringement of a mere "legitimate interest" of the citizen (such as the violation of "due process" in assigning a benefit or levying a tax) the action for damages must be filed within 120 days from the act afflicting the interest.

Competence for judicial review of administrative acts is thus vested in the special administrative courts but following the private law rules in cases of violation of individual rights. Since administrative law is, to a large extent, not codified—with the main exception, as we have just seen, of its procedural aspects—it is one area of Italian law in which precedent undeniably plays an important role. In distinguishing rights and legitimate interests, case law is frequently decisive. Nevertheless, case law fails to provide all the answers.

The Corte di cassazione has the final word on the proper court for administrative suits[15] and may review issues of jurisdiction raised before the administrative courts.[16] In this manner, the highest civil court maintains a certain measure of control over the administrative courts.

4.05 *Relationship between Civil and Constitutional Procedure.* The Constitution of 1948 instituted a Constitutional Court with broad powers to review the constitutionality of legislation and executive acts that have the force of law.[17] Whenever a legitimate and relevant constitutional issue is found to exist in a civil proceeding, the proceeding must be suspended and the Constitutional Court invested with the issue. The competence of and procedures before the Court, as well as the necessary suspension of civil proceedings, are governed by the Constitution, constitutional laws, and ordinary legislation.[18] In addition, the Court has power to lay down rules

15. Codice di procedura civile art. 362, para. 2.

16. Constitution art. 111; Codice di procedura civile art. 362, para. 2.

17. See 2.05. Judgments of the Italian Constitutional Court, like those of Germany and Austria, are binding *erga omnes*. See Cole, *Three Constitutional Courts: A Comparison*, 53 Am. Pol. Sci. Rev. 963 (1959); Cappelletti and Adams, *Judicial Review of Legislation: European Antecedents and Adaptations*, 79 Harv. L. Rev. 1207, 1222 (1966). A more recent study is Dengler, *The Italian Constitutional Court: Safeguard of the Constitution*, 19 Dick. J. Int'l L. 363 (2001).

18. Constitution arts. 127 and 134–37; Constitutional Laws of Feb. 9, 1948, no. 1, and March 11, 1953, no. 1; Law of March 11, 1953, no. 87; Law of March 18, 1958, no. 265.

regulating procedure before it.[19] This rule-making power is unique. Other Italian courts, like European courts in general,[20] have no such power.

Since procedure before the Constitutional Court is not within the compass of this chapter, only a few highlights are noted. Insofar as possible, the Court procedures follow the rules of procedure applicable to the Consiglio di Stato acting in its judicial capacity.[21] Since those rules incorporate by reference several provisions of the Code of Civil Procedure, the procedure before the Constitutional Court is partially based on the Code of Civil Procedure.

When, as in most instances, a case in the Constitutional Court arises out of a civil, criminal, or administrative proceeding, the parties to the case are entitled to present briefs and participate in oral argument. If a state law is in issue, the prime minister—in fact represented by the Avvocatura dello Stato—may participate. The president of the regional executive committee may participate if a regional law is in question.[22]

4.06 *Procedural Standards in the Constitution.*   Many provisions of the Constitution establish minimum standards to which procedure must conform. Since all Italian courts are national courts,[23] these standards are applicable to all judicial proceedings.

The Constitution provides for an independent judiciary.[24] In addition, a number of other provisions bind the legislature and the courts. Articles 13, 14, 15, and

19. This power is granted by art. 14, para. 1, and art. 22, para. 2, of the Law of March 11, 1953, no. 87. The Court's rules are required to be published in the *Gazzetta ufficiale*. Rules have been so published in the editions of March 24, 1956 (item no. 71), May 3, 1958 (item no. 107), Dec. 15, 1962 (item no. 320), and Feb. 19, 1966 (item no. 105).

20. See Kaplan, von Mehren, and Schaefer, *Phases of German Civil Procedure*, 71 Harv. L. Rev. 1193, 1195 n. 4 (1958); von Mehren, *Some Comparative Reflections on First Instance Civil Procedure: Recent Reforms in German Civil Procedure and in the Federal Rules*, 63 Notre Dame L. Rev. 609 (1988).

21. Law of March 11, 1953, no. 87, art. 22, para. 1.

22. Law of March 11, 1953, no. 87, arts. 23, 25. See 2.04 (regional executive committee) and 3.05 (Avvocatura dello Stato).

23. Some courts, such as the Regional Tribunals of Public Waters and the Provincial Administrative Committees, have names that might create the impression that they are organs of regional or provincial government. They are, however, courts of the national government. See 2.06, 2.07.

24. See 3.07.

21 of the Constitution restrict the power of search, seizure, and arrest, providing that unconstitutional acts of this kind are completely ineffective. Although there is disagreement on the meaning of this sanction, the better view is that evidence obtained in violation of these articles is inadmissible.[25]

Article 24 of the Constitution guarantees all persons, whether citizen or alien, the right to sue for the protection of their rights and legitimate interests and to defend any court actions brought against them. It amplifies this right by guaranteeing legal aid to the indigent.[26] In applying article 24 and article 3, which provide broad equal protection of the laws, the Court has invalidated several laws. For example, the requirement that a plaintiff post security for costs was declared unconstitutional,[27] as was the requirement that tax assessments be paid as a precondition to an action contesting the assessments.[28] A law that required courts in certain kinds of landlord-tenant cases to accept as binding the findings of fact of an administrative body was held to violate the rights guaranteed by article 24.[29] The first two of these decisions held in substance that theoretical procedural due process is insufficient. Economic obstacles that in fact deprive individuals of their rights to sue or defend violate the Constitution.[30]

Closely allied to article 24 is article 113, which guarantees a judicial remedy against violations by the state of rights and legitimate interests. This article was designed to prevent the recurrence of abuses that took place during the fascist regime. Along with articles 24 and 3, it was the basis of the decision that struck

25. See Cappelletti, *Efficacia di prove illegittimamente ammesse e comportamento della parte,* 7 Rivista di diritto civile 556 (1961). But see Cordero, *op. cit.* n. 7, at 119 *et seq.,* 125 *et seq.* Cf. *Mapp v. Ohio,* 367 U.S. 643 (1961).

26. See 3.04. Cf. the leading U.S. case *Gideon v. Wainwright,* 372 U.S. 335 (1963).

27. Corte costituzionale, Nov. 29, 1960, no. 67, 5 Giurisprudenza costituzionale 1195 (1960) (critical note by Satta).

28. Corte costituzionale, March 31, 1961, no. 21, 6 Giurisprudenza costituzionale 138 (1961) (critical note by Esposito; approving note by Treves).

29. Corte costituzionale, Dec. 22, 1961, no. 70, 6 Giurisprudenza costituzionale 1282 (1961) (approving note by Cappelletti).

30. Cappelletti, *Diritto di azione e didifesa e funzione concretizzatrice della giurisprudenza costituzionale (Art. 24 costituzione e "due process of law clause"),* 6 Giurisprudenza costituzionale 1284 (1961); Crisafulli, *Principio di legalità e "giusto procedimento,"* 7 Giurisprudenza costituzionale 130 (1962); Sassano, *Il gratuito patrocinio* (2004); Nardi, *Il gratuito patrocinio dei non abbienti nel processo amministrativo, civile, penale e tributario* (2004); Sechi, *Il patrocinio penale dei non abbienti* (2006).

down the requirement of prepayment of tax assessments as a condition to judicial review.[31]

Article 25, paragraph 1 provides that no one may be barred from his "natural court as predetermined by law." The Constitutional Court invalidated a number of provisions of the then-existing Code of Criminal Procedure on the basis of this article.[32] This provision of the Constitution would also seem applicable to civil and administrative proceedings.[33] There is thus at least reasonable doubt about the validity of some rules of civil procedure.[34]

Article 111 imposes a requirement that is unknown in American law: any judicial ruling in any kind of case must be *motivato*—that is, accompanied by a written opinion.[35] This article also guarantees a right of review of errors of law in the Corte di cassazione of all judgments, whatever their nature, and of all judicial rulings affecting personal liberty. Exception is made for decisions of the Consiglio di Stato and Corte dei conti, which are reviewable only on jurisdictional questions.

The Constitution has played an increasingly important role in the interpretation of normal legislation according to the doctrine that a law cannot receive a meaning that would be contrary to the Constitution. In this way norms can be reinterpreted to give them a constitutionally coherent meaning without addressing

---

31. Note 28.

32. E.g., Constitutional Court, July 7, 1962, no. 88, 87 Foro italiano (part 1) col. 1217 (1962), Article 30, paras. 2, 3, and article 31, para. 2, of the Code of Criminal Procedure, under which the prosecutor had the option of remitting to a *pretore* a case that was normally within the competence of a tribunal, and vice versa, were invalidated.

33. See Liebman, *Giudice naturale e costituzione del giudice*, 19 Rivista di diritto processuale 331, 335 (1964); Pizzorusso, *La competenza del giudice come materia coperta da riserva di legge*, 115 Giurisprudenza italiana (part 1, § 1) col. 1313, 1317–18 (1963). But see Andrioli, *La precostituzione del giudice*, 19 Rivista di diritto processuale 325, 329–30 (1964). For the latest doctrines, see Romboli, *Giudice naturale*, in *Enc. Dir.*, XVIII, 2000, at 374; Ghirga, *Riflessioni sul significato di giudice naturale nel processo civile*, in *Riv. Dir. Proc.*, 2002, 805; Tarzia, *Lineamenti del processo civile di cognizione* (4th ed. 2009) at 10; Picardi, *Manuale del processo civile* (2010) at 82; Sassani, *Lineamenti del processo civile italiano* (2012) at 47; Sandulli, *Codice dell'azione amministrativa* (2011).

34. See Pizzorusso, *op. cit.* n. 33.

35. The Code of Civil Procedure is partially superseded by this provision. The code required an opinion for judgments (*sentenze*) (art. 132) but not for *decreti* (art. 135), which are decisions typically made in certain special proceedings. For *ordinanze*, which are rulings on evidentiary and other procedural issues, the code requires a "succinct" opinion (art. 134). The nature of Italian judicial opinions is discussed further below.

the Constitutional Court directly. For instance, the rules on torts have been constructed so as to allow a direct action for damages between private parties if the defendant is assumed to have violated a "constitutional right" of the plaintiff. This doctrine has been peculiarly important, because article 32 of the Constitution provides for protection of the "health" of all citizens (with the original purpose to implement a national health care system).[36] Thus, in an action for damages for personal injury, the plaintiff can receive a sum for the "injury" itself regardless of any further pecuniary loss suffered by him (dec. 184/1986 of the Constitutional Court). For example, a person who suffered an injury can recover damages for her health (*danno biologico*) even if she didn't suffer any difference in income or directly incur any expenses because of the intervention of the national health care system.

4.07 *Noncontentious Cases: Voluntary Jurisdiction.*   One of the central operative concepts in European procedural doctrine is "voluntary jurisdiction." In Germany, the concept has given rise to a law of procedure of code proportions[37] but distinct from the Code of Civil Procedure.[38] In Italy, although the concept of voluntary jurisdiction is widely known and used, the Code of Civil Procedure makes no mention of it except in connection with the recognition of foreign judgments.[39]

---

36. For the general reassessment of tort in Italy and the process of "constitutionalization of private law," see Monateri, *La responsabilità civile* (1998); Barcellona, *Trattato della responsabilità civile* (2011); Alpa, *La responsabilità civile* (2010); Busnelli and Patti, *Danno e responsabilità civile* (3d ed. 2013).

37. Reichsgesetz über die Angelegenheiten der freiwilligen Gerichtsbarkeit of May 17, 1898, as amended. In Italy various monographic studies of the subject exist; in Germany there are not only monographic studies but also textbooks and commentaries. See, e.g., Lent and Habscheid, *Freiwillige Gerichtsbarkeit* (4th ed. 1962); Bumiller and Winkler, *Freiwillige Gerichtsbarkeit* (6th ed. 2006).

38. Known as the Zivilprozessordnung or ZPO.

39. Codice di procedura civile art. 801 governed the recognition in Italy of "acts of foreign courts in voluntary jurisdiction matters"; this article has since been abrogated by the Act of May 31, 1995, no. 218 (art. 73). See Cappelletti and Perillo, *op. cit.* n. 1, at 14.15–14.16. Cf. Brulliard, *L'évolution de la notion de juridiction dite "gracieuse" ou "volontaire*," 9 Revue internationale de droit comparé 5 (1957). For a commentary on the Italian regulation in force, see Vullo, *La giurisdizione italiana in materia volontaria*, in Lupoi et al., *Giurisdizione italiana, efficacia di sentenze e atti stranieri* (2007) at 334; Masoni (ed.), *Guida alla volontaria giurisdizione* (2011); Jannuzzi and Lorefice, *La volontaria giurisidizone* (11th ed. 2006).

It is not easy to define "voluntary jurisdiction." Underlying the concept is the belief that certain proceedings which are typically—but not necessarily—noncontentious may usefully be grouped together for analysis. These include matters as varied as adoptions, declarations of presumed death, judicial approval of the sale of infants' real property, declarations of incompetency, settlement of decedents' estates, and approval of certificates of incorporation.[40] That proceedings of this kind differ in form and substance from typically litigious matters seems clear. Although American law does not use the concept of voluntary jurisdiction, it governs most of the proceedings that Europeans call matters of voluntary jurisdiction by distinct procedures: in many American states, surrogate's, probate, or orphan's courts are instituted to administer many of these matters. European doctrine is not content to analyze these individual kinds of proceedings but seeks to find a unifying concept. The traditional definition, which, however, many scholars do not accept, is that voluntary jurisdiction involves "public administration of private law by judicial organs."[41] The unifying element is that in each of these cases a private law activity cannot be undertaken without an order, authorization, or some other kind of judicial intervention. That the judicial intervention is, or borders on, administration rather than adjudication is illustrated by the following comparative observation. In most American states, certificates of incorporation are approved by administrative bodies, but in Italy, by the courts. In Italy, citizenship is conferred upon aliens by administrative act,[42] but in America, by the courts. In neither country would anyone be unduly disturbed if the competence for these proceedings were reversed.[43]

---

40. For these and other examples, see Cappelletti and Perillo, *op. cit.* n. 1, at 13.05–13.12, and all the references quoted in note 39. See also Verde, *Trattato sulla volontaria giurisdizione* (1989); Santarcangelo, *La volontaria giurisdizione* (2003); Genghini, *La volontaria giurisdizione* (2006).

41. 1 Calamandrei, *op. cit.* n. 12, at § 23. For a similar definition applied to French law, see Morel, *op. cit.* n. 4, at 86.

42. The former regulation (Law of June 13, 1912, no. 555, as amended, art. 4) has been abrogated by the Act of February 5, 1992, 91 (and regulations for its implementation: specifically DPR no. 572 of October 12, 1993, and DPR no. 362 of April 18, 1994). According to the law in force, citizenship is acquired by marriage to an Italian citizen or by naturalization (legal residence is required for a different period of time, i.e., from three to ten years). The administrative act is subject to judicial review upon the application of the interested party.

43. Indeed, in some instances there is a blurring of competence in these matters, as in laws requiring judicial approval for the formation of certain types of organizations.

Book IV of the Italian Code of Civil Procedure regulates various kinds of special proceedings, including typically contentious summary proceedings and applications for provisional remedies. Each of these proceedings, as well as the noncontentious proceedings, is governed separately. In addition, articles 737–42 *bis* govern "proceedings in chambers" to the extent that particular provisions do not provide otherwise. Since most proceedings conducted in chambers involve noncontentious matters, these articles outline the typical procedure used for voluntary jurisdiction.[44]

The procedure is simpler and swifter than in ordinary contentious proceedings. The proceeding is initiated by a simple application addressed to the competent court. Informality is the rule: the formalities of taking evidence are not observed. Article 738, paragraph 3, provides merely that the court "may gather information." After informal discussion, the court rules on the application with a ruling known as a decree, rather than a judgment. Within ten days a party, or the *pubblico ministero*, may attack the decree before the next highest court by a simplified form of appeal known as *reclamo*. Even in this court, the proceeding is conducted informally in chambers.

Decrees issued in chambers do not become res judicata. Any interested party may reopen the issues decided, and the court may at any time modify or vacate a decree previously rendered. However, contract or property rights that have been acquired on the faith of a decree prior to its modification or vacation cannot be divested.[45]

4.08 *Summary Proceedings.* In Italy there are a number of summary proceedings which, like voluntary jurisdiction cases, are deemed to be special

44. In France also, voluntary jurisdiction (*jurisdiction gracieuse*), as opposed to *jurisdiction contentieuse*, is governed by provisions dealing with proceedings in chambers. The Law of July 15, 1944 (revalidated by the Ordinance of Oct. 9, 1945) ("*sur la chamber du conseil*") provided that "la chamber du conseil has jurisdiction: (1) in noncontentious matters, over all claims not involving an adversary and not contestable by a third party; and, furthermore, over all claims in which the parties, not being in disagreement, are required by their status or the nature of the affair, to obtain a court decision." See Cuche and Vincent, *op. cit.* n. 4, at 392–93.

45. Codice di procedura civile art. 742. Similar rules prevail in France (Morel, *op. cit.* n. 4, at 86), and in Germany (Baur, *I princìpi del regolamento della volontaria giurisdizione nella Repubblica Federale Tedesca*, in Centro Nazionale di Prevenzione e Difesa Sociale, *I procedimenti in camera di consiglio* 3, 10, 1962).

proceedings.[46] By far the most important summary proceeding[47] is the ex parte proceeding known as the *procedimento d'ingiunzione*. The proceeding, which originated in medieval Italy,[48] has also been adopted in Germany, where it is known as *Mahnverfahren*.[49] The practical importance of this proceeding is considerable given that it is designed to recover debts based on invoices, which covers essentially the entire sphere of business relations and given that while in a ordinary proceeding one may wait three years to reach a decision, one may normally get an injunction within a few weeks. In this matter many basic business interests are effectively protected by Italian Law, notwithstanding lengthy delays elsewhere in the system.

A summary proceeding may be initiated by a person who asserts a claim (based on documentary evidence, and especially on an invoice) to a liquidated sum of money, a specified quantity of fungible goods, or identified movable property.[50] The claim is asserted by the filing of an application addressed to the court that would be competent for an ordinary proceeding. The application is not served on the alleged debtor: he receives no notice of the proceeding until after a decree is rendered. If the application is in order and accompanied by sufficient evidence, a decree is issued ordering payment (or delivery of the goods claimed) within twenty days of service of the decree. The decree also notifies the debtor that if he does not take steps to contest the decree within that period, it will be executed. For good

46. Among the special proceedings is the proceeding to obtain recognition of a foreign judgment, known as *delibazione*, ruled by the Act of May 31, 1995, no. 218. This proceeding is conducted in the court of appeal. See Pegna, *I procedimenti relativi all'efficacia delle decisioni straniere in materia civile* (2009); Baratta, *Diritto internazionale privato* (2010) at 414.

47. Other important summary proceedings relate to evictions (Codice di procedura civile arts. 657–69) and the protection or reacquisition of possession of property (Codice di procedura civile arts. 703–5; Codice civile arts. 1168–70). See Cappelletti and Perillo, *op. cit.* n. 1, at 13.03, 13.04; Garbagnati, *I procedimenti di ingiunzione e sfratto* (3d ed. 1951); Chiarloni et al., *I procedimenti sommari speciali* (2005); Porreca, *Il procedimento sommario di cognizione: orientamenti, applicazioni e protocolli dei fori italiani* (2011).

48. See Calamandrei, *Il procedimento monitorio nella legislazione italiana* (1926). The proceeding is presently governed by Codice di procedura civile arts. 633–56.

49. Zivilprozessordnung §§ 688–703. This proceeding also exists in several other countries where, however, its scope is more restricted. For comparative study of the proceeding in Germany, Luxemburg, Italy, France, and Holland and its proposed introduction into Belgium, see Horsmans, *La procedure d'injonction ou le recouvrement simplifié de certaines créances dans les pays du Marché Commun* (1964).

50. Documentary evidence is not required for claims for fees brought by attorneys, notaries, and other licensed professionals. Codice di procedura civile art. 633.

cause, the period may be reduced to a minimum of ten or increased to a maximum of sixty days.

If the alleged debtor contests the decree within the prescribed time, an ordinary proceeding is begun, and the decree loses its effect.[51] In the overwhelming majority of cases, however, there is no contest, usually because the debtor realizes he has no defense.[52] Dilatory contests are inhibited by the imposition of costs, including attorneys' fees, upon the unsuccessful contestant.

The summary proceeding provides a rapid means of disposing of a claim, the prima facie validity of which is shown by highly probative evidence. Although the proceeding is conducted without the participation of the alleged debtor, due process is assured by a subsequent opportunity to contest. Summary proceedings, which have no analogue in American law, have great importance and utility in Italy. Perhaps this last statement can best be explained by looking at the rules concerning defaults in the two countries. In America, a debtor who has no defense frequently defaults. His default is deemed to constitute an admission of the validity of the claim, and judgment is summarily entered against him. In Italy, on the other hand, a default in an ordinary proceeding involves neither contempt of the court nor an admission of the validity of the claim. The court must hear evidence concerning the claim. The half million yearly summary proceedings relieve the courts of what would be an intolerable burden if ordinary proceedings with normal default procedures were required in each of them.[53]

4.09 *Provisional Remedies and Duration of Ordinary Proceedings.*   There are a number of distinct proceedings, known as *procedimenti cautelari*, to obtain provisional remedies.[54] The *procedimenti cautelari* are treated in the Code as subspecies

---

51. If the application is rejected, a decree and opinion to that effect is rendered, without prejudice to the commencement of another ex parte summary proceeding or an ordinary proceeding on the same claim. Codice di procedura civile art. 640.

52. The burden of proof in the proceeding contesting the decree is placed on the alleged creditor.

53. See Cappelletti and Perillo, *op. cit.* n. 1, at 11.01–11.08. In addition to summary ex parte proceedings, ordinary proceedings are avoided by the rule that certain legal instruments—for example, negotiable instruments—have the executory force of judgments. See 4.18.

54. See Calamandrei, *Introduzione allo studio sistematico dei provvedimenti cautelari* (1936); Cappelletti and Perillo, *op. cit.* n. 1, at ch. 6; Tarzia, *I procedimenti cautelari* (1990); Iofrida and Scarpa, *I nuovi procedimenti cautelari dopo la L. 80/2005* (2006); Mascia,

of summary proceedings.[55] Provisional remedies are designed to ensure satisfaction of a final judgment, if and when issued.

In every case, prerequisites to a provisional remedy are: (1) that there would be danger to the applicant's rights if the remedial processes of the court were delayed (*periculum in mora*), and (2) that the applicant probably has a right to a favorable final judgment (*fumus boni juris*). The kinds of provisional relief available closely approximate those in the United States.[56] Because of their provisional nature, they are strictly contingent on the commencement and outcome of an action on the merits. If an action on the merits is not commenced within the required period, the provisional remedy lapses.

The frequent resort to and practical importance of provisional and other summary relief become understandable when one considers the period of time it takes to obtain a judgment on the merits in an ordinary proceeding. In many cases it may take two years or more to reach a decision in the court of first instance, and even longer if one includes the court of appeal. This period would be somewhat shorter if cases that do not go to final judgment because of an interim settlement or discontinuance were included in the statistics. Nevertheless, the system remains notoriously slow, and the inefficiency of Italian justice is a challenge that has confounded reformers throughout the country's history.

4.10 *Ordinary Proceedings: Absence of Juries.*   Many of the contrasts between the common law and the Italian procedural system (or any continental system) may be explained by the absence of juries in civil cases. Although the presence of juries in civil cases is rare in England today, the structure of a civil proceeding is still basically the same as when juries sat almost as a matter of course. The rules of evidence and the manner in which evidence is presented are largely the result of adaptation to the presence of a jury. The absence of juries in Italy has resulted in a different

---

I *procedimenti cautelari* (2008); Salciarini and Scarpa, *I procedimenti cautelari: questioni processuali* (2010).

    55. Codice di procedura civile arts. 669-bis–702.

    56. Provisional remedies include sequestration, specified restraining, and mandatory orders governing conduct and the sealing and inventory of assets. See Cappelletti and Perillo, *op. cit.* n. 1, at 6.04–6.12, 6.17. Arrest is not a permissible remedy. In addition, to nominate remedies, article 700 of the Code of Civil Procedure gives the court broad powers to protect an applicant who is threatened by imminent and irreparable damage by any appropriate order. For similar broad powers in Germany, see Zivilprozessordnung §§ 935–45.

development of civil procedure. However, we shall see later that many of the differences are becoming blurred.[57]

4.11 *Discovery and Investigation.*   It is usually a source of surprise to American lawyers to find out that there is almost a total absence of discovery devices available to an Italian litigant prior to the proof-taking stage of a civil proceeding and that Italian lawyers do not make extensive informal factual investigations. This absence of informal investigation and lack of formal discovery devices is a feature common to German[58] and other European litigation and is clearly related to the absence of juries. The impaneling of a jury—a group of laymen who must be released as soon as feasible to go about their normal business—necessitates a concentrated trial, "a day in court." On the other hand, in the Italian system there is no trial in the common law sense; rather, there are a series of separate hearings, often spread over many months. A Korean jurist has aptly described the common law procedure as "the day in court" system and the civil law system as the "dental clinic form of trial."[59] In the European proceeding the judge is the dentist who shrinks from treating all of his patient's ills in a concentrated treatment; rather, he requires periodic visits.

What has been said regarding German procedure also applies to the Italian:

> The fact that there is no "trial" in the sense of a single occasion for the display of evidence affects and compels accommodations in a great many elements of the system. Surprise is not felt to be a substantial danger. Accordingly the lawyer's initial preparation can be less than vigorous, and no pressure is created for out-of-court discovery. As the lawyer's out-of-court investigation is narrow in scope, and what is known to the lawyer is passed on to the court in detailed writings, there is little awkwardness in having the judge take over the chief burden of interrogating witnesses—especially so, as the judge need not conclude the matter in one session but can inform herself step by step over a period of time.[60]

---

57. See 4.15 and 4.20. A limited form of jury trial is used in certain criminal cases, in which two professional judges are supplemented by six individuals chosen from the general public, with one of the judges presiding and a majority vote required for conviction. See generally Freccero, *An Introduction to the New Italian Criminal Procedure*, 21 Am. J. Crim. L. 345, 348–51 (1994).

58. See Kaplan, von Mehren, and Schaefer, *op. cit.* n. 20, at 1199–1202.

59. Chin Kim, *Party Disability to Testify as to the Facts under Continental Code and Anglo-American Systems*, 2 Seoul L.J. 17 (1960).

60. Kaplan, von Mehren, and Schaefer, *op. cit.* n. 20, at 1471.

Naturally, an Italian lawyer makes some investigation before beginning an action. He examines available documents, perhaps makes a physical inspection of relevant premises, and confers with his client. However, only rarely will he interview witnesses. Contacts with witnesses out of court verge on violations of the canons of ethics and could give rise to disciplinary sanctions. Witnesses, however, may be contacted and interviewed by the litigants.

4.12 *The Stages of an Ordinary Proceeding.*   An ordinary civil action in a tribunal unfolds in three stages: introductory, proof-taking, and decision making.[61]

The introductory stage[62] begins with the drafting, filing, and service of the citation that initiates the case, states the legal and factual grounds upon which the prayer for relief is based, and describes the evidence that the plaintiff wishes to be considered. An answer is filed stating the defendant's denials, defenses, setoffs, counterclaims, and evidence. The president of the court then appoints an examining judge, who directs the ensuing proof-taking stage.

In recent decades a sharper line has been drawn between the introductory and the proof-taking stages. New claims may not be propounded, and modification of legal, factual, and evidentiary grounds for the relief initially requested and for the defenses originally raised is only rarely permissible.

Evidence is taken during the proof-taking stage at various hearings,[63] separated by periods of weeks or months. Hearings are closed to the public, but the parties and their attorneys may attend. When the examining judge deems the case com-

---

61. The same procedure applies to the so-called *"giudici di pace,"* except as expressly provided in the Code. Codice di procedura civile art. 311.

62. The introductory stage is governed by Codice di procedura civile arts. 163–74; see Tarzia, *Lineamenti del processo civile di cognizione* (2009) at 336; Mandrioli, *Diritto processuale civile* (22nd ed. 2012) Vol. 2; Lugo, *Manuale di diritto processuale civile* (18th ed. 2012) at 377.

63. The proof-taking stage is governed by Codice di procedura civile arts. 175–274 bis. See general references in note 62. At the first hearing, and again whenever it seems feasible, the examining judge must attempt to bring about a settlement, unless nondispositive issues—for example, in an annulment case—are involved. If a settlement is achieved in court, it is placed in the record of the case and is enforceable as if it were a judgment. For the equivalent rule in Germany, see, e.g., Schönke, Schröder, and Niese, *Lehrbuch des Zivilprozessrechts* 244 (8th ed. 1956). In practice, these conciliation efforts are frequently *pro forma* and are far less effective than in the related German system. See Kaplan, von Mehren, and Schaefer, *op. cit.* n. 20, at 1222–24.

plete, she remits the case to the adjudicating panel, which consists of herself and two other judges.

The decision stage[64] begins with a hearing, open to the public, at which oral argument may be presented before the adjudicating panel. Usually, however, oral argument is waived and briefs are submitted. The panel retires for secret deliberation in chambers, and the decision is made by majority vote. A formal opinion is written and filed; dissenting opinions are not written, and dissenting votes are not recorded.[65] In most cases the judgment awards costs, including attorneys' fees,[66] to the successful party.

64. The decision stage is governed by Codice di procedura civile arts. 275–81. A case may have more than one decision stage; for example, the issue of liability is frequently decided before any evidence is taken on the issue of damages. Once rare, this kind of division of a case has become almost as routine in some American courts as it is in Italy. See Zeisel and Callahan, *Split Trials and Time Saving: A Statistical Analysis*, 76 Harv. L. Rev. 1606 (1963); *Note*, 48 Va. L. Rev. 99 (1962).

65. There are precedents in earlier Italian law for the publication of dissents. See Denti, *Per il ritorno al "voto di scissura" nelle decisioni giudiziarie*, in *Quaderni della giurisprudenza costituzionale, Le opinioni dissenzienti dei giudici costituzionali e internazionali* 1 (1964). Some writers have urged the abolition of the secrecy of judicial votes. See Denti, above; Cappelletti, *Ideologie nel diritto processuale*, 16 Rivista trimestrale di diritto e procedura civile 193, 215 (1962); Anzon (ed.), *L'opinione dissenziente* (1995). Secrecy of judicial voting is common to the major European systems of procedure. See Nadelmann, *The Judicial Dissent: Publication v. Secrecy*, 8 Am. J. Comp. L. 415, 420, 422 (1959), who, at 430, reports Piero Calamandrei, one of Italy's leading proceduralists, as stating that the fiction of judicial unanimity constitutes "an institutional consecration of conformity, a typical example of State unanimity which saves appearances at the expense of conscience." See also Nadelmann, *Non-Disclosure of Dissents in Constitutional Courts: Italy and West Germany*, 13 Am. J. Comp. L. 268 (1964); Heyde, *Das Minderheitsvotum des überstimmen Richters* (1966).

In France at least, some judges have escaped the anonymity of the decision by writing law review comments on cases in which they have participated. See Nadelmann, *French Courts Recognize Foreign Money Judgments: One Down and More to Go*, 13 Am. J. Comp. L. 72, 76–77 (1964).

66. Although there are a number of exceptions (Codice di procedura civile arts. 91–92), it is a fundamental principle, the desirability of which no one in Italy has seriously questioned, that attorneys' fees be paid by the losing party. Italian writers have severely criticized the contrary American practice. See Cappelletti, *In tema di assistenza giudiziaria internazionale nei rapporti fra Italia e U.S.A.*, 26 Annali della Università di Macerata 51, 54–55 (1963). The same general rule applies in other important European legal systems. See, e.g., Kaplan, von Mehren, and Schaefer, *op. cit.* n. 20, at 1201, 1461–67; Jacobsson, *Parts kostnad I*

4.13 *Evidence.* The central phase of a proceeding—the proof-taking phase—is concerned with the taking of evidence. This section examines the admissibility of evidence and the manner in which it is taken. The following two sections attempt to demonstrate how the rules of evidence shape the procedural system and give it its distinguishing features.

Article 115, paragraph 1, of the Code of Civil Procedure lays down the most basic of the rules of evidence: except as specifically otherwise provided, the court may not consider evidence not adduced by the parties or by the *pubblico ministero*.[67] This is called the "dispositive rule" of evidence, to indicate that parties have the freedom to decide what evidence they wish considered and that the court may not substitute its wisdom for that of the parties. The court, as a rule, cannot on its own motion determine what evidence is to be produced or heard, nor may the court rely upon its private knowledge of facts not properly made part of the record.

The dispositive rule has important exceptions. The ancient rule permitting judicial notice, without proof, of notorious facts is recognized.[68] Moreover, certain statutory rules permit the court to act on its own motion to acquire evidence, or at least information. It may call the parties before it to ask them to clarify their allegations, pursuant to a procedure known as the "free interrogatory."[69] It may make a judicial

---

civilprocess 253–54 (1964). For an extensive historical-comparative study, see Chiovenda, *La condanna nelle spese giudiziali* 144 et seq. (2d ed. 1935).

67. The reference to the *pubblico ministero* is limited to those cases in which he is required or permitted to intervene. Codice di procedura civile arts. 69–74. These include cases involving matrimonial status and others that are deemed to involve a public interest.

68. The rule is commonly expressed in the maxim "*notoria non egent probatione*" (notorious facts need not be proven) and is recognized by Codice di procedura civile art. 115, para. 2. See Calamandrei, *Per la definizione del fatto notorio*, in 2 Calamandrei, *Studi sul processo civile* 289 (1930); Taruffo, *La prova nel processo civile* (2012) at 49; Leanza, *Le prove civili* (2012) at 67.

69. Codice di procedura civile art. 117. Although parties themselves are normally disqualified as witnesses, there are certain devices to obtain the parties' version of the facts. Additionally, while the free interrogatory is primarily designed to provide oral clarification of the pleadings, art. 116, para. 2 provides that the court may deduce evidence (*desumere argomenti di prova*) from the parties' answers as well as from their overall behavior in the proceeding. The free interrogatory has analogues in France (the *comparution personnelle* of articles 119 and 324–36 of the Code de procedure civile) and Germany (the *persönliches Erscheinen der Parteien* of section 141 of the Zivilprozessordnung). On the history and the use of the free interrogatory in Italy and elsewhere, see Cappelletti, *La testimonianza della parte nel sistema dell'oralità* (1962); Perillo, Book Review, 49 Cornell L.Q. 169 (1963). See

inspection of places and persons[70] and appoint technical consultants to make surveys, engineering reports, medical examinations, and the like.[71] It may order the parties to take "supplementary oaths"[72] and may request administrative agencies to supply information from their records.[73] In quite exceptional cases the court may, on its own motion, call in witnesses and order the production of documentary evidence.[74]

---

also Taruffo, *op. ult. cit.*, at 385; Leanza, *op. ult. cit.*, at 255; Luiso, *Diritto processuale civile. II processo di cognizione* (6th ed. 2011) at 94.

70. Codice di procedura civile art. 118, para. 1, provides, "The court may order the parties and third persons to consent to the inspections of their persons or of things in their possession that appear indispensable to knowledge of the facts of the case, so long as they may be completed without serious damage to the party or third person, and without forcing them to violate one of the secrets provided for in articles 351 and 352 of the Code of Criminal Procedure." The secrets referred to involve privileged information in the possession of attorneys, clergymen, physicians, government officials, and persons in related professions. See Cappelletti and Perillo, *op. cit.* n. 1, at 8.34–8.36. If a party wrongfully refuses to submit himself or his property to inspection, the court may "deduce evidence" from the refusal. If a third person refuses, the court may merely impose a penalty from €250 to €1,500. Such a trivial penalty is scarcely an effective coercive force; it only limits the authority of the courts, which have no powers to punish contempt. See also 4.18.

71. Technical consultants have their American analogues in expert witnesses. However, technical consultants are not considered to be witnesses but judicial aids whose function is to inspect and evaluate. This is an adjudicatory function that the judges themselves would perform if they had the requisite professional competence. Codice di procedura civile arts. 61–64. When a court appoints an expert to act as a technical consultant, the parties may also retain their own consultants to investigate, evaluate, and report their findings to the court. Codice di procedura civile art. 201.

72. Codice civile art. 2736; Codice di procedura civile art. 240. A party's oath is either supplementary or decisory. The former is put to the party on the motion of the court to supplement the evidence on an issue. The latter is put to the party on his adversary's challenge and can be employed whether or not there is any evidence on the issue. In either case, if the party takes the oath, the facts sworn to are deemed conclusively proved. If he fails to take the oath, the facts he has refused to swear to are deemed conclusively proved to be false. The conclusive nature of party oaths is the most antiquated relic of the medieval system of legal proof surviving in Italy. It survives in several other European systems, including the French, Spanish, and Dutch. Starting at the turn of the century, it was abolished in a number of civil law systems, including the Austrian, German, Russian, Hungarian, Swedish, and Finnish. On its history and present obsolescence, see Allorio, *Il giuramento della parte* (1937); Cappelletti, n. 83, *passim*. For a more detailed discussion in English, see Cappelletti and Perillo, *op. cit.* n. 1, at 8.22–8.23.

73. Codice di procedura civile art. 213.

74. As a rule, however, testimony and the production of documents may be ordered only on the motion of a party. Codice di procedura civile arts. 210, 244 *et seq.*

Courts seldom avail themselves of their powers of initiative. Rarely will the court appoint a technical consultant except on the motion of a party. Free interrogatories and supplementary oaths are used only infrequently. Consequently, despite the presence of some powers of court initiative, the Italian system of evidence can be characterized as one based on party disposition. Among the kinds of evidence that, as a rule, cannot be taken except on a party's motion are testimony,[75] the production of documents,[76] the formal interrogatory of a party,[77] and a decisory oath.[78]

The rules governing the burden of proof determine which party has the burden of adducing the evidence upon which the court will base its decision[79]—that

75. Testimony is governed by Codice civile arts. 2721–26 and by Codice di procedura civile arts. 244–57. See Cappelletti and Perillo, *op. cit.* n. 1, at 8.31–8.43, Taruffo, *op. cit.* n. 68, Leanza, *op. cit.* n. 68, Lugo, *op. cit.* n. 62. The complexities of the rules of testimonial evidence cannot be examined here. Only a few critical remarks concerning the rules are made. Before a witness is called, the party who seeks his testimony must provide the court with a detailed list of facts on which he wishes the witness examined, and the court is restricted almost entirely to this advance formulation. Codice di procedura civile art. 244. Examination of the witness by the judge is stylized and far less searching than examination by counsel in common law systems. As in Germany, no verbatim transcript is made; a summary is dictated by the examining judge to the clerk. See Kaplan, von Mehren, and Schaefer, *op. cit.* n. 20, at 1235–37; Sereni, *L'importanza del processo verbale dell'udienza giudiziaria,* 1 Sereni, *Studi di diritto comparator* 469 (1956). In sum, the rules of testimonial evidence would, more than any other aspect of Italian civil procedure, benefit from radical reform.

76. Codice di procedura civile art. 210, para. 1. As in the case of orders of inspection, the court's coercive power to enforce an order of production is limited to the imposition of trivial fines.

77. Codice di procedura civile arts. 228–32. Formal interrogatories are questions put to a party to provoke admissions. They are of little practical value. There is no sanction for false answers, since they are not given under oath. Answers favorable to the party answering have no evidentiary force and may not be considered by the court. Since the questions on which the party is to be examined are framed by his adversary and made known to him well in advance of the examination, the interrogation lacks flexibility and spontaneity. The court is restricted to the matters on the list and may not enlarge the area of questioning. Because of its impracticality, the French abolished the formal interrogatory in the 1940s, replacing it with the *comparution personnelle,* an analogue of the Italian free interrogatory. However, the French had previously made wide use of the *comparution personnelle,* as had the Austrians and Germans with their similar *persönliches Erscheinen der Parteien* and *Parteivernehmung.* In Italy the free interrogatory is used restrictedly. See Cappelletti, n. 83, *passim.*

78. As discussed in the preceding section.

79. Codice civile arts. 2697–98. See Micheli, *L'onere della prova* (1942); Verde, *L'onere della prova nel processo civile* (2013).

is, which party has the burden of producing documents in his possession, or of requesting the court either to order his adversary or strangers to the proceeding to produce documentary evidence,[80] or to take other kinds of evidence. Broadly speaking, the facts upon which the plaintiff's claim is based must be proved by him; facts upon which affirmative defenses are based must be proved by the defendant.

Although common lawyers are conditioned to think of exclusionary rules of evidence primarily as consequences (and sometimes as obsolete relics) of the jury system, similar rules exist in Italy where the jury system never took root in civil matters. Contrary to the common law, however, Italian law prefers written evidence and hems in testimony with restrictive rules.[81] The most important limitation is the exclusion of testimony by parties, interested third persons, and the spouses, relatives, and in-laws of the parties.[82] The same disqualifications existed throughout the common-law world until they were abolished in many American states and in England over a century ago.[83] The abolition has been a great and universally recognized success.[84]

---

80. Documentary evidence may be either spontaneously produced by a party filing it with the clerk or produced as exhibits in court pursuant to court order by the party or strangers to the proceeding. In addition, documentary evidence may be the object of judicial inspection. Generally speaking, Italian rules of evidence presume the documents to be authentic (without presuming, however, that the statements they contain are true). If the authenticity of a document is contested, a special proceeding must be instituted to determine whether it is false or authentic. Codice di procedura civile arts. 214–27. The presumption of authenticity is in direct contrast with the common law rules governing the introduction of documentary evidence. See McCormick, *Handbook of the Law of Evidence* 395–96 (1954). However, common law rules of proof of documents have been mitigated by pretrial procedures, such as notices to admit and pretrial conferences.

81. See Sereni, *Principi generali di diritto e processo internazionale* 29 (1955). See also Millar, *The Formative Principles of Civil Procedure*, in Engelmann et al., *A History of Continental Civil Procedure* 52, 57 (1927). In addition to the rules of exclusion of testimony discussed in the text, expert opinion is ordinarily received in the form of written reports.

82. Codice di procedura civile arts. 246, 247.

83. On the history of the abolition of disqualifications of parties, their spouses, and interested third persons to testify, see Cappelletti, *La testimonianza della parte nella storia moderna degli ordinamenti processuali anglosassoni*, 28 Studi urbinati 111 (1959–60).

84. See Dillon, *The Laws and Jurisprudence of England and America* 340–41 (1895). ("I believe I speak the universal judgement of the profession when I say that changes more beneficial in the administration of justice have rarely taken place in our law.") See also the preamble to Lord Denman's Act of Aug. 22, 1843, 6 and 7 Victoria, ch. 85, which abolished the disqualification of interested third parties. ("Whereas the Inquiry after Truth in Courts

Other limitations on testimony apply to contract matters. Contracts exceeding a certain value may not be proved by testimony.[85] However, the courts have broad discretionary powers to admit testimony in derogation of this rule, and in practice, it is seldom an obstacle to the introduction of testimony.[86] An additional exclusionary rule has a rather close analogue in the parol evidence rule.[87] In addition, certain contracts and legal acts are void unless in writing.[88] On the other hand, Italy, like France and Germany, is free from analogues to the hearsay rule, the best evidence rule, and the dead man's statutes.[89]

In the next section, we discuss the mathematical and mechanical rules for the evaluation of evidence that prevailed in late medieval and renaissance times and which, in some cases, linger on in modern Italy. Two kinds of legal presumptions, remnants of those times, are still found in Italian law. Some presumptions are conclusive (*praesumptiones juris et de jure*), whereas others are rebuttable (*praesumptiones juris tantum*), resulting merely in an inversion of the ordinary burden of proof.

There are not many conclusive presumptions. A typical example is the rule which conclusively presumes that a child born to a married woman is the progeny of her husband. The rigor of this rule is relaxed only in statutorily defined extraordinary circumstances.[90]

---

of Justice is often obstructed by Incapacities created by the present Law, and it is desirable that full information as to the Facts in Issue, both in Criminal and Civil Cases, should be laid before the Persons who are appointed to decide upon them, and that such Persons should exercise their Judgement on the Credit of the Witnesses adduced and on the Truth of their Testimony.")

85. Codice civile art. 2721. The rule is of ancient French and Italian origin. For a discussion of its history and its influence on the first Statutes of Frauds of England, see Rabel, *The Statute of Frauds and Comparative Legal History*, 63 L.Q. Rev. 174 (1947).

86. The court may permit testimony after taking into consideration the status of the parties, the nature of the contract, and every other circumstance. Codice civile art. 2721, para. 2. In France, the exclusionary rule is far less flexible. See Code civil arts. 1341– 48.

87. Codice civile arts. 2722–24.

88. Codice civile arts. 2725, 1350 *et seq.* The doctrine speaks of these articles as requiring a written *quoad substantiam* to emphasize that the requirement is substantive.

89. See Cappelletti and Perillo, *op. cit.* n. 1, at 8.31, where an analogue, but of a less exclusionary nature, of the opinion rule is also discussed. On German law, see Kaplan, von Mehren, and Schaefer, *op. cit.* n. 20, at 1237 ("hearsay evidence is freely received—and then freely evaluated").

90. Codice civile arts. 231, 232, 235.

Many rebuttable presumptions are codified. The very important presumption of fault established by article 2054, paragraph 1, of the Civil Code is a typical example: the driver of a vehicle not on rails is obligated to pay damages for persons and things injured by the vehicle, unless he proves he did everything possible to avoid the damage.

So-called "simple presumptions" are conclusions drawn case by case from circumstantial evidence (*prova indiziaria*).[91] Unlike conclusive and rebuttable presumptions, circumstantial evidence may be evaluated freely; however, it is not admissible to prove facts that may not be proved by testimony.[92]

4.14 *Noninquisitorial Nature of Proof-Taking.* A commonplace observation about civil law systems is that they are characterized by an "inquisitorial" system of proof-taking as contrasted with the "adversary" system of the common law.[93] There is perhaps a glimmer of truth in this characterization if it is restricted to Germany and Austria.[94] Applied to Italy, however, the characterization is unfounded and misleading.

We have already seen that Italian judges seldom exercise their limited powers to order the taking of evidence not adduced by a party. It has also been noted that courts have limited coercive power to enforce their orders to produce evidence, whether or not the order is based on a party's motion.[95] Although it is true that in

91. Codice civile art. 2729. On the logical nexus between presumptions and circumstantial evidence, see Cappelletti and Perillo, *op. cit.* n. 1, at 8.25.

92. See discussion above.

93. See, e.g., McCormick, *op. cit.* n. 80, at 12; 2 Conrad, *Modern Trial Evidence* 333–34 (1956); 1 Morgan, *Basic Problems of Evidence* 60 (1957).

94. See Pekelis, *Legal Techniques and Political Ideologies: A Comparative Study*, 41 Mich. L. Rev. 665, 666 (1943). (Comparatists "have often treated, on the civilian side, institutions of German law to an extent unwarranted by the importance, however great, of the systems of that type on the Continent," almost as if Europe were "co-extensive with Germany.") On changes in Italian criminal procedure—as a general rule more radical than those in the civil realm—see, e.g., Pizzi and Marafioti, *The New Italian Code of Criminal Procedure: The Difficulties of Building an Adversarial Trial System on a Civil Law Foundation*, 17 Yale J. Int'l L. 1 (1992).

95. However, strong sanctions, including criminal penalties, are available to enforce the "civic duty" to testify.

Italy (as in Germany,[96] France,[97] and most other civil law countries), the judge, and not the attorneys, conducts the examinations of witnesses, the judge in Italy acts merely as a spokesman for the parties. The party who requests that a witness be heard must formulate "in separate articles" the issues of fact on which the witness is to be questioned. Practically, this means that the party is required to submit the questions the judge will put.[98] The questioning lacks the aggressiveness and spontaneity so characteristic of examination and cross-examination by counsel, which is not surprising in view of the fact that the witness usually knows the questions well in advance of the examination.

Examination by the judges is less searching, less inquiring, and therefore less inquisitive than examination by counsel. Historically, judges rather than attorneys were required to examine witnesses because it was felt that their neutrality would prevent overly aggressive and inquisitorial examinations. The power of Italian judges to conduct the examination of witnesses is but a mask that creates the illusion of an inquisitorial system.

If the Italian system is defective, it is because it suffers from insufficient rather than excessive inquisitiveness. The power of the courts is too limited, despite appearances to the contrary. An excessive respect for the parties' freedom of action, in an adversary system that regards a legal action as a strictly private affair of the parties, typifies a social philosophy of extreme individualism, a philosophy that may also explain the political and economic history of Italy and probably of other Latin nations in recent decades.[99] Exaggerated individualism in civil procedure

96. See Kaplan, von Mehren, and Schaefer, *op. cit.* n. 20, at 1234–35. (In Germany "interrogation at proof-taking is conducted mainly by the court," although "the court may allow the parties, and must allow counsel, to put questions direct.")

97. Code de procédure civile art. 265.

98. Codice di procedura civile art. 244. However, the judge may ask questions of his own for the purpose of clarification, provided that he remains within the scope of the "articles" formulated by the parties. Codice di procedura civile art. 253. The parties and their attorneys may attend the examination of witnesses and suggest additional questions to be put to the witness.

99. "Centralization of power and individualism are far from being contradictory and inconsistent. They may sometimes appear as concurrent and complementary concepts. A historical concurrence of this kind probably explains the tyranny of Renaissance Italy and why France has been at the same time a typically centralized and a typically individualistic country. The distant boss, the stranger-judge, and other features of centralized government may be more favorable to the development of individualism than the pressure of govern-

carries with it the extreme Italian conclusion that parties have no duty to confine themselves to the truth and generally have no duty of disclosure.[100] An order of in section or production directed to a party or to an outsider may only be obtained if the document or thing is specifically identified and proof offered that it is in the possession of the person to whom it is directed.[101] Strangers to the proceeding are barely penalized if they refuse to comply. Add to this the lack of discovery devices and the lack of cross-examination, and it becomes clear that neither Italian judges nor litigants have powers to inquire into the facts comparable to those possessed by their counterparts in the United States.[102]

4.15 *Basic Features of Italian Procedure: Historical and Modern.* It has been noted previously that the presence of juries is responsible for many of the characteristics of Anglo-American procedural systems. The concentration of a legal action into a trial, "a single occasion for the display of evidence," was made necessary by the exigencies of the jury.[103] Because of the presence of a jury, most of the evidence is presented viva voce in open court. No intermediary separates the trier of fact and law from the parties and witnesses. Long before the common law existed, the characteristics of immediacy, orality, and concentration were fundamental features of classical Roman procedure (second century B.C. to A.D. third century).[104]

---

ment by neighbors in a decentralized state." Pekelis, *op. cit.* n. 94, at 689. See also Cappelletti, *op. cit.* n. 65, at 200 *et seq.*, esp. 204–12.

100. See the excellent discussion in Pekelis, *op. cit.* n. 94, at 665 *et seq.*, 678 *et seq.*, 685 *et seq.*, where the author connects the absence of a duty of disclosure and of a right to investigation in Latin countries to the individualism of those countries. See also Sereni, *Aspetti del processo civile negli Stati Uniti* 19–20 (1954); and *Basic Features of Civil Procedure in Italy*, 1 Am. J. Comp. L. (1952), at 387 n. 66, where the author underlines the far greater emphasis on the right of privacy in Italian than in American procedure.

101. Disposizioni di attuazione del codice di procedura civile art. 94. This rule prohibits anything remotely resembling a "fishing expedition" for evidence, which is so often necessary to get at evidence. For similar limitations in Germany, see Kaplan, von Mehren, and Schaefer, *op. cit.* n. 20, at 1199, 1217–18, 1240–41, 1246–47.

102. See, for greater detail, Cappelletti and Perillo, *op. cit.* n. 1, at 8.04. Although German procedure is not as deficient as the Italian in this regard, it is still true "that the court proceedings do not in practice serve as an engine of discovery comparable in strength to the modern American methods." Kaplan, von Mehren, and Schaefer, *op. cit.* n. 20, at 1246.

103. See 4.10–4.11.

104. For a comparison of the historical development of procedure in Rome, the common law world, and continental Europe, see Cappelletti and Perillo, *op. cit.* n. 1, at 1.30–1.40;

These features were attenuated in the postclassical era and in Justinian's codifica-tion (A.D. sixth century) and were all but absent from the italo-canonical and *jus commune* procedures that developed in Italy between the twelfth and fourteenth centuries. The *jus commune* was adopted by all of continental Europe and formed the basis of modern European codes.

Italo-canonical and *jus commune* proceedings were typically subdivided into a large number of hearings. The judge rarely, if ever, came into contact with the liti-gants or the witnesses. Testimony was taken by a notary (*notarius or cancellarius*), who prepared a written report for the judge. The decision was thus based on evi-dence filtered through intermediate agencies, and the filtration process frequently distorted the facts.[105] The purpose, as many documents of the era expressly state,[106] was to guarantee the impartiality, objectivity, and neutrality of the judge by keep-ing him out of the thick of the fight. The documentary curtain that separated the court from the litigants and witnesses was designed to protect the judge from pressure from the powerful, an understandable precaution in an era in which each person had a fixed status in a hierarchical society. The documentary system was also designed to permit higher courts to review all the material upon which the decision was based. It was believed that if the court was permitted to base its deci-sion on oral factors and personal observations of the witnesses, the right of review by higher courts would be nullified.

The same purposes were behind the rules by which evidence was weighed. These rules are known as the "system of legal proof," as contrasted with the more modern system of "free proof." In the latter, evidence is weighed by the judge freely, case by case, in accordance with his prudent judgment. In the system of legal proof, the law rigidly predetermines not only what evidence is to be admitted but also what weight it must be given. The age had no faith in the ability of judges to arrive at the truth through empirical data and preferred to provide mechani-cal standards. The court was required to give predetermined weight to testimony based on the number, status, age, and sex of the witnesses. To prove a fact, a given

---

Cappelletti, *Il processo civile italiano nel quadro della comparazione "civil law"–"common law,"* in 9 Rivista di diritto civile 31–64 (1963).

105. Although testimony was given in the spoken language, it was usually recorded in Latin. Anyone who has done translation work will understand the difficulty of making a faithful report.

106. Of major importance is the Decretal of Pope Innocent III of 1216, quoted in Cap-pelletti and Perillo, *op. cit.* n. 1, ch. 1, n. 144.

number of witnesses was required. The testimony of nobles, clerics, and property owners prevailed over that of commoners, laymen, and the nonpropertied. The testimony of an older man prevailed over that of a younger. The testimonies of women were either barred or given one-half or one-third the weight of men's testimonies. These and similar rules for evaluating evidence, in which all evidence was given an a priori arithmetical value (full proof, half-proof, quarter-proof, etc.), were based on what was believed to be common experience. Indeed, perhaps they were fundamentally sound: perhaps truth usually *is* found in the greater number of witnesses;[107] perhaps nobles and clerics were usually less corruptible, more educated, and therefore more reliable than commoners and laymen; older men are perhaps, for the most part, more responsible than younger. To the modern mind, these may be acceptable rules of thumb, but it would be incredible to require judges to use them as absolutes in every case. The idea of legal proof typified the abstract, deductive scholastic philosophy of its age. It arose before men like Galileo and Bacon made their penetrating criticisms of the then-prevalent philosophy. They introduced the idea of trial and error and emphasized empiricism and induction. The system of legal proof, although at variance with the idea of trial and error and unprejudiced direct observation of facts as the foundation of any valid search for truth, nevertheless dominated European procedure for centuries. On the eve of the French revolution, the great French jurist Pothier was still teaching that the testimony of one witness could not prove a fact, no matter how worthy the witness, and that the testimony of two unimpeachable witnesses constituted conclusive proof.[108] However, the system had its critics[109] in revolutionary France; the new regime accepted the principle of free evaluation of evidence.[110]

107. See 7 Wigmore, *A Treatise on the Anglo-American System of Evidence* 244 (3d ed. 2012), quoting A. Heusler: "By reason of long experience with the untrustworthiness of witnesses, a rule of thumb has been made, which denies to the judge his free discretion in the estimation of testimony and lays down a fixed law, not trusting to the often deceptive valuation of each man's credibility, character and the like, but finding its security in the external mark of numbers."

108. See Pothier, *Traité des obligations*, nos. 818–19, in Pothier, *Oeuvres* (1829). Indeed, it was not until 1877 that women witnesses were placed on an equal plane with men in Italy. Law of Dec. 9, 1877, no. 4167.

109. "It is for the judges to weigh the value of testimony." De Voltaire, *Prix de la justice et de l'humanité*, art. 22 § 4, in De Voltaire, *Oeuvres completes* (tome 29) 337 (1785).

110. Its adoption in France during the revolution seems puzzling in view of the suspicion of judges during the revolutionary era. In general, revolutionary legislation attempted

From France the idea spread, and in the nineteenth and twentieth centuries, all of the Continent more or less replaced the system of legal proof with the principle of free evaluation of evidence.[111]

Today the defects of the system of legal proof are too apparent to belabor.[112] However, legal institutions must be viewed in historical context. When the system of legal proof developed, beginning in the twelfth century, it was immeasurably more progressive and civilized than the system it replaced.

Before, and to some extent beyond, the twelfth century, judgments were reached by duels, ordeals, and other "judgments of God." The idea of testimony as the narration in court of facts seen or otherwise known to the witnesses was foreign to the era; "witnesses" were champions who fought for their friend, neighbor, or lord.[113] The transition to a civilized procedure by which triers of fact could evaluate by prudent judgment what we today call evidence was an immense undertaking. The first step was to organize the proceeding, dividing it into precisely defined stages and hearings, prescribing rigidly and formalistically exactly what could and must occur in each stage and hearing.[114] The duel and the ordeal had to be eliminated and replaced by evidence—documents, testimony, and examination of the parties. Every effort was made to prevent judicial discretion in weighing the evidence. How does one explain why this magnificent advance in civilization was accompanied by such rigidity and formalism? The answer stems from the fact that the judges were men of their times, often barely literate and sometimes corrupt; their

---

to eliminate judicial discretion. One solution to the puzzle has been suggested by Dean Wigmore, who finds the answer in the jury system. He notes that the "inherent incompatibility of the jury system and the numerical system" was noted even in France during the debates in the French Constitutional Assembly of 1791 on the proposal to introduce trial by jury; "the arguments turned on this very point, and in consequence the numerical rules were abolished." 7 Wigmore, *op. cit.* n. 107, at 253 n. 30. In addition, the system of legal proof was in conflict with the dominant ideological motif: *egalité*. Consider this motif in relation to the rule giving greater weight to the testimony of a nobleman than to that of a commoner.

111. The principle of free evaluation of evidence does not permit arbitrary or irrational evaluation. Italian law requires the court to state in writing the reason why it has chosen one version of the facts over another. A failure to explain sufficiently, or a contradictory explanation, is ground for reversal by the Corte di cassazione. See Cappelletti and Perillo, *op. cit.* n. 1, at ch. 8, n. 106, n. 287.

112. But see, in defense of the basis of the system, Furno, *Contributo alla teoria della prova legale* (1940).

113. See Cappelletti and Perillo, *op. cit.* n. 1, at ch. 1, n. 136.

114. *Id.,* at ch. 1, n. 137.

tenure was insecure, and they were influenced by outright pressure from, or a tradition of deference to, the politically powerful. It was an era in which men were gradually emerging from barbarism. Better rigidity and formalism than the dangers of arbitrary decisions.[115]

Similar rules were developed in England once trial by ordeal and trial by battle had been eliminated.[116] However, the existence of the jury impeded the full development of binding rules for the evaluation of evidence.[117] Another kind of rule was developed: the exclusionary rules that still prevent the admission of relevant evidence predetermined in the abstract to be unworthy of faith.[118] The exclusionary rules of England had a common foundation with the system of legal proof of Europe. They both had as a basis a suspicion of the ability of the triers of fact to weigh relevant evidence freely. Since there was a common foundation for the two systems of evidence, it is perhaps not surprising that parallel and almost simultaneous reforms began on the Continent at the time of the French Revolution, and in England at about the same time, with the attacks on the legal order made by Jeremy Bentham and his followers.

Despite many reforms, common law systems retained many ancient and often unjustifiable relics of the medieval system.[119] In the civil law system, the transition

115. A noted German legal historian wrote that from the time of the decline of the Roman Empire until the legal renaissance that began in Italy in the twelfth and thirteenth centuries, one cannot speak of impartiality in the administration of justice. In order to repair this centuries-long lack of impartiality, rules of law designed to guarantee judicial objectivity were central to the Italian legal reforms of the thirteenth century; these reforms were adopted in Germany in the fifteenth and sixteenth centuries. Engelmann, *Die Wiedergeburt der Rechtskultur in Italien durch die wissenschaftliche Lehre* 62 *et seq.* (1938).

116. On trial by battle and ordeal in England and its disappearance, see 1 Holdsworth, *A History of English Law* 308 *et seq.* (1922); Maitland, *The Constitutional History of England* (1st ed. 1908); Barrett, *Crime and Punishment in England* (1998).

117. The "numerical" or "quantitative system" of evaluation of evidence reached the courts of common law later, took hold less strongly, and was eliminated earlier than elsewhere, primarily because of its incompatibility with the jury system. See 1 Wigmore, *op. cit.* n. 107, at 236; 7 Wigmore, at 241 *et seq.*, 250 *et seq.* Because of the absence of a jury, the system of legal proof took hold more strongly and for a longer period in English equity. See 1 Wigmore, at 15–16; 7 Wigmore, at 248 *et seq.* See also the quotation from Bonnier appearing in Cappelletti and Perillo, *op. cit.* n. 1, at ch. 1, n. 139.

118. See Millar, *Civil Procedure of the Trial Court in Historical Perspective* 23 (1952).

119. More of these remnants, such as the dead man's statutes, remain in force in the United States than in England. On the slower progress of reform of the law of evidence in the United States, see 2 Cappelletti, *op. cit.* n. 69, at 466–71.

from the system of legal proof to the principle of free evaluation of evidence remained incomplete.[120] The decisory oath continued in force in Italy, France, Spain, and Holland; it was abolished in Austria (1895) and Germany (1933). Almost everywhere, admissions are considered to be conclusive evidence. In Italy,[121] France,[122] Spain,[123] and elsewhere, numerous legal presumptions continue in force. In addition, in France, Italy, and some other systems, there are bars to the admission of testimony. Finally, in Italy, Spain, and a few other countries, parties, their spouses, in-laws, relatives, and interested third persons are disqualified as witnesses.[124]

While the law of evidence was being transformed, other aspects of adjective law were also undergoing change. A great part of the discussions on European legal doctrine in the nineteenth and early twentieth centuries centered on the ideas of concentration, immediacy, and orality in civil procedure. Reformers drew largely from historical discoveries about the nature of classical Roman procedure; they urged the adoption of a revised system of procedure based upon these three central ideas, along with the corollary idea of free evaluation of evidence. The German Zivilprozessordnung of 1877, the Austrian Zivilprozessordnung of 1895, and other procedural reforms were enacted under the banner of these ideas. In Italy, the battle was led by Giuseppe Chiovenda, the founder of the modern school of Italian proceduralists; his students were scholars such as Piero Calamandrei, Enrico Redenti, Antonio Segni, and Enrico T. Liebman.

---

120. It seems clear that in a system in which great trust is placed in the triers of fact, a case-by-case approach to the admission and weighing of the evidence is to be preferred. In classical Roman law the *judex* could consider hearsay and was free to weigh the evidence in accordance with his prudent judgment. See Buckland and McNair, *Roman Law and Common Law* 402 (2d ed. 1952), and other references in Cappelletti and Perillo, *op. cit.* n. 1, at ch. 1, n. 145.

121. See 4.13.

122. Code civil arts. 1349 *et seq.*

123. See Guasp, *Derecho procesal civil* 390–91 (1956); Prieto-Castro, *Derecho procesal civil* 458 (1964).

124. See 4.13 and the French Code de procedure civile art. 262. In France, more than in Germany or Austria, but less than in Italy and far less than in Spain, there are remnants of the system of legal proof. The common observation that American law, unlike the civil law, contains "a system of rules of evidence binding upon the tribunal itself" therefore cannot fully be accepted. The observation is made, e.g., in David and deVries 25, *The French Legal System* 76 (1958) (comparing only French and American law).

If the principles of concentration, immediacy, orality, and free evaluation of evidence have not been implemented completely in other countries,[125] they have been implemented even less in Italy by the code enacted in 1940 and effective in 1942.[126] The reasons why the Italian code lags behind, say, the Austrian Code of 1895, are complex and cannot be analyzed here.[127] In addition to containing various vestiges of the old rules of legal proof, the code also carried over to a large extent the practice of dividing a proceeding into numerous discontinuous hearings. The code attempted to mitigate the effects of this discontinuity by rigidly prescribing the time periods within which procedural acts were to be completed. These periods were fixed in the abstract without reference to the concrete exigencies of the particular case. Mediacy rather than immediacy of proof-taking was substantially preserved but mitigated. Under previous law, evidence was taken by a delegate judge who was not necessarily a member of the adjudicating panel. Under the present code, the examining judge hears all of the evidence and participates in the adjudicating panel so that the other two judges may benefit from his oral report as well as the written record of the case. In great measure, procedure continues to be written. Reliance is placed primarily on the attorney's briefs and documen-

125. See Kaplan, von Mehren, and Schaefer, *op. cit.* n. 20, at 1470–72, especially on the stretching out of proceedings into a series of court sessions in Germany. At 1471 the authors state, "All this creates a danger of undue protraction of litigation, which calls for a large power of control in the court over the pace of the lawsuit." The problem of protraction is more serious in Italy, where courts have far fewer powers of control than in Germany. See Sereni, *op. cit.* n. 100, at 378, 383, 385. For France, see David and de Vries, *op. cit.* n. 124, at 77. ("In non-criminal actions, the word 'trial' is inappropriate; the securing of evidence, the development of the legal contentions, the definition of relevant issues, take place gradually over an extended period of time until the case is ready for final determination; the record so compiled is then submitted to the full court.")

126. The code was the product of decades of preparation. Especially noteworthy is the proposed draft, prepared by Professor Chiovenda in 1919, in which orality and its companion principles were coherently implemented. It was not enacted. Its text and accompanying report is published in 2 Chiovenda, *Saggi di diritto processuale civile* 1 (1931).

127. In part, the conservatism of the code can be explained by the fact that it was prepared primarily by nonfascist legal scholars under a fascist government. To reduce official political and ideological pressure upon the courts, the draftsmen preferred to stress the noncreative function of adjudication, the certainty of law, and rigid separation of powers. They also preferred to conserve rules limiting judicial discretion in evaluating evidence and controlling the pace of a lawsuit. For a more detailed analysis, see Cappelletti and Perillo, *op. cit.* n. 1, at 1.38–1.39. See also notes 178–79 and accompanying text below.

tary evidence. Oral evidence is reduced to writing, and because it is often taken at numerous hearings, with only one of the three adjudicators present at any one hearing, the decision is never the result of the immediate impact of oral evidence and argument.

Certainly, the current Code of Civil Procedure eliminated many of the more serious defects of the old *jus commune* that had not already been eliminated by the Code of 1865 and subsequent amendments. The Code of 1940 (constantly amended in order to reach more effectiveness, up to the latest Law 134/2012) enacted some major technical improvements—for example, its provisions concerning the voidness of defective procedural acts,[128] the form and means of attack on court judgments,[129] default, special proceedings, forced executions, and other matters. Nevertheless, many of the fundamental defects of the old procedure were not eliminated. Nor were they removed by the reform law of July 14, 1950, no. 581 (effective January 1, 1951) or subsequent changes. In some instances these changes mitigated the defects of the Code;[130] in others, however, they introduced new defects.[131]

In conclusion, Italian civil procedure, and especially the rules governing ordinary proceedings on the merits, may still be considered as a modernized and refined version of the procedure of the medieval *jus commune*. The medieval matrix

128. See 4.17.

129. The distinction between decisions made in the form of *sentenze* and those made in the form of *ordinanze* is fundamental. *Ordinanze* are usually rendered by the examining judge rather than the adjudicating panel. Their purpose is to keep order within the proceeding. *Ordinanze* are used to schedule the next hearing and to rule on the admissibility of evidence and like matters. An *ordinanza* is rendered in rather simple form and is not subject to the kinds of attack that may be made against judgments. *Ordinanze* are not preclusive and may be modified or revoked by the panel or the examining judge. Codice di procedura civile arts. 177–78. Under the Code of 1865, many of the rulings now made by *ordinanze* were made by interlocutory judgments (*sentenze interlocutorie*). These were immediately subject to appeal and review in the Corte di cassazione, with the deplorable consequence that every case could proliferate into a number of separate proceedings. See Cappelletti and Perillo, *op. cit.* n. 1, at 1.39; 8.02, esp. note 20 and accompanying text.

130. It mitigated, for example, the too-rigid preclusions attendant upon failure to take procedural steps within given periods. However, this mitigation was not accompanied by greater discretionary powers of judges to fix peremptorily required periods for action based on the concrete circumstances of the case; therefore, there has been an increase in problems concerning the discontinuity of proceedings.

131. See Cappelletti and Perillo, *op. cit.* n. 1, at 1.40.

is evident, often too evident, even though its characteristics, such as the system of legal proof, have been mitigated by legislative, judicial, and doctrinal efforts at reform.

Procedure is only an instrument to arrive at a decision. Those Italian procedural scholars who are most aware of modern trends in philosophical and legal thought concerning the decision-making process are working toward a complete overturning of the inherited defects in procedure.[132] Nevertheless, if the Italian system may still be considered the most interesting and the most representative of all the civil law systems, this is not only because Italy is the place where the civil law originated,[133] but also because Italian civil procedure has not made a complete break with its great past.[134]

Italian procedure is, at the same time, composite, complex, and often contradictory. Instruments developed by modern and refined doctrinal studies stand beside such archaic relics as the decisory oath and the formal interrogatory. In many regions of Italy, builders digging foundations for modern structures often find the remnants of ancient civilizations. Similarly, under many Italian legal institutions lie foundations built hundreds or thousands of years ago, and all the fervor of modern reformers often fails to convince the tradition-minded that new foundations are needed.

4.16 *Attacks on Judgments.* The most important and most frequently used attack on judgments is the appeal; the appeal is addressed to the court that is one step higher than the court rendering the attacked judgment.[135]

---

132. On the work of procedural scholars, see 4.19.

133. On the expansion of the *jus commune*, see 1.16, and Calasso, *Introduzione al diritto commune* 303 *et seq.* (1951); Koschaker, *Europa und das römische Recht* 124 *et seq.* (3d ed. 1958); Vinogradoff, *Roman Law in Medieval Europe* (3d ed. 1929).

134. French procedure, although springing from the *jus commune*, traditionally followed local and national adaptations, reflected primarily in the Ordonnance of 1667, drafted by Colbert and promulgated by Louis XIV, and often called the Code Louis. The Napoleonic Code of Civil Procedure of 1806 is still in effect, although often amended, with important amendments enacted in 1958. It is described by David and de Vries, *op. cit.* n. 124, at 13 (see also 11–12), as "a barely revised edition of the Ordonnance of 1667 prepared by Colbert."

135. Appeals unfold in three stages, in a way similar to the unfolding of a case in a court of first instance. The principal distinction is that, on appeal, decisions on the admissibility of evidence are made by the adjudicating panel rather than by the examining judge.

The fundamental characteristic of appeal in the Italian system, in radical contrast to Anglo-American systems, is that the appellate court is permitted to exercise substitutionary power as well as revisionary power.[136] New claims may not be raised on appeal; new defenses may not be asserted, nor new evidence introduced.[137] Another important rule is that judgments ordinarily may not be enforced until an appeal has been decided, or the parties have waived—by the passage of time or otherwise[138]—their rights to appeal.[139] Because of these rules, a very high percentage of judgments, by Anglo-Saxon standards, have historically been appealed.

Together with ordinary appeals there is the *ricorso in cassazione*, application for review in the Corte di cassazione.[140] The Constitution guarantees all litigants a right to review in this court.[141] Any appellate judgment and any judgment that

---

However, once the decision is made, the evidence is taken, as in courts of first instance, by the examining judge. Codice di procedura civile art. 356.

136. Similar observations have been made about appeal (*Berufung*) in Germany. See Kaplan, von Mehren, and Schaefer, *op. cit.* n. 20, at 1443, 1453–54. To the answers these authors give to the questions "Why should not the appeal be confined to issues of law?" and "Why should it not at least exclude new facts?," we would like to add a historical answer. The status of appeal as more than a review and as a new proceeding, although not ancient, is strongly rooted in tradition. Its basis is the principle of *doppio grado di giurisdizione*, imported from France, according to which a second level of adjudication is considered a matter of right. It is still considered by many in Italy and in other European countries to constitute a fundamental guarantee of a fair hearing. See, e.g., Catala and Terré, *Procédure civile et voies d'exécution* 33 (1965). In addition, the absence of juries eliminates any real barrier preventing appellate courts from readjudicating the factual issues. A leading Italian procedural scholar has criticized this double level of adjudication as no longer responsive to the needs of modern society. 2 Satta, *Commentario al codice di procedura civile* (part II) 183 (1959–62).

137. Codice di procedura civile, art. 345, as amended in 1950, 1990, and 2009.

138. An appeal may not be initiated after the passage of ten to thirty days from service of the judgment. Codice di procedura civile, arts. 325, 326.

139. Codice di procedura civile arts. 282–83, 337. A money judgment may, however, be recorded in order to create a judgment lien even if it is on, or still subject to, appeal. Codice civile art. 2818.

140. Codice di procedura civile art. 360 ss. The procedure has been recently renewed and reformed with the provisons of D.Lgs. Feb. 2, 2006, n. 40; L. May 14, 2005, n. 80; and L. June 18, 2009, n. 69. Ianniruberto and Morcavallo, *Il nuovo giudizio di cassazione* (2d ed. 2010); Cipriani, *La riforma del giudizio di cassazione* (2009); Sassani, *Il nuovo giudizio di Cassazione*, in *Riv. Dir. Proc.*, 2006, 238.

141. Constitution art. 111. See 2.10 and 2.11.

is not appealable[142] can be made the subject of an application for review. An application made after sixty days from service of the judgment is barred.[143] Unlike appellate courts, the Corte di cassazione is limited to reviewing errors of law; it may not review errors of fact. If the application for review is well founded, and the errors not merely harmless,[144] the Court quashes (*cassa*, literally, "breaks") the judgment below. It may not, however, render a judgment of its own. Upon quashing, the Court remands the case to a different court on the same level as the court that rendered the judgment. The court to which the case is remanded is bound to apply the legal principles announced by the Corte di cassazione.[145]

The importance of review in this high court is demonstrated both by the very frequent recourse to it[146] and by the importance of its decisions as precedents.[147] The present role of the court can best be understood from a historical perspective.[148]

The institution of *cassazione* was born with the French Revolution. Prototypes, however, preceded the revolution. In medieval Italian statutes the idea of a *querela nullitatis* had been implemented and had subsequently been accepted by the European *jus commune*. The *querela* involved the review of a judgment for errors of law and differed from appeal in that factual findings were not questioned. In France, a *demande en cassation* similar to the *querela nullitatis* could be made to the sovereign, who would assign the demand to the Conseil des Parties, a section of the Council of Government. The decisions of the *parlements*, the courts of last resort in a number of French cities, were subject to this review. The institution of the *demande en cassation* was an outgrowth of the struggle between the sovereigns, bent on centralizing the realm, and the *parlements*, struggling for retention of local autonomy. The sovereign's power of cassation was one method of guaranteeing enforcement of sovereign enactments.

142. In some exceptional cases, no appeal is permitted. These, however, may be reviewed by the Corte di cassazione. Codice di procedura civile arts. 339, 360, para. 1. If an appeal was available but was not taken within the time allotted, an application to the Corte di cassazione is not permitted.

143. Codice di procedura civile arts. 325, 326.

144. Codice di procedura civile art. 384, para. 2.

145. Codice di procedura civile art. 384, para. 1, provides: "The Court, when it approves an application based on violation or false application of rules of law, announces the principle that the court of remand must follow."

146. See 2.05.

147. See 7.11.

148. For a comprehensive historical survey, see Calamandrei, n. 158.

The origin of modern cassation is in the ideology of Rousseau and Montes-quieu. To them, law was to be all-powerful, all citizens were to be equal in the eyes of the law, and legislative powers were to be rigidly reserved to the legislature. The judge was to be a passive and inanimate *bouche de la loi*, an official who would ap-ply mechanically the pure text of legislation. Pursuant to these ideas, the Tribunal de Cassation was created by the Decree of November 27–December 1, 1790, as a nonjudicial constitutional control organ. The function of the tribunal was to see that the courts strictly applied the letter of the law and did not legislate. The insti-tution of a tribunal of this kind typifies the mistrust of the judiciary that animated revolutionary legislation. Mistrust led the revolutionary lawmakers to prohibit any interpretation of law by judges.[149] This absurd prohibition was abolished by the Code Napoléon. The Tribunal de Cassation was essentially a watchdog body in-stituted to protect the powers of the legislature from judicial usurpation, but the principle of separation of powers required that the Tribunal refrain from usurping judicial powers.[150] Consequently, it was permitted neither to interpret the law in a manner binding upon the courts nor to adjudicate a case. The adjudication was to be made by a court upon remand from the Tribunal de Cassation. Since the court was free to decide the case in the free exercise of its own judgment, it might again make the same decision that was censured by the Tribunal de Cassation. If the decision was once again quashed and then reinstated by the court on the second remand, a *référé obligatoire* to the legislature was necessary. The legislature would enact a binding interpretation of the law applicable to the case, thereby ending the tennis match between the courts and the Tribunal de Cassation.

As the ardor of revolutionary ideology ebbed, the Tribunal de Cassation, re-named the Cour de Cassation, was transformed. With the recognition of the judi-cial power of interpretation by the Code Napoléon, the Cour became the supreme judicial organ with power to review errors of law committed by lower courts. The Law of April 1, 1837, abolished the *référé obligatoire* and provided that if the first court of remand fails to apply the law as interpreted by the Cour de Cassation, the second court of remand must accept as binding the decision reached by this

149. The legislature (*Corps législatif*) was the only body permitted to interpret the law. Whenever a court had doubts about the proper interpretation of the law, it could apply to the legislature for a decree authoritatively interpreting the law. *Référé facultatif*, as this procedure was known, was abolished by the Code Napoléon.

150. See Calamandrei, *Cassazione civile*, in 2 *Novissimo digesto italiano* 1053, 1060–61 (1958).

body after a second review by a larger panel of judges. The decision, at least de jure, is only binding in the particular case. Despite this limitation, a decision made by a court which is supreme and national and which may review the decisions of all other courts inevitably exerts tremendous influence on the decision of similar cases. Starting with the Law of April 1, 1837, "in a constantly more conscious and decisive manner, the Cour de Cassation became what it is today, that is, the Supreme Court . . . ; and it assumed in full that function which today the practice and the doctrine assign to it: that of developing a system of case law" (*élaborer une jurisprudence*).[151] In other words, it has accepted the role of promoting the uniformity of judicial interpretation of the law.

Italy, in the Code of Civil Procedure of 1865, adopted the institution of *cassazione* with substantially the same characteristics that had been developed in France. However, the Italians, until 1923, had five courts (at Turin, Florence, Rome, Naples, and Palermo) of last resort. The Italian Code of Civil Procedure of 1940 accentuated the positive effect of decisions of the Corte di cassazione: the legal principles determined by this court must be applied the first time a case is remanded, and no longer only upon a second remand. Although the Constitution confirms the status of the Corte di cassazione as a judicial organ,[152] its fundamental purpose, as stated in article 65 of the Ordinamento giudiziario, the basic law governing court organization, is that of assuring "the exact observance and the uniform interpretation of the law, the unity of national law."

Given the role of the Corte di cassazione, it seems clear that the traditional contradistinction between the common law and the civil law—made on the basis of the one's possession of the principle of *stare decisis* and the other's lack of it—is not completely based on fact. On the one hand, every common lawyer, especially an American, realizes that the principle has lost its rigidity. On the other hand, the institution of *cassazione* and similar institutions in other civil law countries constitute explicit recognition of the need for uniformity of judicial interpretation of law. In Italy, an office of the Corte di cassazione draws from each of its decisions one or more "*massime*," or headnotes, that express in the form of abstract rules of law the basis of the decision. The comfort an attorney can find in an unequivocal

151. *Id.*, at 1061.

152. Constitution arts. 102, 104, 106, 111. See also article 1 of the Ordinamento giudiziario, Royal Decree of Jan. 30, 1941, no. 12.

and uncontradicted *massima* favorable to his client's position is certainly greater than he can find in an unclear legislative text.

It would be improper, however, to go too far in the opposite direction. By law, precedents, even if set by the Corte di cassazione in united sections, are not binding.[153] In similar cases they have persuasive authority, expressed in the maxim *auctoritas rerum similiter judicatarum* (the interpretative authority of cases that have been similarly decided), but not normative force. A decision is normative only in the concrete case and only to the extent of its res judicata force. Outside the concrete case, every court, whether the lowest or the highest, has the power and the responsibility to apply the law as it thinks it should be applied. "Judges," the Constitution solemnly declares, "are subject only to the law."[154] The rule expressed in the maxim *auctoritas rerum similiter judicatarum* cannot, therefore, be placed among the formal sources of law, although, de facto, Italian courts do exercise law-making power. Legislative foresight is almost always limited and blurred. Consequently, courts and doctrine are not, and cannot be, limited to mechanical and passive interpretive roles. They must exercise the creative and responsible functions of taking abstract statutory provisions and making them concrete. The courts, with the doctrine, must adapt law to the changing needs of society.[155] In the final analysis, these functions de facto involve the creation of law.[156] Modern Ital-

---

153. A panel of nine judges, selected from among judges of the ordinary sections, is known as *sezioni unite*—united sections. One of the grounds upon which such a panel may meet to decide the case is the existence of contradictory precedents for the point in issue; art. 65 R.D. Jan. 30, 1941, n. 12, as modified by L. Aug. 8, 1977, n. 532. Codice di procedura civile art. 374, para. 2. For a historical perspective, see Acampora, *Sulla composizione e sulla competenza delle Sezioni Unite della Corte di cassazione*, in *Riv. Dir. Proc.*, 1957, 393; Pizzorusso, *Corte di cassazione*, in *Enc. Giur.*, XI (1989), at 7.

154. Constitution art. 101, para. 2.

155. See Cappelletti, *L'attività e i poteri del giudice costituzionale in rapporto con il loro fine generico*, 3 *Scritti giuridici in memoria di Piero Calamandrei* 83, 128 *et seq.* (1958). This work contains references to other discussions of this point and a critique of the old and superseded view which sees the function of interpretation as a purely mechanical and syllogistic one and which views the judge as a mere spokesman of the law in accordance with Montesquieu's concept. See 7.10.

156. The observations concerning the French system in David and de Vries, *op. cit.* n. 124, at 113–21, are for the most part applicable to the Italian. The authors state that "decisions of the courts cannot be classed as a formal source of law in France," but "despite the absence of a formal doctrine of *stare decisis*, there is a strong tendency on the part of the French courts, like those of other countries, to follow precedents, especially those of the higher

ian doctrine is well aware of the creative responsibility placed upon it and upon the courts. (The present state of Italian interpretive theory is discussed in Chapter 7.)

Perhaps the best summary of the situation is that of the Constitutional Court in its decision 184/86 which stated the doctrine of the "living law" (*diritto vivente*). Under this doctrine, in order to state the proper meaning of a statute or of an article of the Code, a judge must take into account the way the norm has been interpreted in previous cases. Law is to be thought of as a living and evolving body in which preceding interpretations lie together with the original text and represent the constant unfolding of its meaning. Moreover an actual decision is deemed sufficiently motivated if the judge is making reference to "interpretive precedents," whereas if the judge wants to depart from these precedents, he must give a full, detailed, and complete opinion on why he thinks those precedents do not accurately represent the law. In this way it is much easier for a judge to "follow" the precedents than to depart from them.

Notwithstanding the changes described in the preceding paragraphs, the importance of legislation and the systematic organization of legislation, particularly in codes, should not be underrated. Few jurists in Italy or elsewhere in Europe would seriously think of doing away with the codes, even considering the sometimes doctrinaire abstractions they contain. If legislation does not always provide a sure basis for the solution of a concrete problem, it usually gives the skilled jurist

---

courts." Precedents are not binding, and, indeed, "the decisions of a court . . . can be set aside by the *Cour de Cassation* for 'lack of legal basis' (*défaut de base légale*) if its only source is a prior court decision." Nevertheless, precedent has great persuasive force. "'Persuasive' or 'binding'—the words indicate only a difference in degree of predictability through reference to prior decision. The French judge, not formally bound to follow decisions of superior courts concededly in point, may in theory be freer to disregard a precedent. At least, the absence of the necessity for justifying a decision in terms of existing case law eliminates the elaborate common law techniques of 'distinguishing' cases and of discovering the 'rationale,' the 'holding,' and the 'dictum,' and also the highly detailed statements of fact in the opinion. . . . The *Cour de Cassation* can, of course, always overrule its own prior decisions. But it is equally certain that it will not do so without weighty reasons. . . . The attitude of the lower courts toward decisions of the *Cour de Cassation* is in substance quite similar to that of the lower courts in common law jurisdictions toward decisions of superior courts. Even a single precedent established by the *Cour de Cassation* will usually be followed, though it cannot be cited as the basis for the decision. Certain factors may, however, induce the lower courts to seek reasons for deciding contrary to a prior decision of the *Cour de Cassation*. One such factor may be the expectation that an old decision of the *Cour de Cassation* would not be followed by that court in the light of new conditions."

a highly useful guide to a solution. Although people are no longer as suspicious of judges as they were at the time of the French Revolution, sad recent experience has shown that judicial arbitrariness can be more pernicious than legislative arbitrariness. Judicial arbitrariness, often unsolicited but more often a result of executive pressure, was given a theoretical basis in Germany by the school of "free law" (*freies Recht*), and later by the fanatical mysticism of the "*Führerprinzip*," according to which the fundamental norm to be applied by the judge was the will of the national leader. Arbitrary legislation is usually abstract in terms and general in scope, and it does not act as directly upon the liberty, dignity, and property of the individual as an arbitrary judicial decision. During the fascist period, the less conforming sector of Italian doctrine bravely did battle for the "principle of legality,"[157] for "certainty" in the law, and against the vesting of discretionary powers in the courts. Its purpose was to prevent judicial arbitrariness and to protect judges from political pressures, which were especially to be feared during that period.[158]

In addition to appeal and review in the Corte di cassazione, three less frequently used means of attack on judgments are available. Revocation is the reopening of a judgment that was based upon one of several specified deficient elements, such as fraud of the party or of a judge, perjurious or manufactured evidence, or the lack of decisive evidence, which has subsequently been found.[159] Third-party op-

---

157. The principle of legality, pursuant to which judges are to adjudicate in accordance with law (*secundum legem*) rather than in accordance with conscience (*secundum conscientiam*), prevailed in the Code of Civil Procedure. Article 113, para. 1, provides, "In deciding a case, the court must follow the rules of law, except when the law gives it the power to decide in accordance with equity." A decision in accordance with equity involves a decision in accordance with equity." A decision in accordance with equity involves a decision in accordance with "justice in the concrete case" and has little practical importance except in small claims cases before the *conciliatori*. Codice di procedura civile art. 113, para. 2, art. 114. It has little or nothing in common with the idea of equity in the common law sense.

158. See the writings of Calamandrei, written in the crucial years of 1938 – 42, published in the Rivista di diritto processuale civile and reprinted in volume 5 of Calamandrei, *Studi sul processo civile* 285 *et seq.* (see also 67 *et seq.* and the important position taken at 79 – 90) (1947). See also Lopez De Oñate, *La certezza del diritto* (1942). The defense of judicial and scholarly independence consisted in making a rigid distinction between political and interpretive activity. Interpretive activity was alleged to be a purely technical process divorced from the political purposes of legislation.

159. Codice di procedura civile arts. 395 – 403. Revocation is available in Germany where it is called *Wiederaufnahme des Verfahrens* (Zivilprozessordnung §§ 578 *et seq.*), and in France where it is known as *requite civile* (Code de procédure civile arts. 480 *et seq.*).

position (*opposizione di terzo*)[160] is an attack brought by a stranger whose rights are prejudiced by the judgment of a proceeding or by a successor in interest or a creditor of one of the parties when the judgment is the product of the parties' fraud or collusion. *Regolamento di competenza* permits immediate review in the Corte di cassazione of rulings on the issue of the competence of the court in which an action is brought, thus obtaining a definitive determination of the issue to avoid the useless unfolding of an entire proceeding in an incompetent court.[161]

4.17 *Voidness of Procedural Acts.* Connected with the subject of attacks on judgment is the subject of the voidness of procedural acts. A fundamental rule governing judgments—except in the very exceptional case of inexistence of a judgment[162]—is that the voidness of a judgment may be availed of only within the limits of, and in accordance with the rules governing, the means of attacks on judgment.[163] No collateral attack is permitted. Therefore, if a judgment is appealable and no appeal is taken within the time fixed by law, any nullity of the judgment is cured. One of the consequences of this rule is that if the court lacked jurisdiction, failure to make the appropriate direct attack will cure the absence of jurisdiction.

The curability of errors in this manner is but one manifestation of an antiformalistic trend expressed in the Code of Civil Procedure. The trend, as the rules of evidence show, by no means abolishes all formalism. However, other antiformalistic rules find expression in the Code. Article 156 states that a procedural act containing a defect that the law penalizes by declaring the act void is nevertheless cured if it has achieved its purpose.

160. Codice di procedura civile arts. 404–8. It corresponds to the French *tierce opposition* (Code de procédure civile arts. 474 *et seq.*). Revocation, in many cases, and third-party opposition are permitted even after a judgment has become *res judicata*. The period in which either of these remedies must be applied for begins in these cases from the moment of discovery of the fraud or other facts that form the basis of the application. Other forms of attack are ordinarily barred a short time after service of the judgment.

161. Codice di procedura civile arts. 42–50. Similar to *regolamento di competenza* is *regolamento di giurisdizione* (Codice di procedura civile art. 41), which, however, is not a means of attacking a judgment but of obtaining a prior ruling on the issue of Italian jurisdiction over the parties.

162. The law expressly provides for only one instance in which a judgment is inexistent: a judgment that has not been signed by the court. Codice di procedura civile art. 161, para. 2.

163. Codice di procedura civile art. 161, para. 1.

Consequently, service of process made improperly is valid if it achieves its purpose of notifying the defendant of the commencement of the action.[164] A citation—the instrument that states the plaintiff's claim and summons the defendant into court—although defective, is cured if it serves the purpose of causing the defendant to appear in the action.[165] The defendant may, however, appear in court for the sole purpose of raising the defect of the service, paralyzing in this way the possibility of its cure. We see here the interplay of an antiformalistic principle balanced by a formalistic rule.

Antiformalism also finds expression in the rule, subject to some exceptions, that the voidness of any procedural act may be raised neither by the court on its own motion nor by the party who caused the defect but only by his adversary and only in the first motion or other step following the defective act or notice of the act.[166] The result is that defects not raised quickly are cured.

4.18 *Effects of a Judgment.* The principal effects of a judgment are res judicata and enforceability.[167] In Italy a judgment does not become res judicata until all ordinary means of attack upon the judgment have been exhausted or have become unavailable by lapse of time or waiver.[168] Since in the United States, the prevailing view is that final judgments of trial courts become res judicata when entered,[169] and the means of attack on judgments are more limited,[170] it is apparent that a judgment rendered by an Italian court of first instance is less durable and of lesser consequence.

---

164. Codice di procedura civile art. 160.

165. Codice di procedura civile art. 164.

166. Codice di procedura civile art. 157.

167. There are also certain secondary effects, such as the lien of a recorded judgment, available before a judgment becomes enforceable. See Cappelletti and Perillo, *op. cit.* n. 1, at 9.12.

168. The term "ordinary means of attack" refers to the attacks on judgments, such as appeal and review in the Corte di cassazione, that are available prior to a judgment's becoming res judicata. Codice di procedura civile art. 324. Extraordinary means—on serious and exceptional grounds—are available after res judicata status has been acquired.

169. See Note, *Developments in the Law—Res Judicata*, 65 Harv. L. Rev. 818, 836 (1952).

170. New evidence may not usually be admitted on appeal; also, in the United States (in contrast to Italy), there is usually no absolute right to review by the highest court of the state or of the nation.

Once an Italian judgment has become res judicata, however, it is more difficult to set aside than a res judicata judgment in the United States.[171] For example, in Italy a res judicata judgment may not be set aside on the ground that Italian jurisdiction was lacking or that the court was incompetent.[172] The parties have had ample opportunity to raise the issues of competence and jurisdiction, and to a certain extent, so has the court. Not having raised the issue, the need to put an end to litigation (*ne lites aeternae fiant*) prevails over other considerations. Here we can see the conflict between the value of certainty and the value of justice. It would be utopian for a legal system always to place justice over certainty; each legal system resolves the conflict—often in ways that are not profoundly different—in a manner that it deems most desirable and expedient.[173]

The basic rule of enforcement is that ordinarily no judgment may be enforced except a judgment of an appellate court or a judgment of a court of first instance that has not been appealed and is no longer subject to appeal. It is to be stressed that such judgments have not yet necessarily become res judicata and that review in the Corte di cassazione and other ordinary means of attack may still be available. This rule is subject to a number of important exceptions, such as credits arising out of a labor relation (art. 409 cpc) or cases on leaseholds (art. 447-bis cpc.).

---

171. Means of reopening a judgment after it has become res judicata are available only in extraordinary circumstances, and collateral attack is never possible. See Sereni, *op. cit.* n. 100, at 106. Moreover, the defense of res judicata must be considered by any level of court on its own motion at any state of the proceeding, and the court's failure to consider the defense constitutes reversible error. Cappelletti and Perillo, *op. cit.* n. 1, at 9.13. "The idea that we are here concerned with an interest which is primarily that of the State—*interest reipublicae ut sit finis litium*—has prompted perhaps a majority of the continental systems to remove the matter from the control of the parties, as far as practicable, by requiring the court to take the fact of res judicata into consideration on its own motion." Millar, *The Premises of the Judgment as Res Judicata in Continental and Anglo-American Law*, 39 Mich. L. Rev. 1, 8 (1940); Cohn, *Die materielle Rechtskraft im englischen Recht*, 1 *Festschrift für H. C. Nipperdei* 875, 878–79, 885–86 (1965).

172. See Cappelletti and Perillo, *op. cit.* n. 1, at ch. 9, n. 93 and accompanying text.

173. An interesting difference between the common law and civil law systems concerns the concept of collateral estoppel. See Millar, *op. cit.* n. 171, at 1–36, 238–66; Cohn, *op. cit.* n. 171, at 887. In Italy, and in civil law systems in general, res judicata involves bars and mergers similar to those in the common law but does not encompass collateral estoppel. See Rosenberg and Weinstein, *Elements of Civil Procedure* 925 (1962).

Forced execution of judgments in Italy involves a proceeding separate and distinct from the proceeding in which the judgment to be enforced was obtained.[174] The autonomous nature of enforcement proceedings is partially related to the fact that a judgment or other determination of a court[175] is not the only kind of instrument that may be enforced by execution. A whole series of nonjudicial instruments, mostly promissory notes and other negotiable instruments, may be enforced without either an ordinary action on the merits or a summary proceeding.

Italian law deems these instruments to have such probative force that no preliminary adjudication is required to determine their enforceability. Due process is, however, protected by permitting the execution debtor to take a variety of steps to contest the validity of the instrument and to raise other defenses.[176]

Foreign, non-European judgments are not enforceable until they have been validated in a special proceeding.[177] European judgments, on the basis of EU treaties, are now normally enforceable in all conuntries of the European Union.

Enforcement proceedings are brought on the initiative of the interested party and unfold under the direction of a single judge, rather than a panel.[178] The judge is assisted by the court marshals and, if necessary, by the police.

Italian law has nothing comparable to the idea of civil contempt of court.[179] It has already been noted that certain judicial orders to produce evidence may be ignored with impunity.[180] Similarly, a judgment debtor may with impunity refuse

---

174. Enforcement proceedings are the subject of a three-volume study by Carnelutti, *Lezioni di diritto processuale civile. Processo di esecuzione* (1929–31). This work strongly influenced Book II of the Code of 1940–42, which governs these proceedings. For other references, see Satta, *L'esecuzione forzata* (4th ed. 1963); Fazzalari, *Processi di esecuzione forzata* (1986); Sassani et al., *L'esecuzione forzata* (2010); Campeis (a cura di), *esecuzioni civili* (2002); Di Nanni (acura di), *Codice dell'esecuzione forzata* (2009). For detailed treatment in English, see Cappelletti and Perillo, *op. cit.* n. 1, at ch. 12. In Italy, as in Germany, process in enforcement proceedings "may reach throughout the country." See Kaplan, von Mehren, and Schaefer, *op. cit.* n. 20, at 1257.

175. E.g., a summary ex parte decree. See 4.08.

176. Codice di procedura civile arts. 615–22. See Cappelletti and Perillo, *op. cit.* n. 1, at 12.10–12.13.

177. *Id.*, ch. 14; Cappelletti, *Il valore delle sentenze straniere in Italia*, 20 Revista di diritto processuale 192 (1965).

178. Codice di procedura civile art. 484.

179. See Pekelis, *op. cit.* n. 94, at 667 *et seq.*

180. See notes 70 and 76.

to obey a judgment ordering him to pay a sum of money or to do or refrain from doing a specified act.[181] If the judgment debtor refuses to obey the command of the judgment, his creditor may begin enforcement proceedings. However, these proceedings do not attempt to force the debtor by imprisonment or any other action. Arrest for debt once existed in Italy, but it has long since been abolished.[182] Except for certain specified crimes,[183] failure to obey a court order is not punishable.

With few and very limited exceptions, Italy has no form of enforcement similar to the French system of *astreintes*, which, like arrest for debt, is an indirect manner of coercion. An *astreinte* consists of an order to pay a specified total sum or a per diem sum as a penalty for failure to comply promptly with an order.[184]

In the absence of such coercive measures as contempt penalties and *astreintes*, instances of spontaneous compliance with judgments and instruments enforceable as judgments occur less frequently than they might otherwise. A creditor of a sum of money is therefore forced to have recourse to enforcement proceedings in which the wealth of the debtor may be attached and sold to satisfy his debts.[185] In some cases, instead of a sale, the debtor's property rights are vested in the creditor. Specific enforcement is also available. If specified property is the subject of the

181. This situation illustrates very dramatically the fact that an Italian judge possesses less authority than his American counterpart. See Pekelis, *op. cit.* n. 94, at 667 *et seq.*

182. Abolition was practically completed by the Law of Dec. 6, 1877, no. 4166. The "*contrainte par corps*" of French law, similar to the Italian law's arrest for debt, was almost completely suppressed in 1867. It was almost simultaneously abolished throughout Europe as part of a general humanitarian movement. See Marty and Raynaud, *Droit civil* (tome 2, vol. 1) 685 (1962); Ricca, *Debiti (arresto personale per)*, in 11 *Enciclopedia del diritto* 740 (1962). A residue remains in article 888 of the German Zivilprozessordnung. See Kaplan, von Mehren, and Schaefer, *op. cit.* n. 20, at 1258.

183. E.g., Codice penale art. 641 (fraudulent insolvency). See also Codice penale art. 388; Molari, *La tutela penale della condanna civile* (1960).

184. See Marty and Raynaud, *op. cit.* n. 182, at 687; Cornu, *Institutions judiciaires, procédure civile et voies d'exécution*, in 2 *Les systèmes de droit contemporains. Le droit français* 257, 289 (1960). The negative conclusion concerning the practical effectiveness of the *astreinte* in France (expressed by Pekelis, *op. cit.* n. 94, at 669 *et seq.*) must be reconsidered in the light of the "*développement massif*" which the *astreinte* has undergone in recent years. See Cornu, at 291; Marty and Raynaud, *op. cit.* n. 182, at 701 nn. 4, 5, and accompanying text.

185. Codice civile art. 2740, para. 1, provides, "The debtor answers for the performance of obligations with all his goods present and future." Almost identical is art. 2092 of the French Code civil. In both countries, however, certain goods are exempt from execution. E.g., Codice di procedura civile art. 514.

judgment or other legal instrument enforced, delivery of the property to the claimant, or eviction of the obligor from the property, may be enforced by physical means.[186] If a mandatory or restraining order is not complied with, a person will be appointed by the court to carry out the order.[187] With the aid of the police, this person may, for example, destroy a structure unlawfully built or build an edifice wrongfully not built by the obligor. All expenses of enforcement must be paid by the obligor.[188]

4.19 *Procedural Scholarship: Old and New Trends.*   After this overview of Italian civil procedure and evidence, a few brief observations about Italian procedural science may be useful.

For one hundred years or more, no complaint may properly be made in Italy, as it has been in France,[189] that procedure and evidence have been neglected by legal scholarship. Since the beginning of the last century, procedure has been one of the fields in which the doctrine has been most active and influential. The influence of legal scholarship was not limited to the drafting of the current code;[190] it has also had great impact on the interpretation and practice followed in the courts.[191]

186. Codice di procedura civile art. 605–11; Codice civile art. 2930.

187. Codice di procedura civile arts. 612–14; Codice civile arts. 2931–33. Similar are arts. 1143–44 of the French Code civile.

188. In certain cases, substitution of another person for the obligor is not possible. If the obligor was obligated to perform artistic services, for example, a substitute's performance might be unacceptable. In these cases, damages must be awarded. The obligation to perform a certain act is transformed into a pecuniary obligation subject to being enforced by execution upon the obligor's property.

189. See 1 David, in *Les systèmes de droit contemporains. Le droit français* 129–32 (1960); David and de Vries, *op. cit.* n. 124, at 73–74. See also Vizioz, *Observations sur l'étude de la procédure civile*, in *Etudes de procédure* 3 (1956). Although not very recent, the last essay is very interesting and still mostly valid. At page 18, note 2, Vizioz states that in 1904, Josef Kohler, with justification, wrote that no procedural science existed except in Germany, although a new school was beginning in Italy. Writing in 1927, Vizioz commented that the Italian school had become the equal of, and perhaps superior to, the German. Cf. similar statements in Cornu and Foyer, *Procédure civile* 25–26 (1958); Alcalá-Zamora, 17 Boletín del Instituto de Derecho Comparado de México 625 (1964).

190. Piero Calamandrei, Francesco Carnelutti, and Enrico Redenti, three of the most authoritative Italian legal scholars of this century, were primarily responsible for drafting the code. The relative absence of fascist ideology from the code can largely be attributed to their influence. Cf. Adams and Barile, *The Government of Republican Italy* 142 (1961); Cappelletti and Perillo, *op. cit.* n. 1, at 1.39.

191. Italian procedural doctrine exerts extraordinary influence in Latin America, where hundreds of Italian law books have been translated into Spanish and Portuguese and are

Procedural doctrine was traditionally marked by an excessive emphasis on systematic construction and dogmatics; often purely theoretical in structure, it was for a long time divorced from the social, economic, and ideological bases of the law, a trait that characterizes a great part of Italian legal science until the 1970s. Significantly, none of the numerous classical manuals or commentaries that dealt with civil procedure contained even a minimum reference to judicial statistics. Statistics, of course, are frequently indispensable to an understanding of the law in action. In recent years statistics have become more widely used and important in the ongoing effort to reshape civil procedure and thereby make the legal system more effective.

Notwithstanding the history above, proceduralists have been able to modify some of the characteristics of the traditional Italian doctrine, partly because many of them were active practitioners and therefore in contact with concrete problems, and partly because of the influence of a number of outstanding individuals in the area of procedural studies. The names of Giuseppe Chiovenda (d. 1937) and Piero Calamandrei (d. 1956) are especially significant. Two further generations of scholars, benefiting from the work of these pioneers, have continued to exert their influence even beyond the procedural field: the names of Crisanto Mandrioli, Claudio Consolo, and Francesco Luiso are but three of many that could be mentioned in this context.

4.20 *New Trends in the Law of Procedure: A Comparison in Outline.*   We have reviewed, if summarily, the principal historical developments and the present basic characteristics of civil procedure in Italy, attempting to place our analysis within a larger European framework. Perhaps we can try to draw some conclusions within an even larger comparative framework. We may ask, what are the current trends in adjective law in Italy and generally throughout the Western world? Without resorting to empty generalizations, can any common trends be identified?

Only a more complete analysis can adequately form the basis for a thorough exploration of these questions. However, it seems proper to list here some of the many elements that appear to support the thesis that the common law and civil law

---

used by attorneys and judges in daily practice. The Brazilian Code of Procedure of 1940 was expressly based on the principles propounded by Giuseppe Chiovenda in the code proposed by him in 1919 and never adopted in Italy. See Liebman, *Il nuovo "codigo de processo civil" brasiliano*, in *Problemi del processo civile* 483 (1962).

systems of procedure, separated since the twelfth century,[192] have been converging for many decades.[193] On the common law side, there have been the abolition of the forms of action, the nearly complete disappearance of the jury in English civil cases,[194] the progressive removal of exclusionary rules of evidence, and the fusion of equity and law. On the civil law side, there have been a return, more or less complete, to a system of procedure based on canons of orality, immediacy, and concentration; the more or less complete suppression of the system of legal proof; and the lively doctrinal pressures favoring dissenting and concurring opinions.[195] One must consider, too, the greater diffusion of certain fundamental procedural guarantees that Americans call "due process of law."[196]

Other strong forces give impetus to the harmonization of the various national systems of procedure. These include the demands of international organizations[197] and the pressures generated by globalization,[198] including increasing economic intercourse between nations, deprovincialized cultural development, and less localized human relations; in sum, all those forces that are changing man from a

192. On the cause of this separation, see van Caenegem, *L'histoire du droit et la chronologie—réflexions sur la formation du "Common Law" et la procédure romano-canonique*, in 2 *Etudes d'histoire du droit canonique dédiées à G. Le Bras* 1459 (1965).

193. See Cappelletti, *op. cit.* n. 69, at 64.

194. On the desirability of limiting the use of juries in the United States, see Kaplan, *Civil Procedure—Reflections on the Comparison of Systems*, 9 Buff. L. Rev. 409, 427–28 (1960).

195. See note 65.

196. Interestingly, it was in the course of a study of due process of law that Couture, the noted Uruguayan proceduralist and comparatist, underlined the affinities between the civil and common law systems. These are much deeper and more fundamental than would appear to a superficial observer. See Couture, *La garanzia costituzionale del "dovuto processo legale*," in 9 Rivista di diritto processuale (part I) 81, 99 (1954). See also Cappelletti, *op. cit.* n. 30, at 1284 *et seq.*, and *op. cit.* n. 65, at 218–19.

197. Nagel points out that the treaties of the European communities require the harmonization of the procedural systems of the six member states. See his *Auf dem Wege zu einem europäischen Prozessrecht* (1963). See also Nadelmann, *Common Market Assimilation of Laws and the Outer World*, in 58 Am. J. Int'l L. 724 (1964); Schima, *Gedanken zur Zivilgerichtsbarkeit im geeinten Europa*, in 11 Jahrbuch für internationals Recht 393 (1962); Cappelletti, *op. cit.* n. 177, at 215 *et seq.*, 226 *et seq.*

198. Among the more interesting surveys is Dezalay and Garth (eds.), *Lawyers and the Rule of Law in an Era of Globalization* (2012). On the implications for comparative law, see Mattei, Ruskola, and Gidi, *op. cit.* n. 2. For an Italian language source, see Monateri, *Geopolitica del diritto: genesi, governo, e dissoluzione dei corpi politici* (2013).

local to a universal citizen. Each of these forces, which were beginning to manifest themselves when the original edition of this work was published, have become more powerful in the intervening years. In light of the increasingly greater need for compatible procedural systems, one hopes that both common and civil law jurists will pay close attention to the following statement by Ernest Rabel: "To bridge the gulf between two halves of the legal world . . . is the task of the present generation of lawyers."[199]

199. 1 Rabel, *The Conflict of Laws: A Comparative Study* 64–65 (2d ed. 1958). The author continues: "Hidden behind apparent dissimilarity, there are fundamental likenesses, suggesting international cooperation, though of course not necessarily unification."

CHAPTER FIVE

The Italian Style: Doctrine

5.01 *The Italian Style.* This chapter and Chapters 6 and 7 describe some of the attitudes and assumptions that give Italian law its style.[1] A bare Italian statute or a flatly sketched Italian legal institution is often indistinguishable in appearance from its equivalent in another jurisdiction, but its actual significance is almost always subtly different.[2] Some of these differences are explainable by variations within the formal legal order itself. As an obvious example, the laws concerning

---

1. For an effective use of the concept of "style" as an approach to classification of the legal system, see Zweigert, *Zur Lehre von den Rechtskreisen*, in *XXth Century Comparative and Conflicts Law, Legal Essays in Honor of Hessel E. Yntema* 42–55 (1961). As used in the present work, the term is intended to be purely suggestive and is left undefined. There is no systematic attempt to employ Professor Zweigert's analysis of legal style here, but his basic idea of the essence of style—that which strikes the foreign observer as significantly, arrestingly, different—is similar. Zweigert's ideas are further developed in his by now classic work, Zweigert and Kotz, *Introduction to Comparative Law* (3d ed. 1998); see also Richard Hyland, *Gifts: A Study in Comparative Law* (2012) (applying the concept of legal style and culture to the study of a specific problem in comparative law).

2. "Comparative law scholars know very well that the same norm, transferred unchanged from the order in which it arose to another, can acquire quite different significance and effect . . . through the influence of particular rules and general principles of the new order into which the norm has been transplanted." Bigiavi, *Diritto romano e legislatore italiano*, 10 Rivista di diritto civile (part 1) 14, 23 (1964).

The point is an obvious one, but it bears repetition. A legal norm or institution, abstracted from the culture in which it originated, is a shapeless, empty container. It acquires dimension and content from the legal context. Transfer it to a different legal system, and its

annulment of marriages, even if phrased in exactly the same way, mean something different in a nation in which there was historically no divorce and in one in which divorces are easily obtained.

But a principal source of such differences lies quite outside the formal legal order. It is found in the pervading assumptions and attitudes, lay and professional, about law, in the generally accepted view of what law is, of what the role of the legal process in the society should be, and of how the legal process should be divided up among the various official and unofficial agencies for making and administering law. In a phrase, what gives a legal order character, individuality, a style of its own, is the prevailing legal outlook in the culture of which that legal order is an integral part.

To some extent the Italian legal outlook is peculiarly Italian; there is an Italian style.[3] But much of this outlook is shared by other European cultures with similar attitudes and assumptions, cultures that are products of a similar history and a common legal tradition. Indeed, the Italian style is, in a sense, a paradigm of the civil law. Much of the legal tradition of the contemporary civil law world had its origins and its principal development in Italy.[4] Italy took part in the nineteenth-century

---

meaning will change. Fill an Italian norm with American preconceptions about law and the legal process, and it is no longer Italian.

For a good Italian discussion of the problems involved in attempting to understand another legal order, past or present, see 1 Betti, *Teoria generale della interpretazione* 574–85 (1955).

3. There is no single Italian legal outlook, but there is a dominant one, which these chapters seek to describe. This rather generalized set of attitudes and assumptions about law should not, of course, be confused with the work of professional legal philosophers. For a recent discussion of Italian (and other) legal philosophy, see Fassò, *Storia della filosofia del diritto, vol. 3: Ottocento e Novecento* (2009). For a useful volume emphasizing the Italian Civil Code, see Guido Alpa, *La cultura delle regole: storia del diritto civile italiano* (2000). For an earlier but still helpful discussion of Italian legal thought, including a useful bibliography, see Caiani, *La filosofia dei giuristi italiani* (1955). Piovani, *Consigli bibliografici agli studenti* (1961–62) is another excellent bibliographical survey. For a brief discussion in English, see Bobbio, *Trends in Italian Legal Theory*, 8 Am. J. Comp. L. 329 (1959). For a survey that suggests that the contribution of Italian legal philosophers has consistently been underestimated, if not ignored, see Cohen, *Italian Contributions to the Philosophy of Law*, 59 Harv. L. Rev. 577 (1946). See also Pollock, *The History of Comparative Jurisprudence*, 5 J. Comp. Leg. (n.s.) 74 (1903).

4. See Chapter 1 for a discussion of Italy's role in the history of continental law. For centuries after the revival of Roman legal studies in Bologna, the accepted method of

movement for codification and reform and in the excesses of what one Italian writer has called "code-worship."[5] But Italy is perhaps the only one of the major civil law nations to have received and rationalized the two principal, and quite different, influences on European law in the nineteenth century: the French style of codification and the German style of scholarship. The Italian style, while truly Italian, prominently displays those characteristics that, to common lawyers, typify the civil law.

5.02 *Doctrine.*   The Italian law professor-scholar is the inheritor of a proud tradition reaching back to the Glossators (or even, according to some, to the Roman jurisconsults). This tradition antedates the relatively modern conception of the state as the source of law, legislation as we know it, and a professional judiciary. For a time the preservation, explanation, and evolution of the generally applicable law, to which local customs and statutes were considered exceptions, were almost exclusively in the hands of the teacher-scholar. Although his de facto monopoly has since been destroyed, the teacher-scholar's preeminence among men of the law survives in the civil law world,[6] particularly in Italy. His work, published in the form of textbooks, treatises, commentaries, monographs, and articles, constitutes what Italians call "the doctrine."[7] The towering importance of the doctrine makes

---

teaching and scholarship, and the accepted legal outlook throughout Europe, was known as the *mos italicus jura docendi*, or simply *mos italicus*. For brief discussions of this earlier version of the Italian style, see 1.17; *A General Survey of Events, Sources, Persons and Movements in Continental Legal History* 386–97 (Continental Legal History Series Vol. 1, 1912).

5. Bobbio, *op. cit.* n. 3, at 329, 335. The allusion is to the tendency, attributable to the intellectual forces at work at the time of the French Revolution, to ignore the historic dimensions of the continental legal tradition and to think of it as something that began with the French civil code. The importance of the movement for codification and reform in the nineteenth century is not open to question. But for something over 150 years, civil lawyers (and common lawyers commenting on the civil law) have tended to exaggerate it.

6. On the influence of the jurists in civil law countries, see Lawson, *A Common Lawyer Looks at the Civil Law* 69–76 (1953); David, *Le rôle des juristes dans l'élaboration du droit selon la conception traditionnelle du système de droit romano-germanique*, 1 Festschrift für Hans Dölle 359 (1963). See generally Merryman and Perez-Perdomo, *The Civil Law Tradition: An Introduction to the Legal Systems of Europe and Latin America* (3d ed. 2007).

7. Lawyers and judges also contribute to the doctrine; some of them engage in legal scholarship and publish their work. Both in amount and authority, however, their contribution is of lesser importance. In theory the ideas of a lawyer or judge are entitled to the same hearing as those of a professor, but in fact the professorial origin of a book or article gives

it the logical initial focus of an investigation of the Italian style. Doctrine is not law in Italy in the way that legislation and judicial decisions are law,[8] but it pervades the legal process, strongly influencing legislators and judges, who tend to conform to the doctrinal model not only of what law is but of what their functions are.[9]

The Italian doctrine is not monolithic; the discussion of legal problems is constant, lively, often creative, and is characterized by sharply diverging points of view. But these phenomena exist at the growing edge of a doctrinal area within which a great deal of uniformity persists; there is an identifiable traditional model and orthodoxy. It is variously called "dogmatics," "systematic jurisprudence," and "legal science," depending on the context.

We will use the term "legal science," but with the caveat that it is used to refer to the *traditional, orthodox* doctrine.[10] The books from which students first learn about their law, the books that lawyers and judges use in their daily work, the

---

it an advantage in the competition for a secure place in the world of doctrine. Further, the leaders of the practicing bar are frequently professors, who publish as professors.

8. See Grisoli, *Guide to Foreign Legal Materials: Italian* 48 (1965), for a clear statement of the orthodox Italian view that doctrine is not law. This topic is discussed further in 6.02. A similar distinction is frequently made in American thought between primary and secondary authority. For a critical discussion of such a distinction, see Merryman, *The Authority of Authority*, 6 Stan. L. Rev. 613, 619–21 (1954). A more detailed discussion of Italian legal sources is found in the Appendix to this work.

It is interesting to note that in Italy, where doctrine exerts a more powerful influence on every aspect of the legal process than it does in the United States, doctrine is not formally recognized as a source of law. Provisions on the Law in General art. 1, which lists the sources of law, mentions only statutes, regulations, corporative norms, and usage. This is a *numerus clausus*. Indeed, according to article 118 of the Disposizioni per l'attuazione del codice di procedura civile, judicial opinions may not include citations to legal writers. In California, on the contrary, the law is found in "the treatises of learned men," according to Cal. Code Civ. Proc. § 1899.

9. There is a traditional doctrinal model of the legal process which dictates a sharp division of legislative and judicial powers. Some of the historical sources of that model are discussed at 5.06. Some of its consequences are described herein and in Chapters 6 and 7.

10. In fact, in ordinary usage, the term "legal science" is generally applied to legal scholarship, both traditional and other. A scholar who is critical of traditional Italian doctrine and who thinks "science" is a misnomer for the work of jurists is nevertheless spoken of as a scientist, and his work is still called legal science. The term is retained and is used here in the more restricted sense to emphasize the usually unspoken assumption in the traditional doctrine that the work of the legal scholar is, *and ought to be*, like the work of the physical scientist.

opinions of judges, and much of the legislative process are dominated by it. It is criticized by many thoughtful jurists, and some of these criticisms will be described here, but the critics remain even today the *avanguardia*, the voice of the future rather than the dominant tradition

5.03 *Exegesis and the Pandectists.*   The first Italian codes after unification were modeled on the French Napoleonic codes,[11] and for a time Italian scholarship was also influenced by the French. The dominant current of thought about law of that day has been summed up in the term *exegesis*, by which it was meant that jurists sought to find the solution to legal problems by studying only the provisions of the code. It was thought that the legislative text of each article of the code, if literally studied, should provide the answer to every problem that might arise concerning it. The function of the judge was to find and apply the applicable provision; he was expected not to go outside the code for aid in selection and application, and indeed, it would have been wrong for him to do so. The often-quoted statement of a French jurist of the time to the effect that he knew nothing of the civil law but studied the Code Napoléon is a kind of extreme statement of the philosophy of exegesis, and for a brief period something of the same attitude prevailed in Italy.[12]

It was soon displaced, however, by enthusiastic reception of what has been called the Pandectist school of legal thought. This school developed in Germany, where the Roman law had been formally received in the fifteenth and sixteenth centuries and grew out of the scholarly study of the *Digest* of Justinian (*Pandekten*)

---

11. For discussion of the relationships between the first Italian codes and the Napoleonic codification, see Aquarone, *L'unificazione legislativa e i codici del 1865* (1960), and Chapter 6. It should be recalled that much of what found its way into the French codes was, in turn, based on legal institutions and concepts drawn from Italy. The Roman law, the medievalized Roman law of the Italian schools and the *mos italicus*, canon law and the Italo-canonical law of procedure, and the medieval commercial law growing out of Italian sources were all Italic in origin.

12. See 1.23. "In the same way that our civil code was modeled on the French code, our doctrine modeled itself on the French, adopting its methods of research and orientation. A critical estimate of this doctrine, which was very often limited to the exegesis of norms and avoided conceptual constructions, can therefore not be a positive one. The repetition of reasoning dear to the French doctrine, which in its turn followed, without any appreciable attempt at original reelaboration, in the wake of the great jurists who had provided theoretical support for the Code Napoléon, could not give rise to a scientific movement worthy of the name." Nicolò, *Diritto civile*, in 12 *Enciclopedia del diritto* 904, 918 (1964).

with a view toward the development of a systematic conceptual legal structure. Similar studies were, of course, in the great tradition of continental law, beginning with the Glossators. The principal distinguishing mark of the Pandectists was that they brought this study to the highest systematic level it had ever reached.[13] Their efforts culminated in a number of great works, of which two have been particularly influential: the *Pandektenrecht* of the scholar Windscheid[14] and the *allgemeiner Teil*, or general part, of the German Civil Code (the bürgerliches Gesetzbuch, or BGB).[15]

The Pandectists sought to study the Roman law, as received and applied in Germany, in order to draw pure concepts and principles from it,[16] to establish a systematic legal structure, to build a system. In a word, they conducted what has since been called in Europe the systematic study of the law. In this study attention was not paid primarily to social and economic problems but to the law itself. The attitude was that law was like other phenomena of nature and merited careful

13. See 1.23. Nicolò, *op. cit.* n. 12, at 918, states, "Toward the end of the century, however, the scientific study of the civil law received a new impulse from two independent sources: the reflowering of Romanistic studies and the influence of the *pandettistica*. The German juridical school . . . transformed the Romanistic schemes into an admirable intellectual construction, and created a general doctrine that has for a long time dominated legal thought and that only recently has begun to show its insufficiencies and limits. Everyone knows the influence exerted on the Italian doctrine at the turn of the century by the elaboration of the *pandettistica*."

14. Windscheid, *Lehrbuch des Pandektenrechts* (1862). The ninth edition, revised by Theodor Kipp, was published in three volumes in 1906 and republished in 1963 by Scientia Verlag Aalen.

15. For a description of the background of the German codification and of the BGB, which was enacted in 1896 and became effective in 1900, see von Mehren, *The Civil Law System* 22–30 (1957); Deak and Rheinstein, *The Development of French and German Law*, 24 Geo. L.J. 551, 568–83 (1936).

16. For a good description, see Schmidt, *The German Abstract Approach to Law*, 1965 Scandinavian Studies in Law 133. The conceptual nature of much of the legal science of Germany in the latter half of the nineteenth and the first few decades of the twentieth century was apparent to many continental jurists, and it came to be known as "conceptual jurisprudence" or the "jurisprudence of concepts" (*Begriffsjurisprudenz*). One of the strongest schools of thought that developed out of the reaction against the conceptual jurisprudence came to be called "the jurisprudence of interests" (*Interessenjurisprudenz*). Most works on the jurisprudence of interests are, in part, criticisms of conceptual jurisprudence (just as much of the work of American legal realism is criticism of existing concepts and patterns of thought about law). See, e.g., *The Jurisprudence of Interests* 10, 16–17, 31, 33–34, 51–53, 56, 102–03, 287 (1948).

study in order to discover and explain its inherent principles and their natural relationships. The thing studied was the law, to the exclusion of other materials; the
thing sought was its scientific reconstruction according to its inherent properties.

The work of the Pandectists was sanctified in the famous "general part" of the
German civil code; in this way it became a part of the statutory law of Germany.
But its influence was not limited to that country. The school's leading treatise,
Windscheid's *Pandektenrecht*, was translated into a number of languages and studied throughout Europe; the BGB was studied and copied in many nations, and
German legal science dominated European legal thought for a time. The influence
of the *Pandettistica* was particularly great in Italy. It affected Italian doctrine first,
and through the doctrine it came to dominate the legal process, in legal education, the writings of judges, and the works of scholars. Its effect was not limited
to the civil law. The *Pandettistica* was extended by Italian jurists to the whole of
private law, to much of public law, and to the law of procedure. In the hands of the
Italian jurists it continued to be developed and refined. The body of law studied
was different, but the attitude, the method, and the theoretical structure were substantially the same.

5.04 *Italian Legal Science:Characteristics.*[17]   The traditional attitude is that the law
is a self-contained discipline or phenomenon that can be understood and perfected
by systematic study. It is summed up in the phrase *legal science*, which carries with
it the assumption that the study of law is a science, in the same way that the study
of other natural phenomena—say, those of biology or physics—is a science. The
work of the legal scholar is, like the work of other scientists, not concerned so
much with the solution of practical problems as with the search for scientific truth,
for ultimates and fundamentals; not concerned so much with individual cases as
with generic problems, the perfection of learning and understanding; not, in a
word, with engineering, but with pure science.[18]

17. Piovani, *Dommatica, teoria generale e filosofia del diritto*, 40 Rivista internazionale di
filosofia del diritto 37 (1963), includes a good critical discussion of the nature of the traditional legal science. For a more lyrical exposition of the traditional view of the nature and
functions of Italian legal scholarship, see Capograssi, *Il problema della scienza del diritto*,
2 Opere 401 (1959).

18. "For the jurist, . . . who had always considered the natural sciences a model of scientific research, as science par excellence, to give legal science the appellation of a natural
science meant recognition of the long road he had traveled from pure and simple exegesis

The theoretical structure of legal science consists of general concepts and institutions of a high order of abstraction, arranged and interrelated in a systematic way.[19] The components of the structure, and the relationships between them, are thought to have been discovered by the scientific study of the law.[20] The components are strictly legal, and indeed it is believed that their purity, and hence their validity, would be destroyed by the introduction of nonlegal elements. If at times legal science appears to operate badly, it is only because it is not yet perfected, and accordingly more scientific study is needed.

The legal method, the manner in which the law is applied, is consistent with these assumptions. The work of the judge, like that of the engineer, is considered less demanding, less exalted in function, than that of the scholar—the scientist. The judge's task is thought to be relatively simple: he is presented with a body of

---

of the codes to the systematic elaboration of legal categories, to give a favorable judgment on his recent development and his future possibilities. It was, in sum, a title of honor. . . ." Bobbio, *La filosofia del diritto in Italia*, 8 Jus (n.s.) 183, 194 (1957).

19. For a brief description of the more important concepts, see 5.05. Student teaching manuals contain more extensive descriptions of the theoretical structure. See, e.g., Torrente and Schlesinger, *Manuale di diritto privato* (21st ed. 2013); Ruscello, *Istituzioni di diritto privato* (18th ed. 2014).

All of the cited works describe the conceptual structure of *private law*, the soil in which the traditional doctrine originally grew and flourished. The principal concepts and the method have, however, spread to the public law in Italy (for a discussion of the distinction between public law and private law, see 6.03, 6.04. An excellent exposition may be found in 1 Zanobini, *Corso di diritto amministrativo* (8th ed. 1958).

20. The study is of legal phenomena—the rules of law—typically legislative norms. The purpose is to draw from them the more general legal principles, of which it is assumed the phenomena are concrete representations. "[I]n the great variety of cases and in the inevitable fluctuations of socio-legal phenomena, constant elements are present, so as to allow the construction of a science of law." Biondi, *Metodologia della scienza del diritto*, 13 Jus. (n.s.) 149 (1962). "[E]fforts [are made] to derive from legal data concepts and broad generalizations that aim solely to impose on these data the highest degree of logical systematization; that is, investigations of the internal structure of legal systems in order to achieve a measure of logical integration." Rottschaefer, *Jurisprudence: Philosophy or Science*, 11 Minn. L. Rev. 293 (1927). Similar assumptions form at least part of the intellectual background of case study in American law schools and of much American legal scholarship. See Dickinson, *The Law Behind Law*, 29 Colum. L. Rev. 113, 141–43 (1929). See also de Sloovere, *Analytical Jurisprudence as Related to Modern Legal Methods*, 7 N.Y.U.L.Q. Rev. 88 (1929) (comparing American analytical jurisprudence with continental legal science); Schlag, *Missing Pieces: A Cognitive Approach to Law*, 67 Tex. L. Rev. 1195 (1988).

principles built into a carefully elaborated systematic structure, which he applies to a body of specific norms that are readily understandable and comparatively easy to apply. He need merely reason scientifically. The applicable norms need only to be identified and applied, a labor which, while important, is not essentially creative.[21]

Two of the most widely criticized (in Italy, by Italians) aspects of this legal science are its abstractness and its conceptualism. It is abstract in two senses. First, it is insulated against the intrusion of both social facts and value judgments; sociology[22] and philosophy[23] are foreign to it. Second, it is more concerned with the development and elaboration of a scientific structure than it is with the solution of concrete problems and with the facts of actual cases.[24] Legal science is conceptual in the sense that its structure is built of concepts of great generality.[25] Indeed, one of the objectives of legal science is to discover the true nature of legal institutions (just as pure science in other fields tries to find basic laws), and in the process accidental elements are discarded in the search for the ever more pervasive truth. What is sought might be called, in a highly metaphorical way, a gigantic "equation of state" for law, with only the essential constants, variables, and functions included in the equation; the more universal these elements become, the simpler, and better, the equation.[26]

21. See the discussion of the Italian judicial process in Chapter 7.

22. See 5.07.

23. See 5.09.

24. Among the linguistic problems first encountered by an American who embarks upon the great sea that is the Italian doctrine is the way in which two key words *problem* and *fact* are used in the tradition-oriented literature. *Problem* almost always refers to a theoretical rather than to a practical (whether social, economic, legal, or other) problem. This throws the American reader off his stride, but the use of *fact* to refer to legal norms, to legislation, is even more likely to disconcert him. It is not uncommon to read an Italian law book or article in which the author constantly emphasizes the importance of facts and warns against the dangers of ignoring them but never refers to what an American reader would expect him to mean: to a concrete phenomenon outside the legal system that may have legal consequences. The Italian jurist is, however, being quite consistent with the premises of the traditional doctrine. The norms are the raw material, the phenomena, he studies. They are his facts.

25. For a brief description of the principal concepts, see 5.05.

26. This is, in a sense, what the continental jurist of a traditional cast has sought to construct under the name of "*allgemeine Rechtslehre*" or "*teoria generale del diritto*" (general theory of law). The best known such work in the Italian literature is Carnelutti, *Teoria*

A tradition-oriented Italian jurist could reasonably complain that what has been said so far is more a caricature than a description of Italian legal science. In the interest of balanced description, it should be pointed out that the separation of powers is, for a number of historical reasons, much more sharply conceived in Italy than in common law countries.[27] Because this separation makes it difficult for judges to participate consciously in the creative development of the law, the burden must fall, to a great extent, on the scholar—the jurist who is trained to do this kind of work. The division of labor is also sharper in Italy than it is in the United States: it is the business of lawyers to be practical, of politicians and legislators to relate social need to governmental programs (including laws), and of scholars to be scientific, aloof from politics and practice.

This division of labor implies the more fundamental premise that there are peculiarly scholarly tasks that need doing. Among the most important of these is the erection and elaboration of a theoretical legal structure. Such a structure can contribute much to the simple, efficient, orderly operation of every aspect of the legal process. One of the glaring defects of the common law from the Italian point of view is precisely the lack of such a structure, and hence the common law often seems by comparison to be unnecessarily complex, inefficient, and disorderly.[28]

There are dangers in system-building, and the best of the traditional doctrine displays an adequate awareness of them.[29] The matter has been considered, and a

---

generale del diritto (3d ed. 1951). Kelsen, *General Theory of Law and the State* (1945), is a kind of ultimate logical consequence of the sort of thinking described.

27. See 5.06, 5.09.

28. 1 Sereni, *Studi di diritto comparato* (treatise published in various editions 1908 to 1967). The author also mentions that common law countries lack that admiration for "the *bella legge* and the elegant formula" that is found in Europe and Latin America. *Id.*, at 32.

It has been observed that rationalist thought, secular natural law, and the logical-formal approach to law that achieved partial expression in the Code Napoléon, on the one hand, and the adoption of the metric system of weights and measures and conversion to a decimal currency, on the other, coincided in France. The latter two measures were rejected in England, as was codification. Ascarelli, *L'idea di codice nel diritto privato e la funzione dell'interpretazione*, in Studi di diritto comparato e in tema di interpretazione 165 (1952); Pekelis, *Legal Techniques and Political Ideologies*, 41 Mich. L. Rev. 665, 691 (1943). For a thorough and, on the whole, convincing demonstration that the common law is more and the civil law is less orderly than is commonly assumed, see Lawson, *The Rational Strength of English Law* (1951). See also Radbruch, *Lo spirito del diritto inglese* 36, 39 *et seq.*, 47 (1964).

29. On this point, see the *Prefazione* to 1 Gorla, *Il contratto*, at ix (1954): "I fully recognize the legitimacy of abstractions, generalizations, and conceptual constructions, insofar

conscious decision taken to place greater emphasis on system. Once this question is resolved, the business at hand is to build the best systematic structure possible. It will be composed of concepts; it must be abstract; it will become elaborate and seem artificial. That is the way theoretical structures are.

Thus, to call Italian legal science abstract and conceptual is to state the obvious;[30] the traditional doctrine has chosen to become so in the interest of what many Americans would also recognize to be worthy legal values. Any legal literature must employ concepts and relate them in some systematic way, or be unintelligible. The great books of the common law were for centuries organized around concepts drawn from a system of tenures,[31] or a register of writs.[32] The great American treatises and the Restatement were eagerly welcomed by large segments of the profession precisely because they provided a systematic reconstruction of legal materials according to an acceptable (an Italian might say a scientifically valid) theoretical scheme.[33] To a legal scientist the difference between Italian and American doctrine is not that the Italian is too conceptual but that the American is not conceptual

---

as they respond to certain needs of the spirit (at least for us in *civil law* countries who are habituated to reasoning in this way), needs such as: order, system, the logical development of thought, its discipline. In the present book I have made great use of this method which . . . we may call by the more or less appropriate term 'logical,' seeking, however, to restrict it to the field of satisfaction of these needs. . . . But it always remains that the so-called 'logical method' is only one of the methods, ways, or concerns for approaching legal phenomena, for comprehending them or, better, for making them more comprehensible. But when, leaving the area of satisfaction of such requirements of thought, it is made the sole method, the 'method' par excellence or 'the science of law,' as unfortunately happens frequently among us, then it degenerates, and its bad effects are not slow in manifesting themselves."

30. Pugliatti, *La giurisprudenza come scienza pratica*, 4 Rivista Italiana per le Scienze Giuridiche (ser. 3) 49, 51 (1950), mentions the eagerness of uninformed critics, even in Italy, to "break a lance against the windmills of the systematic jurisprudence."

31. For example, Littleton.

32. For example, Glanville and Bracton. Bracton is a particularly interesting case in point. Much of his work is in the form of a commentary on writs, but some of it is quite different in form and organization and seems to have been copied or paraphrased from the work of Azo, one of the Commentators. See *Select Passages from the Works of Bracton and Azo* (1895); authorities cited in Merryman, *Improving the Lot of the Trespassing Improver*, 11 Stan. L. Rev. 456, 460 n. 16 (1959).

33. For a brief history of the Restatement, which stresses the hope that it would provide order, see Lewis, *History of the American Law Institute and the First Restatement of the Law*, in *Restatement in the Courts* 1 (1945).

enough. From the Italian point of view, a perceptive American scholar who stands apart and objectively surveys the wreckage left by the Realists should not exult; he should weep.[34]

5.05 *Italian Legal Science: Principal Concepts.* The education of an Italian lawyer begins with a systematic exposition of the principal concepts and the structure of the traditional legal science. There is a very extensive literature, ranging from the elementary to the subtle and complex. What follows is an abbreviated version of the discussion that begins every student manual for the first course in private law.[35]

34. For an Italian view of the work of the American legal realists, see Tarello, *Il realismo giuridico Americano* (1962).

Among the wreckage may be found some artifacts that look very much like continental doctrine. Markby, *Elements of Law Considered with Reference to Principles of General Jurisprudence* (2009), is an outstanding example. It is a serious attempt to apply the methods of traditional continental legal science to English law, and it is only one example of what was at one time an important, if not dominant, current of English (and American) legal thought. Other prominent examples are Amos, *The Science of Law* (1874); Austin, *Lectures on Jurisprudence* (5th ed. 1885); Holland, *The Elements of Jurisprudence* (12th ed. 1917, reprinted 2006); Salmond, *Jurisprudence* (12th ed. 1966).

John Austin is generally recognized as the founder of this brand of English jurisprudence. Roscoe Pound states that "when in 1826 John Austin was offered a professorship of jurisprudence in the then newly established University of London, knowing that the common law had little systematic development, whereas the Pandectists in Germany had given modern Roman law a high degree of systematic exposition, he went to Germany and studied." Pound, *Introduction*, 1 Am. J. Comp. L. 1, 4 (1952). For a recent discussion of Austin's work, see Stone, *op. cit.* n. 26, at 62–97.

For a similar manifestation in American scholarship, see Ferson, *The Nature of Legal Transactions and Juristic Acts: Analysis of Common Factors and Variables*, 31 Cornell L.Q. 105 (1945). For a good American criticism of some and defense of other aspects of legal science, see Yntema, *The Implications of Legal Science*, 10 N.Y.U.L.Q. Rev. 279 (1933); Yntema, *Roman Law as the Basis of Comparative Law*, 2 Law: A Century of Progress 346 (1937); and the exchange between Yntema and M. R. Cohen: Yntema, *The Rational Basis of Legal Science*, 31 Colum. L. Rev. 925 (1931); Cohen, *Philosophy and Legal Science*, 32 Colum. L. Rev. 1103 (1932).

35. This description is drawn from the *manuali* cited in note 19. Each of these works presents its author's own views, and it is doubtful that all of the authors would agree on any of the statements in the text, out of dissatisfaction either with what is said or with what is omitted. The text is a composite, oversimplified product, and a respected Italian colleague has called these the "least happy pages" in this chapter. The reader is warned.

The "general part" of such a manual is written for the purpose of providing the student with a conceptual framework that will serve him for his entire professional life as lawyer, judge, or scholar. It is intended to, and does, powerfully influence his legal outlook.

The positive legal order, as distinguished from the natural legal order,[36] is composed of legal norms and the institutions by which they are formulated and applied. The legal norm (*norma giuridica*) has two essential components: a statement of an abstract, generalized, hypothetical fact situation (*fattispecie*) and a statement of a legal consequence. Where an actual fact situation is found by the judge to be congruent with the *fattispecie* of a norm, the legal consequence becomes concretely applicable.

There are various ways of classifying norms, but in a general way it can be said that any norm (and the same is true of any *fatto giuridico*, discussed below) establishes, modifies, or terminates legal relations (*rapporti giuridici*).[37] Where the relation is between a subject (*soggetto*)[38] and the state qua state, the relation is one of public law. Where it is between two or more subjects, it is a private-law relation,[39] and it is to these that the term *rapporto giuridico* is more commonly applied. The legal relation may be of various kinds. To use the terminology of the principal school of American analytical jurisprudence,[40] the one to whom the benefit of a legal relation runs may have a right, a power, a privilege, or an immunity. Italian scholars use different terminology, and the analysis varies among them, but any such interest is normally subsumed under the term "subjective right" (*diritto soggettivo*).[41]

---

36. See 5.06.

37. Cicala, *Il rapporto giuridico* (4th ed. 1959), is a good introduction to the substantial literature on the legal relation.

38. Subjects can be either natural or legal persons, the latter group including a variety of business organizations, foundations, and certain governmental and quasi-governmental entities. The basic legal provisions concerning legal persons are contained in Codice civile arts. 11–42.

39. The distinction between private and public law, which is much discussed in Italy, is really much more complex than this. The state or one of its subdivisions may be, and often is, a party to a private law relation. This public law–private law dichotomy is discussed in 6.03–6.04.

40. See, e.g., Hohfeld, *Fundamental Legal Conceptions* (1923); 1 *Restatement, Property* §§ 1–5 (1936).

41. This is the term usually applied to the interest of the beneficiary (*soggetto attivo*) of a private legal relation. The one against whom that interest runs is called the *soggetto*

Thus, some of the norms of private law establish legal relations between private subjects and create subjective rights. Such relations and rights are usually classified into three major groups: personal (*rapporti personali, diritti della persona*), familial (*rapporti familiari, diritti familiari*), and patrimonial (*rapporti patrimoniali, diritte patrimoniali*). Patrimonial rights include the property and the credits of the subject. All of his patrimonial rights and obligations taken together constitute his patrimony.

Legal relations and subjective rights are, as has been indicated, created directly by norms. According to accepted legal theory, however, there is an additional source of such relations and rights, called the *fatto giuridico*, or legal fact, which includes the *negozio giuridico*, translated here as "legal transaction."[42]

Returning for a moment to the basic content of the norm—the *fattispecie* and the consequence—concrete facts can be divided into two groups: those that alone or in concert with other facts actuate a norm (i.e., fit a *fattispecie*) and those that have no legal relevance or effect. The former are called "legal facts" (*fatti giuridici*). Legal facts are divided into those that occur independently of subjective intention (e.g., the passage of time, birth, death) and are called "legal facts in the strict sense," and those that are the intentional actions of subjects and are called "legal acts" (*atti giuridici*).[43]

In the private law legal acts are further divided into legal acts in the strict sense and legal transactions (*negozi giuridici*). If an act merely produces preordained legal effects, it falls into the former class (e.g., intentional torts). If the act involves the expression of intention directed toward the production of consequences that

---

passivo. In a public legal relation the subject who has a legally recognized interest against the state may have either a "public subjective right" or a "legitimate interest." This distinction is discussed further in 6.03–6.04.

42. The literature on the *negozio giuridico* is immense. Among the traditional landmarks are Betti, *Teoria generale del negozio giuridico* (2d ed. 1960); Scognamiglio, *Contributo alla teoria del negozio giuridico* (1950).

The equivalent concept in German and French doctrine, called *Rechtsgeschäft* and *acte juridique*, respectively, has normally been translated into English as "juristic act." See Holland, *op. cit.* n. 34, at 116–20; Markby, *op. cit.* n. 34, at 125–26. Obviously "juristic act" is not an appropriate translation for *negozio giuridico*, which in the Italian doctrine is only a subclass of the juristic act (*atto giuridico*). Hence "legal transaction" has been used because it avoids such ambiguity and is a reasonably accurate translation of *negozio giuridico*.

43. The term *act* (*atto*) is also commonly used to refer to a written instrument, even though many legal acts are effective without a writing.

the legal order does not preordain but recognizes and effectuates, it belongs to the field of the legal transaction.

The typical examples of the legal transaction are the will and the contract.[44] They are devices by which individuals exercise their legal autonomy. Private property and liberty of contract are recognized by the law. Subjects may dispose of property and enter into agreements, and the law will, within fairly broad limits, enforce such transactions according to their intention. The existence of this kind of autonomy is a necessary precondition of the *negozio giuridico*.[45]

The legal relations resulting from legal transactions are creatures of the law. They have legal effect because they are recognized and enforced by the norms and institutions of the positive legal order. The norms that preordain the effects of legal facts and legal acts, and those that attach legal consequences to the legal transaction, are the real source of the legal relation. Hence all such legal relations are norm-created. Those deriving from the legal transaction are merely less directly dependent on the norm; the legal transaction intervenes, and it is common to speak of the different *levels* at which legal relations are created.[46]

---

44. Another commonly mentioned example is the renunciation of a right. Our conception of an inter vivos conveyance would also appear to fit into the *negozio giuridico* category, but that conception has no equivalent in Italian law. Transfers are made by contract.

Early in the last century, an English scholar, with the aid of a clouded crystal ball, expressed the following thoughts: "It is probable that before long English lawyers will follow the example of continental lawyers, not only in appropriating a name to acts of this class (and whether they are called acts in the law, or juridical acts, or juristic acts, does not seem to me very material), but also in discussing them generally. If we take the commonest examples of this class, contracts, sales, mortgages, wills and settlements of property, we shall find that up to a certain point the principles which regulate them are very nearly the same. . . . Brevity and simplicity, therefore, is attained by discussing these principles once and for all, and this I have endeavored to do to some extent, though in the present condition of English law it is not possible to carry the discussion very far." Markby, *op. cit.* n. 34, at 126–27. See also Lobingier, *Juristic Acts in the Civil Law*, 24 Tul. L. Rev. 178 (1949).

45. Despite efforts to keep the doctrine purely legal and scientific, ideology occasionally creeps in under the cover of an accepted, presumably neutral, concept. This has been particularly true in the case of the *negozio giuridico*, whose dependence for content on the political, economic, and social assumptions of nineteenth-century European liberalism is apparent. This matter is discussed in 6.07–6.09.

46. This view is more accepted in Italy today than the earlier view, developed in Germany, that the individual's will or intention is the source of the legal obligation. On the

A great deal has been written about the *negozio giuridico* and the *rapporto giuridico*. Much of this writing has to do with their legal characteristics and transformations, with general doctrine applicable to all of the more specific institutions that they represent. The course of the discussion is from the general toward the specific. The student studies prescription of the legal relation in general, and only later, in the study of specific kinds of relations, encounters the refinements and variations applicable to them. He learns very generally about the legal transaction, its basic elements of intention, act, and *causa*, and only when he comes to the study of the will or the contract does he encounter the more specific doctrine applicable to those acts.

The *rapporto giuridico* and the *negozio giuridico* are creations of the doctrine. They do not appear in the codes or in special legislation. They are products of the legal science and its effort to achieve a scientific reconstruction of the law. Every *manuale* on private law begins with a description of them and the related concepts of norm, legal act, legal fact, subject, subjective right, and so on. Exposition of these very general concepts and their properties provides the standard introduction to the law; establishes the basis on which later, more specific study builds; and gives the student a frame of reference. Every student begins by learning the fundamentals of the doctrine, and his legal outlook is deeply and permanently affected by it.

5.06 *The Cultural Agnosticism of Italian Legal Science: Positivism.* Such terms as *abstract* and *conceptual* do not fully describe the traditional doctrine. It is pervaded by a kind of cultural agnosticism,[47] a deliberate turning away from other than the purely legal aspects of the culture, that seems strange to an American observer.[48]

Willenstheorie, see *The Progress of Continental Law in the Nineteenth Century* 100–103 (Continental Legal History Series Vol. 11, 1918).

47. "The great majority of the jurists [limit themselves] to an attitude . . . of recognition of their own domain and agnosticism concerning everything that is found outside it." Giannini, *Sociologia e studi di diritto contemporaneo,* 8 Jus (n.s.) 223 (1957).

48. For a symposium on this phenomenon, with primary emphasis on the attitude of jurists toward sociology, see 8 Jus (n.s.) 183–234 (1957). On the separation of legal science and legal philosophy, see the symposium in 33 Rivista internazionale di filosofia del diritto 1–272 (3d ser. 1956). This legal philosophy–legal science schism may lie near the root of the problem. A recent discussion of the relationships between law and culture in Italy sees the legal philosopher, not the legal scientist, as the person qualified to speak on these relationships. See Bagolini, *Cultura e scienza del diritto,* 16 Rivista trimestrale di diritto e procedura

The jurists themselves are often highly cultivated persons; law is part of their culture. But their culture—or at least those aspects of it that can be summed up by terms like *philosophy, sociology, economics, history,* and *politics*—is not part of their law.[49] This cultural agnosticism is displayed in many ways and is only understandable against the history of events and ideas in Italy.[50]

For a number of centuries after the revival of Roman legal studies in the Italian universities, Europe was bound together in a legal community by common acceptance of the Roman law as *jus commune,* or common law. Men came to Italy from all parts of Europe to study *the* law, which was the Roman law as taught in the universities. The language of the law was Latin. Lawyers throughout Europe thus were trained in the same schools, studied the same law, and used the same language. The *jus commune* was the generally applicable law, to which local customs and local legislation were exceptions, and indeed the idea of a purely national law was hardly conceivable. The general law was associated with the concept of the Holy Roman Empire, whose unity was superior to the diversities of local tribes, communities, and nations. The law was both independent of the state and superior to it. Actually the state as we know it did not exist. In most of Europe, society and the economy were organized around the feudal model, and the national tie was far weaker than that of either the feud or the faith.[51]

The growth of the national state from the fifteenth century onward destroyed this legal unity. With the decay of feudalism, the advent of the Reformation, and the demise of the Holy Roman Empire, the centralized monarchy began to emerge as the principal claimant to the loyalty of the individual, particularly in France. The centralized state opposed both the medieval autonomy of classes and lands commonly associated with feudalism and every kind of power outside the state.

---

civile 9 (1962). For a discussion of the equivalent phenomenon in Anglo-American legal practice, see Cotterrell, *The Politics of Jurisprudence: A Critical Introduction to Legal Philosophy* (1989).

49. To avoid any possibility of misunderstanding, it should be emphasized that the intent is neither to state nor to imply that Italian *jurists* are not highly cultivated people or that they are not involved in social, economic, and political affairs. It is Italian *legal science* that is isolated from the rest of Italian life. A professor whose doctrinal writing and teaching are in the mainstream of legal science may at the same time be a tough practicing lawyer or a high government official concerned with a wide range of policy problems.

50. The description of the historical growth of state positivism that follows is based in part on ideas that are more fully developed in Ascarelli, *op. cit.* n. 28.

51. On the *jus commune,* see 1.10 and 1.16.

The state tended to become the unique source of law, claiming sovereignty for itself both internally and internationally. Thus, national legal systems began to replace the *jus commune*, which became a subordinate or supplementary law. Roman law itself was quoted as providing, in the maximum *quod principi placuit habet vigorem*,[52] justification for the legal autonomy of the state that eventually ousted it in favor of a national legal system.

Hence the legislation of the prince replaced the Roman common law. The emphasis on legislative autonomy protected the state against potentially weakening influences during the period of the growth of national authority. The restraining and stabilizing forces of the Roman law and the authority of the Emperor, with their potential braking influence on the misuse of legislative power, were removed from the state, and the age of sovereignty began. Where Roman law was received, as in part of Germany,[53] it was received by will of the prince, and its continued force within the state also depended in theory on his will. But where, as in most of Europe, there was no formal reception of the Roman law, the process of building a national law (usually in the national language) took place under conditions and in the presence of assumptions that presaged European legal positivism. The legislative act was not subject to any higher authority than the state, nor was it subject to any limitation from within the state (such as customary law). The state itself was the only source of law.

What one Italian writer has called "the Sinai complex"[54] developed in this intellectual climate. The domain of the jurist became the legislation of the state, the positive law. If such legislation was enacted according to the rules established

52. *Digest* 1.4.1 (Ulpianus). The maxim is suspect. Mommsen and others have suggested that it is an interpolation by Tribonian, who was in charge of the work of compilation under Justinian. For a summary, see Pernice, *Zum römischen Gewohnheitsrechte*, 20 Savigny Zeitschrift (R.A.) 127, 160 n. 4 (1899).

53. On the reception of Roman law in Germany, see 1.16; and *A General Survey, op. cit.* n. 4. It is difficult for an American to appreciate fully the importance attached by European jurists to this reception. For an Italian assessment, see Pacchioni and Grassetti, *Diritto civile*, in 5 *Novissimo digesto italiano* 800, 802 (1960).

54. Piovani, *op. cit.* n. 17, at 40–41: "Without insisting too much on similarities of this kind one can say . . . that in . . . *giuspositivismo* there is inherent an involuntary parallelism between the authority of Revelation and the authority of legislation, so that the jurist who knows how to see the law only as the totality of legislative imperatives cannot easily free himself from what we may call the Sinai complex." See also Bobbio, *op. cit.* n. 3, at 335 ("code-worship").

by the legislature itself to govern the legislative process, its validity could not be questioned. To do so would be to impair the fundamental assumption of the sovereignty of the state. It was not the jurist's function to look behind or beyond the law. The law was a datum which, like other data, he accepted and studied. In this he was conditioned by preceding centuries of acceptance and study of the *Corpus Juris Civilis* as this kind of law, as legislation of the Emperor Justinian. There was, indeed, new emphasis on the authority of legislation, but what was entirely new was the emergence of the national state as its only source.

In the seventeenth and eighteenth centuries, a new secular natural law arose, based partly on the principles of legal equality and individual justice and partly on a belief in "the chance of deriving the detailed solutions of the law according to the method of Euclidean geometry."[55] It was both the age of the Rights of Man and the age of Reason. The new ideas associated with this secular natural law assumed some limitation on the power of the prince to legislate, and hence the dogma of absolute sovereignty was questioned. Those in power naturally resisted, and the natural law of the Rights of Man became the battle cry of a revolution directed against the evils associated with the extremes of statism.[56]

One might suppose that with the success of such a revolution legal positivism would fall. In fact, however, there was only a short hiatus, after which a new positivism took the place of the old.[57] In France the judiciary had been the object of much hatred. Judicial office was a kind of property right that one could buy, sell, or leave to one's heir. There was a judicial aristocracy that tended to identify with the other elements of the aristocracy, not with the rising bourgeoisie. Often the same identification led to judicial resistance to the further centralization of power in the king, sometimes taking form in a refusal to obey royal laws. The distinction between legislative and judicial functions was not then as clear as it seems today, and

---

55. Lawson, *op. cit.* n. 6, at 31. For fuller discussions, see 1.18; d'Entrèves, *Natural Law* ch. 3 (1951).

56. For a general discussion of the background of the French Revolution, see Lowell, *The Eve of the French Revolution* (1892). For a discussion of the codification of French law after the Revolution, see von Mehren, *op. cit.* n. 15, at 13–22 (1957); Deak and Rheinstein, *op. cit.* n. 15, at 555–58; Friedrich, *The Ideological and Philosophical Background*, in *The Code Napoléon and the Common-Law World* 1 (1956).

57. This form of legal positivism is indistinguishable from what Pound came to call "positive natural law." For his description of the intellectual forces that produced it, see Pound, *The Revival of Natural Law*, 17 Notre Dame L. Rev. 287 (1942).

both powers were lodged in the highest courts, called *parlements*.[58] The protest against the judiciary took form as a protest against judicial arbitrariness, judicial lawmaking, and judicial refusal to be subject to the law. To prevent the recurrence of these abuses, it was thought that lawmaking power had to be forever taken away from the judges and lodged in a representative legislature. Judges had to be made subject to the law, and the judicial function had to be restricted to application of the law.[59]

So a positivism based on the dogma of the state (in the person of the prince) was replaced by one based on the dogma of strict separation of powers. Only the legislature could make law, and it followed that questions about the justice or utility or appropriateness of legislation were questions solely within the legislative jurisdiction.[60] They were not the business of the courts or of legal scholars, many of whom welcomed this opportunity to resist what they considered to be the excesses of natural law.[61] The belief that so sharp a logical distinction could be made between lawmaking and law-applying was an expression of the rationalism of the times, a rationalism that provided support for the idea of codification and support for the assumption of completeness of the code.[62]

58. Most histories of the French Revolution include some discussion of the causes of popular dissatisfaction with the courts and judges of the *ancient régime*. See, e.g., Gershoy, *The French Revolution and Napoleon* 18–22 (1939). See also von Mehren, *The Judicial Process in the United States and in France—A Comparative Study*, 22 Rev. Jur. U.P.R. 235, 244–45 (1953).

59. Montesquieu is usually cited in this connection. See Lowell, *op. cit.* n. 56, at 126–53, for a brief discussion of Montesquieu's ideas, particularly his emphasis on the separation of powers. For a fuller discussion, see 1 Calamandrei, *La cassazione civile* 408 *et seq.* (1920).

60. "The purpose of the science of law is to consider the law that is, and not that which ought to be. At the basis of this theory of legal science is the assumption of a clear separation between validity and value of law, between the rules that can be valid, even without being just (those with which the legal science is alone concerned), and those that can be just without being valid; only the first are the object of the scientific study of the law." Bobbio, *Giusnaturalismo e positivismo giuridico*, 8 Rivista di diritto civile pt. 1, at 503, 508 (1962).

61. It is tempting to attribute some of the extremes of European legal positivism to a reaction against natural law, particularly in Italy, where the natural law of the Roman Catholic Church has exerted an influence quite separate from, but in some ways similar to, that of the secular natural law discussed in the text. On this point, see Falk and Shuman, *The Bellagio Conference on Legal Positivism*, 14 J. Legal Educ. 213, 217–18, 223 (1961); Fassò, *Natural Law in Italy in the Past Ten Years*, 1 Natural L. F. 122, 131 (1956).

62. Ascarelli, *op. cit.* n. 28, at 172–74. See also Campbell, *Legal Positivism* (1999) (presenting responses to and criticisms of positivist legal theory).

In Italy there was not one government at the beginning of the Risorgimento, but many.[63] Legal traditions varied among them, sometimes quite sharply, but it cannot be said that any widely felt hatred of the judiciary was a principal source of revolutionary energy. Indeed, most Italian states had already received the Code Napoléon as a result of French conquest earlier in the century. The principal battle cries were those of unification of the state and independence from foreign domination. Italy was, however, a part of Europe; and the rationalist dogma of strict separation of powers, combined with legislative unification and with codification on the French model, led Italian legal thought in the same directions as the French.[64]

5.07 *Law and Sociology.*   The emphasis on the purely legal, the rejection of the nonlegal as nonscientific, is sharply expressed in the traditional doctrinal attitude toward sociology.[65] There was substantial interest in Italy in law and sociology in the latter half of the nineteenth century; in fact, some of the Italian work of that period in criminal behavior and penology made important contributions to the consideration of problems of criminal policy. But toward the end of the nineteenth century Italian legal sociology began to experience a rapid decline.

A new period began, marked by a progressive restriction of the aims of legal science. More emphasis was placed on formalism. Legal purism became the ideal: the law, it was said, was the business of lawyers; sociology was the business of sociologists. Jurists claimed that sociology was only a pseudoscience which was likely to contaminate legal science, and there was talk of "sociological intrusions" into the law.[66] This defensive attitude toward sociology was only one aspect of a more general phenomenon. Sociology was not the only outcast: religion, morals, philosophy, politics, economics, and history were also rejected. The jurist narrowed his study to the norms—to the provisions of the law itself—in order to interpret

---

63. The best brief discussion of the Italian Risorgimento is Salvatorelli, *Pensiero e azione del risorgimento* (1963). See also Salvatorelli, *A Concise History of Italy* chs. 18, 19 (1940).

64. See 1.20–1.22; Piano Mortari, *Codice (premessa storica)*, in 7 *Enciclopedia del diritto* 227–36 (1960).

65. On the attitude of the traditional doctrine toward sociology see Bobbio, *op. cit.* n. 18; Giannini, *op. cit.* n. 47; Orestano, *Sociologia e studio storico del diritto*, 8 Jus (n.s.) 199 (1957).

66. Giannini, *op. cit.* n. 47, at 223. Giannini states that "one of the most venomous polemic devices in use among legal scientists was that of accusing a certain thesis of sociologism." *Id.*, at 224.

them and arrange them into a system. He restricted his vision to something that was his, to purely legal data.

This emphasis on legal purism was in part a reaction against some sloppy legal-sociological scholarship in Italy, in part a result of the half-political character of the work of jurists identified with the left, and in part the result of a tendency to identify sociology with socialism. More fundamentally, however, it was a logical consequence of the new legal positivism, which was encouraged by the influence of German legal science and was consistent with new currents of Italian philosophic thought. Under these conditions it is not surprising that legal purism had its period of fashion at the turn of this century. But in view of the great social changes that were already under way in Italy, and have since proceeded at a vastly accelerated rate, it is not clear why legal purism was so widely accepted among Italian jurists and why it governed the doctrine, with little effective dissent, for over half a century.

A persuasive explanation has been offered by Norberto Bobbio, a prominent Italian legal philosopher:

> It has also been observed, and I think rightly, that the political atmosphere in which a totalitarian regime matured and prevailed for long years in Italy contributed to the silence that came to fall over sociology. . . . Sociology had found favor at the end of the last century in radical political circles; it was taken up by the socialist intellectuals or those inclined toward socialism. It was frequently considered the scientific way of confronting the social problem, and because of the similarity of the names, it was frequently improperly transformed into a close relative of socialism. Leaving aside any ideological tint, sociology carried with it the requirement that politics be a science. The totalitarian regimes were born, however, under the insignia of irrationalism, of exaltation of talent, of instinct. Politics appeared to them in the garments of a religion, albeit a false religion. The old positivists, now disdained, saw in political man a younger brother of the student of the social sciences; the totalitarians, however, invoked the holy leader, younger brother of the wizard. The first cherished the ideal of a policy elaborated in a cabinet of scientists; the second preferred a rousing dialogue in the public square between the leader and the crowd. One of the practical functions of sociology was to clear the ground of myths that prevented liberation from error and misery; social myths and superstitions were useful instruments of domination in the "age of tyranny." And if history and science were still invoked it was only for the service they could render to the holders of power; but they were the false history of imperial ideology and the false science of racist ideology.[67]

67. Bobbio, *op. cit.* n. 18, at 191–92.

Although the positivist strain remains dominant in Italian thought, a number of competing tendencies retain significant influence. Given the country's Catholic heritage, a significant strain has (not surprisingly) involved natural law theory and the relationship between law, morality, and religion: the distinction between *diritto* (law in the sense of right or justice) and *legge* (law as individual legislative enactments) is a recurring theme in this area. This distinction is most prominent in the work of Giorgio Del Vecchio (1878–1970), Italy's leading natural law scholar, who traced the idea of justice to Greek and Biblical sources and emphasized its transcendent nature above and beyond any temporary legal order.[68] A related stream is represented by Giuseppe Capograssi (1889–1956), who emphasized the "experience of law" as an essential aspect of humanity and the resulting impossibility of containing law within purely scientific categories.[69] The Catholic influence is also visible, if less directly, in the writings of Santi Romano (1875–1947), who suggested that institutions, rather than norms, were the distinguishing feature of all legal systems.[70] With the coming of the Italian Republic several of these themes have reappeared in postwar Italy, as described in Part 5.10, below.

5.08 *History.*   Italian legal thought is also, to the eye of a common lawyer, ahistorical.[71] Although the suggestion that a legal system based in large part on Roman law, canon law, and the customs of medieval merchants lacks the historical dimension may seem bizarre, that is what is meant. Legal history of the sort so familiar to common lawyers through the work of the great Anglo-American legal historians hardly exists in Italy. The careful study of persons and events in relation to the growth, transformation, and decay of specific legal institutions, which Maitland and Holdsworth took as the province of legal history, is characteristic of

---

68. See Del Vecchio, *La giustizia* (1946).

69. See Capograssi, *Il problema della scienza del diritto* (3d ed. 1970).

70. See Santi Romano, *L'ordinamento giuridico* (1946).

71. It also seemed so to Petrarch, who spent seven years as a law student. See his complaint, quoted in Gilmore, *Humanists and Jurists: Six Studies in the Renaissance* 30 (1963). For a further discussion, see Gorla, *Studio storico-comparativo della "common law" e scienza del diritto*, 16 Rivista trimestrale di diritto e procedura civile 25, 48–55 (1962). And see Gorla, *Diritto comparato*, in 12 *Enciclopedia del diritto* 928, 940 (1964) (referring to the "ahistoric" way continental lawyers view their law); Nicolini, *Per una maggiore concretezza negli studi storico-giuridici*, 13 Jus (n.s.) 1 (1963). An updated version of the *Enciclopedia del diritto* is available on CD-ROM.

contemporary Anglo-American legal history, but not of European. In Italy, and in general on the Continent, legal history is something quite different: it is a history of schools of legal thought, first and foremost, and historical persons and events are discussed primarily in relation to these schools. What common lawyers have come to think of as legal history exists to some extent, but it is uncommon. The main stream of historical thought, the legal history taught in the law schools, and the assumptions and attitudes that form the historical outlook of the Italian lawyer, are all something quite different. But the more important evidence that Italian law is ahistorical lies in the prevailing nonuse of history. Textbooks and treatises on the law do not contain the historical component common lawyers have become accustomed to finding in their own literature, and they seem lifeless and abstract by comparison.[72]

A number of factors help to account for this ahistorical attitude. For one thing, Roman law has not traditionally been regarded historically on the Continent. From the time of the revival of Roman legal studies until the last century, the *Corpus Juris Civilis* of Justinian was treated not so much as a stage in the development of Roman law but as a completed legal system having contemporary legal validity. The *Corpus* was studied in order to apply it better to the present,[73] not in order to determine its historical role. The "secular" nature of Justinian's work, its relative freedom from religious, ideological, and political associations, made it more adaptable to the needs of various times and places—so adaptable, in fact, that it could form the basis of a common law of Europe for seven centuries. But this same secularization, by making the *Corpus* seem timeless, also tended to place it outside history. And it should be remembered that during the middle ages the revived Roman system was held in almost superstitious veneration as the

72. "I would almost say that discussions are considered scientific to the extent that they avoid history; it is almost as if the legal order issued improvisedly from the mind of the legislator, like Minerva from the head of Jove." Biondi, *Funzione della giurisprudenza romana nella scienza giuridica e nella vita moderna*, 10 Rivista di diritto civile pt. I, at 1, 11 (1964). And see Orestano, *op. cit.* n. 65, at 210 (listing history among the studies excluded by the purism of the traditional legal science).

73. "Being true medieval men, the Glossators were not motivated by any historical interest in Roman law. To their mind, Justinian's codification embodied the law of their own time; for they adhered to the theory that the Holy Roman Empire was the successor of the old Roman Empire, so that the law of the Byzantine emperor was conceived as the imperial law of their own period." Wolff, *Roman Law: An Historical Introduction* 188 (1951).

perfection of learning, as written reason. It was not something to criticize or to place in historical perspective, but something to learn from; it was a received body of law valid for any time and place. This attitude was encouraged by the medieval scholars, who made the system itself the object of their study and writing, and by the medieval law schools which taught it as *the* law.[74]

Within the ranks of the Romanists themselves there has been a great deal of study of the pre-Justinian Roman law during the last hundred years or so in Italy and in other European countries. These studies have shown that the origins of much of the *Corpus Juris Civilis* can be found in the slow development of Roman legal institutions through centuries of Roman history. In many ways the nearest parallel one can find to the history of the common law, as common lawyers are used to reading it in the works of Maitland and Holdsworth, is in some of the scholarship on the relations between actions and rights during the formative periods of Roman law.[75] But, with some remarkable exceptions, this work has not penetrated very far into the doctrine, and even less into the *manuali*, or textbooks, which law students study. The majority of Italian lawyers and scholars do not regard Roman law historically in the way that common lawyers regard the laws of Henry I. They recognize that many of the institutions of their contemporary legal system have Roman origins, but they seldom go beyond this observation.[76]

Second, the history of Italian law from the revival through the middle ages would be much more likely to engage the historical interest of the Italian lawyer were it not for the dominance of a *jus commune* based heavily on these assumptions about Roman law. The foundation of this European common law was the text of Justinian, and the principal additional sources were the works of scholars who, accepting the authority of the text, wrote glosses or comments on it.[77] Neither the decisions of cases by courts nor the laws enacted by princes were thought of as principal sources of law. They were considered exceptional, less important, sometimes even aberrational, and the scholars often ignored them.

---

74. "For the doctors of the new study the books of Justinian were sacred books, the sources of authority from which all deductions must proceed." Vinogradoff, *Roman Law in Medieval Europe* 57 (3d ed. 1961).

75. See Mattei, Ruskola, and Gidi, *Schlesinger's Comparative Law* (7th ed. 2009); Gorla (*Studio*), *op. cit.* n. 71, at 30 –37.

76. An examination of any of the *manuali* cited in note 19 and of the principal commentaries on the civil code will illustrate the point.

77. See 1.11–1.12; Wolff, *op. cit.* n. 73, at 187–90.

Third, during this period the Italian peninsula was a collection of different kingdoms, duchies, republics, dominions, communes, principates, and the like. It became a nation only slightly more than one hundred years ago. Before unification, warfare among the various inhabitants of the peninsula, foreign invasions, and foreign domination were common. Governments appeared, disappeared, merged; regimes were established, removed, and replaced; boundaries were stretched and contracted. It is one thing to write a history of the common law of England, a jurisdiction that has been free of foreign domination, and has had a more or less stable and unitary identity, for over nine centuries. It is quite another to try to write the legal history of a nation as lacking in unity, continuity, and coherence as Italy.[78]

Fourth, the Italian Risorgimento, although less drastic and bloody than the French Revolution, was still in part a break with the past. Old institutions were systematically and deliberately abolished, and new ones were deliberately and systematically created. It was assumed both that one could destroy old legal institutions and that one could erect new ones in their places by legislative act. These were rationalistic times: man needed only sufficient intelligence and foresight to establish a new legal order. Both the French Code Napoléon and the Italian Civil Code of 1865 incorporated the rationalistic hopes of this era. They were produced in the belief that a legal system could be legislatively created and that, as a corollary, history could be made irrelevant to the law.[79]

---

78. See Gorla (*Studio*), *op. cit.* n. 71, at 50; "This history of formation [of legal institutions] is difficult to follow in our common law, because we do not have a central organ or body such as the Court of London with its Inns of Court; [in our system] disorder reigned, except for the work of the schools, from the Glossators on, which however was not a work of formation but one of reflection on the 'formed,' on that which has already been done, on the past, on the text." And see Gorla (*Diritto*), *op. cit.* n. 71 at 940: "[It is] a strange and paradoxical fact that it is easier, even for us, to know the history of the common law—the well-documented history of a centralized court—than that of our continental law!"

79. See Mattei, Ruskola, and Gidi, *op. cit.* n. 75, at 174–78, 181–82. The statement in the text is extreme. It seems unlikely that all French jurists of the time believed that history could be made irrelevant, but many people of influence, among them many lawyers, did so believe. The Law of the 30th of Ventose, Year XII (1804), sought to repeal all prior law on the topics covered by the Code Napoléon, whether inconsistent with the Code or not. The norms that the Code adopted from prior law had legal effect not because of their prior existence but because of their "legislative novation." See Gény, *La technique legislative dans la codification civile moderne*, in 2 *Le code civil, 1804–1904, Livre du centenaire* 987 (1904).

Of course, rationalism and secular natural law were not the sole driving forces. Nationalism was at work, and neither Roman law nor medieval common law were French.

Fifth, the kind of legal history common lawyers have grown accustomed to reading in the last century is really much more than *legal* history. It is social, economic, political, and legal history blended together, with a dash of anthropology added. Its great strength, which common lawyers take for granted, lies in the synthesis of these points of view about persons and events into a whole that reveals their interrelationships. Taking sociology in a very broad sense, one could say that this kind of legal history is really sociological jurisprudence in historical context. In Italy, where the dominant patterns of legal thought have been inhospitable to sociological jurisprudence, it is not surprising that this kind of legal history is uncommon. It is inconsistent with dogmatic legal science.[80]

Indeed, there is a rather close relation between the fourth and fifth of these points. With the abolition of the old laws and the enactment of the codes, Italian lawyers faced (often, perhaps, unconsciously) the very difficult problem of bridging the abyss that lay between the formal statement of the law and its meaning in application. This is a problem which, for the common lawyer, is greatly eased by reference to the nine centuries of magnificently documented, continuous legal history that lie behind him. It is the foundation upon which he builds.[81] But with codification, history as a source of meaning was abolished for the French jurist, and later, perhaps not so drastically, for the Italian. To play the game by the new rules, he had to find another source of meaning. During the immediate post-Risorgimento period, the ideals of the revolution and the ideas of the secular natural law of the previous century, with their emphasis on liberty and equality, may have helped him bridge the gap. But such general ideals, however worthy, are not of much use in the hard business of establishing a working jurisprudence, and the Italian jurist rebelled against the extremes of an excessive rationalism and

---

Roman law, medieval common law, and the French *coutumes* were identified with feudalism, the power of the aristocracy, and prerevolutionary abuses; hence they should be repealed. Whether the drafters of the Code really sought to replace all existing law *ex novo* is beside the point. The thought of the time assumed that they did.

80. See 5.07; Orestano, *op. cit.* n. 65, at 200–203.

81. "[T]he common law, for historical reasons peculiar to it, offers us a complete and documented history of its formation, with original documents, not corrupted, interpolated, or manipulated, and without breaks in continuity: a history such as no other legal order, in our present state of knowledge, can offer us." Gorla (*Studio*), *op. cit.* n. 71, at 49.

excessive faith in natural law.[82] In this he was aided by the assumptions of the code itself, and particularly by the claim that it was complete.

The dogma of completeness of the code has a number of corollaries, the most obvious of which is exclusion of noncode materials as aids in interpretation. If the code is complete, so the reasoning goes, then the answer to any problem can be found in it. Where the answer fails to leap to the eye, closer examination of the code will find it. Such a process, aided by the covert practice of giving traditional meanings to concepts of obviously Roman or *jus commune* origin, and by the similarity of the backgrounds of those who drafted the codes and those who were called on to apply them, sustained Italian juridical life until the advent of the Pandectist thought and the development of legal science. In this way the dominance of Italian legal science can be viewed as a kind of product of the ahistorical nature of Italian law. What foreigners tend to condemn as the excessive abstractness and conceptualism of Italian doctrine may be traceable to the institution of the new codified legal order. At one stroke a great part of the legal culture was abolished, leaving a great void. Something had to fill the void and fill it according to the rules, including those abolishing the prior law and insisting on the completeness of the new. Legal science filled the void according to the rules.[83]

5.09 *Certainty in the Law.* A final aspect of the dogmatic legal science to be considered here is the repeated emphasis one finds in the literature on the value of certainty in the law.[84] Such an emphasis may be startling to an American lawyer trained in the atmosphere of American legal realism, with its skepticism about the possibility, even the desirability, of certainty.[85] In Italy the attainability and the importance of certainty are seldom questioned. *Certezza del diritto* is an accepted

---

82. See note 61 and accompanying text.

83. The attitude of the French jurist who said that he knew nothing of the civil law but only studied the Code Napoléon, and the statement attributed to Napoleon when he was informed that the first commentary on his code had been published—"My code is lost"—typify the rationalistic belief described. The reaction of Savigny against such views is a famous event in continental legal history. For a good introduction, see Kantorowicz, *Savigny and the Historical School of Law*, 53 L.Q. Rev. 326 (1937).

84. A frequently cited work is Lopez de Oñate, *La certezza del diritto* (1950).

85. See Frank, *Law and the Modern Mind* (2009); Merryman, *op. cit.* n. 8, at 621–29. For an Italian assessment of Frank's views, see Bobbio, *La certezza del diritto è un mito?*, 28 Rivista internazionale di filosofia del diritto 146 (1951).

value. This emphasis on certainty is an expression of the legal positivism already described. Judges are forbidden to make law in the interest of the certainty that flows from having all law produced by the legislator and published in legislative form. Thus, an Italian textbook, in discussing the power of the judge to temper rigid application of the law by equity in hard cases, can say:

> One should not think that recourse to equity is always allowed. The legal order frequently sacrifices the justice of the individual case to the exigencies of certainty in the law, inasmuch as it considers it dangerous to subject itself to the subjective evaluation of the judge, and prefers that individuals know in advance the precepts they must observe and the consequences of inobservance (*the principle of certainty of law*).[86]

And in explaining why there is no general doctrine of abuse of right in Italian law, the same author states:

> [W]here the legislature has not acted, it appears dangerous to entrust the determination of the limits of the subjective right to the discretionary and variable criteria of the judge. It therefore seems better to conclude that, except for the cases expressly contemplated, the requirement of certainty that, as we have seen . . . , is fundamental to the legal order precludes consideration of the abuse of subjective rights.[87]

This insistence on a sharp separation of powers in the interest of certainty is a product of the French Revolution and the Risorgimento, and has its source in a desire to prevent the excesses of judicial arbitrariness associated with the prerevolutionary period in France and, to some extent, in Italy. Its roots also lie partly in the soil of rationalism, in the belief that the law can be made clear and certain, so the individual can know what his rights are without having to wait on the subsequent events of trial and judgment. In this sense certainty is one aspect of the justice that was an object of the European revolution; it expressed the popular longing for a legal system that was fair, uniform in application, clear, and simple. It was primarily a reaction against the injustice of the old order, but it was also partly a reaction against the technicality and professionalism of the law that is the first object of reform in most utopian programs.[88]

The survival of the stress on certainty in the law in today's Italian doctrine can be attributed in part to Italian fascism. A rigid separation of powers is also a

---

86. Torrente and Schlesinger, *op. cit.* n. 19, at 7.

87. *Id.*, at 42.

88. See 5.06.

bulwark against executive interference in the judiciary. Hence, when, under fascism, various overtures were made in the direction of abolishing legal technicalities, of deciding cases according to fascist legal principles, or, most subversive of all perhaps, of relaxing the insistence on certainty, the traditional legal value of certainty became the symbol for those who wished to defend the prefascist legal order. The example of Germany, where the abolition of legality had gone forward under the theory of "free decision" or by reference to the *Führerprinzip*, was before the Italian jurists. Many Italian jurists strongly resisted this tendency, which they feared would make the law merely another branch of the administration, in the name of the traditional values of the doctrine, among which certainty tended to dominate.[89]

The United States and England have a legal history in which the judiciary has traditionally been arrayed on the side of the citizen against arbitrary governmental power. The judiciary was not the principal villain of either the English or the American revolution. And common lawyers have not recently had to endure more than twenty years of a totalitarian government that constantly attacked the barriers placed in its way by a liberally oriented legal system. The emphasis on certainty in Italian doctrine can only be understood in the context of Italian history. In that context it has played an honorable part as the forensic term that summed up basic democratic legal values.

Certainty is not, however, so discussed in the textbooks. It is presented rather as a scientific dogma abstracted from its historical context. Like other aspects of the traditional doctrine, it is purified of nonlegal connotations and becomes a means for resisting any intrusion, whether totalitarian or democratic, of "nonscientific" values into the legal process. It constitutes a further justification of the cultural agnosticism of legal science; if nonlegal factors are allowed to intrude, certainty will be lost.[90] Hard cases and unjust decisions are regrettable, but they are the price

---

89. See 5 Calamandrei, *Studi sul processo civile* ix–xv (1947); Cappelletti, *In memoria di Piero Calamandrei* 55–58 (1957); Cappelletti, *Il processo civile italiano nel quadro della contrapposizione "civil law–common law,"* 9 Rivista di diritto civile (pt. 1) 31, 59 (1963); Falk and Shuman, *op. cit.* n. 61, at 218, 227.

90. "One hears it repeated on all sides that the jurist should not be agnostic, should not stand apart from the political *ambiente* in which he lives and works. And this observation is quite proper if it refers to the jurist when he acts as legislator—that is, to the extent that he performs a *political* function; indeed, the proposition, in the sense indicated, is utterly superfluous, because the legislator in general could not, without betraying his function,

one has to pay for certainty. This emphasis on certainty is sharply expressed in the schism between Italian legal philosophers and Italian legal scientists.

Legal philosophy and legal science are traditionally separate worlds in Italy,[91] in part perhaps because of the purity, and hence the narrowness, of the latter. Discussion of the ends of law, of such ultimate values as justice, was historically excluded from juridical science and left to the philosophers. Hence the traditionally opposed values of certainty and justice, of stability and change, of rest and motion, so frequently contrasted in American legal thought,[92] were not found together in the Italian doctrine. It was one-sided. Certainty was accepted as a "legal" value by the doctrine, but contrasting values were rejected by it. In American legal writing one encounters discussions of the problems of accommodating competing values; in Italy one found little awareness that any competition is going on. What seems odd to the common lawyer is not so much the stress on certainty as the absence of a tempering emphasis on the necessity of reconciling certainty with other important values.

---

legislate against the social conscience. But when one considers the activity of the jurist in his other competence (*interpretation of the constituted* law), one must realize that this is an essentially *technical* activity of elaboration and *explanation* of the objective law, in conformity with the spirit that animates that law, and in which, therefore, the jurist can also perform his critical activity, but also here from the *technical*, and not political, point of view. In this different sense one can justify the assertion that the jurist neither can nor should be a political man; for him the constituted law is a *given*, which he may not put aside.

"If it were not thus, and if the thesis that the *interpreter* should do the work of a *politician* in the act in which he interprets were accepted, a dangerously bad trend would be established, by which the interpreter would eventually deny the application of the norm under the pretext of its inadequacy to the political situation of the moment; that is, a natural-law attitude would be justified ('the law is not law if it is not just law') that would subvert the principle of the obligation of the law, and would make the jurist a revolutionary by profession or by duty of office, compromising that which is one of the fundamental needs of any legal order: its *stability* and its *certainty*." 1 Messineo, *Munuale di diritto civile e commerciale* 24 (9th ed. 1957). (Italics in the original.)

91. See the symposium in 33 Rivista internazionale di filosofia del diritto 1–272 (3d ser. 1956); Piovani, *op. cit.* n. 17; *Atti del II Congresso nazionale di filosofia del diritto* (1956). From this point of view the recent statement of Professor Thomas Cowan seems incorrect, at least as applied to Italy: "I do not mean to say that law completely abandoned philosophy. This did not occur, nor has it yet occurred in civil law jurisdictions." Cowan, *Some Problems Common to Jurisprudence and Technology*, 33 Geo. Wash. L. Rev. 3, 9 (1964).

92. The classic is Cardozo, *The Paradoxes of Legal Science* (1928), reprinted in *Selected Writings of Benjamin Nathan Cardozo* 251–337 (1947).

Like the ahistorical nature of Italian legal thought and the separation of law and social science, the requirement of certainty in legal outcomes has been shaken if never fully abandoned in recent years. Under the influence of Anglo-American thinkers—and reflecting the intellectual ferment of two generations of Italian democracy—scholars have reexamined basic questions relating to the underlying goals of the legal system, the judicial role in statutory interpretation, and the natural law/positivism dichotomy, asking whether the goal of certainty and predictability may be unrealistic or (what amounts to the same thing) whether it may sometimes have to be sacrificed to preserve higher values. To some extent these changes are the result of a counternarrative under which an excessive separation of law and morality, and the resulting excessive deference to positive law, may have exacerbated rather than limited the damage of the fascist period. These and related tendencies are discussed in the following section.

5.10 *The Present State of Italian Legal Science.*   Much of the Italian doctrine may seem strange and unreal to the American observer. The emphasis on system-building; the deliberate search for concepts of a high order of abstraction; the conscious effort to avoid confusing legal with social, economic, or historical facts and objectives; the acceptance of the positive law without questioning its justice or its appropriateness according to other nonlegal criteria; and the emphasis on certainty in the law may all appear to be extraordinary attitudes for sophisticated legal scholars to hold.

Thus, it is easy—too easy—to criticize Italian legal thought. By emphazing its extremes and ignoring its context, one can make it appear ridiculous. But a sympathetic observer who keeps in mind that he is examining the product of a different tradition and a different history will try to understand why these attitudes have dominated Italian legal thought in the first half of this century. Italian legal thought must be judged in the context of the long history of the Italian peoples and the short history of the Italian nation, the revival of Roman legal studies, the European revolution, the Risorgimento, unification, codification, and, most recently, the long years of struggle to retain democratic legal values in the face of the insistent attacks of a totalitarian regime.

In recent decades the growth of foreign influence together with the needs of a new, democratic political order have contributed to a noticeable softening in many of the traditional categories of Italian legal thought. To some extent, the discussion parallels similar debates in other countries, and the work of Kelsen,

Hart, Radbruch—not to mention Rawls, Dworkin, Posner, and other more recent figures—is frequently cited in postwar treatises. But it retains a peculiarly Italian flavor both in its substantive themes and in the abstract, deductive style in which the debate is conducted: the tendency to construct self-contained and comprehensive analytical systems, which display great sophistication but rarely if ever discuss actual cases, is especially striking to a North American observer.

Perhaps the most sophisticated attempt to reconcile international trends with Italian traditions is the work of Norberto Bobbio, a towering figure in legal and political philosophy who died in 2004. In his book *A General Theory of Law*, Bobbio constructs a model of the legal system that incorporates elements of natural law and realist theories against the backdrop of an essentially normativist approach.[93] The notion of law as a particular kind of prescriptive norm, backed by coercive as well as moral sanctions and forming part of a broader, integrated legal order—a bridge as it were between Kelsen's normativism and the institutionalism of Santi Romano and his followers—is especially strong in Bobbio's work.[94]

A more pragmatic approach is provided by Gustavo Zagrebelsky, an important scholar and for several years judge (later chief judge) of the constitutional court. Zagrebelsky's work emphasizes the role of constitutional law in maintaining underlying principles of justice—in putting the *diritto* back in the *legge*, to use the author's own words—and thus provides a crucial link between legal theory and the practical institutions of the modern Italian State. The role of law in protecting democratic institutions and preventing a reversion to fascism is an important if by and large implicit theme of such work.[95]

Italian scholars have also been prominent in comparative law, emphasizing the underlying differences between legal systems and—perhaps motivated by Italy's own experience—the role of legal transplants and hybridity in understanding contemporary legal systems. The work of Rodolfo Sacco and his followers is particularly significant in this area.[96]

Most important of all is a changed described by Bobbio himself:

93. Bobbio, *Teoria generale del diritto* (1993).

94. See *ibid.*, pp. 3–22 (law as rules of conduct), 159–72 (from legal rules to legal order).

95. See Zagrebelsky, *La giustizia costituzionale* (1988); Zagrebelsky, *La legge e la sua giustizia* (2009).

96. See Sacco, *Legal Formants: A Dynamic Approach to Comparative Law*, 39 Am. J. Comp. L. 1 (1991) (First Installment) and 39 Am. J. Comp. L. 343 (1991) (Second Installment).

Finally—and here it seems to me that we touch the principal factor—the return of a democratic regime has stimulated sociological researches just as the long persistence of the totalitarian regime impeded them. It is well known that sociological research is today more advanced in countries long governed democratically. Here I limit myself to one consideration: where it is sought to govern more by persuasion and less by force a more exact knowledge of the interests, needs, and ideas of different groups composing the society is necessary. Sociological inquiry is one of the instruments of this acquisition of knowledge. Democratic policy tends at the limit to become scientific policy, and one of the instruments of this policy is the investigation of the social structures into which the work of the legislature is put.[97]

Even a casual perusal of an Italian law library will bear out the accuracy of Bobbio's prediction, with legal scholars making increasing use of economics, philosophy, and a wide range of empirical methods in their scholarship. The overall tendency is toward broadening the scope of legal scholarship to relate the law to other aspects of society; the progression seems to be from exegesis to traditional legal science to what might be called an "open" jurisprudence. This progression is cumulative; the accomplishments of the exegesists, which were substantial, are retained and reflected both in the structure of the newer Italian codes and in the ease and authority with which Italian jurists deal with difficult problems of statutory interpretation. The accomplishments of traditional legal science, and in particular the systematization and provision of orderly structure in the law, a value common lawyers frequently underestimate,[98] survive. Properly used, legal science provides a sturdy foundation for the study and exposition of legal problems, processes, and solutions—a foundation that can support the study of the law in its economic, social, and historical context.

But, to quote another Italian commentator, "Just as Rome was not built, neither did Byzantium fall, in a day."[99] Although some Italians are critical of the traditional doctrine or seek to progress beyond it, others cling to it. It continues to pervade the literature most frequently used in teaching and practice. The typical *manuale* on private law begins with a general part equivalent in nature and style to the *allgemeiner Teil* of the BGB, in which the theoretical structure is set out and in whose interstices the attitude and the method described become apparent. More

---

97. Bobbio, *op. cit.* n. 18, at 193.
98. See Lawson, *op. cit.* n. 6, at 66–69.
99. Piovani, *op. cit.* n. 17, at 64. See also Bobbio, *op. cit.* n. 3, at 339.

substantial works, such as the standard commentaries on the civil code, display the unmistakable marks of the doctrine. And even the most advanced legal thinkers have to use the language of the legal science, because it is the language of Italian legal scholarship. For all that has changed in the past half century—and will likely to continue to change in the future—the traditional legal science remains an unmistakable and significant element of the Italian Style.

CHAPTER SIX

The Italian Style: Law

6.01 *Introduction.* In Chapter 5, we described some of the more striking (to a common lawyer) features of the dominant force in Italian legal life: the traditional doctrine. This orthodox pattern of assumptions and attitudes, although clearly in decline, still sets the legal tone in Italy and is still characteristic of the Italian style.

In this chapter, the emphasis shifts to certain more specific topics: the theory of the sources of law; the principal divisions of the law; and the ideology, content, and arrangement of the Italian Civil Code of 1942. Each of these topics provides additional perspective on Italian law and on the Italian way of thinking about law.

These topics also provide the occasion for brief discussions of the more obvious examples of the interplay between the traditional view of the legal process and the great political, economic, and social changes that have swept over Italy during the last century. Within the past hundred years or so, Italy has experienced two disastrous wars and three kinds of government: a liberal monarchy, a fascist dictatorship, and a constitutional democracy which has been characterized by recurring waves of governmental instability together with at least one major overhaul of the political system. These events inevitably have left a powerful imprint on the country's law and legal institutions.[1]

---

1. See generally Denis Mack Smith, *Modern Italy: A Political History* (1997).

6.02 *The Sources of Law.*[2]   The formal legislative statement on the sources of Italian law is article 1 of the Provisions on the Law in General,[3] which states, "The following are sources of law: (1) statutes [*la legge*]; (2) regulations [*regolamenti*]; (3) corporative norms [*norme corporative*]; (4) usage [*usi*]." This brief statute, which sums up orthodox Italian doctrine on the sources of law, is as interesting for what it excludes as for what it admits.

Like the traditional legal science of which it is a partial expression,[4] the traditional Italian theory of sources places emphasis on the value of system.[5] The listed sources are treated as constituting a *numerus clauses*; sources of law are sharply dis-

2. The rough equivalent of a theory of "sources of law" in the United States is found in discussions of "primary and secondary authority," usually included in works on legal bibliography. See, e.g., Beardsley and Orman, *Legal Bibliography and the Use of Law Books* 6–14 (2d ed. 1947); Hicks, *Materials and Methods of Legal Research* 52–53 (3d ed. 1942); Jacobstein, Mersky, and Dunn, *Fundamentals of Legal Research* (1994). For a more realistic discussion, see Merryman, *The Authority of Authority*, 6 Stan. L. Rev. 613 (1954).

As in other matters, the Italian theory of sources is more formal and more thoroughly and consciously developed by scholars than its counterpart in the United States. Most manuals and systematic works of scholarship in Italian private law, administrative law, and constitutional law contain discussions of the sources of law. See, e.g., 1 Barbero, *Sistema del diritto privato italiano* 67–84 (6th ed. 1962); 1 Zanobini, *Corso di diritto amministrativo* 59–112 (8th ed. 1958). For more recent authorities, see, e.g., Torrente and Schlesinger, *Manuale di Diritto Privato* (21st ed. 2013); Cerulli Irelli, *Lineamenti di diritto amminstrativo* (2012).

The Italian literature on sources is vast. For an introduction and bibliography, see Sandulli, *Fonti del diritto*, in 7 *Novissimo digesto italiano* 524 (1957).

3. The Provisions on the Law in General (Disposizioni sulla Legge in Generale) are prefixed to, although they are not formally a part of, the Civil Code. Articles 1–9 deal with the sources of law.

The cited provision was enacted in 1942. The republican Constitution was adopted in 1948, and, as the more sophisticated doctrine recognizes, has both increased the variety of sources of law and made some of the major assumptions of the traditional theory of sources untenable. For a good discussion, see Crisafulli, *Gerarchia e competenza nel sistema costituzionale delle fonti*, 10 Rivista trimestrale di diritto pubblico 775 (1960).

Nowhere in the Constitution is there any integrated formal statement of the sources of law and of the relationships between them. This may help to explain why many *manuali* (and some more ambitious works) still treat article 1 of the Provisions on the Law in General as definitive, although the continuing power of the traditional theory of sources is certainly a factor of at least equal importance.

4. For an introduction to the principal relevant characteristics of the traditional legal science in Italy, see Chapter 5.

5. See discussion in 5.04.

tinguished from other materials and events within the legal order, and important legal consequences are assumed to flow from the distinction. Some of the kinds of materials excluded from the group of formal sources of Italian law would also be denied "primary authority" status in the common law, but the process of definition and differentiation is more rigorously, consciously systematic in Italy than it is in the United States.

The standard discussions of the sources of law also display other signs of their origins in the traditional legal science, and indeed the principal exclusions from the category of sources are usually justified by references to state positivism,[6] a rigid separation of powers,[7] and legal purism,[8] all of which are outstanding characteristics of legal science.

The view that the state has a monopoly on lawmaking power excludes a number of internal and external forces from the category of formal sources of law. Italian legal scholarship, despite its pervasive influence throughout the legal process, is an obvious and striking example.[9] Legal transactions (*negozi giuridici*)[10] among individuals and groups, including the bylaws of private organizations, comprise another.[11] Foreign laws, foreign judgments, law produced by international organizations, and international law were traditionally treated as mere facts to which the legal order of the state may or may not attach legal effects, although this approach has been compromised to a degree by Italy's participation in the European Union and other international organizations.[12]

6. Discussed in 5.06.

7. Discussed in 5.06, 5.09.

8. Discussed in 5.06–5.08.

9. "[T]he 'science of law,' whose task is to investigate and explain the law but never to create it, is not a source of law; . . . it is *effective* to the extent it is *convincing*, but it is absolutely lacking in any binding character." 1 Barbero, *op. cit.* n. 2, at 83–84. For a discussion of the role of doctrine in the Italian legal process, see 5.02, 5.10.

10. Described in 5.05.

11. "With these we move even further from the sources of law. Contracts and transactions are not sources of 'rules of objective law,' but of 'legal relations,' of 'subjective relations.'" Hence the erroneous interpretation of a contract, unless such interpretation violates the law governing interpretation, is not subject to attack in the Supreme Court of Cassation, where only the "erroneous interpretation of rules of law" may be attacked. 1 Barbero, *op. cit.* n. 2, at 82–83.

12. "Nor may facts productive of rules of other orders (for example, the laws of another state, the provisions of an international organ) be considered sources of the legal order of

Emphasis on a strict separation of powers justifies the rejection of judicial decisions as a source of law.[13] Lawmaking is one thing; interpretation and application
of laws are quite another. In deciding the case, the judge merely interprets and
applies the law; he does not create it. The decision is binding on the parties, but
does not bind others. *Stare decisis* is rejected. Otherwise judges would become
legislators, and the dogma of sharp separation of legislative and judicial power
would be violated.[14]

In Italy it is recognized that the needs, aspirations, and activities of people—
the political, economic, and social interests seeking legal recognition and
protection—are ultimate sources of law. The legal order of a given time and place
is a partial function of the socioeconomic order. But these "sources of law in the
substantive sense" are distinguished from the formal sources of law. In the same
way, Italian jurists recognize that many of their legal institutions have their origins
in the past and are fully understandable only in the light of history; nevertheless,

---

[this] state. . . . Such facts, which, with respect to the state that receives them, necessarily
assume the position of mere legal facts, are not themselves productive of norms." Sandulli,
op. cit. n. 2, at 533. The lawmaking role of the EU is discussed further below.

13. "[T]he decision of the judge, like judicial activity in general, is not a source of legal
rules but the application of rules to the case. That such application sometimes has the effect
of precedent to which, in practice, other similar cases may conform, does not mean that the
giurisprudenza is a source of law, and it does not mean that a series of decisions conforming
to a given precedent, no matter how long, may not be interrupted by a decision that can
mark a change of direction without signifiying a change in the law. It is all an effect of the
way of looking at the law on the part of those men who have the job of applying it, but it
is not lawmaking, even if, in practice, the technique that governs the efficacy of a judicial
decision may sometimes have the same effect." 1 Barbero, *op. cit.* n. 2, at 83.

"Equity" is also excluded from the sources of law for similar reasons. The power to
mitigate the rigor of the norm according to the circumstances of the concrete case is occasionally granted to the judge by the legislature, but the power is held within narrow limits.
Despite some dissenting voices, "in this sense equity is not a 'means of production' but a
'criterion of application.'" *Id.*, at 81–82.

14. And this, in turn, would, according to the theory under discussion, endanger the
prime legal value of "certainty in the law." The increasing publication (especially online
publication) of judicial decisions, together with the influence of the Constitutional Court
and other appellate forums, have caused the Italian attitude toward precedent to evolve
somewhat in recent decades; this and other aspects of judicial interpretation are discussed
further in Chapter 7.

"sources of law in the historical sense" are also excluded from the group of formal sources.[15] Such distinctions as these are familiar enough to common lawyers, but they have an added dimension in Italy. There, they are magnified in importance by the legal purism of the traditional legal science, which is expressed in what has earlier been described as the cultural agnosticism[16] and the ahistorical nature[17] of Italian legal orthodoxy.

What remains after these exclusions is summarized in the statute quoted above. The only expressly recognized sources of law in Italy are statutes,[18] regulations,[19]

15. 1 Barbero, *op. cit.* n. 2, at 68–69.

16. See discussion in 5.06, 5.07.

17. See 5.08.

18. The Constitution of the Republic of Italy (1948) is, of course, the prime source of Italian law, superior to ordinary legislation because, by its own terms, special procedures are necessary to amend it, and laws contrary to it can be declared void by the Constitutional Court. See 2.09. "Constitutional laws" or "laws on constitutional matters" are contemplated by the Constitution (arts. 71, 72, 116, 117, 132, 138), and require the same procedure for enactment, repeal, and amendment as constitutional amendments (art. 138). See 2.06.

At the level of ordinary legislation the Constitution contemplates not only the typical act of Parliament but also the issuance of decrees by the executive ("the Government") having the force of ordinary legislation. According to article 76 of the Constitution, legislative power may be delegated to the government for a limited time and for a definite object. When promulgated in proper form, these "legislative decrees" (*decreti legislativi*) have the same status, for most purposes, as ordinary laws. Article 77 of the Constitution denies the government the power to issue decrees having the force of law without prior delegation by Parliament, except in "extraordinary cases of necessity and urgency." Such "decree-laws" (*decreti-legge*) are issued by the government "on its own responsibility" and become void *ab initio* unless converted into law by Parliament within sixty days. See 2.07.

The Constitution also contemplates the establishment of twenty regions (art. 131), of which five (Sicily, Sardinia, Trentino–Alto Adige, Friuli–Venezia Giulia, and the Valle d'Aosta) have special legal status.

19. All of the forms of legislation described in the preceding footnote, with the exception of the Constitution itself, are denominated "statutes and acts having the force of statute" by articles 134 and 136 of the Constitution. Only they are subject to constitutional review by the Constitutional Court. The validity of regulations, rules, and similar quasi-statutory norms issued by governmental authority can be attacked only before the administrative or ordinary courts, depending on the case. This gives the distinction between the two categories a very important jurisdictional significance. However, subsequent doctrinal opinion questions the distinction and argues that regulations ought to be subject to a constitutional review. See Mortati, *Atti con forza di legge e sindacato di costituzionalità* (1964). For a good

corporative norms,[20] and usage.[21] Among these recognized sources, a hierarchy exists; they are listed in descending order of importance.[22] At the apex stands the

---

introduction to this distinction and a discussion of regulations as sources of Italian law, see 1 Zanobini, *op. cit.* n. 2, at 59–81.

20. "Corporative norms" were an emanation of the "corporative state" under Italian fascism. They included (1) regulations issued by corporative entities; (2) governmentally approved economic agreements of various kinds (such as a contract between a producers' organization and an organization representing marketers); (3) governmentally approved collective labor agreements; and (4) certain kinds of decisions of the special labor courts created by the fascist government.

Ordinarily, economic and collective labor agreements, on the one hand, and the decisions of courts, on the other, would not be sources of law according to the theory under examination. But, by the laws of the fascist period, such agreements, if governmentally approved, became binding on all persons who were, or subsequently became, engaged in the activities represented by the bargaining groups, whether or not they were or became members of such groups. In common Italian legal parlance these agreements were effective *erga omnes*. Likewise, decisions of the labor courts were, in certain cases, binding on all who fell into the categories formally represented in the action, whether or not they actually belonged to the organizations that were the formal parties.

On the fate of corporative norms when the corporative structure was abolished in 1944, see note 88.

21. The present code uses the term *usi* and the prior code *consuetudine*. They are employed interchangeably. Of all the contemporary sources of Italian law, usage is certainly one of the least important both in degree of authority and frequency of use. Nevertheless, the literature on usage as a source of law is immense—almost, one would say, in inverse proportion to its current significance. This may be explained in part by the greater importance of usage in earlier periods of Italian legal history and in part by the need to explain the seeming anomaly of admitting to the *numerus clauses* of formal sources of law as something that is unwritten and is not created by the state. For good discussions and introductions to the literature, see Bobbio, *Consuetudine (teoria generale)*, in 9 *Enciclopedia del diritto* 426 (1961); Scherillo, *Consuetudine (diritto romano)*, in 4 *Novissimo disgesto italiano* 301 (1959); Astuti, *Consuetudine (diritto intermedio)*, in 4 *Novissimo digesto italiano* 310 (1959); Franceschelli, *Consuetudine (diritto moderno)*, in 4 *Novissimo digesto italiano* 320 (1959). The *Novissimo digesto italiano* is available in an updated edition that includes the Astuti and Franceschelli articles.

22. "The sources and the precepts derived from them are arranged in a 'hierarchy' on the basis of the legal strength they possess.

"The hierarchical scale of sources and precepts has the greatest importance in that, by absolute rule, new acts or facts of legal production can (validly, and therefore 'obligatorially') modify only those precepts drawn from acts or facts of an equal or lower order, and not from those drawn from acts or facts of a higher order.

statute; regulations, corporative norms, and usage have legal effect only within the limits established by it.

This theory of sources, like the traditional legal science of which it is an organic part, has been in visible decline for more than a half century in Italy. Some of the impetus toward revision comes from within the doctrine itself, but much of it is due to the impact of the Constitution of 1948.

The dogma of state sovereignty—the view that only the state can make law—is under attack from two directions. Within the state, according to an influential doctrinal school, there are a number of "legal orders" in addition to that of the state itself.[23] The rules such "private" (nonstate) persons and organizations generate to arrange and conduct their affairs thus qualify, under this view, as "law."[24]

A second challenge arises from the influence of international organizations, particularly the European Union (EU), of which Italy was an original member and which has significantly expanded the range of its lawmaking activities during the past decades. The EU has a substantial direct influence, in that many EU norms and directives are given juridical effect under Italian law, and indirect influence, in that there is an inevitable tendency for the laws of the various EU members to converge in certain areas with the passage of time. The precise effect of EU directives within Italy, and what happens when and if they conflict with internal norms, is a complex question that is beyond the scope of this work, but to the extent that EU rules have effect within Italy, they are, realistically considered, additional sources of law.[25]

"As for precepts derived from acts or facts of equal or less strength, the rule is, in sum, that the subsequent normative act or fact prevails (*lex posterior derogate priori*). On the other hand, the existing precept prevails in the case of new acts or facts when the act or fact from which it originated was superior in strength." Sandulli, *op. cit.* n. 2, at 527; *cf.* Provisions on the Law in General arts. 4–8, 15.

23. The landmark work in support of this view is Santi Romano, *L'ordinamento giuridico* (2d ed. 1951). Santi Romano is generally treated as the founder of the Italian "institutional" school and as principal exponent of a theory of a pluralism of legal orders within the state.

24. This thesis is developed in another landmark: Cesarini Sforza, *Il diritto dei privati* (reprint 1963); *cf.* Codice civile art. 1372: "The contract has the force of law between the parties."

25. On the effect of EU law in Italy, see Daniele, *Diritto dell'Unione Europea: Sisteme istituzionale, ordinamento, tutela giurisdizionale, competenze* (4th ed. 2010).

On the status of foreign law generally, see Alpa, *Foreign Law in International Legal Practice: An Italian Perspective*, 36 Tex. Int'l L.J. 49 (2001). For a historical perspective on the

The classical theory of allocation and separation of powers—that in a well-designed state all formal lawmaking power resides in the legislature—is likewise out of tune with the facts of Italian government. The Constitution, rather than laws enacted by Parliament, is the prime formal source of Italian law. Parliament derives its lawmaking power from the Constitution, and although that document can be amended by parliamentary action, the power of amendment itself is limited,[26] requires a special procedure,[27] and is subject to disapproval by popular referendum.[28] Ordinary acts of Parliament can also be repealed, in whole or in part, by referendum,[29] and proposed legislation can be introduced into Parliament by popular initiative.[30] The Constitutional Court has the power to review legislation for constitutionality. A decision by it that a statute is unconstitutional has effects *erga omnes*; the decision is not, like ordinary judicial decisions, binding only on the parties.[31] A regulation found by an administrative court to exceed the power of the promulgating authority may also be quashed and is thus deprived of any legal effect.[32] These powers, plus the fact that judges in Italy actually do make

---

relationship between Italian and European law, see Antonio Padoa Schioppa, *Italia ed Europa nella storia del diritto* (2003).

26. Article 139 of the Constitution states, "The republican form is not subject to constitutional amendment."

27. Amendments to the Constitution require approval on two separate occasions at least three months apart by absolute majorities of both chambers of Parliament. Constitution art. 138.

28. If the amendment was approved by an absolute majority of two-thirds of the members of each chamber on the second vote, a referendum is not permitted. Otherwise the amendment can be referred to a popular election on the demand of one-fifth of the members of either chamber, by the petition of 500,000 voters, or on the request of five regions. Constitution art. 138.

29. Constitution art. 75. Certain kinds of laws are exempt from popular referendum: fiscal or budgetary laws, amnesties or pardons, and laws ratifying treaties. As for all others, referral to popular election is made on the petition of 500,000 voters or the request of five regions.

30. Constitution art. 71.

31. The basic provisions establishing the Constitutional Court are contained in Constitution arts. 134–37. See 2.09. For a discussion of the effects of the Court on the judicial process in Italy, see Cappelletti, *L'attività e i poteri del giudice costituzionale in rapporto con il loro fine generico*, in 3 *Scritti giuridici in memoria di Piero Calamandrei* 83 (1957).

32. See 2.04.

law in their ordinary work of interpreting and applying the formal sources,[33] further weaken the traditional view of the legislator as sole lawmaker.

The hierarchy of sources, as expressed in orthodox discussions, is seen by recent scholarship to be a vast oversimplification of what is, particularly since the promulgation of the 1948 Constitution, a very complex set of interrelationships that cannot accurately be summed up in so simple a formula.[34] And, finally, there is evidence of growing dissatisfaction with legal purism and its corollary of a sharp separation between law and the rest of the culture.[35]

While little if any hint of these doctrinal developments was found in traditional scholarship about the sources of law in Italy,[36] the traditional theory has plainly lost ground. This "twilight of the myth of the sovereignty of the statute (and of Parliament)"[37] is only one aspect of a growing trend in Italian legal thought that "contraposes a critical view of legal reality to a passé dogmatism . . . enclosed in the most obsolete formulas of legal positivism in an exclusively statal sense, despite the meaning and effect of a Constitution whose innovative import is undeniable."[38]

6.03 *The Divisions of Italian Law.* It is obvious enough that the law can be divided in various ways to serve a variety of functions, and hence it is not surprising that the Italian law is divided somewhat differently than the law is in common law countries. It is equally obvious, although more difficult to demonstrate, that any such division of law is bound to react upon the legal system itself, so the conventional way of dividing labor becomes a part of the law itself, affecting the way that law is formulated and applied.

One of the fundamental distinctions in Italian law is between public law and private law.[39] An apparently similar distinction is frequently drawn in common law

33. This topic is discussed at length in Chapter 7.

34. Crisafulli, *op. cit.* n. 3.

35. See discussion in 5.04, 5.06–5.09.

36. For example, the discussions of Barbero and Sandulli, both cited in note 2, limit themselves to stating the traditional position on every question. There is no indication of the nature of new currents of doctrinal thought or of the impact of the new Constitution in either of these or in most of the *manuali* in general use.

37. Crisafulli, *op. cit.* n. 3, at 810.

38. Salvatore Romano, *Introduction* to Cesarini Sforza, *op. cit.* n. 24, at v.

39. Most institutional works and manuals on civil or private law contain discussions of divisions of the law; they historically began such discussions by emphasizing the public law–private law distinction. See, e.g., 1 de Ruggiero and Maroi, *Istituzioni di diritto civile*

jurisdictions, but the similarity is to some extent deceiving. With common lawyers these terms generally have, at most, a kind of conventional or descriptive significance; they are a way of talking about law that is sometimes convenient but seldom more than that. Serious debate and extensive scholarship about the nature of public and private law, the differences between them, and the area of application of each of them are uncommon in the United States. The contrary is the case in Italy.

Such a distinction can be conceived of as descriptive or normative; it may simply be a convenient way of summarizing legal results, or it may be a way of achieving them. It is one thing to conclude that a matter concerns public law because the law treats the interest of the state as superior, in the concrete instance under discussion, to that of the individual. It is quite a different thing to say that since the matter concerns public law, it must follow, in a given case, that the interest of the state is elevated to a higher plane. In Italy the distinction between public and private law is both descriptive and normative, and the classification of a problem or a legal relation as appertaining to one or the other can have significant legal consequences. It can, first of all, determine which of two potentially applicable bodies of substantive law will in fact be applied. If an agreement between a public body and an individual is found to fall into public law, the rules applicable to contracts in the private law do not apply, and the agreement is not considered to be a contract in the usual sense; it is something else: a creature of public law.[40] The interest of the individual in a private law relation is called a right (*diritto oggettivo*), but his interest in a public law relation is often called a "legitimate interest,"[41] something quite different. Finally, although some public law problems may be decided by the ordi-

---

15–17 (9th ed. 1961); 1 Messineo, *Manuale di diritto civile e commerciale* 54–858 (9th ed. 1957); Torrente, *Manuale di diritto privato* 9–10 (5th ed. 1962); Trabucchi, *Istituzioni di diritto civile* 8–10 (15th ed. 1966). Similar discussions may also be found in institutional works on public law. See, e.g., Monaco and Cansacchi, *Lo stato e il suo ordinamento giuridico* 8–16 (9th ed. 1962); Mortati, *Istituzioni di diritto pubblico* 86–93 (6th ed. 1962); 1 Zanobini, *op. cit.* n. 2, at 23–26; *cf.* Zanobini, *Diritto pubblico*, in 5 *Novissimo digesto italiano* 1021 (1960). For a more recent example, see Caretti and DeSiervo, *Istituzioni di diritto pubblico* (10th ed. 2010).

40. For a discussion of contracts in public law, see 4 Zanobini, *op. cit.* n. 2, at 465–512; Virga, *Teoria generale del contratto di diritto pubblico*, in 9 *Enciclopedia del diritto* 979 (1961); Sepe, *Contratti della pubblica amministrazione*, in 9 *Enciclopedia del diritto* 986 (1961).

41. On the distinction between subjective right and legitimate interest in Italian law, see Galeotti, *The Judicial Control of Public Authorities in England and Italy* 13–16 (1954); 1 Zanobini, *op. cit.* n. 2, at 181–99; Bozzi, *Interesse e diritto*, in 8 *Novissimo digesto italiano* 844 (1962).

nary courts, many of them are exclusively in the jurisdiction of an entirely separate group of courts—the administrative courts—and once a problem falls within that jurisdiction, it stays there, subject to different procedures and remedies.[42]

It hardly needs to be pointed out that a normative distinction between public and private law that has implications of this kind is of resounding importance. It affects the distribution of de facto power between individual and state and defines the legal limits of individual autonomy in economic and social matters. Further, classification of a problem or an interest as public or private places it in a doctrinal context. The applicability of fundamental attitudes of public or private legal thought, the relationships with other private law or public law problems or interests—matters which may often be determinative of resolution of conflicts— will depend on the initial classification. Hence discussion about the true nature of the distinction and of the areas of application of public law and private law principles and attitudes are of the greatest practical importance, even though they are normally carried on in the abstract and conceptual terminology of juridical science.

The typical description in the *manuali*, to the effect that public law governs the organization of the state and its relations with the citizen, relations in which the state is in a position of superiority to the citizen, while private law concerns the relations between private individuals who are in a position of equality with respect to each other,[43] thus fails to convey the true flavor of the distinction. Nor does it indicate the relative nature of the dichotomy and the effect of recent history on it.

6.04 *Changing Conceptions of Public and Private Law.*[44]   The distinction between private and public law that exists today in Italy has its ideological origins in the nineteenth century. The civil law, which at that time was the core of private law, was codified in the Code Napoléon, the Italian Civil Code of 1865, and the bürgerliches Gesetzbuch of 1896. The dominant legal concepts in all of these codes were individual private property in land and individual freedom of contract. The codifiers

42. See 2.06, 4.04.

43. This is the statement of Torrente, *op. cit.* n. 39, at 9. The other cited manuals and institutional works use similar language.

44. On this topic, see Orlendo Cascio, *Il "nuovo volto" del diritto privato*, 10 (II) Rivista di diritto civile 65 (part 2) (1964); Giorgianni, *Il diritto privato ed I suoi attuali confini*, 15 Rivista trimestrale di diritto e procedura civile 391 (1961); Nicolò, *Diritto civile*, in 12 Enciclopedia del diritto 904 (1964). For a more recent example, see Torrente and Schlesinger, *op. cit.* n. 2.

believed these rights to be natural rights of man. In the legal thinking of that century, the statement and elaboration of these rights in the codes served as legal guarantees against state intrusion into areas properly left to individual autonomy. The thinking was of the kind we might now describe as extreme individualism. The civil codes were thought of as serving a sort of constitutional function by establishing a legal order in which individual private property and individual freedom of contact were fundamental rights. Private law meant that area of the law in which the sole function of government was the enforcement and the protection of those rights.

Accompanying this fundamental attitude were various corollary assumptions. Among these were a rather primitive view of the economy, in which the principal actors were private individuals, and an extremely limited conception of the appropriate sphere of governmental activity. The various forms of association of individuals for concerted activity, such as corporations and labor unions, and the expanded participation of the government in the country's economic and social life that are common today were not contemplated. The doctrine of that period, later raised to a highly systematic and abstract level by the Pandectists and then enthusiastically received and further refined by Italian jurists, helped to preserve these essentially nineteenth-century attitudes until the middle of the twentieth century.[45] The fundamental conceptions of the juridical science—*diritto soggettivo* and *negozio giuridico*—are nineteenth-century notions.[46] They assume both the central importance of the individual and the limited function of government. They are the juridical formulation of the role of individual autonomy in the law, and their area of effectiveness is coterminous with the area of effectiveness of the private law.

As a result of these developments, the traditional polarization of Italian law into public and private law continued. Despite frequent recognition by others that this ideology was out of tune with contemporary Italian political, social, and economic life, it did not begin to encounter any effective opposition from established legal scholars until after the fall of fascism. The traditional dichotomy of public law and private law, like the traditional theory of sources, is now being reexamined.

A few of the more important changes that have stimulated this reevaluation deserve brief discussion. First, the postwar government was established in Italy under a Constitution not only recognizing but emphasizing the relations of government

---

45. On the Pandectists and Italian legal science, see 1.23, 5.03.

46. On these and other major concepts in the Italian doctrine, see 5.05.

to the economy and the society.[47] The individualistic state of the nineteenth century has slowly but surely been replaced by the social state of the twentieth. The role of government has expanded far beyond earlier conceptions. The social and economic life of the nation is controlled by state activity to a much greater extent, decreasing the area for the free play of individualistic conceptions of private autonomy.[48] One way of viewing this change is to see fundamental private law concepts as having been modified by the addition of social or public elements, and such terms as the "socialization" or the "publicization" of private law are frequently encountered. Although a doctrinally more conservative writer may insist that the "legal" content, as distinguished from the social or economic content, of private law rights remains unchanged,[49] such a distinction has only limited utility. In fact, the content of fundamental rights has been substantially altered.

Second, a rigid Constitution[50] was adopted, and a Constitutional Court with power to review the validity of legislation was established.[51] Fundamental rights of property and of economic activity are defined in, and protected by, this Constitution, and although elaboration of the constitutional provisions has only begun, it is clear that the Civil Code has been deprived of its constitutional function. That function has been transferred from the most private of private law fields to the most public of public law. In a sense this might be described as a "depublicization" of private law, as purifying it of a primarily public function.

Third, the intervention of the state in the economic life of the nation has to a growing extent been carried on by the direct participation of state entities or corporations engaging in the conduct of enterprise and using the legal forms of private law, notwithstanding a significant decline in the state role since its peak in the early postwar period.[52] In this way the private law exerts a growing force on public

47. See 2.05.

48. See notes 96–107 and accompanying text.

49. See 1 Messineo, *op. cit.* n. 39, at 54–58 (referring, at 57, to "the so-called 'publicization' of private law" and insisting that "as long as subjective rights of individuals, as *individuals*, are recognized, there will be private law").

50. For a translation of the Italian Constitution of 1948, see http://www.senato.it/documenti/repository/istituzione/costituzione_inglese.pdf.

51. For a brief description of the nature and functions of the Constitutional Court, see 2.04 and authorities there cited.

52. The best-known example is ENI (Ente Nazionale Idrocarburi), headed, until his death in 1963, by Enrico Mattei. For an informative discussion of ENI and Mattei, see Accorinti, *Quando Mattei era l'impresa energetica* (2006); Votaw, *The Six-Legged Dog* (1964).

activity carried on not through the more traditional medium of the administration but through the conduct of industrial and commercial enterprise by state organs or by corporations controlled by the state. This tendency has been summed up by some administrative law scholars as a "privatization" of public law, as an expansion of the role of private law at the expense of administrative law.

Fourth, so-called intermediate groups—associations of persons engaged in concerted activity—have become increasingly important, not only in the life of the nation but also in its law. The earlier conception of a legal world composed primarily of individuals and the state has had to be expanded to take into account the role played by groups that are neither one nor the other but something intermediate between them.[53]

Fifth, the older conception of property as the relation between the individual and a thing, typically land, has had to be modified as the importance of other forms of property, with different characteristics, has grown, and as the separation between power and property associated with investments in corporate securities has been recognized.[54]

Finally, Italian law has witnessed the growth of fields that defy classification as either public or private law. For example, navigation law, labor law, and agrarian law, together with various other regulatory fields, are a mixture of both public and private elements, hybrids that defy traditional classification.[55] Chairs and institutes in these fields exist in the major Italian universities, and journals devoted to them are published regularly. Their existence tends further to blur the distinction between private and public law.

Hence, without attempting to penetrate too deeply into the matter, one can say that a rather drastic reshaping of the traditional conceptions of private and public law is under way in Italy. The distinction continues, for the reasons already men-

---

In fact, however, IRI (Istituto per la Ricostruzione Industriale) was more important in historical terms and is a better example of the point made in the text. For a brief description, see Pini, *I giorni dell'IRI* 67 (2004); Giacci, *Istituto per la Ricostruzione Industriale*, in 9 *Novissimo digesto italiano* 262 (1963).

53. See Rescigno, *Le società intermedie*, 10 Iustitia 335, 356 (1957); *Gruppi sociali e lealtà*, 133 Pubblicazioni dell'Università di Pavia, Studi nelle Scienze Giuridiche e Sociali 175 (1958).

54. See Nicolò, *Codice civile*, in 7 *Enciclopedia del diritto* 240, 248–49 (1960).

55. For a discussion of the peculiar nature and importance of these "autonomous" fields, see Cappelletti, *Il problema processuale del diritto agrario alla luce delle tendenze pianificatrici delle costituzioni moderne*, 18 Rivista di diritto processuale 550, 554–56 (1963).

tioned, to have great practical importance. Even under the impact of the forces tending toward newer definitions, substantial areas remain clear, and the great majority of problems and interests remain easily classifiable into one field or another. But at the frontier between them there is great flux, and few Italian scholars today would attempt any functional definition of private law or public law.

6.05 *Other Divisions of Italian Law.* The normative effect of the distinction between public and private law in Italy tends to overshadow its descriptive effect, but it does also serve a descriptive function. It serves to sum up a division of labor, a separation of the law into smaller parts to facilitate teaching, scholarship, and discussion. But the normative overtones tend to make the distinction a rather sharp one, even when used in a descriptive sense. A teacher of private law in Italy does not, as a rule, attempt to teach or study the public aspects of the equivalent subject. For example, a teacher of property law probably will not discuss property taxation, regulation of urban land use, or the constitutional protection of property rights. These are all parts of public law, and he or she leaves them to specialists in that area. On the whole, most private law instructors restrict their attention to the purely private aspects of the subject.

The teacher also tends to make somewhat sharper distinctions, even within private or public law, between procedure and substance and between one substantive field and another. On the whole, the importance and the nature of such distinctions seem to be considerably more emphatic in Italian than in American legal thought. From the academic and doctrinal point of view, it is not typical for the scholar to follow a problem where it leads, regardless of boundaries; over time this attitude has become an important assumption of the doctrine and hence a part of the law itself. Indeed, in extreme cases, distinctions of this sort are conceived of as embodying reality, as indicating a classification that is not merely conventional but is based on the nature of the material itself. Hence one occasionally finds doctrinal discussion about the autonomy of certain subjects, even where the field under discussion would seem to have been the result more of historical accident than of any compelling scientific considerations. In an aggravated case a writer may insist that only one of various proposed arrangements of the law is correct.[56]

---

56. On the "autonomy" of commercial law, see 1 Messineo, *op. cit.* n. 39, at 60. ("Now, the autonomy of *commercial* law must be preserved, notwithstanding the abolition of an autonomous commercial code; the question is not of *legislative* autonomy, but of *scientific*

Italian law is thus divided for scholarly purposes into public law, private law, and a group of hybrids that have elements of both. Public law itself is divided into constitutional law, administrative law, criminal law, procedure (both criminal and civil), ecclesiastical law, and, more recently, financial law. Private law is divided into civil law and commercial law.

6.06 *The Codes.*   Italy is a code jurisdiction. This means not only that codes are in force but also that certain attitudes about their nature and functions prevail. Some of these attitudes were mentioned in the discussion of the Italian doctrine, and others will be mentioned briefly below. However, no attempt will be made here to enter into a detailed discussion of the code idea. The subject has been relentlessly pursued in the literature, and the interested reader will have no difficulty finding reading matter.[57]

There are four principal codes in force in Italy: the Civil Code,[58] the Code of Civil Procedure,[59] the Penal Code,[60] and the Code of Criminal Procedure.[61] These

---

autonomy: it concerns, not the *code* of commerce, but the *law* of commerce.") Tamburrino, *Manuale di diritto commerciale* 1–12 (1962). For an opposing view, see Nicolò, *op. cit.* n. 44, at 904, 905–7. On the autonomy of agrarian law, see Arcangeli, *Il diritto agrario e la sua autonomia,* 3 *Scritti di diritto commerciale e agrario* 337 (1936).

57. For useful discussions and references, see Ascarelli, *L'idea di codice nel diritto privato e la funzione dell'interpretazione,* in *Studi di diritto comparato e in tema di interpretazione* 165 (1952); Lawson, *A Common Lawyer Looks at the Civil Law* 45–63 (1953); Vassalli, *Motivi e caratteri della codificazione civile,* in 3 (pt. 2) *Studi giuridici* 605, 607–9 (1960); von Mehren, *The Civil Law System* 31–80 (1957); Rescigno, *Codici: storia e geografia di un'idea* (2013). A good introduction to the history of the Italian Civil Code is Alpa, *La cultura delle regole: storia del diritto civile italiano* (2009). See also Hartkamp and Hondius, *Toward A European Civil Code* (2004); Collins, *The European Civil Code: The Way Forward* (2008).

58. Codice civile, approved by the Royal Decree of March 16, 1942, no. 262, and in force as of April 21, 1942. By the same decree, the Disposizioni sulla legge in generale (Provisions on the Law in General) were approved. A reliable but unofficial translation is Beltramo, Longo, and Merryman, *The Italian Civil Code and Complementary Legislation* (2d ed. 1990). The original Italian version is available online at http://www.unicam.it/ssdici/codice.html.

59. Codice di procedura civile, approved by the Royal Decree of October 28, 1940, no. 1443, and in force as of April 21, 1942.

60. Codice penale, approved by the Royal Decree of October 19, 1930, no. 1398, and in force as of July 1, 1931.

61. Codice di procedura penale, D.P.R. September 22, 1998, n. 447. On the 1998 revision, see Amodio and Selvaggi, *An Accusatorial System in a Civil Law Country: The 1988 Italian Code of Criminal Procedure,* 62 Temp. L. Rev. 1211 (1989); Pizzi and Marafioti, *The New Ital-*

are in addition to narrower codes that deal with particular subjects (tax law, environmental law, etc.).[62] While the Code of Criminal Procedure was redrafted in 1988, the remaining three date to the period before 1948, although some have been extensively amended. As in other European code jurisdictions, the codes are dwarfed by the bulk of the noncodified legislation in force, much of it fragmentary and ad hoc, but some quite systematic and indistinguishable in form from the codes themselves. Of this great mass of legislation outside the codes, some, called "special legislations," expand and supplement provisions of the codes themselves. For example, the provisions of the Civil Code on negotiable instruments are rudimentary;[63] for the full legislative statement on the subject one must in addition go to a *testo unico* or special legislation.[64] But other large areas of the law lie quite outside the codified topics. This has become particularly true in recent decades with the development of ever-widening areas of regulatory law, some that lie within the codes and some that lie outside them. Even if one thinks of codes as serving a kind of primary legislative function—as stating basic propositions that special legislation amplifies—they cover only a part of the law. Much of public law, in particular, is uncodified even in this sense. There is, in other words, a great deal more to Italian law than the codes might suggest.

6.07 *The Civil Code of 1865.* When common lawyers refer to the civil law, they generally intend to indicate either the legal systems originating in continental Europe or a distinction between criminal and civil law. To a European jurist, however, the term *civil law* has quite a different meaning. It refers to the content of the first three books of the *Institutes* of Justinian (of persons, of things, of obligations) and to the content of the major nineteenth-century civil codes. All of these have substantially the same subject matter, which is roughly what American law

---

ian Code of Criminal Procedure: The Difficulties of Building an Adversarial Trial System on a Civil Law Foundation, 17 Yale J. Int'l L. 1 (1992).

62. A particularly longstanding example is the Navigation Code, which dates to the 1940s. Codice della navigazione, approved by the Royal Decree of March 30, 1942, no. 327, and in force as of April 31, 1942. This code regulates maritime and air transport, both internal and international.

63. Codice civile arts. 1992–2027 (1942) govern negotiable instruments.

64. The law on bank checks and related instruments is the Royal Decree of December 21, 1933, no. 1736, consisting of 123 articles. That on notes is the Royal Decree of December 14, 1933, no. 1669, containing 105 articles.

schools teach in courses on persons and domestic relations, property, succession, contracts, unjust enrichment, agency and partnership, torts, and the remedies by which interests falling into these fields are judicially protected. The belief that this group of subjects is a related body of law which constitutes the fundamental content of the legal system is deeply rooted in Europe and the other parts of the world that have received the essentially Roman civil law, and it is one of the principal distinguishing marks of what common lawyers call the civil law system. Expansion of governmental activity and the increasing importance of public law have not seriously altered this outlook. Civil law is still the fundamental law.[65]

The Italian Civil Code of 1865 was not the first civil code in Italy. Before unification, the separate jurisdictions that later formed the Italian nation had various experiences with codes. The Austrian Civil Code of 1811 was in force in some parts of the north, various more or less indigenous attempts at codification were made in other parts of Italy, and during the period of Napoleonic conquest, the Code Napoléon was imposed on most of the peninsula.[66] Thus, when political unification made the need for legislative unification obvious, the idea of a code was already familiar to Italian jurists. Both because the experience under the Code Napoléon had been satisfactory and because the areas under Austrian domination were not yet a part of the Italian nation, the Napoleonic Code became the model for the Italian Civil Code of 1865. Although a number of changes were made on the basis of French and Italian experiences with the Code Napoléon, it is fair to say that the Italian Code of 1865 was not substantially different from its model.[67]

Thus, unified Italy enacted a Civil Code without the intensive discussion of the nature and the desirability of a code that one might expect to precede so important a legal step.[68] This readiness for a code was in part a reflection of the fact that the traditional source of law in continental Europe, and above all in Italy, was an authoritative text: the *Corpus Juris Civilis*. The Italian legal mind was trained by centuries of references to this text as the authoritative source of law. When, on unification and the creation of the new Italian state, it became necessary to establish a national law, the legal mind turned naturally to the idea of a code, or written systematic scheme.

65. On the history and nature of the concept of civil law, see Nicolò, *op. cit.* n. 44; Pacchioni and Grassetti, *Diritto civile*, in 5 *Novissimo digesto italiano* 800 (1960).

66. On the history of codification in Italy prior to unification, see 1.19–1.21; Aquarone, *L'unificazione legislative e i codici del 1865*, at 1–6 (1960).

67. See 1.22–1.23; Aquarone, *op. cit.* n. 66, at 38–42.

68. Nicolò, *op. cit.* n. 54, at 240, 241.

The Code Napoléon was chosen as a model not only because of its earlier imposition by the French but also because of its compatibility with Italian needs. In
Italy there was a rising *borghesia* with new ideas about the relations between the
citizen and the state and about the balance between individual liberty and state
authority. The French code, with its emphasis on private property and liberty of
contract—in general, the recognition of wide areas of individual autonomy—was
the embodiment of these ideals. Its indifference, if not hostility, toward intermediate associations (an attitude which is a kind of corollary of the individualistic
emphasis of the Code Napoléon), its treatment of land as the principal form of
wealth, and its emphasis on liberty of commerce were all consonant with the economic structure of the new Italian state. The structure of the family in Italian life
was compatible with its treatment in the code. The Roman law background of
many of the legal concepts was familiar to Italian jurists. The principal lacuna
was the lack of anything approaching a developed labor law, but this could hardly
concern a nation just embarking on the industrial revolution. In sum, the Code
Napoléon was acceptable because its fundamental outlook was similar to that of
the new Italian state.[69]

Thus, the need of the new Italian state for a unified civil law took shape in a code
that was bourgeois in outlook,[70] Roman and *jus commune* in content,[71] and French
in form. In one sense the new code was out of date soon after its enactment. The
reception of German juridical science had a profound effect on Italian doctrine
and was undoubtedly a factor in the call for reform of the much less scientific
French style of code.[72] The code's foreign origin must have lessened the inertia that
a more indigenous codification would have had. The later incorporation into the
Italian state of territories governed by Austrian law may further have weakened the
position of the 1865 Code.[73]

---

69. On the ideological and social compatibility of the Code Napoléon with the unified
Italy of the 1860s, see Nicolò, *op. cit.* n. 54, at 242–43; see also 1.22.

70. "[T]he code of a *western, bourgeois* people." 1 Messineo, *op. cit.* n. 39, at 56. (Italics
in original.)

71. For a discussion of the *jus commune*, see 1.10, 1.16.

72. For a discussion of the nature of the German legal science and its reception in Italy,
see 5.03–5.05.

73. For example, the Veneto region was incorporated after the defeat of Austria in 1866,
and the provinces of Trento, Bolzano, Trieste, and Istria after World War I. All these areas
were, before incorporation into Italy, subject to Austrian law. By the law of December 30,
1923, no. 2814, a Royal Commission on Reform of the Codes "*in occasione della unificazione*

Most important, however, were the great economic and social changes that took place in Italy after unification. Among these were the formation of large commercial and industrial enterprises, the growth of an industrial labor class, and the emergence of Italy as a participant in international trade and international politics. During the same period the often vague and radical programs of the political left began to take shape as calls for enactment of social legislation and for limitations on individualism in the interest of more equitable distribution of wealth and status.[74]

Some of the pressure for reform may have been eased by the enactment of special legislation and by the 1882 revision of the Commercial Code of 1865. Actual work on revision did not begin until after the World War I, when it originated as part of a larger program of reconstruction following the disastrous impact of that conflict on all phases of Italian life.[75]

6.08 *Ideology and the Civil Code of 1942.*   One of the principal obstacles to adequate appreciation of the originality and excellence of the Civil Code of 1942 is the fact that it was enacted under the fascist government of Benito Mussolini. It is often difficult to separate the image of the man and his regime from one's attitude toward the codification. The tendency is to assume either that the code is not to be taken seriously or that it is tainted by the totalitarianism that produced it. The first assumption is unfounded, as even a casual reading will demonstrate. There remains the equally serious doubt about the acceptability of its ideological content.[76]

It should be emphasized that the new code was not a revolutionary document. There was some new material, but there was also much that is hardly distinguish-

---

legislative con le nuove provincie" was formed. The intensive work on what became the 1942 Civil Code originated in that commission.

74. For good discussions of the relation between these economic and social changes and the pressure for reform, see Aquarone, *op. cit.* n. 66, at 43–60; Nicolò, *op. cit.* n. 54, at 243–44.

75. The formal beginning may be traced to the establishment in 1917 of a postwar commission, which included a subcommission on legal, administrative, and social questions. Vittorio Scialoja, one of the great names in Italian private law scholarship, presided over its work. It was succeeded by a Royal Commission on Reform of the Codes in 1923. See note 73.

76. This doubt was shared in some quarters in Italy. "They were certainly wrong, and it is surprising that there were learned and qualified men among them, who after the fall of fascism and the end of the war called loudly, but without adequate serious arguments, for the immediate abrogation of the Civil Code and a return to the preexisting legislative system." Nicolò, *op. cit.* n. 54, at 240, 248.

able from similar provisions of the Civil Code of 1865 and the Commercial Code of 1882. Many of the novelties had their origins in the doctrine and jurisprudence that had accumulated under the older codes, and the principal work of the new codifiers was modification and adaptation of the older codes to incorporate these developments. The older codes, with their natural law, rationalist, and individualist emphases, formed the basis from which the work began. The work of codification itself began shortly after World War I, before Mussolini came to power.[77] It was in the hands of established jurists whose education and professional formation preceded Italian fascism.[78] Much of their work was in completed form before the government began to take an interest in the ideology of the code. During this initial period, from 1923 to 1937, the Reform Commission drafted the parts on persons and the family and succession, which were enacted without substantial change as books one and two of the new code. In addition, the commission drafted a part on property and a proposed new commercial code.[79] During the same period, a separate Italian–French joint commission drafted a proposed joint code of obligations.[80] Although none of these latter three projects was enacted in the form of the drafts, the years of careful study and formulation they represented gave their fundamental content a direction that was not easy to change.

During the second period, beginning in 1939, there was mounting pressure from the more active fascists for integration into the code of so-called "general principles of the fascist legal order."[81] Despite party-sponsored confer-

77. See note 75.

78. Those who participated in the work of the postwar commission and in the work of the Royal Commission on Reform of the Codes, established in 1923, were recognized legal scholars before Mussolini became a major force in Italian politics. The work of the commissions continued under the control of such men until its completion.

79. Vassalli, *op. cit.* n. 57, at 609–12; Nicolò, *op. cit.* n. 54, at 243–45.

80. This was published in 1928 and was, according to Nicolò, a failure. See Nicolò, *op. cit.* n. 54, at 244. The draft was originally published as Commissione reale per la riforma dei codici & Commission française d'études de l'union legislative entre les nations alliées et amies, Progetto di codice delle obbligazioni e dei contratti, Testo definitivo approvato a Parigi nell'ottobre 1927 (1928). For a brief discussion in English, see Note, *Franco-Italian Draft Code of Obligations*, 10 J. Comp. Leg. & Int'l L. (3d ser.) 311 (1928).

81. Nicolò, *op. cit.* n. 54, at 246, refers to "the attempt by many persons, and unfortunately by some qualified jurists, to codify the general principles of the 'fascist legal order' as a premise of the Civil Code, an ill-conceived and obviously contradictory attempt that would have resulted only in the statement of abstract demagogic formulas, good for a

ences,[82] however, no very coherent statement of these principles was ever produced, and the vagueness of the programmatic calls for establishment of a fascist legal order made resistance to any such effort to contaminate the new code easier. In fact, many Italian jurists resisted the effort with remarkable success.[83] In the process they were assisted by the resistance of the legal science to the intrusion

---

political manifesto but not for a serious work of legislation." Vassalli, *op. cit.* n. 57, at 613 n. 2, mentions "the most active elements of the party, unhappy about the severely technical criteria followed in the work of codification and desirous of the solemn affirmation of so-called 'general principles of law' which could be nothing but the consecration of more or less defined" fascist ideologies.

82. A congress was held at the University of Pisa in May 1940. Its proceedings were published as *Atti del convegno nazionale universitario sui principi generali dell'ordinamento giuridico fascista tenuto a Pisa nei giorni 18 e 19 maggio 1940*, and are dismissed by Vassalli in four words: "*scritti pieni di fervore*" (writings full of fervor). Vassalli, *op. cit.* n. 57, at 613 n. 2.

83. "The great majority of Italian jurists who took part in this second, more intensive phase of the work of codification took advantage of their cultural education and technical experience to prevent political ideology . . . from prevailing in the reform . . . and it must be frankly recognized that in large part they were successful." Nicolò, *op. cit.* n. 54, at 246.

There were, of course, some exceptions. For example, one writer, in discussing the new Book V of the code, on labor, wrote that this section would help to bring "the fatherland [*patria*] to the forefront of the civilizations with the wisest laws," that in it "the legitimate aspirations of labor toward a higher social justice find solemn recognition and protection, and a new decisive thrust is given to the expansive march of the Italian economy," and that "in the book of labor corporative principles are realized in a form that is original politically as well as legally. In the scheme of the Charter of Labor the concept of labor is purified and freed from the class struggle." And in his report on the draft of Book V, the Minister of Justice wrote, "The historical reasons that have until now justified the autonomy of the Commercial Code must be considered overcome by the fascist corporative order. . . . In the regulation of the enterprise, the discipline of labor, almost ignored in the codes in force, must become an essential part. The precept of Il Duce: 'In our century labor will no longer be the object, but the subject, of the economy' should, that is to say, be translated into a legal norm."

What is chiefly remarkable about such effusions is their irrelevance to the substance as opposed to the presentation of the code. They are not so much explanations of the reasons for the form of the new code as they are attempts to turn to their advantage forces over which the fascists had little control.

For alternative views of law in the fascist period and the influence of the regime's ideology, see Schwarzenberg, *Diritto e giustizia nell'Italia fascista* (1976); Teti, *Codice civile e regime fascista: sull'unificazione del diritto private* (1990).

of nonlegal or nonscientific elements, and by its insistence on the preservation of legal values.[84]

Certain effects of fascism were of course apparent in the original iteration of the code. One of these took the form of insertion of the Charter of Labor of 1927[85] as a kind of prologue to the code, to serve as a source of "general principles of the legal order of the state" that were to guide the interpretation and application of its provisions.[86] This was abrogated after the fall of fascism in 1944.[87] Another was the "corporative norms" that were included among the listed sources of law and occasionally referred to in the code (obviously these "norms" were related to the quasi-governmental bodies that were an aspect of the corporative state under fascism) were likewise modified and adapted without altering the content or structure of the code.[88] However, certain collective labor agreements adopted prior to 1944 remained in effect, and it is to these that the term *corporative norm* has its only real reference in the code. Similarly, Book 5 of the code contains both the articles on labor, and capital and management. As is discussed in section 6.15, this is, in

84. Nicolò, *op. cit.* n. 54, at 246, mentions "those positions of cautious innovation that had emerged before or independently of fascist political doctrine," "a few, frequently simply verbal, concessions to the ideology of the moment [in order to] keep the code on the traditional path, utilizing doctrinal constructions," and the "enlightened technicism" of the jurists who dominated the work of codification.

85. For a brief description of the Charter of Labor, see Corrado, *Carta del lavoro*, in 2 *Novissimo digesto italiano* 967 (1958).

86. Article 12 of the Provisions on the Law in General contains a reference to "general principles of the legal order of the State" as a source of authority for decision when ordinary interpretation and analogy fail. For a fuller discussion, see 7.06.

87. The abrogation of the Charter of Labor was effected by the Legislative Decree of September 14, 1944, no. 287, one of a number of decrees repealing or modifying fascist laws and institutions.

88. By the Legislative Decree of November 23, 1944, no. 369, the fascist "corporations" were deprived of all norm-creating powers. Existing corporative norms were, however, continued in force. These were, for the most part, officially recognized collective bargaining agreements (and other economic agreements, such as marketing agreements between producers' and retailers' associations) which had, as a result of such recognition, *erga omnes* effect. It was clear that to deprive these agreements of such effect would result in economic chaos, since they were an integral part of the economic structure of Italy. Hence article 1 of the Provisions on the Law in General, listing corporative norms as a source of law, was left standing. No new corporative norms could be created, but the great range of those in existence, which provided the economic fabric of the nation, were continued in force.

part, a reflection of the fascist doctrinal view, of which labor and capital were two parts of the same process. The racist provisions of the code were removed from it without obvious side effects, although it has been argued that they distorted Italian law and jurisprudence in certain respects These expressions of fascist policy never became organic parts of the code.

The more substantial part of the governmental program of revision was not uniquely fascist in origin. It consisted of a desire to reform the private law in the interests of increased national production, more adequate distribution of wealth, and greater social justice. All three of these goals were to be achieved through the expansion of the role of the state. These attitudes were not unique to Italy. In fact, they dominated political, economic, and social thought throughout the world, particularly in Europe and America. The processes of redefining private property; of placing new limits on liberty of contract; of recognizing the importance of labor; of promoting commercial, industrial, and agrarian productivity; and of recognizing and encouraging the formation of associations of individuals in economic and social activity were all aspects of the evolution of Western thought in the twentieth century. It is true that the 1942 Code is permeated by such new emphases; indeed, they are its outstanding characteristics.[89]

Despite being enacted under a fascist regime and containing some provisions and norms that reflected fascist doctrine, at its core the 1942 Code is not a fascist document. More important, once a certain amount of fascist superstructure had been cleared away, a solid juristic accomplishment remained: a body of law built on the foundations laid in the nineteenth-century codes and reflecting some of the more prominent trends in the thought of the twentieth century. It has been said that the Code Napoléon was a great code because it interpreted and embodied the ideals of the French Revolution. It cannot be said that the Italian Civil Code of 1942 played any such revolutionary role. The circumstances under which it was prepared called forth all the resources of legal conservatism to protect it from becoming a programmatic fascist document rather than a progressive code.[90] This same conservatism prevented it from becoming more than mildly progressive.[91]

89. Nicolò, *op. cit.* n. 54, at 248–49.

90. See note 84 and accompanying text.

91. "Naturally this enlightened technicism, while on one side impeding the spread of dangerous tendencies, also produced its own inconveniences, and in particular a certain conservative spirit toward the privatistic legislation that was being elaborated . . . so as to preclude a more profound renovation of the law." Nicolò, *op. cit.* n. 54, at 246.

It is not the law of tomorrow but rather the orderly development of the older law in the light of the more significant new trends in social and economic thought.

6.09 *The Civil Code of 1942.*[92]   The 1942 Code is, predictably, a blend of the old and the new. Like the code it replaced, it is more French than German in form and style. The desirability of including a "general part" embodying the concepts and structure of the traditional legal science was considered and rejected, partly on the reasoning that this was the domain of legal scholarship, not of legislation. It was thought more appropriate to leave to the jurists themselves the development and refinement of a general legal structure of the sort assumed by the legal science.[93] In some ways, however, the 1942 Code does show important consequences of the impact of the legal science on Italian legal thought. Advocates of the view that much of that science is implicit in the new code point, in particular, to the provisions on contracts in general.[94] These can be read as the expression and utilization of that generalized conception of the *negozio giuridico* which is so prominent a feature of the Italian legal dogmatics.[95]

Private property and liberty of contract continue to occupy central positions in the Civil Code of 1942.[96] Both in the statement of these fundamental concepts and in the development of the technical legal institutions in which they figure, however, there has been a substantial effort to modify the extreme individualism

92. The best discussion of the formation of the 1942 Code is Vassalli, *op. cit.* n. 57. Professor Vassalli participated in the work from its beginning in 1917 until its completion. The discussion in Nicolò, *op. cit.* n. 54, is also authoritative.

93. The committee charged with revising the French Civil Code has also decided against inclusion of such a "general part," and some German lawyers would like to see it excised from the BGB. Lawson, *op. cit.* n. 57, at 167–68.

94. Codice civile arts. 1321–1469bis (1942) (comprising title II of the fourth book of the code) deal with "contracts in general." Article 1324 provides that the provisions on contracts in general apply, to the extent compatible, to unilateral inter vivos acts having patrimonial content. Thus, the great bulk of inter vivos legal transactions (*negozi giuridici*) are subject to a single, uniform legislative regime which can be read as a statutory expression of the general doctrine of the time of codification on the *negozio giuridico*.

95. For a brief explanation of the Italian legal science and the *negozio giuridico*, see 5.05. For a thorough theoretical exposition, see Betti, *Teoria generale del negozio giuridico* (1960).

96. The continuing importance of these institutions in Italian private law is perhaps best illustrated by the statement of Professor Vassalli that if private property is renounced, there is no point in having a civil code. Vassalli, *op. cit.* n. 57, at 614 n. 1.

that characterized its predecessor.[97] The interest of the property owner has been redefined with emphasis on "the limits and . . . the obligations established by the legal order."[98] The basis for expropriation by the state has been broadened to authorize taking of property "that affects national production."[99] Parties have contractual autonomy "within the limits imposed by law,"[100] but if the contract does not fall into one of the enumerated classes specifically recognized under the code,[101] it will be enforced only if "[it is] directed to the realization of interests worthy of protection" by the legal order.[102] These limitations on property and contract were further expanded in the 1948 Constitution.[103] Taken together, the property and

97. "The crisis of the right of property, in the form given it by the Napoleonic Code, has been pointed out by sociologists, politicians, philosophers, and jurists, some of whom saw in it the crisis of the subjective right itself; in many quarters there was talk, first in vague terms, then more concretely, of the need to recognize a social function of property. . . . The code has certainly not ignored these clear symptoms; in fact, it has given the law of property a systemization that is in substance quite far from the untouchable myth of the Napoleonic Code." Nicolò, *op. cit.* n. 54, at 240, 248–49.

98. Codice civile art. 832 (1942). The full text of this article reads, "The owner has the right to enjoy and dispose of things fully and exclusively, within the limits and with observance of the duties established by the legal order." For useful discussions of this statute see the commentaries on article 832 in Scialoja and Branca, *Commentario del codice civile* (2012); *Commentario del codice civile* (2013). Both of these multivolume works are excellent and provide useful means for beginning the study of specific provisions of the Civil Code.

99. Codice civile art. 838. For discussions, see the commentaries cited in note 98.

100. Codice civile art. 1322.

101. These enumerated enforceable contracts are called typical or nominate; nonenumerated contracts, called atypical or innominate, may or may not be enforceable. See 6.13.

102. Codice civile art. 1322.

103. See 2.05. Article 2 "recognizes and guarantees" fundamental, inviolable human rights but imposes "duties of political, economic, and social solidarity." Article 3 imposes the task on the Republic of removing economic and social obstacles that limit the "participation of all workers in the political, economic, and social organization of the country." Article 4 guarantees a right to work and adds that "every citizen shall have the duty of exercising . . . an activity or pursuit that contributes to the material or spiritual progress of society." By article 9 the Republic promotes scientific and technical research and protects "the scenic beauty and the historical and artistic heritage of the nation." Article 36 states that workers are entitled to "remuneration proportionate to the quantity and quality of their work, and in any case sufficient to provide a free and dignified existence for themselves and their families." Article 38 gives those unable to work a right to maintenance and assistance, and guarantees the right to adequate insurance against accident, illness, disability, old age, and unemployment. Article 39 provides a scheme for making collective labor contracts

contract provisions of the 1942 Code and the 1948 Constitution reveal a tendency toward a social conception of private interests. Related to this trend are provisions directed toward the recognition and protection of social groups and interests, among which the most important may be considered the more liberal treatment of natural children,[104] the broad powers of the domestic relations judge,[105] protection of the weaker party in bargaining situations,[106] and, most important of all, the introduction of an integrated and comprehensive group of provisions recognizing and regulating the labor relation.[107]

The concept of the civil law is Roman in origin; that of the commercial law is medieval. The beginnings of commercial law are found in the practices of Italian merchants, the statutes of medieval Italian corporations, and the laws of the Italian communes. The commercial law developed with the revival of commerce in the Mediterranean area after the Dark Ages and spread from Italy to other parts of Europe.[108] It was the object of separate codes in France, Germany, and Italy in

---

binding *erga omnes* on both employers and workers, although this scheme is not in effect owing to the lack of implementing legislation.

Articles 41 to 44 are particularly interesting. Article 41 states that "private enterprise . . . shall be free" but cannot be carried on in conflict with "public interest," and is subject to such controls as are prescribed by law "in order that public and private economic activities may be directed and coordinated for the benefit of society." Article 42 recognizes and guarantees private property, subject to "the law, which determines the manner of its acquisition and enjoyment and its limits in order to assure its social function and render it accessible to all." By article 43, property affected with a public interest may be expropriated (with compensation) and retained by the state or transferred "to public bodies or to communities of workers or users." Article 44 gives the state broad powers with respect to agrarian land tenure and reform, including the power to impose obligations and limitations on private land ownership.

Even though some of these provisions may seem more rhetorical than substantial, they create both a constitutional justification for broad programs of economic and social reform and an altered climate for the interpretation and application of existing laws. For a discussion of this latter point, see 7.10.

104. Constitution art. 30; Codice civile arts. 231–90.

105. Codice civile arts. 273, 307, 318, 320–21, 336–37, 344–89, 392–97, 402–13.

106. See Codice civile art. 1448, providing for rescission in certain cases of unequal bargaining position.

107. See Codice civile, fifth book, particularly arts. 2060–81, 2222–46. See also 6.14.

108. On the origins of European commercial law, see Ascarelli, *Corso di diritto commerciale*, chs. 1–2 (3d ed. 1962); Mitchell, *An Essay on the Early History of the Law Merchant* (1904); Ferri, *Diritto commerciale*, 12 *Enciclopedia del diritto* 921 (1964); Trakman, *The Law*

the nineteenth century. France and Germany still have separate commercial codes, but in Italy the Commercial Code was abolished in 1942, and its contents included in the Civil Code of the same year. Even though there is no longer a separate commercial code, the field has survived for academic purposes, and the tendency persists to think of it as autonomous in subject matter.[109] From the code point of view, however, the distinction no longer exists; the Civil Code of 1942 contains both the civil and the commercial law. And, as a result of the way the legislative consolidation was carried out, a substantial modification of important differences between the two fields took place.

Civil and commercial law had different origins, dealt with different matters, and, for a large part of their histories, had separate jurisdictions and judges.[110] As a result, the doctrines and emphases in the two bodies of law are quite different. Hence a merger of the two into one code—if it was to be an actual merger and not merely a consolidation of dissimilar provisions—had to resolve divergent attitudes toward, and treatments of, similar institutions. The problem was particularly acute in certain parts of the law of property, contract, and associations. The attitude of the Civil Code about these might be summed up by saying that it envisioned the individual owner of land as the typical subject of the law. Under the Commercial Code, however, the protagonist, who historically had been the merchant, was in the doctrine of the commercial law scholars at the time of codification: the enterprise.[111] The civil law saw the contract as a device by which the individual managed domestic and personal affairs; the commercial law saw it as the means by which commerce and industry were carried on and credit was extended.

Merchant: The Evolution of Commercial Law (1983). See generally Levi, *La commercializzazione del diritto privato: il senso dell'unificazione* (1996).

109. The term generally used is *scientific autonomy*. For an introduction to the extensive literature on the topic, see the works cited in note 56; Vassalli, *op. cit.* n. 57, at 617 n. 1; Ferri, *op. cit.* n. 108, at 924–26.

110. Commercial jurisdiction and commercial courts were abolished in Italy in 1888. Since that date, the ordinary courts have had jurisdiction in commercial matters.

On the growth of Italian doctrinal sentiment in favor of unification of civil and commercial law in the nineteenth century, see the sources cited in note 57.

111. The entrepreneur is defined in Codice civile art. 2082 as one who "engages professionally in an economic activity organized for the purpose of production or exchange of property or services." For discussions of the significance of this conception, see note 163 and accompanying text; Ascarelli, *op. cit.* n. 108; Franceschelli, *Imprese e imprenditori* (3d ed. 1964); Tamburrino, *op. cit.* n. 56; Ferri, *op. cit.* n. 108.

The result of the resolution of these divergent approaches toward fundamental institutions has been described in the Italian literature as the "commercialization" of the private law. What this means is that where the civil and the commercial attitudes toward an institution seemed to demand modification of one or the other, the commercial view prevailed.[112] The phenomenon is clearest, perhaps, in the law of contracts, where general principles having their origin in the commercial law now govern all of contracts law, but the effects are felt throughout the code. For example, agriculture, formerly governed by property and contract institutions based on the civil law, was redefined as agrarian enterprise, and, through association with the enterprise concept, became commercialized.[113]

This phenomenon of commercialization of the private law of Italy can be viewed as a logical consequence of the increased importance of the economic sector in the life of the nation. The government in power at the time of the 1942 codification was deeply involved in a variety of attempts to increase the national productivity. The merger of the two fields into one code, the dominance given the commercial approach over the civil where conflict existed, and the establishment of the concept of enterprise as a cornerstone of the code all may be viewed as partly impelled by this force. The enterprise, taken as organized commercial activity, is a concept around which revolves a body of law congenial to the efficient organization and operation of commerce and industry.[114]

112. The process of commercialization of the private law in Italy has been going on since the latter half of the nineteenth century and is closely related to the transformation of the Italian economy that followed unification. See Ascarelli, *op. cit.* n. 108, at 74–78; Ferri, *op. cit.* n. 108, at 923–24. For a reference to a possible countertendency toward "civilization of the commercial law," see Massimo Bianca, *L'autonomia dell'interprete*, 10 Rivista di diritto civile (part 1) 478, 485–86 (1964).

113. At the time of codification it was hoped that the unitary enterprise concept could include agrarian enterprise so agriculture, industry, and commerce all would be subject to the same legal regime. Ascarelli, *op. cit.* n. 108, at 123–25, indicates some of the difficulty of including agriculture but finds the attempt on the whole successful. Ferri, *op. cit.* n. 108, at 926–27, finds the attempt artificial and would restrict its application in the agrarian sector to "industrialized agriculture."

114. For a discussion of Italy's economic policies under the fascists, see the sources cited in notes 85–88. For a similar discussion, with emphasis on labor, see Neufeld, *Italy: A School for Awakening Countries* 395–443 (1961). For a discussion of the relationship between postwar economic policy and the concept of the enterprise in the 1942 Civil Code, see Ascarelli, *op. cit.* n. 108, at 133–35.

The express recognition and regulation of a wide variety of associations of persons into groups forming subjects of the law is another important aspect of the 1942 code. It is related both to the increased importance of the commercial law in the private law and the diminished emphasis on the individual as the principal, if not sole, subject of the private law. Whereas collective action of any kind was hardly conceived of as an object of the law's attention under the 1865 Code, the 1942 Code contemplates not only the acceptability but the normality of collective action in agrarian as well as commercial and industrial matters. The individual and the state are no longer the main objects of the law's attention; between them now stands the association of persons organized for collective action of one sort or another.[115] Often the association is in fact a mixture of individual and state interests molded into the form of a private enterprise.[116]

Hence it might be said that the existing code is more scientific, more social, more commercial, and less exclusively individualistic than its predecessor. These changes are woven into the code and form an inseparable aspect of it. Although much of the work was done in haste and under difficult political and ideological conditions, the quality of the effort to synthesize new attitudes and emphases with both old and new legal materials to produce an organic whole—to produce a code—was very high. There are obvious defects to be found in its conception, articulation, and organization,[117] but the effort was, on the whole, a successful one. The Italian Civil Code of 1942 retains and builds upon the achievements of earlier European codes and incorporates new developments in the law and the doctrine.

115. Nicolò, *op. cit.* n. 54 at 242, refers to the "hostile indifference toward those forms of associative life which today are interposed . . . as intermediate entities between the individual and the state" that characterized the Code Napoléon and the Italian Civil Code of 1865. The 1942 Code contains extensive provisions on collective forms of commercial enterprise (companies of various kinds), arts. 2247–2574, 2595–2641; provisions on collective labor and management organizations, arts. 2060–81; and provisions for consortiums in agriculture, arts. 850, 862–63, 914, 918–21.

116. On this kind of "public enterprise" in Italy, see Adams and Barile, *The Government of Republican Italy* 190–96 (1961). For a history and description of the most widely discussed of these enterprises (the Ente Nazionale Idrocarburi, or ENI) and of the man who made it so (Enrico Mattei), see 2.05; sources cited *op. cit.* n. 52.

117. For brief critical statements, see Vassalli, *op. cit.* n. 57, at 606 ("[I]t is technically far from perfect and does not fully reflect the state reached by legal studies in Italy during that period"); Nicolò, *op. cit.* n. 54, at 247.

6.10 *The Architecture of the Code: Overview and General Provisions.* The internal arrangement of anything as comprehensive and systematic as a contemporary civil code is affected by the substantive view taken of the materials arranged. The facade of such a code is a product of its foundations. The purpose of the remaining part of this chapter is to conduct a rough survey of some of the most important of these relationships within the Italian Civil Code of 1942. Such an "architecture of the code," while it cannot go very far in explaining the substantive content of Italian civil law, offers additional perspective on the way Italians think about their law and hence on the Italian style.

The architecture of the code can be easily reconstructed by looking at the headings of the code, as set out in the Summary of Contents. The code begins with sixteen articles of Provisions on the Law in General,[118] which are generally treated as a part of the code, but technically are not. The Provisions on the Law in General originally consisted of 31 articles, but articles 17–31 were removed in 1995 as part of Law No. 218 reforming the Italian system of conflicts of law. The code then contains six "books" or main divisions. The contents of the first four books, taken together, reflect the traditional European concept of the civil law;[119] books five and six are innovations.

118. Articles 17 through 31 of the Provisions on the Law in General were repealed by article 73 of Law No. 218 of May 31, 1995.

119. The French Civil Code is divided into a brief introductory section and five books: I. Of Persons; II. Of Property; III. Of the Different Ways in Which Property Rights Can Be Acquired; Of Securities; Provisions Applicable in Mayotte. The third book actually contains the provisions governing intestate succession, wills, inter vivos gifts, torts, unjust enrichment, marital property, contracts, landlord and tenant, agency and partnership, bailments, pledges, liens, mortgages, creditors' rights, and the limitation of actions.

The German Civil Code contains five books: I. General Part; II. Obligations; III. Things; IV. Family Law; and V. Inheritance. While the organization of this code is substantially different from the French, the subject matter is similar. The principal difference is that the general part (Book I) of the German Code has no equivalent in the French Code. On the nature of the "general part," see 5.03.

The first four books of the Italian Civil Code of 1942 (Persons and the Family, Succession, Property, Obligations) are broader in scope than the French and German Civil Codes to the extent that material on commercial obligations formerly found in a separate commercial code is now incorporated into the fourth book (Obligations). Similar subject matter is still found in separate commercial codes in France and Germany.

6.11 *The Architecture of the Code: Book I.*   The first book, on persons and family, contains few surprises for the common lawyer. Although specific institutions
appear to differ in nature and effect from their common law analogues, the area
of concern is roughly the same. The principal exceptions are title II, containing
general provisions dealing with legal persons and some fairly detailed rules concerning the internal affairs of nonbusiness organizations, matters which common
lawyers generally consider more closely related to business associations than to
persons and the family; and title III, on domicile and residence, matters which
common lawyers would ordinarily assign to conflict of laws. From the titles of
the various parts of this book, with the exceptions noted above, one can conclude
that both its subject matter and its principal institutions are quite similar to those
found in the common law.[120]

One aspect of Book I worth further consideration is the evolution of Family Law
within the italian legal system. Originally the code reflected an authoritarian and
patriarchial view of the family, where the wife was subordinate to the husband.[121]
This was, in part, a result of reliance by the drafters on the 1865 code, whose drafters in turn relied on the Code Napoléon of 1804.[122] The 1948 Constitution of the
Italian Republic changed some of the principles of family law in stating that "marriage is based on the moral and legal equality of husband and wife."[123] A scattered
and unsystematic case law developed between 1948 and 1975 that did not drastically
change the underlying conception of family law.[124] It was not until the 1975 Family Reform Act modified sections of the code that this conception systematically
changed. Some of these changes included the introduction of a joint relationship;
the introduction of no-fault separation; and the equality of children born within
and outside of the marriage.[125] It also introduced principles that reflected a desire

120. This does not, of course, mean that the law of persons and the family is the same
in Italy as in the United States. There are many important differences, ranging from the
obvious (e.g., no divorce in Italy) to the subtle (e.g., the consequences of the institution
of forced inheritance for many aspects of family law). On the latter point, see Merryman,
Policy, Autonomy, and the Numerus Clausus in Italian and American Property Law, 12 Am. J.
Comp. L. 224 (1963).

121. Parisi and Frezza, *The Evolving Principles of Italian Family Law*, 9 Digest 1, 1 (2001).

122. *Ibid.*

123. Constitution art. 29(2).

124. Parisi and Frezza, *op. cit.* n. 121, at 3.

125. *Ibid.*

for economic equality, including the abolition of the dowry; replacement of asset seperation with common ownership as the default patrimonial system; and new norms on the adminstration of commonly owned assets.[126] These changes also required modification of the rules of succession. This evolution of Family law in the Italian system entails one of the largest departures from the original 1942 code.

6.12 *The Architecture of the Code: Book II.* The second book is quite a different matter. The Italian law of inheritance is fundamentally different from that of the common law, primarily because of the existence of two institutions: forced inheritance and universal succession. Forced inheritance, or *legittima*, is common in continental law and consists of the right of certain relatives of a property owner to inherit from him on his death. In Italy, for example, one-half of the decedent's property is reserved for his child, if he has only one, and two-thirds, if he has two or more.[127] This obligation cannot be avoided by making inter vivos gifts; such gifts are considered to be part of the decedent's property for purposes of the *legittima* and may be reclaimed from the donee if needed to satisfy the claim of the legitimate heir.[128] This interrelation between gifts and forced inheritance helps to explain why gifts (*donazioni*) are included in this book rather than in the third book, on property, or in the fourth book, on contracts, and it also provides a partial key to the importance and difficulty of distinguishing between gifts and nondonative transactions in Italian law.[129] Only donative transactions are subject to the *legittima*; the typical business or exchange transaction, even one so imprudent as to diminish the owner's total wealth (his patrimony, in Italian law) substantially, cannot be revoked in the interest of the legitimate heir.[130]

The institution of universal succession has at its base the concept of succession to the obligations, as well as to the wealth, of the deceased. Subject always to the

126. *Ibid.*, at 9. See Codice civile art. 159–230bis for provisions on the patrimonial system in the family.

127. Codice civile art. 537.

128. See Codice civile art. 555.

129. For a thorough discussion of these and related problems, see 1 Gorla, *Il contratto*, preface, 1–326 (1954).

130. For a discussion of some of the implications of the *legittima* for that hardy perennial of the comparative law literature, the nonexistence of the trust in the European civil law, see Merryman, *op. cit.* n. 120.

legittima, the heir[131] may be designated by the will or by the rules of intestate succession, but this designation is not binding on the heir; he may either accept the status of heir,[132] with its concomitant obligation to pay debts and legacies, or reject it.[133] The concept of a decedent's estate as a legal entity which pays debts, taxes, and legacies and which is subsequently distributed after administration under the supervision of a court is unknown in Italian law. The heir can, however, limit his liability to the extent of the decedent's property by qualifying his acceptance "with benefit of inventory."[134] Without such a qualification, the property of the accepting heir also becomes available to pay the obligations of the deceased. The theory is that the heir literally "succeeds," or occupies the place of, the deceased.

6.13 *The Architecture of the Code: Book III.*   The subject of the third book is property. Both this book and the Italian law of property are dominated by the concept of ownership, a concept foreign to the common law.[135] The principal relevant characteristics of this concept as employed in Italian law are its absoluteness, in contrast to the common law concept of relativity of title, and its resistance to fragmentation, in contrast to the common law propensity for dividing up property interests into estates, into legal and equitable title, into beneficial and security title, and the like. Both of these characteristics resound throughout the Italian law of property and cannot be fully explored here, but some of the more obvious implications bear directly on the content and arrangement of the code.

For one thing, nothing remotely comparable to the common law concept of the estate exists in Italian law. Indeed, except for certain limited property interests which historically have been considered to be real rights, as distinguished from personal rights, the concept of an "interest in property" hardly exists. One either owns a thing or he does not; there is no middle ground, and this theory is main-

---

131. Only the heir succeeds; a legatee does not. Hence the distinction becomes one of substantial importance. For an introduction to the Italian learning on this distinction, see Codice civile art. 588; commentaries cited in note 98.

132. See Codice civile art. 459.

133. See Codice civile art. 519.

134. See Codice civile arts. 484, 490; Cappelletti and Perillo, *Civil Procedure in Italy* 359 (1965); Balena, *Istituzioni di diritto processuale civile* (2012).

135. For a thoughtful discussion of the nature and significance of the fundamental conceptual distinction between civil law ownership and common law estate, see Lawson, *Introduction to the Law of Property* (1958).

tained even in the face of the limited group of real rights just mentioned. These real rights are the various servitudes,[136] more or less equivalent to common law easements and profits; the *superficie*,[137] which has no exact equivalent in the common law; the *emphyteusis*,[138] likewise unknown in the common law but similar in effect to a perpetual lease; and the usufruct,[139] which approximates in general effect a life estate.[140] None of these is conceived of as affecting the ownership of the property. The owner of land subject to a usufruct for life is no less owner of it according to Italian law.[141] Whereas common lawyers would say that there are two estates, a life estate and a reversion, an Italian conceives of the situation as one of ownership subject to a real right.

Other interests that common lawyers would consider estates do not even have the status of real rights. Most prominent among these is the lease. In Italian law the lease is not a conveyance of an estate or interest in the land; it is merely a contract, creating personal rights. Hence the code provisions concerning leases are not found in this book but in the next one, on obligations.[142]

Finally, the great range of what common lawyers call future interests—reversions, remainders, executory interests, and the like—simply do not exist in Italian law. Nor does the trust, or anything like a division between equitable and legal title, appear.[143] Security interests exist but are included in the fourth book, on obligations,[144] or in the sixth book, on protection of rights,[145] rather than in this one. Gifts, as already mentioned, are included in the second book, on succession.

---

136. Codice civile arts. 1027–99.

137. Codice civile arts. 952–56. The *superficie* is the right to build, maintain, and own a structure on, over, or under another's land. For a full discussion, see the commentaries cited in note 98.

138. Codice civile arts. 957–77. See generally Cariota Ferrara, *L'enfiteusi* (1950).

139. Codice civile arts. 978–1020.

140. Two other minor real rights, use (*uso*) and habitation (*abitazione*), are governed by Codice civile arts. 1021–26.

141. For a thorough discussion, see Pugliese, *Usufrutto, uso e abitazione* 23–44 (1956).

142. Codice civile arts. 1571–1654.

143. For a brief discussion of the absence of future interests and trusts in Italian law, see Merryman, *op. cit.* n. 120.

144. Codice civile arts. 1960–64 (antichresis).

145. Codice civile arts. 2784–2807 (pledge), 2808–99 (mortgage) 2900–2906 (actions for protection and preservation of security interests).

It is also interesting to note that title II, chapter III of this book, on the methods of acquiring ownership, deals only with the so-called original titles.[146] Transfer of ownership is not included, and the reason is again one of fundamental difference in outlook. In Italian law the concept of a conveyance, such as the deed, does not exist. The device for effectuating a transfer of real rights or of ownership is the contract, whether the transaction is one for value or is a gift. Thus, the provisions governing the typical transfer of land are found in the fourth book, on obligations.[147]

6.14 *The Architecture of the Code: Book IV.*   This is the largest of the six books of the code by a substantial margin. It includes material we would ordinarily classify into contracts, torts, sales, bills and notes, agency, landlord and tenant, bailments, banking, insurance, suretyship, creditors' rights, unjust enrichment, and conveyances. The first question a common lawyer asks when confronted by so heterogeneous (to him) a collection of provisions is what unifying concept, if any, operates to bring them together in this place. The answer is the generalized conception of obligation.[148]

The idea is that a party to a contract, a tortfeasor, and one who ought to perform under principles of what common lawyers generally call unjust enrichment all owe an obligation, and that such obligations, whether deriving from contract, tort, or unjust enrichment, are legally more or less the same in nature. This concept is not peculiar to Italian law but is found also in French and German law and is based, according to a distinguished commentator, on a misunderstanding of Roman law, although, he adds, "A place must be found for the tendency to ruthless analysis which is often encountered among academic thinkers."[149] Whatever the source, the idea of obligation or, perhaps better, of the obligatory relation, seems firmly rooted in Italian law and doctrine.

---

146. Codice civile arts. 923–33 (occupation and invention), 934–47 (accession, specification, union and commixation), 1158–67 (usucaption—roughly equivalent to adverse possession).

147. Codice civile arts. 1537–41 (sale of immovable things).

148. The outstanding works on obligations in the Italian literature are Barassi, *Teoria generale delle obbligazioni* (2d ed. 1948, repr. 1963–64) (3 vols.); and Betti, *Teoria generale delle obbligazioni* (1953) (4 vols.). A more recent work is Gazzoni, *Obbligazioni e contratti* (2006).

149. Lawson, *op. cit.* n. 57, at 162.

Given the conception of the obligation, the content and arrangement of the fourth book begin to seem more logical. First, there are certain provisions on obligations in general,[150] provisions presumably applicable to all obligations, regardless of sources. Then come provisions on contracts,[151] then those on unjust enrichment,[152] and then those on torts.[153]

Confusion reappears, however, when one notes that of the 886 articles in this book, only 17 deal with torts and 15 with unjust enrichment, while 148 concern obligations in general, and a massive 706 govern contracts. It is difficult to avoid the impression that the fourth book is primarily a contracts book, with unjust enrichment and torts constituting rather undeveloped appendages. The fact is that the law of contract is much more fully elaborated in the code than either of the other sources of obligation, but it is also true that parts of what common lawyers consider tort law appear elsewhere in the code. In particular, some property torts, or rather their equivalents, are treated in Book III; there, what common lawyers would think of as trespass, nuisance, and conversion are governed by provisions on the protection of ownership, the protection of real rights, and the protection of possession.[154] The protection of the right of privacy in the first book is another example.[155] In addition, there are private remedies in damages for many penal offenses against persons and things, and an investigation of the applicable provisions of the Penal Code[156] and Code of Criminal Procedure[157] amplifies the more general provisions of the Civil Code.

The fact remains, however, that the elaboration of contract norms in the fourth book seems considerably out of proportion to a common lawyer. This is partly due to the broader scope of contracts in Italian law, including matters common lawyers would put into property (leases, bailments) or commercial law (sales, negotiable instruments, banking). Further, it is due to the importance in Italian law, and indeed in the civil law generally, of the so-called "typical" contracts, or rather the

150. Codice civile arts. 1173–1320.
151. Codice civile arts. 1321–2027.
152. Codice civile arts. 2028–42.
153. Codice civile arts. 2043–59.
154. See codice civile arts. 948–51, 1079, 1168–70. There is also a rough equivalent of the bill *quia timet* in arts. 1171–72.
155. See Codice civile arts. 7–10.
156. See 4.03; Codice penale arts. 185–98.
157. See Codice di procedura penale Book VI.

"typicality" of certain contractual transactions. The conception goes back to the formative period of the Roman law, to a time when it, like the early common law of England, was primarily a law of actions rather than of rights. Only certain kinds of promises were enforced in this Roman law; there was no generalized conception of contract and no comprehensive contract remedy. Rather, certain kinds of promises could be enforced through the appropriate actions.[158]

Although this historical foundation has undergone twenty centuries of evolution, it has left its mark on the civil law, and in Italy today one distinguishes between the typical or "nominate" contracts, on the one hand, and the remaining undifferentiated scheme of enforceable contracts classified as "innominate," on the other.[159] Of these, the former are by far the more important, including in their scope the great majority of normal promissory relations. Each of these has its own group of applicable rules,[160] and the classification of a transaction as of one "type" rather than another has significant legal consequences. Although there are provisions on "contracts in general,"[161] provisions that might lead one to think of the specific types as mere elucidations of fundamental contract principles, in fact they are more post hoc in nature, embodying the result of attempts to draw general principles from the variety of typical contracts.

Finally, the law of typical commercial contractual relations is largely contract law. With the merger of civil and commercial law in the codification of 1942, commercial contracts were added to the typical civil contracts, substantially increasing the bulk of the contract provisions of the new code.[162]

6.15 *The Architecture of the Code: Book V.* The fifth book, with the somewhat misleading title "Labor,"[163] contains matter common lawyers would include in business associations, corporate finance, securities regulation, unfair competition,

---

158. See Lawson, *op. cit.* n. 57, at 113–35, 148–52.

159. This is clear from the code provisions themselves. Codice civile art. 1322, para. 2, provides that "parties can also make contracts that are not of the types that are particularly regulated."

160. For specific provisions dealing with the various "types" of contract, see Codice civile arts. 1470–1986.

161. Codice civile arts. 1321–1469bis.

162. Vassalli, *op. cit.* n. 57, at 617.

163. Earlier in its development, this book had the more descriptive title *Of Labor and the Enterprise*, but this was shortened to *Of Labor* in the version ultimately enacted.

trademarks and trade names, copyright, patents, government regulation of business and property, as well as labor law in a very broad sense, taken to include regulation of professional activity. Here, again, the common lawyer faces the initial problem of trying to discover the organizing concept that has led to the inclusion of such apparently disparate matters within the same book of the code.

The answer can be found in the confluence of a number of factors. First, the decision to abandon the Commercial Code and combine its contents with those of the Civil Code raised obvious problems of arrangement. Certain parts of the Commercial Code had substantial analogies in the Civil Code and thus could be merged with them. Hence, as we have seen, much of the law of commercial obligations was eventually incorporated with the law of civil obligations in book four of the code. Other parts of the Commercial Code could not be fitted so easily into the traditional structure of the Civil Code, however, so new categories became necessary if a genuine merger was to be carried out.

Second, labor law in the traditional sense was very slow in developing in Italy, and the earlier codes said very little about it.[164] By the time of the 1942 codification, the pressure for a more detailed codified labor law, aided by the program of the government in power and its professed regard for labor, was very great. This body of law was viewed as primarily private rather than public in nature, so a place had to be found for it in the new Civil Code, which was to be a unified code of private law.[165]

Third, the legal concepts of the entrepreneur and the enterprise (*imprenditore* and *impresa*) were adopted as fundamental institutions under the new code. According to the formulation ultimately adopted, the entrepreneur is "a person who engages professionally in an economic activity for the purpose of production of or exchange of property or services."[166] The enterprise is not defined as such, but as used in the code, it refers to the activity of the entrepreneur. These two new legal concepts[167]

---

164. See 1.22; Nicolò, *op. cit.* n. 54, at 240, 242.

165. In Italy, as in many other nations, labor-management relations were historically thought of as governed by a contract formed between private entities engaged in a free bargaining process. This attitude survived under fascism and was embodied in the 1942 Civil Code. There has been significant evolution in this attitude in recent decades. See Varesi and Tursi, *Lineamenti di diritto del lavoro* (2012).

166. Codice civile art. 2082.

167. For a brief discussion of the history of the concept of *impresa* in Italian law, see Casanova, *Impresa (in generale)*, in 8 *Novissimo digesto italiano* 348 (1962).

were enthusiastically received and used by a government interested in increasing national productivity.[168]

Fourth, in the early decades of the last century, Italy experienced a great deal of governmental intervention in agriculture, and in the process a great deal of law specifically concerned with agriculture was developed.[169] These laws were, however, scattered among the codes and in special legislation. Pressure from the specialists in agrarian law and the interest of the government in increased agricultural production combined to support an integrated, codified statement of agrarian law.[170]

Fifth, under the Charter of Labor and other programmatic documents, the government sought to establish a conception of the economy in which employers, employees, and government worked together. From the governmental, and also from the fascist doctrinal point of view, labor, on the one hand, and capital and management, on the other, were simply parts of the same process: the production and exchange of goods and services. One of the more prominent features of the corporative state was an attempt to create rule-making bodies that represented both employers and the employed. Thus, it was not unusual at the time to conceive of labor and enterprise as closely related not only in the economy but also in law.[171]

These factors converge in Book V. Labor and the enterprise are the dominant institutions, and everything else is somehow related to either one or the other. Professional activity and the work of artisans are included and regulated because such activities are a form of labor. Competition is regulated because it relates to the conduct of the enterprise. Agrarian law is included by treating agriculture as

---

Italian scholars attach considerable significance to the *impresa* concept, which is a creation of the Italian doctrine. Nicolò, *op. cit.* n. 54, at 240, 249, says of it: "Property and the enterprise, as parallel categories, constitute, together with the complementary category of labor, the fundamental concepts of our code, and from this point of view they accurately represent the primary aspects of our social organization and our economic structure." Franceschelli, *op. cit.* n. 111, at 7, states, "The entrepreneur . . . came to be at the center of the new national economic structure and of the norms developed to . . . discipline that structure."

168. On the ideology of the fascist government and its impact on the Civil Code, see 6.08.

169. There are chairs in agrarian law in the universities and a considerable literature, including a regularly published periodical, the Rivista di diritto agrario, which has been appearing for more than 50 years. For a brief introduction to the subject in Italian law, see Bolla, *Diritto agrario*, 12 *Enciclopedia del diritto* 846 (1964); Costato, *Trattato di diritto agrario* (2011).

170. See Carrara, *Impresa agraria*, in 8 *Novissimo digesto italiano* 358 (1962).

171. It will be recalled that the Charter of Labor, which was a programmatic document setting out the theory of the corporative state, was prefixed to the 1942 Civil Code.

agrarian enterprise. Business associations are included because they concern the form of the enterprise. Little imagination is needed to understand how such broad and flexible rubrics could also include such matters as securities regulation, patents, copyright, and trademarks and trade names. In this way, what remained of the Commercial Code was combined with the "private" law parts of labor law and agrarian law to produce a novel synthesis.[172]

It is important to note the role of the directives of the European Union which have required various changes to the provisions of Book V. Although these changes affect numerous areas of law, they tend to be most significant in those areas (company law, copyright, etc.) that involve substantial cross-border transactions. These changes reflect continent wide preferences, as opposed to being directly reflective of Italian legal theory and structures.

6.16 *The Architecture of the Code: Book VI.*   The organization of Book VI, on the protection of rights, is understandable only in historical and practical terms. This book contains provisions on recording land and some other property transactions, on evidence in civil actions, on the enforcement of judgments, on pledges and mortgages, and on prescription and decadence (expiration) of rights. In the 1865 Code, the equivalent provisions were more or less appended to Book III, which bore the title *On the Ways of Acquiring and Transferring Ownership and Other Rights in Things*, and included all of the law of obligations, much of the law of inheritance, and a large part of the law of property. The drafters of the 1942 Code wished to group these institutions together in some more organic way. Neither that wish nor the assertion that these were "institutions of a prevalently instrumental character, having the function of protecting and preserving subjective rights"[173] can conceal the fact that this book is a kind of receptacle for miscellaneous provisions that were not, for one reason or another, put elsewhere in the code. They were included in the Civil Code because of their suitability or because traditionally they had been so included in the past. They were put into this book because they had to be put someplace, and the criticisms made of it by Italian jurists[174] seem justified.

---

172. This synthesis was not greeted with unanimous approval at the time and is still criticized by some conservative scholars. See 1 Messineo, *op. cit.* n. 39, at 59: "That 'book,' in fact, has mixed together, forcing them against nature, institutions that are, from the technical point of view heterogeneous." But see 3 Vassalli, *op. cit.* n. 57, at 617–21 n. 1.

173. Nicolò, *op. cit.* n. 54, at 247.

174. See 1 Messineo, *op. cit.* n. 39, at 60. But see 3 Vassalli, *op. cit.* in 57, at 626–27 n. 1.

CHAPTER SEVEN

The Italian Style: Interpretation

7.01 *Three Kinds of Interpretation.*   There are certain similarities between the judicial functions in Italy and in common law jurisdictions. In each the court is required to decide a concrete case according to authoritative rules, and in each the judge must identify, interpret, and apply the rules in the context of the case. Interpretation is necessary whether the authority to be applied is judicial or legislative in origin; in this sense common law and the civil law judges face the same problems, regardless of the source of the norms they must seek to bring to bear on the problems before them. In both systems a simplistic view of the judicial process as mere mechanical application, in the one principally of precedents and in the other principally of statutes, continues to influence the thinking not only of laymen but also of a large segment of the profession. And in both systems the literature on the nature of the judicial process is extensive. In the United States one talks about the judicial process; in Italy the discussion is of the interpretation and application of statutes (*interpretazione ed applicazione della legge*).

But the apparent similarities in the judicial processes themselves mask differences in emphasis and outlook. Like and unlike multiply at various levels of comparative analysis and from different perspectives. In fact, the act of interpretation is the point at which doctrine and law intersect. It is the focus, the culmination, of the forces represented by the formally recognized sources and institutions of law and by the prevailing attitudes toward them, attitudes that have much to do with their actual force and effect. Hence all that has previously been said about doctrine[1] and law[2] takes on new meaning when considered in relation to interpretation.

Judicial interpretation is only one of three kinds of interpretation traditionally discussed in continental works on the subject, the others being *doctrinal interpretation* and *authentic interpretation*.[3] Doctrinal interpretation is the work of scholars. Authentic interpretation is performed by the formal source of the statute itself: the legislature. Common lawyers are generally unfamiliar with the special significance of doctrinal and authentic interpretation during specific periods in the history of the civil law; a brief discussion of the subject should provide a useful background for an explanation of the current theories of judicial interpretation in Italy.

The history of Roman law includes a long and highly creative period during which the opinions of legal scholars were authoritative. These scholars, who came to be called jurisconsults, would give opinions in concrete cases, and these opinions would then become the explicit bases for decisions in those cases. Such opinions were frequently written down and collected and had a certain power as precedent. Doctrinal interpretation was a vital—perhaps the most vital—force in the evolution, explanation, and preservation of the law.[4] It played a somewhat similar role after the revival[5] of Roman law in the Middle Ages,[6] and after its reception in Germany at the end of the fifteenth century.[7] Each of these periods, in its own way, represents a kind of golden age of doctrinal interpretation.

1. See Chapter 5.

2. See Chapter 6.

3. See, e.g., Rotondi, *Interpretazione della legge*, in 8 *Novissimo digesto italiano* 893, 897–98 (1962). For a comprehensive recent work on interpretive theory, reflecting both Italian and global trends, see Modugno, *Interpretazione Giuridica* (2009). Other contemporary authors are cited in 7.12.

4. For discussions, see 1.03; Bonfante, *Storia del diritto romano* 397–430 (4th ed. 1958); Grosso, *Lezioni di storia del diritto romano* 297–303, 382–84, 390–405 (5th ed. 1965); Wolff, *Roman Law: An Historial Introduction*, ch. 4 (1951).

5. On the revival of Roman legal studies, see 1.08–1.11; Vinogradoff, *Roman Law in Medieval Europe* ch. 2 (3d ed. 1961); Wolff, *op. cit.* n. 4, at 183–90.

6. See 1.11; Wolff, *op. cit.* n. 4, at 204.

7. On the reception, see 1.16; Wolff, *op. cit.* n. 4, at 193–206. Wolff mentions the practice of referring legal problems to scholars, at 204.

In the later Empire, the authority of doctrinal interpretation and the prestige of scholars declined.[8] The culmination of this trend was the command in the *Corpus Juris Civilis* that no commentaries on it should be written, and that judges, when in doubt about the meaning of a law, should refer the matter to the emperor. He alone, in Justinian's own words, had the authority "to make and to interpret laws."[9]

Napoleon's despair at the appearance of commentaries on his code is well known.[10] For a brief period after the revolution, French courts were required to refer questions on the meaning of laws to the legislature for interpretation.[11] Similarly, various early (eighteenth-century) efforts at codification in Italy contemplated referral of problems of interpretation to the prince for authoritative solution.[12] In modern times Italian courts, unlike those in France and Germany, have been forbidden to cite the works of legal writers in their opinions.[13] Both in

8. For discussion of some of the reasons for this decline, see Wolff, *op. cit.* n. 4, at ch. 5.

9. The relevant provision is Const. Tanta 21. On contemporary interpretation of this ban on commentaries, see Wolff, *op. cit.* n. 4, at 180–81. For earlier imperial legislation limiting the authority of doctrine to a few named writers, see the "law of citations," Code Theod. 1.4.1–3, discussed in Wolff, at 159–62.

10. See, e.g., the statement quoted in Friedrich, *The Ideological and Philosophical Background*, in *The Code Napoléon and the Common-Law World* 1, 15–16 (2008), and the remark attributed to the emperor when he was informed that the first commentary on his Civil Code had been published, "Mon code est perdu," quoted in Gény, *Méthode d'interprétation et sources en droit privé positif* 16 (English transl. of 2d ed. 1963).

11. The reaction in France is usually described as based in part on antagonism toward the courts, in part on hostility toward Roman and feudal law, and in part on a rationalistic belief in the possibility of creating a clear, simple, coherent, complete statutory system. It led to such laws as the Decree of Aug. 16–24, 1790, art. 12, reserving to the legislative assembly the power to interpret the laws. Later, the Tribunal de Cassation was established as a nonjudicial organ to control the courts. Law of Nov. 27–Dec. 1, 1790. For a thorough discussion, see 4.16; Gény, *op. cit.* n. 10, at 49–56.

On the development of the Corte di cassazione in Italy, see Calamandrei, *La cassazione civile* (1920); Meccarelli, *Le Corti di Cassazione nell'Italia unita* (2005).

12. See the discussion of this aspect of the compilations of King Vittorio Amedeo and his eighteenth-century successors in Schupfer, *Manuale di storia del diritto italiano* 575–76 (1895). See also Statuto Albertino art. 73 (1848) (first promulgated as a constitution for Sardinia and Piedmont and later employed as the constitution of unified Italy): "Interpretation of the laws, in a manner obligatory for all, belongs exclusively to the legislative power." On legislation in Italy prior to the nineteenth century, see 1.19.

13. Disposizioni per l'attuazione del codice di procedura civile art. 118 (1942). The same rule existed under the 1865 Code. See 4 Mortara, *Commentario del codice e delle leggi di procedura civile* 93–94 (3d ed. 1910).

the Empire during the time of the *Corpus Juris Civilis*[14] and in Europe during the age of codification and reform,[15] the number and diversity of doctrinal points of view and the mass and varying quality of doctrinal writing were described as evils to be corrected by compilation and codification.

From this point of view the two great periods of codification in the long history of the civil law were, to some extent, periods of reaction against the doctrine. The *Corpus Juris Civilis* and the codifications of eighteenth- and nineteenth-century Europe were, in a sense, attempts at a massive "once and for all" authentic interpretation. The codes attempted to substitute legislation for doctrine, and were accompanied by the hope, and sometimes by the admonition, that doctrinal interpretation of the new law was to be avoided.[16]

Hence doctrine is excluded from the *numerus clausus* of sources of law in Italy, as it is generally in civil law jurisdictions;[17] doctrinal interpretation is not authoritative in any formal sense. To the foreign observer this might seem to indicate that the work of legal scholars is irrelevant to the Italian legal process. In fact, it is not. As was pointed out in Chapter 5, the work of legal scholars dominates the Italian legal process. Realistically speaking, the law in Italy is to a large extent what the scholars say it is. It could hardly be otherwise. Laws must be interpreted. Authentic interpretation, reference back to the lawmaker, has never been and could never be more than a sporadically useful solution to the problems inherent in the interpretation and application of statutes in concrete cases. Continental judges are severely restricted by the traditional view of the judicial process (happily perpetuated by scholars) and by their lower stature to a relatively narrow interpretive function. Someone has to do the job. The scholars, who draft the codes, who develop the conceptual structures within which the law operates, who write the doctrine and teach it to their students, and who have the great scholarly tradition of the civil law behind them, do it. Their formal authority is nil; their real authority is great.

7.02 *The Folklore of Judicial Interpretation.*   Like the American, the Italian legal system operates in an atmosphere of assumptions that, although demonstrably

---

14. See the complaint about commentators on the *edictum perpetuum* in Const. Tanta 21, and Wolff, *op. cit.* n. 4, at ch. 5.

15. See discussion in Schupfer, *op. cit.* n. 12, at 612–34.

16. The point should not be overstated. The reaction against doctrine was only one of a number of forces at work in either period. The fact remains, however, that it was a force. See authorities cited in notes 14–15.

17. See 6.02.

unsound, tend to persist because they are firmly rooted in the culture.[18] This kind of folklore serves a variety of functions, some laudable and other regrettable. Although it exists in its most exaggerated form in the lay mind, it tends, somewhat refined, to dominate the thinking of the profession itself; alternately idealized and caricatured, it becomes the starting point of much scholarly discussion. One who would begin to understand the conventional terms of scholarly discourse about interpretation in Italian law must first become familiar with the folklore. It takes different forms, depending on whether one contrasts the work of judges with that of scholars or with that of legislators.

From the time of the Roman jurisconsults on, the history of continental law has been one in which the role of the judge is unfavorably contrasted with that of the scholar-jurist. Jurisprudence (in the continental sense: the reports of judicial decisions) follows and is dominated by the doctrine, just the reverse of what is generally thought to be the natural order of things in common law jurisdictions. The civil law judge is not a hero figure (or a father figure), as he tends to be in England and the United States. The great names of the common law are those of judges; the great names of the civil law are those of scholars.

18. Arnold, *The Folklore of Capitalism* (2010), is a delightful, penetrating discussion of the way some of these assumptions operate in the United States. For a discussion of how equivalent assumptions operate elsewhere in Europe, see Wieacker, *Foundations of European Legal Culture*, Am. J. Comp. L. (1990); Lopez-Rodriguez, *Towards a European Civil Code without a Common Legal Culture—The Link Between Law, Language, and Culture*, J. Int'l L. (2003). For discussions and criticisms of the Italian folklore, see Ascarelli, *L'idea di codice nel diritto private e la funzione dell'interpretazione*, in *Studi di diritto comparato e in tema di interpretazione* 165 (1952); Ascarelli, *Giurisprudenza costituzionale e teoria dell'interpretazione*, 12 Rivista di diritto processuale 351 (1957); Massimo Bianca, *L'autonomia dell'interprete: a proposito del problema della responsabilità contrattuale*, 10 Rivista di diritto civile (part 1), at 478 (1964); Calamandrei, *La funzione della giurisprudenza nel tempo presente*, in 6 *Studi sul processo civile* 89 (1957); Cappelletti, *L'attività e i poteri del giudice costituzionale in rapporto con il loro fine generico*, in 3 *Scritti giuridici in memoria di Piero Calamandrei* 83 (1958); Meneghello, *Il formalismo nella interpretazione giuridica*, 15 Jus (n.s.) 226 (1964); Torrente, *Il giudice e il diritto*, 16 Rivista trimestrale di diritto e procedura civile 1261 (1962).

For a still earlier realistic discussion of judicial interpretation in Italy, see Pacchioni, *I poteri creativi della giurisprudenza*, 10 Rivista del diritto commerciale (part 1) 40 (1912).

There is a good brief discussion of the problems of interpretation in French law in Stone, *The Province and Function of Law* 149–65 (1961). Stone refers repeatedly to the work of François Gény, whose most important book is cited in note 10. Gény wrote in reaction against the extremes of the folklore of judicial interpretation in France at the turn of this century.

In Italy, under the influence of the assumptions of the traditional legal science, this contrast between the scholarly and the judicial functions has assumed the particularly sharp form already discussed.[19] The scholar is the scientist, and the judge, at best, merely the engineer. The scholar provides the systematic, scientific legal structure that the judge accepts and applies. The work of the scholar is creative and exalted; that of the judge, although important, is on a lower plane. The judicial function is not really a creative one. Jurisprudence not only is dominated by doctrine but attempts to imitate it, with consequences that will be discussed below. These views have inevitably evolved in recent decades, but the difference from Anglo-American practice remains quite pronounced.

This attitude, fundamental to the folklore of interpretation, has some interesting by-products. The literature of interpretation, produced out of the abstractness, conceptualism, and cultural agnosticism that characterize Italian legal science,[20] is rendered even more unreal by the fact that it is produced by persons who have no experience in the business of deciding cases.[21] The scholars having, so to speak, occupied the field, the judge, who might be able to supply useful insights into the judicial process, abandons it to them on the theory that they are better qualified than he.[22] The more exalted role of the doctrine, as compared with the jurisprudence, leads naturally to the emulation of the one by the other. The form and style of Italian judicial opinions are closely imitative of doctrinal writing. The way for the young judge to get ahead is to write opinions that show his ability to move easily in the doctrinal *ambiente*. The abstractness and conceptualism typical of the doctrine are prominently displayed in judicial writing and the publication of judicial opinions. The factual emphasis, the concreteness, that common lawyers associate with such writing is absent. Opinions often contain no coherent state-

19. See 5.04.

20. See 5.04, 5.05.

21. "It is one thing to interpret, it is another to talk about interpretation," Meneghello, *op. cit.* n. 18, at 227.

22. After World War II, many Italian judges joined in the growing movement toward reconsideration of the folklore of judicial interpretation. See the articles by Torrente and Meneghello, *op. cit.* n. 18. Both men were judges: Andrea Torrente was president of a section of the Supreme Court of Cassation; Bruno Meneghello a tribunal judge. Even if these men had espoused a traditionally limited view of their power and responsibility, the mere fact that they entered into the dialogue at all indicates that some change in attitude toward the role of judges is under way in Italy. In fact, however, they both argued for broader recognition of the creative part judges play in the legal process.

ment of the facts of the case, and even those that do are seldom published with the facts intact. Instead, at the point where the facts might be found, one encounters the disheartening term *omissis*, signifying that a part of the opinion is omitted. The emphasis is not on the facts but on production of the polished maxim (*massima*), and this abstract and conceptual statement, divorced from its factual context, may be the only part of the opinion to be published.[23]

The folklore of the strict separation of legislative and judicial power leads to an even more extreme oversimplification of the interpretive act and a further diminution of the stature of the judiciary. Behind this attitude, whose origins have previously been indicated,[24] is the dogma that only the legislature can make law. With its companion assumptions that the code is complete and that the legislature can enact laws that are simple, clear, and easy to apply, this premise makes the judge into a kind of expert clerk. Interpretation is not a problem because the meaning of the statute in application is obvious. While the doctrinal folklore admits that the judge must interpret and tells him how to do so, the legislative folklore, at the extreme, denies that there is any interpretive function.

This attitude has as an obvious corollary the denial that a decision has any legal effect beyond the case itself. The dogma of strict separation of powers and the doctrine of *stare decisis* are clearly incompatible: a judiciary that could make decisions binding in future litigation would encroach on the legislature's monopoly on

23. For extensive discussion and criticism of these characteristics of the preparation, publication, and use of *massime* and judicial opinions, see the following writings by Gorla: *Contratto a favore di terzi e nudo patto*, 5 Rivista di diritto civile (pt. 1) 585, 598–603 (1959); *Lo studio interno e comparativo della giurisprudenza e i suoi presupposti: le raccolte e le tecniche per la interpretazione delle sentenze*, 87 Il Foro Italiano (part 5) 73 (1964); *La struttura della decisione giudiziale in diritto italiano e nella "Common Law,"* 117 Giurisprudenza italiana (part 1) 1, col. 1239 (1965); *Nota*, 88 Il Foro Italiano (part 1) 433 (1965). Current Italian practice regarding publication of opinions and their precedential value is discussed in 7.11.

This practice is clearly related to the abstractness that is typical of, although it is not restricted to, Italian legal scholarship. See 5.04. One Italian colleague puts part of the responsibility on codification, with its tendency to simplification and abstraction of facts—to reduction of concrete facts to the abstract legal *fattispecie* of the norm. See 5.05. The attempt is to reduce legally relevant facts to the minimum in the interest of abstract order at the expense of pragmatic concreteness, the rule at the expense of the exception, and the category or class at the expense of the individual.

24. See 5.06.

lawmaking. Hence precedent is not binding in Italian law. The apparent inconsistency between this attitude toward judicial precedent and the constant insistence on the value of certainty in the law troubles the common lawyer.[25] To him certainty means foreseeability of result, and *stare decisis* is a means by which this is guaranteed. But in Italy the emphasis on certainty has its historical origins in distrust of the judiciary and in the conviction that lawmaking should be kept out of the hands of judges. Certainty is endangered by the growth of judicial power and hence of judicial arbitrariness. So the need for certainty becomes an argument *against* the doctrine of *stare decisis*, and by extension against lesser degrees of influence of the decision beyond the case itself. Foreseeability of result is of course important, but it is guaranteed in other ways. According to the legislative folklore, it is assured by the clarity and simplicity, and hence the certainty, of legislation. The doctrinal folklore finds it in legal science, in the structure erected by the doctrine for the guidance of the judge. An able judge will, by following the directions provided by the scholars, arrive at the same result another judge would in the same kind of case.

One who mentions the readily demonstrable fact that Italian judges sometimes reach different results in otherwise indistinguishable cases receives the candid admission that this is true. From a fundamentalist point of view, however, there are only three possible explanations: one (or perhaps both) of the judges was mistaken; the legislation is imperfect; or the doctrine is imperfect. The remedy is either to get better judges who will not make such mistakes or to improve the legislation or the doctrine, whichever is at fault.[26] *Stare decisis* is not an admissible approach to the problem.

---

25. For a discussion of the emphasis on certainty in Italian doctrine, see 5.09.

26. Almost everyone, however, thinks that different opinions and opposing solutions are due to contingent factors, to imperfect formulation of the statutes, to lack of preparation of operators of the law, and, above all, to a lack of logical rigor [on the part of the operators]. It is considered a perfectly clear truth that every fact has its own objective reality; to discover it, it is enough to know how to avoid deceptive appearances. It seems perfectly logical that each norm has, of necessity, one and only one meaning and that differences concerning it can only be the fruit of sophistry and equivocation, which can easily be eliminated by correct reasoning. In substance, given a well-drafted law and a certain fact, it is supposed that any judge, young or old, conservative or progressive, educated or ignorant, in any part of the globe, now or a hundred years ago, should arrive at the same conclusion." Meneghello, *op. cit.* n. 18, at 228.

The traditional image of the judicial process is thus one of something mechanical and automatic, of slot machine jurisprudence. Applying juridical logic—the way of legal thinking supplied by the folklore[27]—the judge is driven inexorably to the proper decision, As a prominent Italian jurist has described it:

> There is everything in the statute: all is foreseen in advance. The legal order (it is said) does not have lacunae. The legal system is like an immense cabinet, in which each compartment contains the provision for a certain fact situation: the work of the judge consists above all in the qualification of the facts found, that is, in finding which of the thousands of fact situations foreseen by the law is the one to which the facts found correspond. Once having found this coincidence, the judge need do nothing except open the little box in the compartment (which is the article of the code that applies to the case), and find inside, like a prescription, the ready solution. This is the famous logical mechanism by which every decision can be schematized in a syllogism: the major premise is the statute, the minor premise is the facts: it is enough that the facts coincide with those contemplated by the statute for the conclusion to come out by itself.[28]

This kind of thinking has its equivalent in the United States. Common lawyers have their own folklore of the judicial process and their own theory of automatic decision.[29] But there is a striking difference in status between the common law judge and the Italian judge, who is thought to be merely the operator of a machine designed and built by scholars and legislators.[30] The tendency is to think of him as just another kind of civil servant. Judicial appointment is not a reward for distinguished academic or government service or for eminence in practice; it is not the crowning achievement, the ultimate recognition, that it often is in the common law world. Judges tend to think of themselves as the folklore pictures them, and,

27. For a thorough criticism of "juridical logic," see Calogero, *La logica del giudice e il suo controllo* in *Cassazione* (2d ed. 1964). For an excellent discussion in English directed toward French practice, see Stone, *op. cit.* n. 18, at 149–65. For the same author's discussion of fallacies of the logical form in common law reasoning, see *id.*, at 166–212.

28. Calamandrei, *op. cit.* n. 18, at 95. Meneghello, *op. cit.* n. 18, at 228, speaks of "an electronic calculator. Inside the machine there is a program made up of substantive and procedural legal rules; one introduces the facts in their proceduralized form and pulls a lever; the decision issues forth."

29. For a discussion and references, see Merryman, *The Authority of Authority*, 6 Stan. L. Rev. 613, 621–29 (1954).

30. In fact, it is common practice in Italy to refer to judges as "operators of the law." See, e.g., the quotation from Meneghello in note 26.

through the operation of the principle of self-justifying expectations, to conform to the folkloric model.[31]

7.03 *The Practice of Interpretation.* It is unlikely that Italian jurists have ever had much confidence in the extremes of the folklore. At an earlier time it might have seemed more important to act as though the folklore were valid, but it is doubtful that many thoughtful scholars ever really believed in it.

It is too obvious that the practice is sharply different from the folklore. For one thing, the illusion of the self-applying statute, the legislative norm that is so clear its application is an automatic process, was long ago dispelled by the facts. Ever since 1865, the Italian courts have been engaged in hearing and deciding disputes whose resolution depends on the meaning to be given to a legislative norm. Such litigation is frequently appealed, and reversals of lower court decisions are far from uncommon, particularly in the postwar era where opinions of the Constitutional Court as well as the Supreme Court of Cassation and other appellate courts must be taken into account. Hardly a norm in the Civil Code has escaped the need for a judicial interpretation to supply a meaning that was unclear to the parties, to their counsel, and to the judges themselves.[32]

31. See 3.07. To the same effect in Germany and France, see von Mehren, *The Judicial Process in the United States and Germany—A Comparative Analysis*, in *Festschrift für Ernst Rabel* 67 (1954); von Mehren, *The Judicial Process in the United States and France—A Comparative Study*, 22 Rev. Jur. U.P.R. 235 (1952). For more recent discussions, see Lasser, *Judicial Deliberations: A Comparative Analysis of Judicial Transparency and Legitimacy* (2010); Clark, *Comparative Law and Society* (2012).

Under article 135 of the Constitution of 1948, judges of the Constitutional Court may be chosen from professors of law and practicing lawyers as well as from the judiciary. By article 106 of the Constitution (and by law before 1948), professors and practicing lawyers are eligible for appointment to the Supreme Court of Cassation. By article 104, professors and lawyers are represented on the Consiglio superiore della magistratura, which is a kind of supreme judicial council for the nation.

The growing importance of the Constitutional Court and the practice of appointing professors and lawyers to it indicate that the prestige of judges of that court will, in time, approach that of judges in the United States and England. There is somewhat less evidence on which to base a prediction that the same kind of transformation will take place elsewhere in the Italian judiciary.

32. The amount of accumulated published judicial interpretation of codes and other legislation in Italy is impressive. For an introduction to Italian case law, see http://www.law .nyu.edu/library/research/foreign_intl/foreigndatabasesbyjurisdiction/italy/.

Likewise, the dogma that the code is complete (no lacunae) and coherent (no conflicting provisions) fails to survive even a cursory glance at the jurisprudence. The books are full of decisions in which the court has had to fill gaps in the legislative scheme and reconcile apparently conflicting statutes. The claim of legislative prescience becomes nonsense in view of the constant appearance of new problems, clearly unforeseen by the legislature, demanding judicial solution. Although the text of the statute remains unchanged, its meaning in application often changes in response to new social pressures. The ideal of certainty in the law becomes an illusion in the face of the uncertainty that exists in fact, where determination of the rights of parties frequently must await the results of litigation.

The evidence is overwhelming. The Italian judge is not, in practice, relieved by clear, complete, coherent, prescient legislation from the necessity of interpreting and applying legislative norms. Like his common law counterpart, he is engaged in a vital, complex, and difficult process. He must characterize problems and also select and apply to them norms that are seldom, if ever, clear in the context of the case, however clear they may seem in the abstract. He must fill gaps and resolve conflicts in the legislative scheme. He must adapt the law to changing conditions. The code is not self-evident in application, even (or, rather, particularly) to the thoughtful judge.

But, according to the folklore, the judge need only turn to the doctrine to find the systematic guidance that will relieve him of the uncertainties of interpretation. Here again the facts belie the hypothesis. Despite the best efforts of judges to follow doctrinal instructions, otherwise indistinguishable cases are frequently decided differently by different Italian courts, and often the same case will be decided differently on appeal. The scholars themselves are frequently in disagreement not only about important elements of the doctrine but also about the proper result in concrete cases. The doctrine is not monolithic; there are wide variations in point of view within it. But even where the scholars appear to speak with a single voice, their words must be interpreted by the judge. The doctrine may not so much clarify the judge's problem as complicate it.

Thus, despite the best efforts of the scholar and the legislator, the judicial decision in Italy is far from automatic and the application of the law to the case far from mechanical. There is too much litigation turning on questions of law to be explained away as the intransigence of parties, the maintenance of lawyers, and the ineptitude of judges. The code is not clear, certain, complete, and coherent; interpretation is necessary, and the doctrine is not a sure guide to interpretation.

The judge plays an important role in the creation and evolution of Italian law, a fact which the jurisprudence amply demonstrates.

7.04 *The Tension between Folklore and Practice.*   The greater the scope of judicial interpretation, the greater the de facto power of the judge. And the greater his power, the greater his responsibility. According to the folklore, judicial scope, power, and hence responsibility are all sharply limited. In practice they are substantial. The resulting tension causes serious problems for the Italian legal process.

Consider the judge who is persuaded by the folklore. She must decide hard cases; she must make law. But, unaware of what she is doing, she is liable to do it all wrong. Unconscious of her lawmaking power, she decides irresponsibly. Putting her faith in an omniscient legislature and the infallibility of judicial logic, she sets major and minor premise together and watches the decision trot forward, not recognizing it as her own. In this process of inadvertent lawmaking, the product is bound to show the signs of its origin.

Consider the judge who is aware of his lawmaking power but unwilling to take the responsibility it entails. The folklore becomes his refuge. Given an opportunity to find a better way to solve the social problem before him, he instead selects a more traditional interpretation, pleading that his hands are tied. It is not for him, a mere judge, to change the law, even if a change is obviously desirable and is one that might more appropriately be made by evolutive interpretation than by legislation. And so he adds judicial to legislative *immobilismo*, blocking the development of the law in the name of the separation of powers, certainty, and other traditional verities.[33]

Consider the thoughtful judge, aware of her power and willing to accept the responsibility of its conscious exercise. She must clothe her work in the traditional costume, conceal what she is doing behind the camouflage of the folklore, or run the risks of reversal on appeal, of castigation by scholars, of injury to her career. The folklore tends to limit what the good judge can do.

These problems are intensified by the fact that prior decisions, contrary to the folklore, do in practice have some effect on future cases. Cases are in fact reported, sometimes fully, more often in highly abbreviated form. Courts do cite prior decisions, or *massime*, from them. Although a formal doctrine of *stare decisis* does not exist, an informal practice that closely resembles it does. This fact, which makes

---

33. On *immobilismo*, see 7.10.

every decision a precedent, increases the lawmaking power of the judiciary and magnifies the tension between the folklore and the practice of interpretation.

This tension helps to explain some of the peculiarities of the Italian use of precedent. The idea that a judicial opinion is a third art form, which has its own characteristics and can stand on its own feet, seems unacceptable. Instead, the opinion is disguised to look as much as possible like doctrine and legislation. The abstractness of Italian opinions and the frequent use of the *omissis* where the facts might be found have already been mentioned. The published opinions of the Supreme Court of Cassation and the lower ordinary courts thus read more like excerpts from treatises or commentaries on the codes than the reasoning of a court in deciding a concrete case.

Until quite recently, most opinions of the Supreme Court of Cassation were not published even in this form. Instead, brief abstract statements from them, indistinguishable in appearance from typical legislative norms in the codes, are the normal form of publication of judicial decisions. These *massime*, divorced completely from the facts of the cases and from the reasoning of the court, go into a general repository of similar *massime* called the *massimario*. There, looking much more like a collection of statutes than judicial precedents, they stand available to the lawyer or judge, who will sometimes apply them to cases quite different from those out of which they arose.

All the dangers of the use of headnotes and dicta that seem so real to the common lawyer are encouraged by the Italian practice. A formal doctrine of precedent being inadmissible, precedents are made to look like statutes, and, like statutes, they are generally phrased and generally applicable. The way of someone who wishes to restrict a *massima* to its original context is very hard. If the opinion is published, the facts are probably omitted. He must go to the opinion in the files of the court to find the complete text, but even the files do not always contain a complete statement of the facts. He must then go to the record and the pleadings in order to find them. In the nature of things this leads to constant use of the bare *massima*. The process of reconstructing the facts is too difficult.

7.05 *The Problems of Interpretation.*   Italian jurists are aware of the inadequacy of the folklore as a model of the legal process. They are conscious of the disparity between folklore and practice and of the difficulties the resulting tension creates. The discussion about interpretation is an ancient one in Europe and goes on in Italy against a background of European and, recently, American thinking and writing.

Interrupted by the years of fascism, when some Italian jurists espoused traditional theories as a defense against executive interference in the judicial process,[34] the discussion became particularly lively again since establishment of the Republic of Italy, enactment of the Constitution of 1948, and creation of the Constitutional Court.

The debate about interpretation can be put in terms of three more or less classic problems: the problem of interpretation in the strict sense—of the unclear norm; the problem of lacunae—of the nonexistent norm; and the problem of evolution—of the norm whose meaning changes, while its text remains constant. To these a fourth—rationalization of the use of precedent—should be added. All of these draw attention to the variation that exists between folklore and practice, and all involve reexamination of the traditional distribution of power between legislator and judge.

The problem of interpretation in the strict sense assumes, as is abundantly clear, that it is not always obvious how a norm should be applied to a case. The judge is faced with a choice of possible interpretations and, by exercising that choice, runs the risk of making, rather than applying, law. Under a strict doctrine of separation of powers, she should not decide, but it is settled law in Italy that he must. The judge is not permitted to say *non liquet*, the law is not clear, and dismiss the action.[35] She must interpret the applicable norm.

The problem of lacunae is distinguished from that of interpretation in the strict sense by rather sharply (and, it would seem, sometimes artificially) contrasting the existence of an applicable unclear norm with the nonexistence of any applicable norm. Here again the judge should not decide, according to the orthodoxy of interpretation, but here again he must. The problem of interpretation is to supply meaning to the norm; that of lacunae is to supply the norm.

The range of points of view about these problems is very wide, from the simplistic discussion in the *manuali* through various ingenious attempts to rationalize folklore and fact to frontal assaults on traditional views.[36] The serious contempo-

---

34. See the discussion and authorities cited in 4.16, at n. 180; 5.09.

35. Codice di procedura civile art. 112; Codice penale art. 328; Torrente, *Manuale di diritto privato* 27 (6th ed. 1965).

36. Critical discussions of the folklore of judicial interpretation are cited in note 18. For a more traditional discussion by an established and highly respected scholar, scc Betti, *Interpretazione della legge e degli atti giuridici* (2d ed. 1971). Rotondi, *op. cit.* n. 3, at 893, is a brief and representative statement of the traditional view. For an excellent discussion of

rary discussion can be summed up as a polemic between those who seek to mediate between fact and tradition and those who attack tradition in the name of fact. But before turning to this current debate, it is necessary to consider article 12, Provisions on the Law in General, which states:

> *Interpretation of statutes.* In interpreting the statute no other meaning can be attributed to it than that made clear by the actual significance of the words, according to the connection between them, and by the intention of the legislature.
>
> If a controversy cannot be decided by a precise provision, consideration is given to provisions that regulate similar cases or analogous matters; if the case still remains in doubt, it is decided according to general principles of the legal order of the State.[37]

The first paragraph is the legislative instruction to the judge on interpretation in the strict sense; the second is a similar instruction on the problem of lacunae. The meaning of the first paragraph, in particular, seems to be clear enough: the judge applies the applicable statute according to its literal meaning and legislative intent; other approaches to interpretation are prohibited. However, this provision is a statute and, like other statutes, is itself subject to interpretation. This interpretation about interpretation has led to some interesting products.

For one thing, it seems to be generally conceded that "to be applied to the concrete case the legal norm must be interpreted. . . . Application of a legal norm that has not been interpreted cannot be logically conceived. . . . Even the most

---

newer (at the time) continental trends in the theory of interpretation and conscious rejection of them in favor of a traditional view of the judicial process, see Ferrara, *Potere del legislatore e funzione del giudice*, 3 Rivista di diritto civile 490 (1911). For a reaction to the modern trend toward realism in discussing the judicial process in Italy, see Tedeschi, *L'insufficienza della norma e la fedeltà dell'interprete*, 8 Rivista di diritto civile (part 1) 536 (1962).

For an example of a discussion of interpretation in the *manuali*, see *Istituzioni di Diritto Privato (Diritto Civile)* 22 (16th ed.) (2012).

37. This provision reproduced, with some modification, a similar provision in article 3 of the Preliminary Provisions of the 1865 Civil Code. That, in turn, was based on a provision of the Albertine Code, which was, in turn, taken from the Austrian Civil Code of 1811, arts. 6–7. On the nature of the modifications, see note 49.

Neither the French Code Napoléon nor the German bürgerliches Gesetzbuch contains equivalent statutory directions to the judge on interpretation. However, the doctrine on interpretation in those countries is substantial, particularly in Germany. For excellent discussions and introductions to the literature, see the articles by von Mehren cited in note 31. There is a good discussion of French practice in David and de Vries, *The French Legal System* 113–21 (1958).

perspicuous and clearly formulated norm needs interpretation."[38] This being true, "the actual significance of the words" being an illusion, "the intention of the legislature" becomes the key to meaning. Here, however, it seems to have been settled for some time that the reference is not actually to legislative intent but to the "intention, spirit, objective content of the norm itself."[39] For legislative intent substitute personification of the norm. Or, as another writer has put it, "It is usual . . . to compare the norm to fruit which, detached from the tree, assumes its own identity, distinct from the tree that produced it."[40] The actual occasion for its enactment—the *occasio legis*—is irrelevant. What the interpreter seeks is the *ratio legis*.[41] Some of the consequences of this universally accepted interpretation of the first paragraph of article 12 of the Provisions on the Law in General appear below. Here it will only be observed that one of its results is to deprive the words "no other meaning . . . than" of much of their potential effect by opening the door to other methods of interpretation than a search for the literal meaning or the actual legislative intent. All norms are unclear, and the norm can have a different content than that which the legislator had in mind.

7.06 *Lacunae.* The second paragraph of article 12 contains three important concepts: lacuna (no "precise provision"), analogy, and general principles of the legal order of the state. The first sums up the problem and the latter two the methods of solving it.[42]

A great deal of ingenuity has gone into consideration of the problem of lacunae, some of it for the purpose of demonstrating that it does not exist. It will be recalled

---

38. Rotondi, *op. cit.* n. 3, at 896. All of the discussions cited in note 36 make this point, with varying degrees of emphasis, as do those cited in note 18. The statement of Meneghello, *op. cit.* n. 18, at 226, is particularly good: "If the norms are clear and the facts simple and incontrovertible, application becomes a quasi-automatic function, but if problems are presented an intellectual effort is necessary to resolve them. It might seem that the first case is normal and the second the exception, an almost pathological legal condition; but reflecting a bit it becomes clear that in the conditions we call normal, professors, judges, lawyers, universities, courts, reviews, textbooks, reports, etc. would be completely useless and that effectuation of public ordering would be a simple administrative and police affair."

39. Rotondi, *op. cit.* n. 3, at 896.

40. Torrente, *op. cit.* n. 35, at 23.

41. *Ibid.*

42. For an excellent critical introduction to the topic of lacunae and to the extensive literature on it, see Bobbio, *Lacune del diritto*, in 9 *Novissimo digesto italiano* 419 (1963).

that the problem offends the folklore by positing both the incompleteness of leg-islation—the existence of lacunae—and the judicial creation of norms to fill the gaps left by the legislature.

Three theories have achieved some prominence as proofs that there are no lacu-nae. One of them distinguishes between legislation and the legal order as a whole. There may be lacunae in a code or *testo unico*, the reasoning goes, but not in the legal order, a much broader category of which legislation forms only a part. Legis-lation, in other words, is not always complete, but the legal order is.[43] That order includes not only the specific group of statutes under consideration in the case but all the norms in force, whether in legislative or other form.

Two other approaches, which closely resemble each other, insist on legislative completeness. There are no lacunae, according to the first, because every norm has a double effect: to govern some activity and to leave the ungoverned activity unaffected. There are only two possibilities: either the law applies to the activity in question or it does not. There can be no lacunae, taken as lack or insufficiency of legal regulation, because where the law applies there is no problem and where it does not the activity is legally indifferent. The banks of a stream are not lacu-nae in the stream.[44] The other hypothesis supposes that every specific norm is accompanied by an unexpressed general norm that excludes, by negative impli-cation, what the specific norm does not include.[45] In sum, the first assumes as a general proposition that all that is not expressly governed is legally irrelevant; the second that all that is not expressly forbidden (or permitted) is legally permitted (or forbidden).

It has been argued, in response to these two theories, that they constitute an extension of the principle *nulla poena sine lege*, usually restricted to criminal law, to all law. But the Italian legal order does not admit such broad application of the principle. In fact, there are not just two possible aspects to the norm, but three: the area regulated, that not regulated, and that similar to the area regulated but not legally irrelevant or governed by any general principle of negative implication. The interpreter, in the absence of a "specific provision," has not one but two pos-sible courses of action: the argument by analogy and the argument *a contrario*.

43. See *id.*, at 419–21.

44. Santi Romano, *Osservazioni sulla completezza dell'ordinamento statale* (1925).

45. See Donati, *Il problema delle lacune dell'ordinamento giuridico* (1910).

The choice between them is a problem of interpretation in the strict sense, and the true lacuna comes into being only on rejection of the argument *a contrario*.[46]

Once a lacuna is found to exist, the interpreter is told to try to decide the case first by recourse to analogic interpretation, by reference to "provisions that regulate similar cases or analogous matters." Theoretically this requires the judge to draw from the "similar cases or analogous matters" the legal principle inherent in the legislative norms that govern them and apply it to the case before him. The assumption that such broader principles are implicit in specific norms leads to the conclusion that the law, even though not complete, is self-sufficient. The process is called "logical expansion." Lacunae are filled from within the legislative scheme rather than from without. Analogic interpretation is a process of auto-, rather than heterointegration, and so there is no need to resort to the creative power of the judge.[47] This is on the whole the prevailing view.

If analogy fails, then the interpreter, according to article 12 of the Provisions on the Law in General, decides the case according to "general principles of the legal order of the State." The chief dispute over the interpretation of this expression is between those who would find such general principles outside the positive legal order—in natural law or some other type of ideal system[48]—and those who would look for these principles within it. The terms of the statute are loaded in favor of the positivists—the judge is not to look to general principles of *law* but to general principles of *the legal order of the State*—and theirs is the dominant view.[49] Thus, the process of drawing broader principles from specific legislative norms is merely a first step; such principles themselves contain equally valid but more general implicit principles, and so on up the scale.

46. Bobbio, *op. cit.* n. 42, at 421–22.

47. *Id.*, at 422–23.

48. For a representative statement of this view, see del Vecchio, *Sui principi generali del diritto*, in 1 *Scritti sul diritto* 205 (1958).

49. In the Preliminary Provisions of the 1865 Code, article 3, the reference was to "general principles of law." The same terms were used in article 14 of the Albertine Code. But in article 7 of the Austrian Civil Code of 1811, which is the source from which the Italian provisions were drawn (see note 37), the reference was to "the principles of natural law."

In article 1 of the Swiss Civil Code, the judge is instructed, in the absence of an applicable legislative provision, to look first to the customary law and, failing that, to apply the rule he as a legislator would adopt.

This process of logical expansion is, of course, the fundamental method of the traditional legal science.[50] The general principles of article 12 of the Provisions on the Law in General and the conclusions of scholars as a result of their scientific study of the law consequently are identical under this view of the meaning of article 12. The scholar, by bringing such principles to light, is engaging, at least indirectly, in the judicial process and hence making his contribution to the law in action. The judge, in the process of interpretation, is contributing to the science and hence performing a scholarly function. But since both are merely drawing forth principles that are implicit in the legislation, they are not making law. The dogma of strict separation of power is preserved.

7.07 *Evolutive Interpretation.*   The neatness with which all of this fits together may account in some measure for the massive uniformity one traditionally encountered in the standard discussions of interpretation. Since World War II, however, attacks on this image of the judicial process have multiplied in number and intensified in force.[51] They have concentrated on a problem that is not expressly governed by article 12 of the Provisions on the Law in General and has not yet been discussed here: evolution of the meaning of a textually constant statute. Like that of lacunae, the problem of evolutive interpretation is an ancient one, and the contemporary discussion in Italy goes on against a background of centuries of thinking and writing.

The extreme folkloric view would be that evolutive interpretation is not a permissible judicial function. If only the legislator can make law, only he can change it. This formulation is now generally repudiated in favor of theories that justify evolutive interpretation, the dispute shifting from its legitimacy to its nature. In a very general way, it may be said that two points of view are in conflict. One, the most widely held, argues that the judge, even in evolutive interpretation, merely interprets the statute. The lawmaking power remains in the legislature under this view, and the folkloric model of the legal process is thus preserved. The other view is that the judge makes law when he interprets evolutively. This necessarily leads to a drastic reformulation of the Italian legal process. What appears on the surface to be a kind of scholarly quibble is really the focus of a much more far-reaching and significant discussion.

---

50. See Chapter 5 in general and 5.03 in particular.
51. Some of the most important of these are cited in note 18.

Those who take the conservative view marshal a number of arguments. One, which explains some but not all evolution in statutory applications, posits a kind of interdependence of laws. The statute is not interpreted alone, isolated from other statutes, but in the context of the statutory scheme of which it is a part. The obvious necessity for this kind of interpretation, which none would question, is proof of the organic, interrelated nature of the body of laws. But, like all the law, this corpus of legislation is in constant flux, and a change in one part of it affects the others. Thus, the meaning of a law whose text remains constant will change as a result of legislation not directly affecting it; every legislative act has some amending effect on existing legislation. Evolutive interpretation merely recognizes and effectuates legislative change.[52]

7.08 *The Betti Thesis.* The above theory does not purport to rationalize all evolutive interpretation with the orthodoxy of the strict separation of powers, but the one about to be considered does. This theory finds its most effective expression in the work of Emilio Betti, probably its most resourceful and sophisticated advocate.[53] In effect, it explains how a judge may properly give a statute a meaning different from the one it appears to have, without making law. Perhaps the prime example of such drastic interpretation is found in the interpretation of article 12 of the Provisions on the Law in General itself. It will be recalled that the first paragraph of that statute says that "no other meaning" can be given to a statute than "that made clear . . . by actual significance of the words . . . and by the intention of the legislature." As has already been pointed out, this statute also is subject to interpretation. The theory under discussion interprets it to mean that statutes may

52. Rotondi, *op. cit.* n. 3, at 898–99. The best-known exponent of evolutive or "dynamic" interpretation in the United States is William Eskridge, although his theories differ in emphasis if not essence from his Italian colleagues. Eskridge, *Dynamic Statutory Interpretation* (1994).

53. For a biographical sketch of Professor Betti, see 2 *Novissimo digesto italiano* 383 (1958). His principal work on legal interpretation is *Interpretazione della legge e degli atti giuridici* (1949). He is the author also of a unique two-volume work, *Teoria generale della interpretazione* (1955), in which he discusses the interpretive process in general and a wide variety of specific "types of interpretation" (philological, historical, translative, dramatic, musical, etc.). Legal interpretation is discussed in Volume 1, at 801–66. His works are serious, impressively erudite, and not easy to read. A good summary of his views on evolutive interpretation is presented in Betti, *Interpretazione della legge e sua funzione evolutiva*, 10 Jus (n.s.) 197 (1959).

be interpreted by other means than resort to the literal text and legislative intent and that the resulting effect may be something quite different from what the words seem to say and what the legislature seemed to intend. This interpretation of article 12 then becomes the rationale of interpretation of other statutes.

In barest outline the reasoning is this:[54] by "the intention of the legislature" is meant the *ratio legis*, or reason of the law, rather than the *occasio legis*, or occasion for the law. The statute has a life of its own, a life given it by the legislature. It imports not only the specific norm but also a larger content, of which its legislative form is only a partial representation. This "surplus of content" includes a value content. Latent in the text are legislative consideration and valuation of conflicting social interests. These, being a part of the norm, must be found by the judge. Since the enactment of the statute, society has, inevitably, undergone change. So, as a second step, the interpreter must determine whether, and in what way, the play of the social interests latent in the norm has been affected by changed conditions external to it, and the interpretive result will follow from this process. Just as the logical content of a statute varies with changes in other statutes—by external legislative change—so its value content varies with external social change. Logical expansion of the norm, by finding the broader legal principle of which the norm is only a partial expression, leads to solution of the problem of lacunae. "Axiological expansion," by discovering the social values of which the norm is a partial expression, leads to solution of the problem of evolution.

In the conclusion to the article from which this explanation has been drawn, Betti states:

> I have presented criticism and ideas which, on the one hand, are opposed to those of persons who would attribute to the judge a task that cannot be his, the task of setting norms, and which, on the other hand, seek to justify in the interpretation of the judge an effect, and therefore an evolutive function, that is not limited, should not be limited, to the pure recognition of the literal sense. He must extract from the entire order all that excess of content, not only logical but especially axiological (*value content*), that is inherent in general principles of law and in all those supreme values that have found only partial expression in individual norms.
>
> It is as necessary, therefore, to be sufficiently clear-sighted about the evolutive function of interpretation of statutes (and, in general, of interpretation directive of conduct

---

54. This description is drawn from Betti, *Interpretazione della legge e sua funzione evolutiva, op. cit.* n. 53.

in conformity with a preestablished system) as it is to remain aware of the tie of subordination that always binds the interpreter to the objectivity to be interpreted, in this as in other fields of the spirit. The contradiction between evolution and subordination (which imports conservation) is only apparent.[55]

7.09 *The Ascarelli Thesis.* After World War II, a number of Italian scholars began to take a substantially different view of the nature of evolutive interpretation and, indeed, of the entire interpretive function. The names most often mentioned are those of Tullio Ascarelli[56] and Piero Calamandrei,[57] the former a commercial lawyer and the latter a proceduralist. Both were towering figures in the Italian legal world, and both have had substantial influence on contemporary Italian legal thought.

Ascarelli denies the univocality of norms.[58] To him the problem is not to apply the norm to the exceptional hard case, but to any case. It is always equivocal, and indeed its abstractness, which permits a kind of stability in the face of change, also permits its application to concrete changing reality. The norm is merely a *text* which the judge must interpret. It only becomes a norm, in the sense of a

55. *Id.*, at 215. For another example of a traditional rationalization of evolutive interpretation by an eminent Italian scholar, see Santi Romano, *Interpretazione evolutiva*, in *Frammenti di un dizionario giuridico* 119 (1953).

56. For a biographical sketch of Ascarelli (d. 1959), see 1 *Novissimo digesto italiano* 1021 (1958). In addition to his work as a commercialist, Ascarelli was deeply interested in comparative law, an interest he developed during his stay in Brazil (from 1938 until the fall of Italian fascism) A stimulating collection of his writings on comparative law is contained in Ascarelli, *Studi di diritto comparato e in tema di interpretazione* (1952).

57. For a brief biographical sketch of Calamandrei, see 2 *Novissimo digesto italiano* 664 (1958). For a more substantial biographical appreciation by a student and disciple of Calamandrei, see Cappelletti, *In memoria di Piero Calamandrei* (1957). Two of Calamandrei's shorter books have been translated into English: *Eulogy of Judges* (1942) and *Procedure and Democracy* (1956). Calamandrei's legal writings are now being republished in a ten-volume *Opere giuridiche*, edited by Cappelletti; the first two volumes were published in 1966.

58. This statement of Ascarelli's views is based on Ascarelli, *Giurisprudenza costituzionale e teoria dell'interpretazione*, 12 Rivista di diritto processuale 351 (1957); *In tema di interpretazione ed applicazione della legge (lettera al prof. Carnelutti)*, 13 Rivista di diritto processuale 14 (1958). For the reaction of a more traditionally inclined major Italian jurist to Ascarelli's thesis, see Carnelutti, *Postilla*, 12 Rivista di diritto processuale 363 (1957); *In tema di interpretazione ed applicazione della legge (risposta al prof. Ascarelli)*, 13 Rivista di diritto processuale 22 (1958).

binding rule, on interpretation and application to the concrete case. Once applied, that application becomes just another text, a point of beginning for new formulations.

He attacks also the view that denies the influence of the judge's values in interpretation, saying, "It is vain to deny the weight of the interpreters' values, that it is they in fact who determine eventual new interpretations, new norms, genuine development in the law even in texts remaining literally unchanged, that the law changes . . . in an inexhaustible process in which legislator, judge and jurist participate."[59] To talk of the declarative nature of interpretation is to overstate the admitted need for continuity in development and to deny the actual nature of evolutive interpretation.

Ascarelli also rejects the notion of a surplus content of the norm, whether logical or axiological. To him the interpreter begins with an inevitably equivocal text and achieves a norm which is the confluence of his value judgments, traditions, hopes, prejudices, and general conceptions, under the directing influence of the "vectors" of general principles and legal categories.

Ascarelli concludes by arguing that much effort is misdirected into trying to establish or maintain the fiction of the univocal norm, into disputes about the nature of given institutions, and hence about nonexistent problems, in the search for certainty. In place of all this, he believes efforts should be directed toward making the judge more aware of what he is in fact doing so that he can consciously examine and more objectively and explicitly evaluate the presuppositions and values that actually influence his interpretation.

This exposition of Ascarelli's thesis has been so summarily exposed because of its similarity to the commonplaces of American legal realism. Its influence in Italy has been substantial, but it is rather abstractly developed and hence just as applicable, on the whole, to any civil law jurisdiction. The Calamandrei thesis, although also valuable outside Italy, is primarily concerned with Italian practices and problems, is illustrated by description of Italian cases, and is much less abstract in tone. In addition, Calamandrei goes beyond Ascarelli by suggesting how Italian judges should use their creative power.

---

59. *In tema di interpretazione ed applicazione della legge (lettera al prof. Carnelutti)*, 13 Rivista di diritto processuale 14, 17 (1958).

7.10 *The Calamandrei Thesis.*   Calamandrei's concern is with the Italian Constitution of 1948.[60] Even today, that document is far from an unqualified success, but in 1955, when these words were written, it was even less so:

> Only a part of its provisions, perhaps less than a half, have been actuated. Since the law, like nature, abhors a vacuum, old laws have been left in force to fill the place of [those provisions still unactuated]. Hence it is difficult to orient oneself in this uneven panorama, where venerable archeological ruins stand beside new construction projects still encumbered with scaffolding, and where heterogeneous legal sources produced by three different historical periods live together in disconcerting promiscuity: some norms of a constitution of democratic inspiration with social tendencies; some pre-fascist laws of liberal inclination; and many fascist laws with a strongly authoritarian mark. The jurist who goes in search of the road in this landscape devastated by a still recent cataclysm, and who, according to his function, asks nothing other than to be faithful and obedient to the laws of his country, finds himself bewildered and uncertain. He hears laws that speak to him of liberty, others that talk of authority; on one side he encounters provisions that seem to exalt free private initiative; on the other, provisions that place the accent on social solidarity. Here, he comes across the needs of regional autonomy and of decentralized administration, and there, the reaffirmation, by way of old organs still in force, of a traditionally centralized system. On the one hand he reads the program of a rigid constitution where individual rights are secured under the armor of the principle of legality; on the other he encounters in full effect the preeminence of those discretionary powers by which rights of liberty were transformed into flaccid rights, reduced in substance to desires without any legal guarantee.
>
>   How ought the jurist to conduct himself confronted with such disparate voices, such . . . contrasting conceptions? And what can be the function of the jurisprudence in that clash between the old and the new?

Calamandrei thus asks himself, why does the situation he describes exist and how should it be remedied? He finds both the principal fault and the principal hope of correction in the judicial process. He finds Italian judicial practice "rich in dialectic virtuosity," but, as a result, "less sensitive and open to the human requirements of the individual case than in other countries, particularly those of the common law." One must admire certain decisions that are "monuments of

---

60. This discussion is based on his famous article *La funzione della giurisprudenza nel tempo presente* (1955), in 6 Studi sul processo civile 89 (1957). All of the quotations and paraphrases in the text are taken from that article.

legal doctrine," but they leave one with a feeling of discontent and unease, "a secret question that does not find an answer in that display of erudite dialectic." He
quotes a judge who told him, "We decided unanimously, because juridical logic
required it, but when we parted we were all full of sadness."

This juridical logic is the most valuable instrument of justice as long as it remains an instrument, but it becomes its own most dangerous enemy when allowed
to dominate. At present, formal logic has got the upper hand. This is perhaps
a secular legacy of the scholastic tradition, "not yet exhausted in our university
education, in which jurisprudence was nothing but a chapter of logic, understood
as the art of language." Even today, after so many centuries, the way in which an
Italian judge approaches a case is essentially different from, almost the reverse of,
the approach of an English or American judge. With them, the fact is what counts;
justice is justice to the extent it is adequate to the case; the solution for the case is
sought not in general criteria but in the equity that is better adapted to concrete
circumstances, not in abstract logic but in social values.

"In our jurisprudence," on the other hand, "it appears that everything is a
question of abstract logic." Even where the judge has interpretive functions to
perform, "this work of supplemental jurisprudence is . . . traditionally considered not as work of creation" but as mere interpretation, "as research, among
general and abstract statutes, for something that is already there by intention
of the legislature" to be "discovered and recognized," not created. "Our jurisprudence is essentially conceptual." Application of the statute to the case means
discovery within the norm of those narrow and more detailed norms that are
already there. The judge is like one who patiently seeks to sort out the individual
fibers of a rope. The rope is the law and the ever smaller threads the jurispruden-
tial *massime*. "But rope and thread are logically of the same fiber." The judge in
disentangling the threads adds nothing of his own except his patience and pre-
cision. "The jurisprudence in our reports is prized not as a dispenser of justice
adequate to the requirements of the individual case, but as a revealer of *massime*
good for the future," to be used by other judges and lawyers in their search for
the useful formula.

> Think, oh colleagues, on the form our work as lawyers takes when we prepare an argu-
> ment: our work consists not only in tracking down in the legislative chaos the statute that
> best serves our thesis, but also in going with our little lamp into the jurisprudential forest
> that has grown up around each statute, in search of the jurisprudential *massima* that ac-
> commodates itself most to our case. [These *massime*] by force of inertia are confirmed

by other judgments [and in fact acquire authority similar to that of statutes], and neither lawyer nor judge can free himself of them.

I confess to you . . . my distrust, which sometimes approaches terror [of juridical logic]. I have the suspicion that in general we jurists . . . abuse the logic. Even in the field of justice we have inherited, perhaps more from medieval scholasticism than from Roman *aequitas*, a tendency toward systematic architecture: we build castles of concepts to provide a dignified dwelling for justice, and we do not notice that little by little they are transformed into barred prisons from which she is unable to free herself.

Think about how *massime* are formed in practice. In origin they are the result of an inductive process, from an individual case to a judgment that claims a general character. Even though it is claimed that the legal order is complete, the statutes cannot foresee all the cases that reality, much richer than the most fervid imagination, brings before the judge. Thus, even in a system of legality, every law leaves a certain margin of discretion to the judge within which he becomes, even if he does not realize it, a "creator of law." Even the most precise and minute law leaves to the judge, in the reconstruction of the facts and in the search for the relation between the facts and the precept, a certain freedom of movement and choice. Here the judge must find the answer not in the statute "but in his conscience." The system of legality is not the abolition of judicial choice but its control and rationalization.

The Italian judiciary, according to Calamandrei, does not employ this power of controlled choice with courage and resolution. The judge shrinks from openly stating that he has, within the limits of the statute, decided for reasons peculiar to the case. Instead, he feels the need to disguise this and to draw a general principle from it, a *massima* that seems appropriate for application in future cases. "His conscience is not at peace" if he does not transform the unique case into terms typical of juridical logic and "draw from that case a general principle of which his decision can appear to be an application." By force of inertia, it is applied by other judges in future cases. But since the specific facts and reasons for the original decision are not included in it—since it has been "logic-ized"—a *massima* that was born to justify the decision of a certain case is made, out of regard to formal coherence, to apply to a case in which the facts and considerations of equity and policy are quite different, and perhaps opposed.

Calamandrei argues that cases would not be decided in this manner if the judge did not give the effect of law to the logical construction of his predecessors. Juridical logic can be compared to an instrument used by the old portrait painters when exact reproduction of the subject was highly valued. It was a wooden frame with a network of silk threads at right angles. By using this to view the subject, it was easier to obtain the exact proportions. The syllogisms of the jurist serve a similar purpose. But if the number of threads is increased too much, and the apertures through which justice is viewed made too small, at a certain moment justice can no longer be seen behind the tangle of the jurisprudence.

Even in a system of legality, he goes on, the statute offers the judge the means to interpret creatively. Evolutive interpretation, analogy, and general principles are windows that open on the world. By using them, the judge can, within the limits of the law, keep the law abreast of changing times. There are periods of relative social stasis in which it is possible and right for the judge to remain faithful to the statutes, but there are also times of rapid transformation in which the judge should have the courage to be a precursor, a standard-bearer. Italy finds itself in such a period, but there is much legislative inertia. Hence it is even more important that the judge should exercise his creative function. But almost always "we face another kind of inertia, . . . a waiting contest . . . between the legislative and judicial powers, . . . a kind of connivance in immobility." Someone proposes an urgent reform in Parliament, perhaps a change in one article of a statute. The competent minister replies that this ought to be left to evolutive interpretation by the judges. But when one knocks on the judge's door, he hears the reply that the laws are written and that the judge can do nothing but wait until the legislator decides to change them.

> Now I think that this conspicuous immobility of the judges—who, in response to the neglect of the legislators, almost seem to enjoy applying to the very letter decrepit old laws that no longer correspond to the changed needs of society—is incompatible with the useful and trustful cooperation that should exist between powers in a democratic regime.
>
> I understand that in an authoritarian regime . . . the judges . . . might limit themselves to applying the statutes as dictated, without adding or taking away anything, in order to leave all the responsibility to [the legislator], especially when infamous laws, like those of racial persecution, are involved. But in a free regime, in the presence of a constitution in which the judiciary is a power placed on the same plane as the legislative, this agnostic jurisprudential attitude, this great pleasure taken in pointing out the inadequacy of the statutes and of making all the blame fall on the inertia of the legislature, is no longer consistent with the constitutional duties of the judiciary.

The Constitution, with its programmatic provisions, is not addressed solely to the legislature to transform into statutes. It is also addressed directly to the judiciary so that, through the openings provided by general principles and evolutive interpretation, it can bring the social demands that the Constitution embodies and consecrates into effect in its decisions without waiting for the legislature. The much-discussed distinction between perceptive and programmatic constitutional norms,[61] which has served to prevent realization of the document's most essential dispositions, should not be considered an obstacle by the judiciary. Instead, these provisions should serve as orienting principles in judicial practice.

Thus, even if the legislature remains inert, the judges can make the spirit of the Constitution—what are today called *valori costituzionali* (constitutional values)—live in their decisions. They can transform it in their daily work into the reality of human relations. This does not mean abandoning the spirit of legality. To be inspired by the Constitution in order to refuse to apply old formulas is the true democratic legalitarianism. A free and autonomous judiciary, courageously inspired, ought to be proud to perform such a function.

The U.S. Constitution, originally composed of only a few written articles, has been strengthened, developed, and perfected day by day by the dedicated and courageous jurisprudence of the Supreme Court. It can be said that "in America the Constitution has become, through a labor of almost two centuries, a monument created by the judiciary." The Italian judiciary can do the same.

This, then, is the Calamandrei thesis. Judicial interpretation is creative, so the judge is responsible for the conscious exercise of his power as lawmaker. That power must be exercised within the limits imposed by the principle of legality, in the interest of continuity, but it must also be exercised with careful regard for individual justice in concrete cases. The glorification of juridical logic and the production and use of *massime*, which contribute to the extremes of the logical-formal conception of interpretation, lead to judicial irresponsibility, to unjust decisions, and to immobility in the law. The law must adapt itself to new social demands. Judges can aid in such adaptation; indeed, it is their function to do so. The agnostic, formal, conceptual structure of the traditional doctrine, which rejects such social values as unscientific and avoids direct encounters with the justice of the concrete case, is inadequate as a sole source of analogy and general principles. The values that ought to guide the interpretive process are not found in the doctrine,

---

61. Programmatic norms, in Italian constitutional doctrine, are those held to require governmental action in order to produce effects. Preceptive norms, on the contrary, establish operating rules. The distinction is similar, in effect, to that drawn in the United States between self-executing and non-self-executing norms. See 2.03.

but in the new democratic Constitution of Italy, and the judges ought to draw on that document in their daily work.

Calamandrei and others such as Ascarelli argue for a conscious redistribution of power and responsibility between judge and legislator. But unlike others, Calamandrei goes on to advocate deliberate utilization of the Constitution as a source of analogy and general principles. Not only are traditional attitudes about interpretation brought into question, but the whole dogmatic doctrinal structure, with its assumptions about the nature and functions of law, its methodology of logical expansion, and its paraphernalia of abstract concepts, is accused of inhibiting judges from the proper performance of their true role. Whereas Betti builds a model of the legal process that rationalizes fact and folklore, Calamandrei proposes an entirely new model which, in the name not only of fact but of individual and social democratic values, is incompatible with traditional attitudes toward doctrine, legislation, and jurisprudence.[62]

The work of Betti, Ascarelli, and Calamandrei is now several decades old and does not encompass the full range of the current discussion of interpretation in Italy. It does present three of the most influential positions. Of the three views, Betti's is the most nearly representative of the way Italians traditionally thought about the judicial process. The more realistic theses of Ascarelli and Calamandrei—supported by external influences and changes in Italian legal practice—have, however, achieved growing influence in recent decades, as will be observed below.

7.11 *Precedent.*   According to the traditional doctrine, judicial decisions are not a source of law.[63] One way to put this proposition is to state that judicial decisions are not binding precedents in subsequent cases; another is to say that decisions of courts affect only the parties and have no effects *erga omnes*. However the matter is put, it is obvious that the traditional Italian view of precedent is an organic part of the traditional view of the legal process, with its emphasis on legislative su-

---

62. Meneghello, *op. cit.* n. 18, at 226, arrives at similar conclusions by an even more drastically realistic route; he calls upon contemporary thought about linguistics, the nature and areas of applicability of the scientific method, the limitations of scientific certainty, Heisenberg's Uncertainty Principle, Gödel's Proof, Wittgenstein, Russell, and Whitehead.

63. See the discussion of sources of law in 6.02. The sharpness of this distinction between sources and nonsources is similar to the distinction in the legal folklore of the United States between primary and secondary authority. For a discussion, see Merryman, *op. cit.* n. 29, at 619–28.

premacy and a sharp separation of powers. The judicial function is limited to the interpretation and application of the law. If the decision of a court is a precedent or is otherwise effective beyond the limits of the case, it is engaging in a function reserved to the legislator.[64]

This theory of the limits of the judicial process, like other aspects of the folklore of judicial interpretation, is in conflict with the facts in Italy. A decision by the Constitutional Court that a law is unconstitutional, although made in the context of a concrete case, does have *erga omnes* effects; the law is, as a result, invalid.[65] The decision is binding not only on other Italian courts but throughout the Italian legal process. The same is true of a decision by the Council of State that a regulation or other administrative act is invalid.[66] It is, of course, quite possible to consider these powers of the Constitutional Court and the Council of State exceptional, to distinguish them from the judicial function in general, and to argue that elsewhere in the Italian judicial process the decisions of courts have no effects beyond the cases in which they are rendered.

There are other factors, however, that call the validity of the folklore into question. The Supreme Court of Cassation is the highest court of judicial, as distinguished from administrative and constitutional, jurisdiction. It is at the apex of that part of the Italian judiciary most like common law courts in function. Article 65 of the 1941 Law on the Judiciary places the obligation of assuring the "uniform interpretation of statutes" and the "unity of national law" on the Supreme Court of Cassation. At an earlier time there were five such courts, all on the same level of authority, and considerable disparity existed among their interpretations. A principal argument for a single such court was the desire for an authoritative final voice on the interpretation of the law, and the statute cited expressly confers that function on the Supreme Court of Cassation. Even though the decisions of that court are not "binding" in theory, few judges would knowingly adopt a different interpretation. They may not be bound, but the pressure to conform is irresistible.[67]

It is also relevant to note that the Public Prosecutor may, under article 363 of the Code of Civil Procedure, attack a civil decision "in the interest of the law." The

64. See, e.g., Rotondi, *op. cit.* n. 3, at 897.

65. See discussion and authorities cited in 2.09, 4.05, 6.02.

66. Discussed in 2.11, 4.04, 6.02.

67. For a good discussion of this function of the Supreme Court of Cassation, see 2 Calamandrei, *op. cit.* n. 11, at 48–85. See 4.16.

purpose of such an attack, which does not affect the interests of the parties to the case, is to avoid allowing an erroneous "precedent" to remain at large. Although this procedure is hardly ever used, it exists *in posse* and clearly implies that decisions have effect as precedents.[68]

Finally, and most important of all, Italian courts regularly cite and apply *massime* and decisions (of lower courts, as well as of the Supreme Court of Cassation) in their opinions. The practice is widespread. Whatever the folklore may say about the value of precedent, the fact is that courts do not act very differently toward reported decisions (and *massime* from them) in Italy than they do in the United States. When an Italian judge cites a prior decision, he presumably thinks that it is relevant in some way to the decision of the case before him.[69] It is true that, as the Italian discussions of precedent uniformly point out, he is not formally bound by the prior decision. He is, however, affected to some extent by it.[70] To that extent the prior decision is, in realistic if not in formal terms, a precedent.[71]

It is an interesting fact that Italian scholars traditionally did not focus on these matters. The literature on the question of whether the judge makes law for the case when he interprets statutes is, as was shown above, extensive. The literature on

68. 2 Calamandrei, *op. cit.* n. 11, at 104–30; 4.16. See also Codice di Procedura Civile art. 360 bis (inadmissibility of appeals to Supreme Court of Cassation when the rule being challenged is consistent with the Court's jurisprudence and no basis for a change in such position has been presented).

69. For a discussion of the assumptions implied by a citation, see Merryman, *op. cit.* n. 29, at 614–16.

70. For an enumeration and discussion of the variety of reasons why judges use authority, even though not "bound" by it, see *ibid.*, at 621–29.

71. In addition to the views of Calamandrei discussed in 7.10, see 2 Calamandrei, *op. cit.* n. 11, at 57–85, and the articles by Gorla cited in note 23. And consider the following statement by Torrente, *op. cit.* n. 35, at 21 n. 1: "Judicial interpretation . . . , especially if it is contained in decisions of the Cassation, which is the supreme judicial organ, or is repeatedly accepted in the pronouncements of lower judges, has notable importance for other judges who are called on to decide analogous controversies; they will not depart from them, or they should not depart from them, unless they are convinced of the wrongness of the principle that was affirmed in other decisions. One speaks in this connection of *auctoritas rerum similiter indicatarum.*" To the same effect see Cappelletti and Perillo, *Civil Procedure in Italy* 49 (1965): "Although Italian law does not formally embrace the principle of stare decisis, court decisions . . . do have persuasive authority." For a skeptical view of the use of precedent in Italy, as seen from a North American perspective, see Mazzotta, *Precedents in Italian Law,* 9 MSU-DCL J. Int'l L. 121 (2000). See 4.16.

whether he makes law beyond the case, by creating a precedent that will affect the actions of persons or organizations and the decisions of courts in future cases, is not. Most discussions of interpretation say little or nothing about precedent. The reader is told that precedent in Italy, in contrast to common law countries, is not binding, and the matter is left there.[72]

One writer, Colesanti, probing more deeply into the effect of decisions as precedents, distinguishes between the normative effect of a case or *massima* and its "interpretive value."[73] Its normative value is limited to the case itself, but its interpretive value gives it life beyond that case, a power to "impose itself on the critical perception of a future judge" and to be useful to him in the solution of new cases. It is legitimate to "distill from the particular facts the rule valid for the decision of future cases." In this way, over time, a mass of "decision-rules" is formed. Their normative import does not extend beyond the cases decided, but their value "on the level of interpretation" does. In this way they assume authority as "precedents."[74]

Such "decision-rules," he continues, exist in the presence of a tendency toward uniformity of decision. When a new case arises, there is a strong probability that the same basis of decision will be invoked, leading to a series of conforming decisions. The mere fact that a rule has been applied in a previous case gives it a certain "authority," satisfying the drive toward certainty in the law by a "constant jurisprudence." On the other hand, the freedom of the judge to decide whether or not to apply the old *massima* allows the case law to develop, to be refined, to meet new demands. An inherent problem in the use of *massime* is the tendency to allow them to have normative effect. But "our legal order, inspired by the principle of legality, and on the other hand permitting no limitation on the judge but the statute, forbids conferring normative effect, even indirectly by way of *massime*, on the jurisprudence. [The *massime*] have their effects on the level of interpretation and their survival is conditioned on their persuasive force."[75]

It is apparent from this discussion that such a distinction between the normative effect and the interpretive value of *massime* and decisions is a fairly subtle one. Colesanti himself recognizes that it is not carefully observed in practice and that

---

72. See, e.g., Rotondi, *op. cit.* n. 3, at 897.
73. Colesanti, *Giurisprudenza*, in 7 *Novissimo digesto italiano* 1101, 1102 (1961).
74. *Id.*, at 1102–3.
75. *Id.*, at 1103–4.

the tendency is to use *massime* and decisions much as they are used in common law countries. He concludes that the theoretical differences between the value of precedent in the civil law and in the common law tend to obscure substantially similar practices. The folklore of the Italian judicial process demands that decisions and *massime* be freely evaluated by the judge; in practice they are treated as normative not only by subjects of the law but by judges themselves.[76]

In the past two decades, the issue of precedent has been called into further question by technological change. While semiofficial reporters like the Foro Italiano and Giurisprudenza Italiana continue to report only selected cases or holdings—frequently interspersed with academic notes and comments—a large volume of judicial opinions are now published by free or paid electronic websites that are widely available in and outside the country. Intellectual currents, including Anglo-American legal theory and internal Italian developments, have further chipped away at the traditional resistance to a precedence-based jurisprudence. But traditions change slowly, perhaps more so in procedural than substantive matters. Courts can only cite things that are written down: the continuing practice of many Italian judges and reporters to omit detailed factual discussions, focusing instead on the *massima* of the particular case, makes precedents difficult to apply in the Anglo-American sense. There is also the matter of judges' training, which encourages them to look for guidance in the codes or commentaries rather than prior holdings. Here as elsewhere, the country's practice remains an uneasy mixture of global tendencies and the traditional "Italian style," with one or the other predominating, depending on the issue and actor in question.

7.12 *Conclusion.*   Although the views of a Calamandrei or an Ascarelli are far from dominating contemporary Italian thought concerning interpretation, one can observe that great changes in the Italian judicial process—and hence in the entire legal process—have taken place in the last generation. A variety of factors are at work. After more than two hundred years, the specter of the ancient-régime judge walks less often and with less effect.[77] The years of self-imposed restraint under

---

76. Colesanti also discusses the problems created by the abstractness of *massime* and the tendency to treat them as normative in situations dissimilar from those out of which they arose, thus supporting the criticisms of Calamandrei, described in 7.10, and of Gorla, in the articles cited in note 23.

77. See 5.06 for an explanation of the effect of this specter on continental legal thought in the nineteenth century.

fascism are long since over, and a democratic constitution has been in existence for more than sixty years.[78] Attitudes toward the separation of powers are becoming more flexible.[79] There is a Constitutional Court, manned by judges who have the authority to override the legislature, and some of this power filters down to the lower courts in the form of a power to declare a constitutional objection "not manifestly unfounded"[80] or apply constitutional values to broader issues. The tension between folklore and fact continues to grow, and despite the ingenuity of apologists for the traditional view, folklore is losing its grasp, while the power of fact increases. There is a new concern for individual justice, achieved at the expense of dogmatic certainty, and a concern for the implementation of social policy by judges as well as legislators. Two generations of scholars and judges, many of them students of such men as Ascarelli and Calamandrei, now fill the university chairs and the bench. New concepts and attitudes enter through windows opened by comparative legal study and by Italy's participation in international organizations. Although some Italian scholars still seek to rationalize contemporary judicial practice with a traditional model of the legal process, employing such devices as "logical expansion," "axiological expansion," and the "interpretive value" of precedent, there is increasingly general recognition that Italian judges have broad interpretive power and that reported decisions and *massime* have effect as precedents. The dispute is less about the facts than about the characterization to be given the facts and the conclusions to be drawn from them.

The change in emphasis is seen in the legal academy as well as day-to-day practice. Works by Ronald Dworkin, H.L.A. Hart, and William Eskridge now take their place in libraries next to those of the great Italian commentators, while a new generation of Italian scholars has attempted to integrate outside influences with local tradition. Among these, the names of Enrico Diciotti, who emphasizes the

78. Although the Constitution was enacted in 1948, a number of its provisions were for a time ineffective because of the lack of implementing legislation. The impact of the Court was thus perhaps more gradual than might otherwise have been expected.

79. One author, as early as 1934, argued that judicial review of the substantive validity of legislation was not inconsistent with the separation of powers, properly conceived. Esposito, *La validità delle leggi* (1934). See also the interesting discussion of the separation of judicial and legislative powers in Battaglia, *I giudici e la politica* 3–13 (1962).

80. See 2.09 for a description of, and citations to the literature on, the Constitutional Court and the role of lower courts in referring questions to it. For an extensive discussion of the Constitutional Court and its interpretive function, see Cappelletti, *op. cit.* n. 18, at 83.

role of values in interpretation and expresses skepticism regarding the existence of inherently "true" or "correct" interpretations;[81] Riccardo Guastini, who emphasizes that legal rules (*norme*) are the products rather than objects of an interpretive process;[82] and Francesco D'Agostino, who regards the creative role of judges as central to a broader postmodern theory of law, stand out, although several others have made notable contributions, as well. There remains, here as elsewhere, a peculiarly Italian feel to such efforts.[83] While Anglo-Americans tend to regard judicial interpretation as supreme, Italians remain more likely to see it as one of several types of interpretation, including that by scholars, practicing lawyers, and the legislature itself. Foreigners may find it odd to see scholars asking "What is interpretation?" or "Who is an interpreter?," while rarely if ever discussing individual cases. Yet, the change in approaches—or perhaps more accurately the completion of the changes begun in the immediate postwar era—remains significant notwithstanding these continuities: here again an essentially hybrid style has developed, with foreign influences filtered through a domestic prism resulting in a unique and unmistakably Italian synthesis.

7.13 *Toward a New Italian Style.*   Doctrine, law, and interpretation, as the terms have been used in these chapters, are merely names for different aspects of the same process. The work of the scholar, the legislator, and the judge does not go on in isolation; each affects and is affected by the other. Together they comprise only a part, although a very important part, of a legal process that extends far beyond them, to the limits of the culture of which that process is itself only one manifestation.

Certain themes have constantly recurred throughout this discussion. Of these, the orthodox doctrine and the Constitution may be taken as particularly significant because they are symbols of the forces of tradition and of change. Before 1948 the traditional legal science *was* the Italian constitution in a very real sense. It dictated a model of the legal process to which scholars, legislators, and judges conformed. Norms and concepts came to mean what the doctrine said they meant, and the doctrinal view of fundamental institutions like property and contract operated as a limitation on government in the interest of nineteenth-century liberalism. Cul-

---

81. See Diciotti, *Verita' e certezza nell'interpretazione della legge* (1999).
82. See Guastini, *Il diritto come linguaggio* (2001).
83. See D'Agostino, *Filosofia del diritto* (2d ed.) (1996). A good summary of interpretation theory is Modugno, *Interpretazione Giuridica, op. cit.* n. 3.

turally agnostic, rigidly "scientific" and dogmatic, the doctrine excluded not only Catholic natural law but also every form of secular idealism, functionalism, utilitarianism, and pragmatism, and every intrusion of history or sociology, as nonlegal. A variety of forces lay behind the doctrine and gave it its character, and some of these have been described. But the doctrine was the medium through which these forces acted, and after a time it developed its own independent momentum.

If the doctrine was the stronghold of the forces of tradition, the Constitution of 1948 became the banner of the *avanguardia*. It represented the release from long years of repression under fascism and the accumulation of decades of frustrated desire for reform. It embodied principles of individual and social justice of the sort the traditional doctrine rejects as "nonlegal." It established the institution of judicial review of legislation for the first time in Italy, destroying the dogma of legislative supremacy and increasing the status of the judiciary. It redefined fundamental legal institutions in terms quite different from those of the doctrine. It provided a basis for theories of interpretation that are more realistic and more value-conscious than those provided by the older model. It provided an alternative source of analogy and general principles of law. It was both cause and symbol of a modernizing revolution in Italian law.

The revolution in legal styles was part of a much broader historical and cultural transformation. The first postwar generation saw an economic miracle and what has been aptly called a cultural renaissance in Italy. Names like Antonioni, Fellini, Moravia, Olivetti, Pavese, Quasimodo, and Tommasi di Lampedusa became familiar symbols of the creative energy that was released by economic revival and the fall of Italian fascism.[84] Together with an open society and a newly democratic polity, these changes gave rise to a new internationalism with important consequences for specific legal institutions and the legal order as a whole.

The second postwar generation—that beginning somewhere around 1980— has witnessed a less dramatic break with the past but had no less important consequences.[85] The advent of a European as opposed to a purely Italian consciousness, of which the European Union and its institutions are merely the most obvious examples, has given rise to new juridical structures and a new way of thinking

84. "It has become a cliché to speak of a post-fascist cultural renaissance in Italy." H. Stuart Hughes, *The United States and Italy* 236 (2d ed. 1965).

85. See generally Paul Ginsborg, *Italy and Its Discontents: Family, Civil Society, State* (2006).

about legal issues. The increasing prevalence of English, and the prominence of the Internet and other electronic media, have revolutionized the use of source materials and brought Italy closer than ever to global intellectual currents. A new generation of scholars, moving easily between countries and languages, have blurred the distinction between legal systems to the point where some question whether it is meaningful to speak of Italian as opposed to Europea or Western law altogether.

Writing in 1967, the original authors of this book remained confident that an "Italian style" in doctrine, law, and interpretation still existed, notwithstanding the unmistakable changes in the first postwar generation. The characteristic attributes of this style were those identified in the preceding chapters: an extreme form of legal purism and a correspondingly rigid separation between law, morality, and social science; a rigid conceptual structure and an insistence upon legal certainty; and an elevation of doctrine over jurisprudence at all levels of the legal system. The authors concluded by noting the postwar trend toward a more "open" jurisprudence, including a deemphasis on legal purism and logical formalism, an expanded role for the judiciary, and increased respect for democratic values, even if these concepts had at times to be "smuggled" into the existing scholarship in the guise of incremental adjustments to traditional norms.

A generation later, the trends above, together with some (notably the Internet) that could not have been foreseen by the original authors, have come to fruition. Today the question is no longer whether an Italian style exists but whether and to what extent it can survive in an increasingly interconnected world. The answer, not surprisingly, depends on what values and institutions are in question. Italian law will continue to become more international and eclectic in nature: its scholars will blur distinctions between law and social science, its judges become more assertive and less deferential to other bodies. An elite of internationally minded scholars and practitioners may even come to think of themselves as European or "global" rather than Italian in character. But habits of thinking change more slowly than surface labels. For all their newfound sophistication, Italian lawyers continue to approach legal issues in a distinctive manner—a deductive, logical style which proceeds from general to specific matters and emphasizes abstract patterns over real-world fact situations—that differs in tone and substance from that in common and even other civil law jurisdictions. Concepts like the *fattispecie* or *negozio giuridico*, with their associated historical baggage and the unique approach to law and legal problems that they bring with them, will not quickly fade from the Italian scene. Institutions like the *manuali* and the *magistratura* will continue to distinguish Italian practice from that in neighboring countries. Here the question of Italian style merges into the more general question of law's future in a globalized world: a high degree of superficial convergence masking the persistence of profound differences in thought and behavior, which—like the differences between cultures generally—become visible only upon close observation but are nonetheless vital and all too real.[86]

86. The "Europeanization" or "Globalization" of Italian law is, of course, hardly a new phenomenon, as any comparativist will attest. See Monateri, The *"Weak" Law: Contaminations and Legal Cultures: Italian Report to the Bristol Conference* (2000) at http://www.jus.unitn.it/cardozo/Review/Comparative/weak.htm.

Appendix: A Note on Italian Source Materials

The First Edition of this book included three appendices: the Constitution of the Italian Republic (Appendix A); the principal headings of the Italian Civil Code (Appendix C); and a more ambitious item entitled "The Progress of a Civil Action," which traced a case involving a bicycle accident in October 1951 from the initial action in the Florence *Tribunale* through an appeal to the *Cassazione* in 1960 and final resolution in 1962 (Appendix B). (All fifty documents in this latter appendix, with a combined length of 120 pages, are translated into perfect and at times poetic English.)

The availability of online sources renders materials of this nature somewhat redundant, but it seems appropriate to provide further guidance regarding source materials for those who wish to pursue the subject more extensively. A question of language presents itself at the outset. Even today, there are fewer English-language sources on Italian law than one might think. The Italian Constitution is available at http://www.senato.it/documenti/repository/istituzione/costituzione_inglese.pdf. There is a translation of The Italian Civil Code and Complementary Legislation by Mario Beltramo (Oceana Publications 1990) which may, however, be difficult to locate and does not appear to be available online (Professor Merryman was a participant in an earlier version of this project). There are also several good secondary guides to Italian legal materials, although at some point these usually bring you to Italian-language materials of one kind or another. Among the best secondary guides are those provided by the NYU Law School at http://www.nyulawglobal.org/globalex/italy.htm and by the U.S. Library of Congress at http://www.loc.gov/law/help/guide/nations/italy.php. There is also a useful English-language entry on Italian law at the European Union website at https://e-justice.europa.eu/content_member_state_law-6-IT-en.do?clang=en. These are basically annotated bibliographies and include only limited explanation, but they provide some measure of "one-stop shopping" and are a useful way of getting started with the primary sources.

Italian case law is harder to come by, partially as a result of translation problems, partly because (as explained above) judicial decisions have historically occupied a somewhat lesser role in Italian than in Anglo-Saxon law. The Constitutional Court publishes English summaries of its decisions, together with other information about the Court, at http://www.cortecostituzionale.it/ActionPagina_320.do. Newspapers and other mass media frequently cover Italian trials, but they tend to select items with prurient or cultural appeal (e.g., the Amanda Knox Trial) rather than lasting legal import.

It also bears noting that there are several earlier English-language treatises on Italian law which—although different in scope and emphasis from the present work—are nevertheless extremely useful for many purposes. Jeffrey S. Lena and Ugo Mattei (eds.), *Introduction to Italian Law* (2002), includes useful introductory materials together with chapters on various specific areas of law. G. Leroy Certoma, *The Italian Legal System* (1984), is another useful introduction although inevitably somewhat dated in nature. Although not limited to Italy, John Henry Merryman and Rogelio Perez-Perdomo's *The Civil Law Tradition: An Introduction to the Legal Systems of Europe and Latin America* (3d ed. 2007) is required reading for any serious student of the subject.

Italian-language materials are, of course, more plentiful: the problem here is not finding materials but deciding which ones are most useful (or, for those not available gratis, which are worth paying for). The following is an admittedly unscientific list that may nevertheless prove useful for those who can read Italian and wish to delve further into the original sources. URLs change frequently. if any of these links do not function, simply search for the Italian name at www.google.it or an equivalent site, and it should appear quickly.

Codes

Civil Code (Codice Civile)
http://www.altalex.com/index.php?idnot=34794
http://www.diritto.it/codici/1

Civil Procedure Code (Codice di Procedura Civile)
http://www.altalex.com/index.php?idnot=33723
http://www.diritto.it/codici/3

Criminal Code (Codice Penale)

http://www.altalex.com/index.php?idnot=36653

http://www.diritto.it/codici/2

Criminal Procedure Code (Codice di Procedura Penale)

http://www.altalex.com/index.php?idnot=2011

http://www.diritto.it/codici/4

Government

The website www.normattiva.it provides a kind of "one-stop shopping" by including links to various governmental sites as well as to contemporary legislation and regulation.

President (Capo dello Stato)

www.quirinale.it

Prime Minister's Office (Presidenza del Consiglio dei Ministri)

www.governo.it

Parliament

www.parlamento.it

Ministry of Justice

www.giustizia.it

Courts

Corte Suprema di Cassazione

www.cortedicassazione.it

Corte Costituzionale

www.cortecostituzionale.it

Judiciary (Consiglio Superiore della Magistratura)

www.csm.it

Legal Scholarship (Dottrina)

www.ittig.cnr.it

Secondary Sources/Internet Portals

In recent years there has been a proliferation of Internet portals frequently bearing clever names like www.diritto.it, www.altalex.com, www.filodiritto.it, and the like, together with more focused sources emphasizing specific areas of law. Some of these are tied to specific law or accounting firms, and some (but not all) may charge fees for specific services. As a general rule, these sites are designed for practitioners rather than scholars, and they are more useful for answering specific questions than for gaining a more general impression of Italian law. Nevertheless, if one is interested in a particular area and does not know exactly what institutional source to consult, they may be useful in getting started.

As always, the value of any and all of these resources depends on the task at hand. If one is conducting research on behalf of an Italian client, one is obviously advised to consult an Italian lawyer: even with the best language skills written materials can convey only a portion of the legal landscape. If, on the other hand, one's goal is to attain a deeper insight for comparative or scholarly purposes, the materials above should suffice to make a good start and, if not to provide all the relevant answers, then at least suggest what the right questions might be.

Index